The Life and Mind of John Dewey

by George Dykhuizen

Introduction by Harold Taylor

Edited by Jo Ann Boydston

Carbondale and Edwardsville

Southern Illinois University Press

Feffer & Simons, Inc.

London and Amsterdam

Library of Congress Cataloging in Publication Data

Dykhuizen, George, 1899–
The life and mind of John Dewey.

Includes bibliographical references.
1. Dewey, John, 1859–1952. I. Title.
B945.D44D94 191 [B] 73–4602
ISBN 0–8093–0616–6

Polly V. Dunn and Elizabeth M. Evanson of the Southern Illinois University Center for Dewey Studies have vetted the text and notes of this book.

Printed in the United States of America

To **H. Y. D.**

Contents

List of Illustrations

between pp. 226 and 227

Acknowledgments

THE WRITER has stated in the appropriate places in the notes his indebtedness to many persons who have aided in the preparation of this volume. In addition, he wishes to express his gratitude to Roberta (Mrs. John) Dewey for the generous amount of time she gave for interviews and for permission to examine her husband's unpublished papers and manuscripts.

He is deeply indebted also to members of the John Dewey family: Frederick A. and Elizabeth (Mrs. Frederick A.) Dewey, Jane, Lucy (Mrs. Wolf Brandauer), and Sabino and Florence (Mrs. Sabino) Dewey for their many acts of hospitality and for information about their father.

For permission to quote in whole or in part unpublished letters to which they are the literary heirs he is under obligation to Laura T. Buckham, Dr. McKeen Cattell, Dr. Paul V. Harper, Edith Harris, Ronald B. Levinson, William J. McGill, and Henry C. Torrey. Special thanks are due Mr. Meyer Halpern, executor of Roberta Dewey's estate, for permission to quote from the unpublished Dewey letters used in the book.

For their courtesy in allowing him to use unpublished letters to which they have proprietary rights, the writer is indebted to the following institutions: Butler Library, Columbia University; Milton S. Eisenhower Library, The Johns Hopkins University; New York Public Library, Manuscript Division, Astor, Lenox and Tilden Foundations; Joseph Regenstein Library, the University of Chicago; Michigan Historical Collections, the University of Michigan; Hoose Library, the University of Southern California; Guy W. Bailey Library, the University of Vermont; and the State Historical Society of Wisconsin.

The author is indebted to Professor Norio Miura of Tohoku Gakuin University, Sendai, Japan for his kindness in translating into English the Japanese material used in the book and to his colleague, David C. Lai, for translating the Chinese material.

Also deserving his gratitude are the editors of the *Journal of the History of Ideas* for permission to incorporate in the book in slightly altered form the following articles which appeared in their *Journal*: "John Dewey: The Vermont Years"; "John Dewey at Johns Hopkins (1882–1884)"; and "John Dewey and the University of Michigan."

Similar gratitude is due the editors of the *Journal of the History of Philosophy* for permission to use in somewhat changed form the two following articles which were published in their *Journal*: "John Dewey: The Chicago Years" and "John Dewey in Chicago: Some Biographical Notes."

Acknowledgment is also made to the Committee on Institutional Grants of the University of Vermont for generous financial assistance in the preparation of the book.

Jo Ann Boydston, director of the Center for Dewey Studies, merits special recognition for her painstaking and conscientious editing of the manuscript.

If space permitted, it would be a pleasant task to list the names of numerous other persons who in one way or another were helpful to the author as he wrote this biography.

George Dykhuizen

Introduction

By Harold Taylor

TO HAVE lived one's way in the Western world from the middle of the nineteenth century into the middle of the twentieth, and to have had a major part in shaping the intellectual character of the time through which one lived, is not only an extraordinary achievement in itself, but an achievement with many additional consequences. In John Dewey's case, one of these lies in the development of a philosophical framework for social thought which fuses social science with psychology and the natural sciences in a modern form of logic and empirical philosophy. Another lies in the lessons to be learned by students of social history from a life so entirely devoted to teaching, writing, and philosophical thinking in the environment of the university and its surrounding communities.

Another consequence, as important as any other, is that when the story of the philosopher's life and the body of ideas it has generated is told in detail, piece by piece, as in George Dykhuizen's meticulous account of Dewey's career, it makes the intellectual history of the Western world more tangible, and, in a certain way, more manageable. It shows intellectual and cultural changes in the process of being made, and indicates how the generalizations of a philosopher who is close to his own time infiltrate the culture and become part of the intellectual equipment of the generations in dealing with their own problems. One can feel a personal link with the past as one goes back year by year in gradual stages from a present Dewey helped to create to a point in nineteenth-century time, remote when looked at as a period in history, but close at hand when seen as the beginning of a set of experiences of a young man growing up in nineteenth-century Vermont and maturing in a wider America, until the experiences touched the whole world of the twentieth century. One is allowed to enter into those experiences as if they were his own, and to understand how intellectual history looks from the inside.

Reading the autobiography of Bertrand Russell has the same effect, or rather, a parallel effect, since Russell's life began later (1872) and lasted longer (1970), gathering strength and influence as it went, linking a late-nineteenth-century boyhood in Victorian England to the major events in world society as they moved their way toward the 1970s. The parallel continues when one realizes that both Russell and Dewey spent the whole of their lives as philosophers working within an intellectual environment which included university scholars, scientists, artists, and writers of all kinds. The extent of their influence on the world began in the fact that they *were* philosophers, that they possessed a common insatiable desire to settle for themselves the answers to basic philosophical questions, and that they wrote so constantly in response to that desire.

At the time of the celebration in New York City of Dewey's contributions to twentieth-century society on his ninetieth birthday, Dewey declared that no matter what else he had done, in politics, education, social movements and the development of new social institutions, he thought of himself as one who "first, last, and all the time, engaged in the vocation of philosophy." His other interests, he said, were "specifically an outgrowth and manifestation of my primary interest in philosophy," and his aim in life had always been to obtain "a moderately clear and distinct idea of what the problems are that underlie the difficulties and evils which we experience *in fact*; that is to say, in *practical* life."

Neither Dewey nor Russell was content to stay inside the academic environment which gave to each man a confirmed and honored place in his own society. Whatever was happening in the world they took as fit subject for inquiry and comment. Their major contributions to the formal philosophical disciplines—in aesthetics, logic, political and social thought, education, ethics, and epistemology—won them the respect of the world's organized intellectual community. But the total influence they exerted in national and international affairs had its origin in the fact that they were continually involved in analyzing and making public judgments about political, social, and cultural developments in their own societies and in the world at large. They were also ready to join with others in forming activist organizations, against war, on behalf of intellectual freedom and social justice, for educational and social change, and for the cause of liberalism in social institutions.

In this sense they were engaged intellectuals in the style

called for by Malraux and Camus, whose experience in war, in a captured and occupied country, and in the politics of the post-war period was much more direct. It may be that the death of Russell and Dewey marks the end of an era in which a single philosopher with a comprehensive view of the world can be acknowledged on a world scale as a spokesman for mankind. The study and practice of philosophy has now become so technical and academic an exercise that even the idea of the philosopher as a thinker capable of developing a view of the world which could influence the course of history has been lost in the thickets of the academy.

In the case of Russell, the task of writing a consecutive account of his life was willingly taken up by Russell himself in the three-volume autobiography in which he acts as his own personal historian, explicator of texts, and sympathetic critic of his own ideas and conduct. He took pains to present himself to the world in the way he wished to appear. Through writing his *History of Western Philosophy* (New York: Simon and Schuster, 1945), Russell also managed to give the world a fairly good account of his views on the major figures in Western intellectual history and to assign them to their place in history according to the degree to which they approached his own answers to philosophical questions. Of Dewey, for example, he said in summing up Dewey's life and work,

> He is a man of the highest character, liberal in outlook, generous and kind in personal relations, indefatigable in work. With most of his opinions I am in almost complete agreement. Owing to my respect and admiration for him, as well as to personal experience of his kindness, I should wish to agree completely, but to my regret I am compelled to dissent from his most distinctive philosophical doctrine, namely the substitution of "inquiry" for "truth" as the fundamental concept of logic and theory of knowledge. (P. 819)

Russell then goes on to argue his own point of view against Dewey by the use of what Dewey (and a good many others) considered to be distortions of his position, and the use of examples which twisted Dewey's meaning.

2

Dewey was less inclined than Russell to write about himself, produced no autobiography, very little introspective information, even in his letters, and did his best to keep himself out of subjective evaluations of the philosophers and writers on whose ideas he commented. As Russell says, Dewey was a man of the highest character, generous and kind in his personal relations, and not only indefatigable in his work, but absorbed in it to a degree that amounted to a form of self-denial. When he travelled abroad, to Japan, to China, to Mexico, Turkey, the Soviet Union, there was little room for the pleasures of the traveller at leisure in new landscapes and ambiences. His travels were more like intellectual expeditions, in which he headed straight for the university lecture halls and classrooms to explain his ideas and explore issues in philosophy, conferring with his new colleagues on educational and social problems, learning to understand the cultural and political conditions in which they lived, using his expeditions as a further means of developing his own ideas.

Abroad and at home, he wrote constantly of what he had learned, usually in pieces for the *New Republic,* for which he wrote 160 articles and five letters from 1915 to 1935. He raised intellectual journalism to the level of philosophical discourse. His lectures in Japan in 1919, for example, became his *Reconstruction in Philosophy,* his lectures at Harvard in 1931 became *Art As Experience.* Everything he did turned into an exercise in further philosophical writing. His books came out of his lectures, his lectures came out of his teaching, his ideas came out of his day-to-day experience with other ideas, practical situations, and contemporary events. His method of thinking was to put himself into situations in which answers had to be given to questions raised by the situation, in the classroom, the lecture-hall, the union meeting, the public forum, in letters to friends, students, colleagues—and then to refine the answers through speculation and analysis as he wrote. He wrote his way toward understanding.

When he went on vacation to his summer home, he spent almost all of his time writing more philosophy rather than using the interlude as a way of recovering from the strenuous year of teaching, lecturing, and writing from which he had just emerged. Out of it all came forty books and more than seven hundred articles on so wide a variety of subjects and with such a range of insight as to command the respect and admiration of the entire intellectual community, including those who were his critics.

A paradox lay in the fact that although his devotion to the study of philosophy occupied him every day, every week, every year, his generosity in giving his time to students, colleagues, and liberal causes was so great as to become legendary. His life and his work were all of one piece. His personal pleasures were in the work and in the relation with those to whom he gave so freely of his time and energy. His honesty in personal and intellectual relations was so complete and chivalrous as to verge on saintliness, although he would have laughed to be confronted with so extravagant a term as a description of his character.

Yet the power of his mind was strengthened and energized by that honesty, since it meant that he not only faced up to ideas contrary to his own with the open courage of an honest man, but kept on pursuing variations of his own ideas in an effort to make them clearer to himself and to others. It also meant that his intellectual influence matched the power of his mind, since it was so clearly a mind that could be trusted, one which tried to resolve doubts by further inquiry and exposition, not by denials and polemics or by questioning the qualifications of the doubter. When he replied to criticisms of his views it was in a genuine effort to explain to his critics and to others what it was he actually meant and why he came to the views he held. Although he was a lively and tough thinker in polemical situations, he kept his polemics to a minimum and used his explanations as a means for exploring and developing his own thought.

3

In the absence of an autobiography by Dewey, the opportunity and privilege presents itself to scholars and intellectual historians to reconstruct from the materials at hand as accurate an account as possible of Dewey's life and thought while so much of the biographical material is comparatively fresh and there are friends, relatives, colleagues, and students whose memories and memorabilia can help to supply the details. The eighty warehouse boxes filled with Dewey's personal papers which were added last year to the archives of the Center for Dewey Studies at Southern Illinois University—books, manuscripts, notes, pictures, films, records, tapes, and other items—provide a wealth of material for further study and biographical use.

In the meantime, George Dykhuizen has been painstaking and indefatigable in his own way in putting together the present book and in giving his readers access to information available only in a book of this kind. Mr. Dykhuizen's work in setting down the factual details of Dewey's career in an orderly way and summarizing Dewey's ideas as they developed in his writing make an important contribution to an understanding of Dewey's life and thought and of American intellectual history. For many of us who have been deeply influenced by Dewey and have had the privilege of his personal friendship, it has not ordinarily been possible to know in detail the story of his life, or to become aware, except in a general way, of the extraordinary range of activities in which he was involved as he went from period to period in his career as a professor of philosophy and an activist in world affairs.

In my own case, I first came across Dewey's ideas as an undergraduate student of philosophy at the University of Toronto. There the British tradition of teaching and of education prevailed, resting on the assumption that nothing that had been said in philosophy or had happened in history during the previous thirty to forty years was established deeply enough in its historical roots to be accepted as more than conjecture. The consequence for those of us who were philosophy students together in the mid-1930s was that we ran through all the contemporary philosophers —James, Russell, Dewey, Whitehead, Bergson, and one or two others—in a single course taught in the senior year. The rest of the year and the whole of the previous three dealt with the historical figures, from the pre-Socratics to Hegel and Kant, stopping short of contemporary intellectual and social events on the grounds that they were too recent to be properly evaluated.

Another result was that the study of philosophy, as in Dewey's student days in the 1880s, was reduced to the study of the history and sequence of Western ideas, and the role of the student was reduced to a program of learning how to describe and comment on the ideas. The purpose in undertaking the study of philosophy in a university was assumed to be either to become a scholar in the field and possibly a professor of philosophy, or to become liberally educated by a knowledge of what the major philosophers had had to say. In neither case was the student asked to come to grips with the issues in contemporary society, or even in the societies of the past, through the employment of his own critical intelligence and of what he had learned in his philosophical studies.

It therefore came as shock to me to discover in Dewey a philosopher who deliberately threw over that tradition and considered philosophy to be a means not of dealing with the problems of philosophers but with the problems of man in his existential situation. Not until I arrived at the University of Wisconsin to teach philosophy under the chairmanship of Max C. Otto, a close friend and colleague of John Dewey, did I come to realize how radical and far-reaching were Dewey's ideas about education, social institutions, and the pursuit of philosophy itself. I discovered that the more I learned through the personal experience of teaching students and examining the ideas with which we were mutually concerned, the more I found in Dewey to encourage and support my own intellectual development and to extend the range of possible inquiry into issues of whose relevance to contemporary life I had been only dimly aware. Such feelings of gratitude and appreciation have been shared by thousands and thousands of students and teachers over these past eighty years.

I wish now that in those earlier days I had had a chance to find in one place Mr. Dykhuizen's story of what Dewey did from year to year, and how, for example, in the early days in Chicago (1894–1904) he combined his work in the study of philosophy with the practical application of his ideas in organizing and administering a school for children. There are some deep lessons to be learned by the beginning teacher from the simple and direct way in which Dewey made a complete integration of his work in philosophy, psychology, and practical pedagogy as chairman of the philosophy and education department at the University of Chicago.

4

I recall one conversation with Dewey during the latter years of his life, when I had come as president to Sarah Lawrence College, an institution which reflected basic elements of Dewey's educational philosophy in its structure and in its approach to teaching and learning. We had been talking about the way in which a concern for the practical problems of education and how to make it work forced the administrator to answer questions which were actually questions in philosophy. We had also been deploring the fact that so few college presidents and administrators had educational convictions and intellectual interests or a social philosophy which informed their work in administration.

It was a familiar Deweyan view that the reason students and teachers should be mutually involved in working out their own educational plans was not only for the experience they could gain in the practice of democracy, but for the insight they could reach in the study of human values and social philosophy. If education is to be defined in Dewey's terms as philosophy in action, then the study of philosophical questions must arise naturally from the experience of students and teachers with their own education.

The problem as I presented it to Dewey was a double one. First, if education is philosophy in action and philosophical insight is to come from practical experience in education, then how did he explain the absence of such insight in the entire sweep of American college presidents and high school administrators, most of whom had had nothing *but* practical experience with educational problems yet seemed to be fairly short on insight. The second part of the problem was simply one of finding the time and context for the administrator or teacher (or student, for that matter) to speculate on the meaning of his continuous practical experience. As I had discovered after one short year at Sarah Lawrence, so much time had to be spent on the practical problems that there was no room left for speculation.

Dewey's reply was that the aim of all education was to develop a body of knowledge and a philosophy with which to deal with whatever came up in one's life, to make of oneself an instrument of continuous learning. "I never learned how to separate the two, running the school and doing philosophy," he said, "and I wasn't a good administrator. But I wouldn't have traded the experience of the school for anything. If you want to know about education you have to practice. But I hope you will know when you have had enough practice and will get back into philosophy. The way for you to do that is to stop being president and start teaching again. It's the teaching that does it."

Dewey then went on to talk about the necessity of putting the country's universities into the hands of university presidents who had social and intellectual interests, and recalled the time in his student days when it was common practice for university presidents to teach a course in philosophy, usually moral philosophy mixed with religion, to the whole senior class. He said that his own method of thinking was to keep telling other people what he meant, and that he thought he was more radical now that he was approaching ninety than he had ever been before, because he had had more experience in explaining why existing conditions had to be changed.

It was not until I came to Mr. Dykhuizen's full record of biographical events that I realized how completely true were the things Dewey had said that day. In the educational system of the late nineteenth and early twentieth century, the central problem had become one of freeing the structure and content of the curriculum in schools and colleges from the rigidities and standardization of teaching methods and subject matter. William Rainey Harper at the University of Chicago was the kind of energetic president of whom Dewey could approve, and by 1894 when Dewey took up his work there, he immediately began to combine his studies in education, psychology, and philosophy with the operation of an elementary school, and to introduce the ideas of Pestalozzi, Froebel, and Herbart, along with his own, into the curriculum of teachers and into the practices of the schools.

His writing on education came out of his practical experience, from his talks to and with teachers, parents, colleagues, his direct work with children, and the development of curricula and educational policy. The more he learned, the more he wrote about it. By 1902 he had written *The School and Society, The Child and the Curriculum,* and the basic monographs *Interest in Relation to the Training of the Will, The Reflex Arc Concept in Psychology, Principles of Mental Development as Illustrated in Early Infancy,* among other articles related to the central educational issues. In his theory of functional psychology and his advocacy of education which begins with the interests and activities of the individual child, Dewey had laid the foundation for the progressive reform of American education.

5

In reading Mr. Dykhuizen's record of what Dewey did in his young manhood—in Vermont as a student, in Pennsylvania as a high school teacher, at Johns Hopkins as a graduate student, in Michigan as a young instructor—one is struck by the fact that from the beginning his was a continuing struggle for emancipation and liberation from ideas in philosophy, religion, and education which were universally accepted as norms for intellectual behavior. There was a persistence about him, even in his earliest years as a student, in taking all ideas seriously while at the same time examining them for what truth might be found in the examination. President Buckham of the University of Vermont, in writing to President Gilman of Johns Hopkins University in 1883 about the twenty-four-year-old Dewey's qualifications as a teaching fellow, said of him then, "John Dewey has a logical, thoroughgoing, absolutely independent mind. He is sound and sweet all through—is true and loyal in matters of religion, and without any crotchets, or drawbacks of any kind, so far as I know. He is very reticent, as you see—probably lacks a due amount of self-assertion. This is the only question that would arise in the minds of those who know him—whether he has the amount of dogmatism that a teacher ought to have. I am inclined to think that the confidence in him implied in an appointment would reinforce his own confidence in himself and go far toward overcoming the defect."

The acceptance of the idea that a qualified philosophy student and teacher should be loyal and true in matters of religion and possess an appropriate amount of dogmatism indicates the intellectual base-line from which Dewey was beginning his career in teaching and philosophy, and the distance he so swiftly travelled on the path toward emancipation. One can also see the beginning of Dewey's rejection of dualisms of all kinds in an intellectual landscape strewn with dualisms and fixed ideas about religion, metaphysics, society, and philosophy itself. What Buckham saw as a lack of "a due amount of self-assertion" was in fact the sign of an original inquiring mind, a suspension of easy belief at a time when such ease was to be deliberately sought by those entering the profession of philosophy.

6

In the cycle of intellectual and cultural change from the 1880s to the 1970s, it is instructive to follow the further course of Dewey's emancipation, and to see over and over again, the degree to which Dewey was ahead of his time. His comment on China, after he had visited there in 1919, for example, illustrates a capacity for sensitive perception which he carried with him wherever he went. "Simply as an intellectual spectacle," he said, "a scene for study and surmise, for investigation and speculation, there is nothing in the world to-day—not even Europe in the throes of reconstruction—that equals China."

Dewey's own intellectual struggle for liberation can be seen as a symbol of a general movement toward wider and more liberal views of cultural and social change which at every point in twentieth-century history have been in conflict with institutional dogmas and new forms of authoritarian thinking. Whether or not one agrees with Dewey's instrumentalism and pragmatism, or with his view of logic as a theory of inquiry, one cannot fail to take account of his formulation, as early as 1890, of the idea that thinking and reflecting are part of a "process of tentative action" and that moral ideals are working hypotheses for social and personal action. To put it another way, when the dogmatism is removed from the conception of moral ideals and ideologies, what remains is a set of ideas for social and intellectual experiment and a mandate for nonviolent revolution.

The history of Dewey's development as a thinker is also the history of twentieth-century cultural and social change on a world scale. If there are to be solutions to ideological, racial, political, and economic conflicts, they will have to rest on a philosophy of pluralism and nonviolent revolution of the kind proposed by Dewey. Otherwise they will go on finding their solutions in various forms of mass killing.

Up through the years to the 1930s, the problems of the 1900s kept recurring in new forms and constantly expanding the range of their effects, until they had reached the matrix of a worldwide economic depression and a second World War. As the problems developed before and after the First World War, then following the postwar settlements—the growth of the industrial and urban society, the shifts in political coalitions and international alliances, the beginnings of colonial disintegration and social revolution, the development of an organized working class, the growth of fascism—Dewey's ideas and activities developed with them.

Here is a sample of his activity. He became involved in starting a new political party in the 1920s, in organizing unions for teachers, in developing new curricula in social studies, in organizing the American Association of University Professors, in clarifying and acting on issues of academic freedom and the relation of democracy to education, in organizing the civil liberties movement, in founding the New School for Social Research. The reader will find the list extended to an extraordinary length in Mr. Dykhuizen's account of his career. Dewey worked always at the advanced edge of social change, helping to create a cultural environment in the United States out of which liberal institutions could grow. In doing so, he introduced the idea of activism into the American academic community.

At every point in the social development of the country during these past eighty years, Dewey's living influence has been felt, up to and including the 1940s and '50s when his ideas were being attacked on three fronts at once—by the Hutchins-Adler educational traditionalists, the Communist Left, and right-wing politicians and their adherents who blamed Dewey for everything from the decline of the American high school to the loss of faith in religion and capitalism. What in fact he had done was to lay the philosophical foundation for contemporary liberalism in politics and social change, and supply a full set of instruments for practising it.

In a large sector of contemporary politics and social thought, those instruments and that philosophy are again under attack, although the terms of reference go beyond Dewey's formulations and engage the whole structure of liberal institutions and the concept of liberalism itself. At one level a political attack is made on 'permissiveness', which is held responsible for the loss of belief in the work ethic, for the break-up of the American family, for threats to law and order, for the development of a welfare state and a citizenry lacking goals and initiative. At another level it is an attack on the idea that through social legislation and community action in housing, education, employment, and racial integration, progress can be made in curing the problems of poverty, inequality, and social injustice. At another it is an attack, by the use of mass statistics and computerized data, on the central thesis of Dewey's educational philosophy, that education can and does change society. At its deepest level it is a loss of faith in the idea that the combined efforts and shared experience of democratic citizens of good will can solve the problems of a mass society.

Yet the clarity, compassion, and humanity of Dewey's central themes in philosophy persist within the culture. They find their expression not only in his books, but in the ideas and commitments of generations of citizens who have grown up within a society whose liberalism he helped to create. If there are failures in the social system, they come from the inadequacy of present institutions to cope with the size and scope of the social revolution, not with Dewey's philosophy of social change. Dewey urged over and over again the reconstruction and critical evaluation of existing institutions, he wanted to know what was being done "to release specific capacities and co-ordinate them into working powers," his insistent question was, "Just what response does *this* social arrangement, political or economic, evoke, and what effect does it have upon the disposition of those who engage in it?" (*Reconstruction in Philosophy* [New York: Henry Holt and Co., 1920], p. 197).

In the evolution of the social order from the old to the new, generations of presidents, politicians, educators, corporate managers, artists, labor leaders, writers, teachers, intellectuals, students, and citizens come and go, leaving something behind them and adding something, good or bad, to the flow of history. In the flow, the cause of human betterment succeeds and fails concurrently. Advances at one point are matched by retreats at others. But the necessity for change continues, propelled by human events and needs which are in some ways manageable, in other ways uncontrollable. The fundamental question for the character of the change is not merely one of survival for the human race, but whether or not the circumstances of survival can be arranged so that they respond to universal human needs and are nourishing to the human spirit.

The generation of young Americans of the 1960s who began to take their lives and their education into their own hands and to take up the work of educational and social change on their own terms, are the philosophical descendants of John Dewey. What they want and what they are determined to have are the kinds of educational and social institutions for which Dewey fought. If the students are unaware that the ideas they have developed found their earlier expression in Dewey's work of eighty years ago, and that they are now rediscovering educational insights already available in his philosophy, this can be counted, not as a failure on their part to have understood the history of philosophy, but as an affirmation of the persisting worth of the ideas themselves in the context of a society with its own continuities.

All his life Dewey did his utmost to remove sentimental and specious reasoning from the discourse of liberals who felt that all that was needed to make a new world was faith, trust, hope, and a political party that would pass liberal legislation. He knew as well as Marx or Lenin the necessities of history, the power of economic and social forces which take on a life of their own, the power of institutions to make men into symbols of the institutions which moulded them. He knew as well as any of his critics that simply to release children into free situations in which each could wallow untended in his own emotions was psychologically and socially stultifying.

But he also knew that unless men and women can find within themselves as a function of their lives the will to act and the energy to change, and unless they persist in making and remaking their own institutions to match new needs and circumstances, they will be trapped in a social order designed to denigrate their very humanity. What it comes down to *is* a matter of faith in intelligence and in creative energies liberated into humane acts. In the long run, that is all that does matter. Dewey knew that and he said so. He not only said so, but he showed by his life, his thought, and his actions that the world can be made to respond to the demands of reason and the imperatives of justice. Even if this were not the case, he would argue that to be truly human it is necessary to go on trying.

The Life and Mind of John Dewey

1. Boyhood and Youth in Vermont, 1859–1879

JOHN DEWEY'S roots penetrated deeply into Vermont. Three generations of his forebears were Vermont farmers and each of his parents was born and raised on a farm in Vermont. Being Yankees, these forebears had the characteristics traditionally attributed to the early New Englanders; they were industrious, shrewd, self-reliant, thrifty, without pretense or show, independent in their thinking, puritanical in their conduct, and deeply pious. Being Vermonters, "the most impregnably Yankee of all Yankees,"[1] they had these traits in intensified form. "John Dewey," wrote Irwin Edman on the ninetieth anniversary of Dewey's birth, "is a homespun, almost regional character. To this day, on meeting him, one would imagine oneself talking with a Vermont countryman."[2]

Dewey's father, Archibald Sprague Dewey, broke with family tradition when, in his early twenties, he left the family farm in Fairfax and entered the grocery business in Burlington. He made this move at a time when Burlington was changing from a small village of three or four thousand to a city of fourteen thousand and the second largest lumber depot in the country. Archibald's business flourished under the impact of this growing population as well as because of his friendliness and handsome appearance.

Archibald Dewey was forty-four years old, well established in business, when he met and married Lucina Artemisia Rich, twenty years his junior. Like Archibald, Lucina came from a farm family, but one considerably more prosperous and prominent than his.[3] Her grandfather, Charles Rich, was a Congressman in Washington for ten years; her father, Davis Rich, was a member of the Vermont General Assembly for five years.

Two sons were born to Archibald and Lucina in the early years of their marriage, John Archibald and Davis Rich. The older of these died in an accident at home when he was two and a half years old. To ease the painful memories, the parents shortly afterwards moved to another residence where, on 20 October 1859, John Dewey was born.[4] A fourth and last child, Charles Miner, was born in 1861.

If events had proceeded normally, Dewey would have spent his preschool years with family and friends in the quiet of Burlington. But the Civil War intervened, breaking up and unsettling the family for almost six years. Archibald responded immediately to President Lincoln's call for volunteers, enlisting with the First Vermont Cavalry as quartermaster. After three years of separation from her husband, Lucina moved the family to northern Virginia where she and the children could be near Archibald; not until two years after the war's end was the family together again, settled in Burlington.[5] Archibald, having sold his grocery business when he entered the armed forces, now bought a share in a cigar and tobacco shop of which he became sole owner a few years later.

The city in which Dewey spent his childhood and youth had a charm and natural beauty matched by few other New England communities. Situated on the slopes of the hill that rises gently from the shores of Lake Champlain, it overlooked the Green Mountains to the east, Lake Champlain and the Adirondacks to the west. The majority of the people, including Archibald and Lucina, belonged to the middle class, neither exceptionally rich nor unusually poor. Great wealth and abject poverty, however, did exist among minorities, as reflected in their dwellings. Handsome homes and estates with well-kept grounds, gardens, and stables dotted the residential areas, especially in the hill sections, while near the industrial areas along the lakeshore were the tenements of the very poor, many of them "unfit for habitation," "the abodes of wretchedness and filth," "haunts of dissipation and poverty."[6] Awareness of these conditions was brought home forcefully to the young Dewey boys by Lucina's philanthropic work among the poor and underprivileged of Burlington.

Dewey had opportunities unusual for a child growing up in a Vermont community at this time for varied cultural contacts, because Burlington's population, unlike that of the typical Vermont village, was a culturally mixed one.[7] There were the "old Americans," descendants of families long established in Vermont or some other part of New England, and there were the foreign-born, immigrants from Ireland and Quebec, numbering almost as many as the native-born.[8] During Dewey's adolescent years, his family lived in a neighborhood of "old Americans" but adjacent to neighborhoods of Irish and French Canadian immigrants. Dewey inevitably had contact with the children of these families in grade school, on playgrounds, and in casual neighborhood relations. Such association with boys and girls of cultural and income groups quite different from his own undoubtedly provided liberalizing influences. Though Dewey grew up a typical product of "old American" culture, he had a breadth of social horizon and a depth of understanding for members of other cultural groups not ordinarily encountered in a youth with a Vermont background.

Dewey had ample opportunity to mix with the élite of the "old Americans," who dominated the city's political and economic life, and the wealthier and better educated of whom also determined the city's cultural and social life. "Burlington," wrote one of its citizens, "has long been the home of many wealthy persons, who, with the people of refinement always to be found in a college town, form a cultivated society which keeps the city rich in social attractions and prominent in leading social entertainments."[9] Though this portion of the "old American" population constituted a sort of social and intellectual aristocracy in Burlington, it claimed to have a minimum of snobbish exclusiveness. "We claim for Burlington," wrote a member of this group, "the prevalence of a social equality, as complete and untrammeled as can be found in the smallest country village anywhere in New England. Intelligence, virtue, and a reasonable degree of good manners, will at once admit a new comer of any rank or occupation into any circle which he or she may choose to enter."[10] Through associations in home, school, church, literary circles, and study groups, Dewey's parents were identified with the "cultivated society" of Burlington. John and his brothers came in turn to know and be known by most of the members it comprised. Thus it was not unusual that President Angell, who had left the presidency of the University of Vermont for the presidency of the University of Michigan when Dewey was twelve, should write thirteen years later when he was offering Dewey an instructorship in philosophy in 1884 at the University of Michigan, that he well remembered Dewey as a child and that he wished to be remembered to Archibald and Lucina.[11] "The Vermont and the New England of Dewey's boyhood and youth are gone," wrote one of Dewey's biographers. "But he still carries with him the traces of its social environment, not as memories but as habits, deep preferences, and an ingrained democratic bias. They show themselves in his simplicity of manner, his basic courtesy, freedom from every variety of snobbism, and matter-of-course respect for the rights of everyone in America as a human being and a citizen." [12]

While the family was on the move during the war, little could be done about John's formal schooling even though he had reached school age. But with family life back to normal, Dewey began his grade-school studies with the opening of the fall term in September 1867.[13] These he started under unfavorable conditions. Burlington still retained its local school districts in which public education had deteriorated to a degree little short of scandalous. Crowded classrooms, low standards, lax discipline, irregular attendance, poorly prepared teachers, run-down school buildings were the general rule.[14] The class in which Dewey enrolled, for example, had fifty-four pupils whose ages ranged from seven to nineteen.[15] But the efforts of public-spirited citizens who for a long time had been working for change finally bore fruit; when Dewey began his second year, an up-to-date, city-wide system with graded classes, uniform standards and practices was in operation.[16]

Dewey took the traditional subjects: reading, writing, arithmetic, spelling, grammar, history, geography. He did not mind assignments in reading; in fact, he liked his texts because he found in them much that was new and informational, but recitations generally bored him. For, despite the improvement in the organization of Burlington's schools, classroom procedures continued to be traditional, mostly dull and uninspiring. The indictments of some superintendents read like those which Dewey was later to make against the American classroom generally. There was "too much of learning and teaching parrotwise." [17] The reading was more "a mere pronouncing, or mispronouncing of the words, a lifeless, monotonous, droning utterance of syllables, than . . . intelligent, appreciative, sympathetic expression of thought." [18] The children were often restless; among the older pupils, there prevailed "a languid and shiftless way, and a trifling, frivolous way of study." [19] Although Dewey was rarely among those who caused disturbances, as his almost perfect record for deportment shows,[20] his yawns and fidgetings mingled with those of his classmates in unconscious protest against the monotony he was forced to endure. Nevertheless, Dewey did well in his work. He was allowed to advance rapidly and to catch up first with his own age group, then with the next older, so that he completed his grade-school work at the age of twelve.

Persons who knew Dewey during these early school years have said he was quiet and reserved, but liked fun and was always ready to participate in the play and games of the playground and neighborhood.[21] Shy with strangers, he was friendly and companionable with those whom he knew well. His teachers found him courteous, well-mannered, conscientious, and likeable; some entered his name as "Johnny" instead of "John" on their class lists.

Burlington's school reorganization had extended to the high school, improving it considerably by the time Dewey entered it in September 1872. Two plans of study were open to him: a terminal English course designed for students not going to college and a college preparatory course. Dewey enrolled in the college preparatory course because he vaguely thought he might want to go to college, because his mother had always hoped he would go, and because his closest friends were enrolled in it.

The college preparatory course was heavily weighted in favor of the classics. Dewey was required to take four years of Latin and three years of Greek. In addition he had to take two years of French grammar and composition, one year of English grammar and composition, two years of mathematics; most of his electives were in English literature. As his work was of high quality, he was allowed to double up in his studies to finish the four-year course in three.

Dewey's high-school years marked the time when his interests were expanding; he sought the company of books. In this he was encouraged at home. Both his parents were fond of reading and had over the years accumulated a sizeable collection of books. The recently opened public library offered additional opportunity for reading. Neither Archibald nor Lucina placed any restrictions on their sons' reading, so that John was free to read any books that caught his fancy.

But he was not yet the devotee of books, the bookworm he was later to become. Like most youths growing up in Vermont, Dewey spent much of his leisure time out-of-doors where he acquired a love for nature and the outdoor life that persisted throughout his lifetime. As a boy, he spent many days each summer on his grandfather Rich's farm in Richville, some twenty miles south of Burlington. During his grade- and high-school days when he lived only three blocks from Lake Champlain, he spent much time in and on its waters and along its shores. When he was older and in college, he made frequent hikes to the Green Mountains. The two highest peaks, Mount Mansfield and Camel's Hump, were approximately thirty miles from Burlington; a trip through their foothills and a climb to their summits involved overnight camping with careful preparations. Dewey also worked at odd jobs after school and during the summer, finding work chiefly in the lumber yards tallying lumber.

Dewey had considerable freedom in his studies, reading, and out-of-door activities, but he was carefully restricted in other ways. Although both parents were interested in the moral and religious upbringing of their sons, Archibald was more tolerant and easy-going in this respect than was Lucina. In his fifties when his sons were growing boys, he had considerable understanding of the problems of youth. He would not have been shocked, as Lucina would have been, had he discovered his sons surreptitiously playing ball or marbles on a Sunday afternoon in violation of a city ordinance that forbade such play on the Lord's Day.[22] Relations between father and sons were friendly and cordial; Archibald delighted his sons with anecdotes of his youth and with accounts of his experiences during the Civil War. Some of Dewey's most pleasant memories of his childhood related to his father. "I still recall," he wrote at ninety, "his bringing back to Burlington [from southern Illinois] some lotus pods and we used to rattle the seeds in them, large, flat, sort of crownshaped pods." [23]

Lucina was a kind and generous person, but narrow and strict in her views of morals and religion.[24] As a young woman she had been won over to the evangelical pietism that had taken hold in many parts of the country around the middle of the century; her deepest concern was the moral and spiritual welfare of her sons. She wanted to instill in them her own devout and earnest godliness. At her knees John learned the prayers of childhood and heard stories from the Bible; in her company he went regularly to church and then to Sunday School; at her urging he joined the First Congregational Church in Burlington at the age of eleven; and it was she who wrote for him a typically pietistic note when he was seeking membership: "I think I love Christ and want to obey Him. I have thought for some time I should like to unite with the church. Now, I want to more, for it seems one way to confess Him, and I should like to remember Him at the Communion." [25]

Lucina's concern did not weigh too heavily on John in his early years, but as he grew into adolescence, he began to rebel against the limitations she imposed on him. Lucina condemned dancing, card-playing, pool, billiards, drinking, gambling, and forbade her sons doing these or visiting the places where they were allowed. She questioned her sons constantly concerning their activities, tirelessly reminding them of their moral and religious obligations. Particularly distasteful to Dewey was her recurrent question whether he was "right with Jesus."[26] As if in retrospect of these years, Dewey wrote in one of his earliest articles: "Religious feeling is unhealthy when it is watched and analyzed to see if it exists, if it is right, if it is growing. It is as fatal to be forever observing our own religious moods and experiences, as it is to pull up a seed from the ground to see if it is growing."[27]

Perhaps Lucina's over-solicitude for her sons had an element of abnormality. Psychiatrists would be tempted to say that it grew out of a feeling of guilt and a desire to atone for what she judged to be her sin of negligence in the death of her first-born son.[28] But to her more pious friends and neighbors Lucina seemed the ideal mother for college boys. In a book entitled *Freshman and Senior* published by the Congregational Sunday-School and Publishing Society, Lucina Dewey appears in the character of Mrs. Carver, the wise and understanding counselor of college youths, as solicitous of their moral and spiritual good as of their academic welfare.[29]

That Dewey did not abandon all religion at this time in reaction to his mother's narrow pietism and excessive religious emotionalism is due in large measure to the liberal evangelicalism he was finding in church and college, a form of Christianity more palatable to his developing intellect than was his mother's religion. Like other forms of Protestantism, liberal evangelicalism recognized the Bible as the final test of Christian doctrine. But it rejected the notion that it must be read and interpreted literally or in terms of some historic denominational creed. It believed, instead, that Scripture must be read in the light of experience and intelligence. "Liberal evangelicalism," wrote the Reverend Lewis O. Brastow, its exponent in Burlington's First Congregational Church while Dewey was a member there, "assumes that human intelligence may venture to deal with the facts of revelation and of religious experience and bring back valid results."[30] An intelligent or reasonable approach, however, is not to be identified with a narrow, rationalistic one that judges religious truth a matter for the intellect alone. "A broadly rational estimate of Christianity," said Brastow, drawing on intuitionalist philosophy, "will take into account its adaptation to the whole complex nature of man, not to his intelligence alone. It will find its verification and vindication not merely in the conceptual or speculative understanding, but in the moral and religious nature as well."[31]

Liberal evangelicalism, as presented by Brastow, taught that God the Father is revealed in Christ. To preach Christianity is to preach Christ and redemption. To be a Christian is to accept Christ as an ethical ideal, as master and redeemer, and to grow in Christian perfection. To be redeemed is "to be delivered from the dominating lower life of the flesh, to be rescued to the higher life of the spirit, and to be shaped into a spiritual manhood." But "the rescue and reconstruction are not wholly of individual men in their isolation from their fellows, but of men in their associate life. It is the building in and the building up of men into the body of Christ. . . . No man ever finds completeness in himself. . . . We come to the perfect man, to the perfect stature in Christ, only in our associate life. Men must be won to a common life and built up together in it." [32]

These evangelical teachings came to Dewey during the most impressionable years of his life, sinking deeply into his mind and conscience where they remained a long time.[33] The dualisms involved in some of these teachings, such as that between "the lower life of the flesh" and "the higher life of the spirit," and that between the person one is and the perfect man in Christ one ought to be, became for Dewey a few years later a source of considerable mental and emotional disturbance, as did the dualisms he encountered in his college studies of intuitionalist philosophy. But during his years of graduate study, Dewey believed that he found in Neo-Hegelianism a philosophy that softened the oppositions in liberal evangelical teachings without impairing their Christian content. As a Neo-Hegelian, Dewey took a renewed hold on his evangelical faith; during most of the time that he occupied the chair of philosophy at the University of Michigan, he expressed his religious thinking in terms of the evangelicalism he had learned in his youth. He spoke of "that perfect and living will of God as made known to us in Christ"; [34] he referred to Jesus as "the Teacher of all who know, the Light which lighteth every man that cometh into the world"; [35] and he reaffirmed as man's moral ideal "the perfect and matchless character of Christ." [36] He believed that "the evangelist, ignorant though he be, who is in constant contact with the needs, the sins, the desires and the aspirations of actual human nature is a better judge of religious truth than the man of science, if a truly speculative life has shut him off from sympathy and living intimacy with the fundamental truths of the common nature of man." [37] Only when Dewey developed his instrumentalism did all vestiges of evangelicalism disappear. But the idea learned in his youth that "we come to the perfect man, to the perfect stature in Christ, only in our associate life," reappeared in his mature philosophy as the concept of "shared experience," or, as one writer has expressed it, the "religion of shared experience." [38]

As Dewey neared the end of his high-school studies, he and his family understood that he would go on to college. It was true that he had no definite idea as to what career he wanted after he had finished. But he had shown marked ability in his high-school work; he had a studious and reflective bent; and he was happy in the world of books.

There was never any question as to the college he would attend. It would be the University of Vermont, located in Burlington, the alma mater of most of those in Burlington who had gone to college. Though the charter of the university stated that preference should be given to no religious sect or denomination, the rules and regulations governing the life of the institution reflected the "old American," Protestant, Congregational bias of the faculty and administration. Students were required to attend morning devotions in the college chapel; the members of the faculty were required to take turns leading the devotions; each student was expected to attend the church of his choice on Sunday and to refrain from any activity that would desecrate the day. The use of alcoholic beverages on university premises was forbidden; smoking was permitted in the rooms of students but not in the public rooms of the university; students were warned of possible expulsion should they be found frequenting billiard saloons or "other objectionable places of resort." "The conduct of the students towards all men," read a statement of the university, "is to be regulated by those plain rules of politeness, honor and religion, which are binding on every free and virtuous community." [39]

Despite these overtones of New England Puritanism, Dewey did well to pick the University of Vermont for his undergraduate training. Founded in 1791, it was the fifth oldest college in New England, antedated only by Harvard, Yale, Brown, and Dartmouth. Under its fifth president, James Marsh, it enjoyed an enviable reputation among its sister institutions in New England. Marsh was one of the leaders of the transcendentalist movement in America; as president of the university, he was mainly responsible for introducing radically new programs in studies and discipline. These developments, as Marjorie H. Nicolson noted in "James Marsh and the Vermont Transcendentalists," marked the university as "an institution so important that for years it was considered the center of the most advanced thought in New England, and looked upon by other colleges as daring in its innovations."[40] In 1865, the newly established State College of Agriculture was united with it, adding courses in the agricultural and mechanical arts to its offerings.

The university had always been small; its undergraduate student body never exceeded ninety-four during the years Dewey attended. The faculty numbered eight, all old-type college professors, men of broad scholarship who brought to their subjects a rich store of knowledge gained from the study of other fields. They were well known to Burlington's "old American" community because of close associations in neighborhood, church, civic, and cultural affairs. Goodrich, Perkins, Torrey, and Buckham, for example, were old friends of Archibald and Lucina Dewey and had known John and his brothers from the time they were children. The faculty believed in the sanctity of the human mind and its right to think freely and independently; they encouraged their students to be themselves and to think their own thoughts. Goodrich's lectures in the classics, recalled a former student, aimed not at making perfect classicists but independent thinkers: "His lectures were full of subtle 'digs,' questions, suggestions" designed to stimulate the individual to think.[41] The faculty believed, too, that a student's character as well as his mind should experience growth and refinement while in college; they taught with this in mind. The classroom, with one of these teachers and with ten to fifteen students, came close to exemplifying the old definition of a university—Mark Hopkins at one end of a log and a student at the other. In a speech at the university many years later, Dewey mentioned his "stimulating contacts with teachers who were devoted scholars in their fields."[42]

Dewey was not quite sixteen years of age when he entered the university in September 1875. His earlier shyness had diminished somewhat and he felt more at ease in company, but he was still quiet and reserved with persons he did not know well. He rather envied his two brothers, who were much more adept than he in meeting the demands of a social occasion. His older brother, Davis Rich, though studious like himself, was a good conversationalist with much social poise and charm. His younger brother, Charles, was not only completely at home in a group of young people but also usually the life of the party.[43] Dewey enjoyed fun and appreciated humor, but he reacted with chuckles and smiles rather than with the hearty laughs or uproarious guffaws of adolescents. He was at his best in the classroom or in the discussions and debates of formal or semiformal gatherings. He had a fund of knowledge derived from his reading; his ability to present ideas with logic and precision, even though in a hesitating and drawling manner, won him admiration and respect. Dewey joined the Delta Psi fraternity when he was a freshman, enjoying the social contacts as well as the formal meetings with discussions on serious topics. Easygoing and casual about his appearance, Dewey frequently caused titters because of a crooked tie, an unfastened garter, or a broken shoelace. His gentleness, unfailing courtesy, modesty, obvious sincerity, and genuineness made him well liked; his friends of those years spoke of him always with regard and affection.

The widespread horseplay among students in Dewey's day caused a real discipline problem for the faculty. Though Dewey was not one to start a disturbance, he was not one to stand aloof once it began. Faculty records show that he was among those penalized for tying the door of a classroom thus imprisoning the instructor, and for taking part in a concerted absence from military drill.[44]

Because his college preparatory course in high school with its heavy dose of Latin, Greek, and mathematics had fitted him for the classical course in college, Dewey enrolled in it. The studies in this curriculum, as in the other curricula of the university, were largely prescribed. The students, Dewey recalled, "went through a list of courses one after the other, without its even occurring to us that they were prescribed, so much were they a matter of course." [45]

Most of the subjects of the first three years held only casual interest for Dewey. The Greek and Latin classics, mathematics, rhetoric, English literature merely continued on an advanced level his high-school studies which had lost much of their freshness and appeal. Besides, they were oriented to the past and only infrequently related to the present. The sciences he was required to take were new and interesting, especially the biological sciences that touched upon the controversies on evolution current in academic and religious circles.

The major portion of Dewey's reading, however, was devoted to books and periodicals dealing with matters of widespread current interest. He was at this time, he said, "an omnivorous reader," reading whatever books and magazines were of interest and available to him in the college and city libraries.[46] Dewey's favorite periodicals were the three English ones to which the university subscribed: the *Fortnightly Review*, the *Nineteenth Century*, and the *Contemporary Review*. These journals regularly contained articles on outstanding economic, political, social, moral, religious, and philosophical problems, written by such men as Darwin, Huxley, Wallace, Tyndall, Leslie Stephen, G. H. Lewes,

Frederic Harrison, and their opponents in press and pulpit.

Because of the large amount of time spent with these writers, Dewey's grades suffered. His average for these first three years was 83.5 per cent, with grades ranging from a 69 in Herodotus and a 70 in algebra to an 88 in botany and a 92 in physiology.[47]

In *Democracy and Education* Dewey wrote: "A knowledge of the past and its heritage is of great significance when it enters into the present, but not otherwise. And the mistake of making the records and remains of the past the main material of education is that it cuts the vital connection of present and past, and tends to make the past a rival of the present and the present a more or less futile imitation of the past."[48] This same thesis Dewey maintained again in the 1930s and 1940s in his debates with Hutchins, Meiklejohn, Stringfellow Barr, and others.[49] In defending his position Dewey drew on firsthand experience in a way his opponents could not.

The studies of his last undergraduate year marked a turning point both in Dewey's college career, and also in his life. He was confronted with problems that held a deep fascination for him; in quest of their solution he was led eventually to the pursuit of philosophy as a professional career.[50] Dewey's interest in his senior-year studies is reflected in his marks, which surpassed, in overall average, any he had previously received. His average for the year was 92.35 percent, high enough to give him a four-year average of 86 percent, to win him election to Phi Beta Kappa, and to place him second in his graduating class of eighteen.[51]

The senior-year course of study was designed to introduce students to the fundamental problems of human existence, supplying the capstone to the intellectual structure of the students' preceding three years. The courses were offered by the Department of Philosophy under two headings: political and social philosophy; mental and moral philosophy. The first were not strictly courses in political and social philosophy but rather studies in the history of civilization, political economy, constitutional history, international law, and the Constitution of the United States. Required readings included Guizot's *History of Civilization*, Woolsey's *International Law*, Pomeroy's *Constitutional Law*, Walker's *Science of Wealth*. Books used as references were: Hallam's *International Law*, Mill's *Principles of Political Economy*, and Fawcett's *Manual of Political Economy*. The courses in mental and moral philosophy were the traditional ones at the time: psychology, logic, metaphysics, moral science, evidences of religion, and, in addition, theory of fine arts, and Plato.[52]

Dewey's interest as an undergraduate, he has said, lay largely in the field of political and social philosophy[53]—an interest reflected in "The Limits of Political Economy," the essay he prepared as his senior commencement oration. But problems of metaphysics and of mental and moral philosophy also appealed to him; his first two published articles, written during the two years immediately following his graduation, were on metaphysics rather than social philosophy.

The professor of political and social philosophy while Dewey was a student was Matthew Buckham, also president of the university. Buckham brought to his subjects a considerable background of knowledge along with an aptitude for teaching. He always expressed his ideas in language "so chaste and captivating as to give to his teaching, his public speech, his conversation the charm at once elevating and instructive, to which so many of his students and friends have paid tribute." [54] Buckham made generous use of the Socratic method in the classroom, believing that "the modern teacher cannot do better than to study the didactic art of Socrates." [55] He encouraged the students to ask questions, offer opinions, and to enter into the defense of them. Being "conscientious in all of his civic duties and a loyal member of his political party," [56] he frequently digressed from the scheduled lesson to discuss current social and political problems on all levels. Buckham was socially conservative, reflecting the attitude of Burlington's "old Americans" generally. He was rather impatient with "self-constituted social reformers" and their socialistic utopias.[57] He recognized that individualism might have gone too far in many instances, and he admitted that "thinking men are not now looking in the direction of a further developed individualism for the bettering of man's estate." [58] But he did not believe a radical reconstruction of society was called for: "Society does not need revolution; it needs further development of the principles of its true life. It is imperfect; it tolerates many abuses; it groans under many grievous wrongs; but all this is because men do not yet fully believe and practise the three great Christian social principles: the infinite worth of every man; the solidarity of all men in Christ; the supremacy of righteousness conceived as love." [59]

Dewey undoubtedly absorbed much of Buckham's mature and pious wisdom. But it is unlikely that he accepted without qualification Buckham's doctrine that the evils of rampant individualism can be cured by improving man's moral and religious nature while leaving the structure of society as it is. His reading of current periodicals, especially the more radical *Fortnightly Review*, had made him aware that a rapidly developing industrialism required new controls and new organizations to safeguard the rights of those being victimized. The articles on Comte, especially those by Frederic Harrison, turned Dewey's attention to the great French positivist and led him to read Harriet Martineau's edition of Comte's *Positive Philosophy* in the university library. "I cannot remember," wrote Dewey, "that his law of 'the three stages' affected me particularly; but his idea of the disorganized character of Western modern culture, due to a disintegrative 'individualism', and his idea of a synthesis of science that should be a regulative method of an organized social life, impressed me deeply." [60]

H. A. P. Torrey, nicknamed "Hap" or "Happy" Torrey by the students, was Dewey's professor of mental and moral philosophy. An ordained Congregational clergyman, Torrey left his parish in Vergennes, Vermont, in 1868 to accept the chair of philosophy at the university, a post made vacant by the death of his uncle, Joseph Torrey. Henry Torrey had taken his undergraduate work at the University of Vermont, where his uncle had introduced him to transcendentalist philosophy. Deeply religious, Torrey could recall with great clearness "the moment of his illumination." [61] He joined the First Congregational Church in Burlington when a sophomore in college, remaining a faithful and active member for forty-two years. Unlike Buckham, Torrey remained aloof from civic affairs and confined his off-campus activities to the church. "I remember him," recalled a former student, "as a philosopher living in a congenial atmosphere, untouched by the material and the sordid; having little and wanting little; satisfied indeed with what he had; poor as the world estimates men; but rich beyond all calculation in those rare possessions which satisfied his soul." [62] Dewey's impressions of Torrey are worth recording: "Mr. H. A. P. Torrey was a man of genuinely sensitive and cultivated mind, with marked esthetic interest and taste, which, in a more congenial atmosphere than that of northern New England in those days, would have achieved something significant. He was, however, constitutionally timid, and never really let his mind go. I recall that, in a conversation I had with him a few years after graduation, he said: 'Undoubtedly pantheism is the most satisfactory form of metaphysics intellectually, but it goes counter to religious faith.' I fancy that remark told of an inner conflict that prevented his native capacity from coming to full fruition." [63]

Torrey belonged to the intuitionist school of thought, believing that the dominance of the emotions in human nature carried deep significance for philosophy. "May it not be," he asked, "that the great impulses of hope, desire, and aspiration, unsatisfied in the temporal life, have, like natural instincts, some answering reality in the future? If, trusting them here, our human lives are elevated and enriched, may it not be sane and rational even, in respect to the larger issues, to believe where we cannot prove?" [64] "With intelligent tenacity he held fast to what he regarded as the fundamental principles of consciousness, refusing to be swept away from these moorings." [65]

Intuitionism maintains that the mind is endowed with certain "innate ideas," "primary beliefs," "fundamental principles of cognition" that are the necessary presupposition of all our knowledge of the true, right, beautiful, or divine. The mind accepts these intuitions not because it can rationally demonstrate their validity but because they come to it with a force of conviction the mind is powerless to resist. The mind believes, for example, in God, freedom, and immortality not because it can rationally demonstrate their existence but because its deepest moral and religious impulses declare that they must be real and because they serve as necessary starting points for whatever moral and religious knowledge we might attain.

Intuitionism, thus, provided a reasonable basis for belief in moral and religious realities, freeing men from the skeptical doubts induced by current positivistic and empirical philosophies. It was natural, therefore, that it should be widely acclaimed in academic and religious circles as the champion of morality and religion as well as a defense against the agnosticism, materialism, atheism, and pantheism prevailing in many quarters. Dewey recalled "the almost sacrosanct air that enveloped the idea of intuitions" in his day, and how "the cause of all holy and valuable things was supposed to stand or fall with the validity of intuitionalism." [66]

Torrey selected texts that presented intuitionalism from several points of view; when Dewey was in college these were: James Marsh's works on Psychology, including the *Memoir and Remains,* edited by Joseph Torrey, Noah Porter's *Elements of Intellectual Science,* Hopkins's *Outline Study of Man,* Thomson's *Outline of the Laws of Thought,* Calderwood's *Handbook of Moral Science,* and Joseph Torrey's *A Theory of Fine Art.*[67] Henry Torrey's own deep interest in Kant, on whose *Critique of Pure Reason* he had cut his philosophical teeth, kept the author of the *Critiques* constantly in the foreground of his classroom discussions. Dewey acknowledged the influence on him of Torrey's lectures on Kant. "Thanks to my introduction under your auspices to Kant at the beginning of my studies," he wrote to Torrey, "I think I have had a much better introduction into phil. than I could have had any other way. . . . It certainly introduced a revolution into all my thoughts, and at the same time gave me a basis for my other reading and thinking." [68]

Though an avowed intuitionalist, Torrey subscribed to no particular philosophical system; in this respect, he was an eclectic, taking philosophical truth wherever he judged he had found it. "I cannot say," his longtime colleague and close friend, Matthew Buckham, remarked, "that he was a Cartesian, or a Kantian, or a Hegelian, or a Lotzian; but he was a philosopher, and a ripe one." [69] But, "his eclecticism," we are told, "was that of perfect sanity and self-control." [70] "No unjustified inference, no sweeping induction, no extreme conclusion could command the assent of this judicious finely-poised mind." [71] Unable to find or to work out for himself a satisfactory speculative system, Torrey was unwilling to impose one on his students. "In all the studies of this division," read a catalogue statement of the department, "the end sought is the awakening and training of the powers of reflective thought. The student is encouraged to raise questions and to present difficulties, and the aim of instruction is not so much to impart a system, as to stimulate and guide philosophical inquiry." [72]

Encouraged thus to think for himself, Dewey did so, only to find he did not share the enthusiasm for intuitionalism of those around him. "I learned the terminology of an intuitionalist philosophy," he wrote, "but it did not go deep, and in no way did it satisfy what I was dimly reaching for." [73] Intuitionalism's solutions to the problems of God, man, and the world seemed to Dewey too shallow; its arguments, he felt, frequently proceeded more from a robust religious faith than from an awareness of the philosophical problems involved. What disturbed Dewey particularly was the opposition intuitionalist psychology or mental philosophy sets up between intuition and reason. The domain of intuition, of man's deepest moral, religious, and aesthetic impulses, intuitionalism declares exempt from rational and scientific analysis because it involves realities to which ordinary philosophical and scientific thinking does not apply. What the feelings and emotions proclaim defies philosophical and scientific verification, with no validation other that that given by the "soul" itself. Dewey, on the other hand, believed that intuitions ought not be taken as final. Rather, they ought to be interpreted and subjected to verification by the intellect. In religion, for example, Dewey felt "that any genuinely sound religious experience could and should adapt itself to whatever beliefs one found oneself intellectually entitled to hold—a half-unconscious sense at first, but one which ensuing years have deepened into a fundamental conviction."[74] Dewey could not persuade himself that intuition and reason were rivals; he dimly felt that reason would confirm valid intuitions and that valid intuitions would function as hints or clues to reason as to where truth might lie.

Dewey was equally skeptical of the dualisms set up by intuitionalist metaphysics, the most popular version of which was Scottish commonsense philosophy. Indeed, the attachment between Scottish philosophy and Christianity had become so close that many persons considered them necessary parts of the same system; to reject the one was to discard the other. Scottish realism sharply distinguished God and the world, the divine and the human, the infinite and the finite, man and nature, soul and body, the self and society. Its principle of identity postulated for beings and things a self-identity, a mutual exclusiveness, that no machinery of external relations, however ingenious, could overcome. Dewey sensed that a valid metaphysics would picture reality as unified, its several parts interdependent and functionally related. The model he had in mind was the biological organism, suggested to him by the junior-year course in physiology with Huxley's *Elements of Physiology* as the text. "Subconsciously, at least," Dewey reported, "I was led to desire a world and a life that would have the same properties as had the human organism in the picture of it derived from study of Huxley's treatment."[75]

The most widely accepted alternative to intuitionalist philosophy during the 1860s and 1870s was sensationalistic or empirical philosophy. This doctrine was particularly popular in scientific circles and in more "tough-minded" philosophical quarters. The case for sensationalism, positivism, and empiricism, with accounts of their implications for morals and religion, was ably presented in the *Fortnightly Review*, the *Nineteenth Century*, and *Contemporary Review*. Articles on materialism, agnosticism, naturalism, and humanism appeared regularly under titles such as "The Metaphysics of Materialism," "Materialism and Its Opponents," "Modern Materialism: Its Attitude toward Theology," "An Agnostic's Apology," "The Scepticism of Believers," "The Religion of Positivism," "The Place of Conscience in Evolution," "Evolution as the Religion of the Future," "The New Psychology." The position taken by most of the writers, especially those scientifically trained, was positivism in science and agnosticism in religion and philosophy; Leslie Stephen claimed for these views the distinction of being the convictions of all sensible men.

That Dewey read these articles, there can be no doubt; indeed, the titles which he assigned to his first two published articles, "The Metaphysical Assumptions of Materialism," and "The

Pantheism of Spinoza" are reminiscent of titles that had appeared in the periodicals. Dewey's daughter has said that the English periodicals supplied "the chief intellectual stimulus of John Dewey at this time and affected him more deeply than his regular courses in philosophy."[76]

Because empiricism either dissolved the reality of spiritual objects or rendered them unknowable, Dewey could not accept it. He was, at this stage of his development, too "tender-minded" to disavow all belief in transcendent spiritual realities or to admit that knowledge of them lay beyond the grasp of the human mind. Being at this time ignorant of Hegelianism, Dewey believed that he had no recourse other than to fall back on the intuitionalism and metaphysical dualism with which he was familiar, despite his many misgivings concerning them. The "inward laceration" he said he experienced at this time attests his deep awareness of the dualisms and oppositions in his thinking; it accounts for the "intense emotional craving" for a unifying philosophy to surmount these dualisms. When, a few years later, he judged that he had found such a philosophy in Neo-Hegelianism, it is understandable that he should eagerly embrace it. In so doing, he experienced "an immense release, a liberation."[77]

With the conferring of degrees, Dewey became a Bachelor of Arts, ready to enter upon the next stage of his career. Like many of his classmates in the classical curriculum he had decided on high-school teaching, at least for a time. But as the days and weeks of the summer wore on, he became more and more uneasy. Those who had jobs to offer regarded him as too young and inexperienced to take charge of boys and girls in many cases almost as old as he. Friends and relatives outside Burlington were consulted but with no results. Then, late in September, a relative who was principal of the high school in Oil City, Pennsylvania, wired Dewey that a position had unexpectedly opened up in her school, paying forty dollars a month, which he could have if he desired. Dewey quickly accepted the offer, leaving soon after for Oil City.

2. Instructor in High School, 1879–1882

DEWEY ARRIVED in Oil City at a time when the petroleum industry in Pennsylvania was rapidly developing. This development, begun in the 1850s, had reached a climax around 1865 when more than six hundred oil companies were found in the state.[1] Venango County, where Oil City was located, was one of the areas ranking highest in production; its many derricks and drills became a familiar sight to Dewey. In Oil City itself and in the surrounding territory, "derricks peered up behind the houses, thronged the marshy flats, congregated on the slopes, climbed the precipitous bluffs and clung to the rocky ledges." [2]

Because Oil City was at the mouth of Oil Creek where it emptied into the Allegheny River, all oil coming down either stream had to pass through Oil City. The village was thus the natural center for the shipment of oil, with nearly a mile-long stretch of boat landings and oil wharves at the mouth of Oil Creek and at convenient points along the Allegheny.

Flatboats, barges, and rafts of all kinds were towed up Oil Creek by horses. After being loaded on the banks of the creek with oil either in bulk or barrels, they were floated down the stream by a crew of two or three men and tied to the landings. From here the boats carrying bulk oil were towed by steamer towboats to Pittsburgh to be refined, while those loaded with barreled oil remained tied up till the filled barrels could be transferred by horse and wagon to warehouses and storage lots on the wharves. So great was the traffic in oil that "there were millions of dollars worth of oil stacked up in barrels on the wharves, and in the boats alongside, at almost anytime, for a number of years." [3]

The workers engaged in transporting and transferring oil lived in shanties at the mouth of the river or on barges moored to the shore. This neighborhood, the "shanty town" of Oil City, provided most of the business for the eating places, saloons, and dance halls bordering the area. The laborers, especially the teamsters, were noted for a proficiency in "lurid profanity" that manifested itself particularly when horses and wagon wheels became bogged down in the knee-deep mud on the flatlands, including some of the city's streets.[4]

Growing from a cluster of twelve families totalling about fifty persons in 1860,[5] Oil City in 1880 had a population of 7,315.[6] As was to be expected, its manufacturing and business enterprises were geared mostly to the needs of the petroleum industry. Barrel works, oil well supply stores, refining companies, and lumber yards appeared, so that "everything from the drill point to gasoline was soon made within the city limits." [7]

The Oil City Exchange, organized in 1869 to facilitate transactions among producers, dealers, investors, and speculators in oil, did a flourishing business during the 1870s. To provide more ample quarters a new Oil Exchange Building was erected and formally opened in April 1878, less than eighteen months before Dewey arrived. "The volume of business was immense, the clearances often amounting to ten or fifteen million barrels a day. Only the New York and the San Francisco stock exchanges surpassed it. During fluctuations the galleries would be packed with men and women who had 'taken a flyer' and watched the antics of the bulls and bears intently. Fortunes were gained and lost. Many a 'lamb' was shorn and many a 'duck' lamed. It was a raging fever, a delirium of excitement, compressing years of ordinary anxiety and haste into a week." [8]

With interest in oil and in investments in oil at such a high pitch, it was natural that two brokers living in his boarding house should strongly advise Dewey to borrow money and invest in Standard Oil, already the giant among oil companies. Dewey, more intellectually than investment minded, passed up the advice; instead, he "borrowed books and used the oil in a lamp." [9]

As the city grew during the 1860s and 1870s, elementary schools were added to the one or two already in the district. But not until 1875 was a high school organized to meet the needs of children wanting to continue their education. The work of the school was carried on three years in rented rooms until a three-story brick and stone structure was completed in 1878 at the corner of Central Avenue and Fourth Street; in this building Dewey met his classes during the two years he was in Oil City.[10]

Like so many high schools of this period, Oil City High School kept no permanent records, thus very little is known about

Dewey's experiences there.[11] The only evidence the high school has of Dewey's teaching is two commencement programs, one for 7 June 1880, the other for 10 June 1881. Each of these lists Dewey as one of a three-member teaching staff and as assistant principal. The two other instructors were women—Miss E. A. Kent and Miss Affia Wilson, Dewey's cousin. The 1880 program lists six students graduating; the 1881 program mentions thirteen.[12] These figures would indicate that the total student body was not large, probably between seventy-five and one hundred.

During his two years at the high school, Dewey taught classes in Latin, algebra, and the natural sciences.[13] Since his college studies had included four years of work in each of these fields, Dewey had little difficulty handling these subjects on the several high-school levels. On the other hand, as he had had no professional training or practice in classroom teaching, his inexperience must have at times been apparent to teacher and students alike.

The students were in general well-behaved. Those who might have been tempted to take advantage of Dewey's youth and inexperience were disarmed by his friendliness, sincerity, and modesty, so that whatever disturbances there may have been were minor. Contrary to notions popular in Oil City school circles long after Dewey had left, reports from former students indicate that Dewey was well-liked and respected by his students, who took no more liberties with him than with the other two teachers.

Affia Wilson stood ever ready to help and advise her young cousin on both personal and professional matters, often in the presence of students, causing suppressed amusement among them and embarrassment to Dewey. When students twitted him about his over-solicitous relative, Dewey made no attempt to hide his displeasure.[14]

Since class preparation did not require an excessive amount of his attention, Dewey had ample time for other matters. Activities around the landings and wharves on the shores of Oil Creek must certainly have interested him; he would frequently have been on the creek bridge with others who watched the barges and boats making their way downstream. His love for the outdoors probably sent him on trips with friends to the surrounding hills and nearby oil wells. The Oil City Opera House, first built in 1872 and completely remodeled in September 1878 just a year before he arrived, gave Dewey an opportunity to attend performances by "many of the best known theatrical stars."[15]

Dewey had at this time an experience he later recalled for Max Eastman. He said it was a "mystic experience" that came,

Eastman reported, as "an answer to that question which still worried him: whether he really meant business when he prayed." The essence of the experience was a feeling of oneness with the universe, a conviction that worries about existence and one's place in it are foolish and futile. "It was not a very dramatic mystic experience," Eastman continued. "There was no vision, not even a definable emotion—just a supremely blissful feeling that his worries were over." Eastman quoted Dewey, "I've never had any doubts since then, nor any beliefs. To me faith means not worrying. . . . I claim I've got religion and that I got it that night in Oil City." [16]

However real this experience may have been to Dewey, it brought about no marked change in his religious practice. For the next dozen years he maintained membership in a church, attended religious services; when he prayed he did so as though he really meant business. When he later abandoned evangelical Christianity, embracing first absolute idealism with its emphasis on the unity of existence, then humanistic naturalism with its stress on the continuity of man and nature, he did so primarily for intellectual and philosophical reasons rather than for emotional or mystical considerations.

Dewey continued to maintain the interest in philosophy that had begun during his senior year in college, now spending much of his spare time reading in this field. Though social issues had been his primary concern while an undergraduate, and despite the fact that Oil City provided a superb opportunity for him to observe the social problems arising from raw, uncontrolled industrialism, his efforts were directed to problems of metaphysics.

His attention was drawn to metaphysical materialism, then being debated in philosophical and literary journals to the considerable concern of those interested in conserving traditional moral and religious values. Examining what he considered the unconsciously held assumptions of materialism, Dewey concluded the logical development of these would result not in a materialistic monism but in a dualism of mind and matter and an intuitionalist theory of mind—theories within whose framework traditional moral and religious values could find a secure lodging.

Dewey put his ideas together in an article entitled "The Metaphysical Assumptions of Materialism" which he sent to W. T. Harris, editor of the *Journal of Speculative Philosophy*, on 17 May 1881 just a few weeks before the close of the school year in June. Dewey's letter which went with the manuscript was important because the reply it evoked was influential in turning him to the pursuit of philosophy as a professional career. He wrote:

> Enclosed you will find a short article on the Metaphysical Assumptions of Materialism, which I should be glad if you could make use of, in your Review. If you cannot, if you will be so kind as to inform me, stamps will be sent for its return.
>
> I suppose you must be troubled with many inquiries of this sort, yet if it would not be too much to ask, I should be glad to know your opinion on it, even if you make no use of it. An opinion as to whether you considered it to show ability enough of any kind to warrant my putting much of my time on that sort of subject would be thankfully received, and, as I am a young man in doubt as to how to employ my reading hours, might be of much advantage. I do not wish to ask too much of your time & attention however.[17]

With the close of the school year in June, Dewey left Oil City for Burlington where he awaited Harris's reply.

Dewey did not return to Oil City for a third year. He had accepted an offer to teach during the winter term in a small academy in Charlotte, Vermont—a village sixteen miles south of Burlington; he had also arranged with Professor Torrey for private tutoring in the philosophical classics and in philosophical German during the months he was not teaching.

Upon his return home, Dewey did not remain idle. During the summer and fall months he continued his study of philosophy, directing his attention to the pantheism of Spinoza as argued in the *Ethics,* probably prompted by the many articles that had appeared on the bicentenary of Spinoza's death in 1677. Dewey's examination led him to conclude that as a theory of knowledge Spinoza's pantheism breaks down. Spinoza starts with a definition of Substance, proceeding to demonstrate in geometrical fashion that it is an Absolute Perfect Being in whom all things exist. But in proving this, Spinoza's doctrine cannot account for things as we find them. It denies that they are what they seem to us to be and elevates them into the Divine. Why they seem to us to be other than they really are, Spinoza's doctrine cannot explain. The result of Dewey's study was a second article, "The Pantheism of Spinoza," which he forwarded to Harris, even though he had not yet learned the fate of the first manuscript which he had sent, saying:

> Enclosed you will find some thoughts upon Spinoza's *Pantheism* tending to show its inadequacy as a theory of knowledge. As they seem to me to bring out one or two things commonly overlooked in criticisms of Spinoza, I send it to you thinking perhaps you may find it a suitable article for your Journal.[18]

The day after this note was mailed, the long awaited letter from Harris concerning the article on Materialism arrived. That letter is not extant, and so we do not know the exact words that helped launch Dewey on a career in philosophy, but Dewey's next letter indicates Harris's reply had been encouraging.

> Yours of 17th inst. is at hand. Thanks for your favorable opinion. I should be glad to have you print it, if you desire. As I do not take the Journal myself, if you do print it, I should be glad to have a copy or two. Yesterday, previous to receiving your communication, I sent another article to you upon the Pantheism of Spinoza. I should be glad to have you make any use of that which you see fit. I am a young man, having studied Philosophy but a comparatively short time and do not particularly [care] for pay for any articles that you think worthy of print.[19]

Harris, busy with other matters, let time slip by without replying to Dewey. Finally, after more than eight months of waiting, Dewey wrote Harris asking whether he had reached a decision on the Spinoza article, offering at the same time to help Harris in work connected with the *Journal of Speculative Philosophy*:

> As it has been some time since I have had the pleasure of hearing from you, I take the liberty of writing to ask if you have found time as yet to look over the article upon Spinoza, and when there is any probability of the other article being published? Your duties as head of the Concord Summer School must, of course, keep you very busy, and, as I have considerable leisure time, if I can help you in any way by proof reading or anything of the sort I shall be very glad to do so. I should be much pleased if you would feel perfectly free to call upon me at any time when I could aid you in any way. Do you wish any translations for the Journal? I have been reading recently K. Rosenkranz' brief introduction to Kirchmann's ed. of Hegel's Encyclopädie, which seems to bring out clearly both Hegel's relation to Kant & his own leading principles. If you desire, I should be glad to send a translation.[20]

How Harris responded to Dewey's offer of help, we do not know. But he used both of Dewey's articles in his *Journal*—the one on Materialism in the April 1882 issue[21] and the one on Spinoza in the July issue of the same year.[22] In later years, Dewey referred to these articles as "highly schematic and formal," saying, "My deeper interests had not as yet been met, and in the absence of subject-matter that would correspond to them, the only topics at my command were such as were capable of a merely formal treatment."[23]

When Lake View Seminary in Charlotte, Vermont, started its winter term, Dewey began another period of high-school teaching. His task was somewhat difficult because he had to guide the school in the period after a recent reorganization. The Methodist

Episcopal Society had maintained a school in Charlotte from 1840 to 21 November 1880 when fire destroyed its building. During the ensuing year parents and others interested in providing secondary education for the town's children raised money by voluntary subscription to erect a new building on the site of the old, also reorganizing the school under the title of Lake View Seminary. The Lake View Seminary Association, formed to provide continuing support and to oversee general school operations, invited Dewey to take charge of the school during the winter term of 1881–82.[24]

Charlotte was similar to villages scattered throughout rural Vermont. Literally a crossroads, but commanding a magnificent view of Lake Champlain, it had the seminary, one church (Methodist), two general stores, a shoe shop, a blacksmith shop, and about twenty dwellings.[25] Dewey stayed with a family in the village during the school week, going home weekends on a train that passed through the village on its way to Burlington and Montreal.

The school had between thirty and thirty-five pupils, ranging in age from thirteen to twenty, mostly from farm families. Many were ill-prepared for the work they undertook and belonged more properly on lower levels of study, which led to much frustration for both pupils and teacher, creating the general opinion among the townspeople that Dewey's teaching was not "average good." [26]

While most of the children were well-behaved, the older boys were mischievous and unruly, and played all manner of pranks on each other and their teacher. Dewey's attempts to control the situation were only partly successful; the impression in the community was that he was too inexperienced, too gentlemanly in manner, to be an effective disciplinarian. "I remember two things in particular about Mr. Dewey's teaching," recalled Miss Anna L. Byington, one of the pupils, "how terribly the boys behaved, and how long and fervent was the prayer with which he opened each school day." [27]

Hired only for the winter term at Lake View Seminary, Dewey was free the other months to pursue his plan of reading philosophic classics and discussing them with Professor Torrey. These conversations usually took place during their walks in nearby woods. Teacher and pupil came to understand each other to a degree not possible in the classroom: the teacher expressed himself more freely and fully, while the pupil discovered the man and the thinker behind the professor. Recalling these days with Torrey, Dewey wrote: "In our walks and talks during this year, after three years on my part of high-school teaching, he let his mind go much more freely than in the class-room, and revealed potentialities that might have placed him among the leaders in the development of a freer American philosophy—but the time for the latter had not yet come." [28] The pupil in his turn talked and questioned more freely, making the teacher aware of powers of mind in the pupil that he had only dimly suspected in the classroom.

Dewey and Torrey frequently discussed John's future. They agreed that he should not continue teaching on the secondary school level; Torrey suggested that he make philosophy his life's career, a daring suggestion because universities at this time seldom employed as professors of philosophy men who had not been thoroughly grounded in Christian theology. Yet the proposal had merit: Dewey had an absorbing interest in philosophy and his first efforts in the field had earned the praise of W. T. Harris. After some deliberation, Dewey decided to follow Torrey's suggestion; he immediately laid plans for graduate study in philosophy at The Johns Hopkins University.

Dewey's deep gratitude to Torrey for his help during this year in Burlington is shown in his statement many years later: "I owe to him a double debt, that of turning my thoughts definitely to the study of philosophy as a life-pursuit, and of a generous gift of time to me during a year devoted privately under his direction to a reading of classics in the history of philosophy and learning to read philosophic German." [29]

One matter that troubled Dewey was how to finance his studies. He had not been able to save much from his teaching salary, and his father, retired for some years from business, was in no position to help him. Learning that The Johns Hopkins University was offering twenty $500 fellowships to graduate students, Dewey applied for one, asking Torrey to write in his behalf. Torrey's letter to George S. Morris who taught philosophy at the Johns Hopkins concisely sums up Torrey's judgment of Dewey's qualifications:

> Allow me to recommend Mr. John Dewey as a candidate for a Fellowship in the Johns Hopkins University in the department of Philosophy. Mr. Dewey was graduated with honor at the University of Vermont in the year 1879. While in college he showed a decided aptitude for philosophy, and since his graduation he has made it his special study. With a marked predilection for metaphysics, Mr. Dewey seems to me to possess in a rare degree the mental qualities requisite for its successful pursuit. I feel sure that his high character and devotion to philosophy would ensure the best results if the opportunity were afforded him to cultivate his powers in that direction.[30]

When word came during the summer that he had not received the award, Dewey immediately applied for a lower paying scholarship. His letter to President Gilman of the Johns Hopkins reflects Dewey's concern:

> I am very anxious to continue my studies in Philosophy and Psychology and though much disappointed in not obtaining a Fellowship, wish greatly that you could give me one of the scholarships, as that would enable me to carry on my studies during the next year. Of course, I should not make the request if I were not so situated pecuniarily as to make it almost impossible to go on without aid and I feel confident that if I were to secure that aid, I could render a good account of it, and of myself.
>
> I have rec'd the circular of instruction for the coming year and find that I have read almost all the books recommended as preparatory—and others, more than an equivalent for those which I have not. If you will kindly inform me as to my prospects of getting aid, and under what conditions it is given I will be extremely obliged.[31]

Again Dewey suffered disappointment when he failed to receive the scholarship. But, having by now fully made up his mind to go to the Johns Hopkins, he decided to borrow the $500 an aunt had offered to lend him. He thereupon sent in his application for admission, receiving word in a short time that he had been admitted to the graduate division for advanced study in philosophy.

3. The Johns Hopkins University, 1882–1884

DEWEY was almost twenty-three years old when he began his graduate studies at the Johns Hopkins in September 1882. He chose the Johns Hopkins for his advanced training because of its reputation as the one institution in America where opportunities for graduate study were at all comparable to those offered by European universities. Founded in 1876, only a few years before Dewey entered, the university was a pioneer in graduate study, in teaching by means of seminars and laboratories, in encouraging research by faculty and advanced students, and in sponsoring scholarly publications.

During its early years the university had a small but select body of graduate students. "To look through the list of first students at the Johns Hopkins University is to obtain a preview of the men who were to become the distinguished members of the faculties of American universities in the thirty or forty years that followed."[1] The graduate student body when Dewey first entered the university numbered one hundred and twenty-five; this jumped to one hundred and fifty-nine the following year. Classes were generally small, especially in philosophy, where enrollment ranged from two to eleven. This made for exceptionally close personal relations, creating a situation in which exchange of ideas among students and instructor commonly prevailed.

The campus of the university when Dewey attended it lay only a few blocks from the heart of Baltimore's business area; it has since disappeared as the city closed in. The seven or eight academic buildings were in or facing the block bounded by Howard, Eutaw, Monument, and Little Ross streets, the last of which no longer exists. Near the campus was the Peabody Institute whose sixty thousand volumes of scholarly reference material supplemented the limited collection of books in the library of the university. As the university had no dormitory system, students were scattered among the private rooming and boarding houses in neighborhoods adjacent to the campus. The places Dewey lived while he attended the university have long since been torn down, their places taken by parking lots or business structures.[2]

The expectation that advanced students as well as faculty would engage in original research was a great stimulus to scholarly activity, lending the university an atmosphere of excitement not matched elsewhere. Josiah Royce, who had preceded Dewey at the Johns Hopkins by a few years, wrote that "the beginning of the Johns Hopkins University was a dawn wherein ' 'twas bliss to be alive.' . . . The air was full of rumors of noteworthy work done by the older men of the place, and of hopes that one might find a way to get a little working-power one's self." [3] Dewey, addressing a group at the University of Michigan shortly after his arrival there, declared, "What more than anything else strikes the student at Baltimore is the atmosphere of activity and ambition in things intellectual. There is no mental laziness nor deadness. The student is treated not as a bucket for the reception of lectures, nor a mill to grind out the due daily grist of prepared text-book for recitation, but as a being in search of truth, which he is to discover for himself, the proper encouragement and advice as to means and methods being furnished by the instructor." [4]

Dewey found the intellectual climate at the Johns Hopkins highly invigorating; he devoted himself unstintingly to both his course work and scholarly research, producing, in addition to his doctoral dissertation, three articles accepted for publication while he was still a student.[5]

With an endowment of nearly three and one-half million dollars, a very considerable one at that time, the Johns Hopkins made generous provisions for its several departments. Philosophy was the lone exception. President Daniel C. Gilman of the university, caught up in the general enthusiasm for science at the time, was reluctant to spend much money on philosophy, being inclined to give it to departments whose fields of study were more empirically grounded. Besides, he felt that graduates in philosophy had little chance of getting positions teaching philosophy in American colleges and universities, which continued to employ as instructors only those trained in Christian theology. As a gesture of friendship, he tried at first to dissuade Dewey from majoring in philosophy.

The lack of administrative support for philosophy was reflected in the small number of advanced courses given by the department. Confined to History of Philosophy, Logic, and Psychology, there were just enough in number to satisfy requirements for major work in the department.[6] Such areas as Ethics, Economics, Political and Social Philosophy received only incidental treatment or no treatment at all. "No one realizes more than I," Dewey wrote, "the great benefits of the courses given here, but no one realizes more than the instructors I presume their inadequacy in extent to cover the ground which a *University* ought to cover."[7]

Partly to offset the lack of course offerings in political, economic, and social philosophy and partly because of his interest in social problems, Dewey selected history and political science as his minor fields of study. The courses he took in these areas during his two years of graduate study were: Institutional History (two semesters), Sources of English History, Comparative Constitutional History, American Institutions and American Economics (two semesters), and International Law. These courses, in some instances, covered the same ground as the senior year requirements at the University of Vermont.[8] But Dewey was expecting that the advanced courses at the Johns Hopkins would probe more deeply into the facts and also give a philosophical interpretation of them. That the courses did not do this he felt was their weakness. "I am taking as a minor subject," he wrote W. T. Harris, "the theory of state, international law &c., in the historical department, & am in pretty close contact with the men there. It was the largest, & in the character of its students about the strongest dep't. in the Univ., but there is no provision to give them the philosophic side of their own subjects. The philosophy of history and of social ethics in its widest sense is untouched, & as long as it remains so, they don't get more than half the good of their own courses it seems to me."[9]

The course offerings in logic by Charles S. Peirce were quite different from what Dewey expected, proving a disappointment to him. He had come to the Johns Hopkins prepared to study "philosophic logic," the different forms of knowledge, their origins and development, their interconnection, and their comparative value as embodiments of truth. The logic Peirce taught was largely mathematical logic and scientific methodology. "I am not taking the course in Logic," Dewey wrote to Torrey shortly after he had become settled in his studies. "The course is very mathematical, & by Logic, Mr. Peirce means only an account of the methods of physical sciences, put in mathematical form as far as possible. It's more of a scientific, than philosophical course. In fact, I think Mr. Peirce don't think there is any Phil. outside the generalizations of physical science."[10] Dewey took the course during his second year, more from necessity to fill in his program of study than from genuine interest. As the course neared its end, he complained to W. T. Harris that "Mr. Peirce lectures on Logic, but the lectures appeal more strongly to the mathematical students than to the philosophical."[11] Only after some twenty years of further study did Dewey recognize the great significance of Peirce's work in logic, making it the basis of his own.

The courses in psychology at the Johns Hopkins were in line with the new trends in this field. G. Stanley Hall, the instructor, was a man of broad academic training and interests. His advanced studies had been first in theology, but a growing skepticism had led him to abandon this for philosophy and literature. The appearance in 1874 of Wundt's *Grundzüge der physiologischen Psychologie* aroused his interest, and he went to Germany to study under its author. Convinced that the "new psychology" had a promising future, he decided to make it his primary interest. Upon his appointment to the chair of psychology at the Johns Hopkins in 1882, Hall established two courses in physiological and experimental psychology, adding a course in speculative psychology called Psychological and Ethical Theories. He was also asked to give a seminar in "scientific pedagogics" for those who intended to teach. Dewey took all these courses, performing, in addition, some independent experiments in the psychological laboratory that Hall had set up. These experiments, as Dewey described them, had to do with attention, "one set to determine, if possible, what effect fixing attention upon one thing very strongly, has upon a 'remainder' in consciousness, & the other the effect attention has in producing involuntary muscular movements—something after the 'mind' reading fashion."[12]

Dewey's greatest satisfaction by far came from the courses he took under George Sylvester Morris, professor of philosophy at the University of Michigan, who had been coming to the Johns Hopkins since 1878 to lecture for part of each year on the history of philosophy. Morris had gained prominence in philosophical circles first with his translation in 1872–73 of Ueberweg's *History of Philosophy* and then with subsequent writings.[13] After studying in Germany under Trendelenburg, he had on his return worked out a version of Neo-Hegelianism which, as Dewey recalled, combined "a logical and idealistic metaphysics with a realistic epistemology."[14] His courses under Morris during his first year of graduate study were: a seminar in Science of Knowledge, History of Philosophy in Great Britain, and Hegel's Philosophy of History.

The second year they were: a seminar in Spinoza's *Ethics* and History of German Philosophy "with special reference to the movement from Kant to Hegel."

Dewey described the first two courses in a letter to Torrey shortly after he had begun his graduate studies:

> My work under him [Morris] is four hours a week in the history of Phil. in Great Britain—from Bacon to Spencer; and twice a week in the Philosophical Seminary, as it is called. The latter I think will, in many ways, be the more profitable. It is "for the study of texts relating to the Science of Knowledge." The method of working is this. We begin by reading Plato's *Thaeetetus* [*sic*] (in translations) and along with it are given subjects relating to matters suggested by the text—the writings of Heraclitus, Democritus, Protagoras, &c. One subject is given to each, & he is expected to look up the fragments that remain of that author's writings, consult leading authorities, &c., and then give an account of it before the class. We then take up Aristotle's *De Anima* & treat in a similar manner. By the time of finishing we will be supposed to have a pretty good knowledge of Greek Phil. & from original sources as much as possible—at least of Gk. Phil. in so far as it relates to the question of the origin, meaning &c. of knowledge. . . .
>
> His lectures upon Brit. Phil. will be rather of a critical character than descriptive, & tend to show the inadequacies, contradictions &c. of Sensationalism & Agnosticism.[15]

He discussed the courses in Spinoza and German philosophy in a letter to W. T. Harris:

> Just at present I am working with Prof. Morris in two courses—one, lectures on German Philosophy, beginning with Leibniz. He has but half a year, and so this year the bulk of the course has been from limitation of time confined to Kant. Just now he is upon Schelling, and will give I suppose a short outline of Hegel before concluding. The other course is upon Spinoza's Ethics, which has been studied *seminarisch.* Dr. Morris & each of the students in turn takes up the hour in expounding certain propositions—explaining them in their reference both to Spinoza's system and to philosophic discussion in general. Thus the course has been the means not only of giving a very good knowledge of Spinoza, but of elucidating the logic of Pantheism and "identity" systems in general, special attention having been called of course to the difference between mathematical & philosophic procedure and method. Both courses have afforded me as much instruction as interest.[16]

Morris's teaching personality deeply impressed his students. Believing wholeheartedly in what he taught, he presented his ideas with a force and sincerity his students did not easily forget. "My chief impression of Professor Morris as a teacher, vivid after the lapse of years," wrote Dewey in 1915, "is one of intellectual ardor, of an ardor for ideas which amounted to spiritual fervor. His very manner as he lectured on a theme dear to him was like an exemplification of his own attachment to the Aristotelian theme, that the soul is the form, the entelechy, of the body."[17]

Dewey's initial grasp of Morris's general philosophical position is reflected in a letter written after only a few weeks of class sessions with Morris:

Prof. Morris, as one would judge from that article in the Princeton,[18] on "Phil. & its problems" is a pronounced idealist and we have already heard of the "universal self." He says that idealism (substantial idealism as opposed to subjectivistic, or agnosticism) is the only positive phil. that has or can exist. His whole position is here, as I understand it. Two starting points can be taken—one regards subject & object as in mechanical relation, relations in and of space & time, & the process of knowledge is simply impact of the object upon the subject with resulting sensation or impression. This is its position as science of knowing. As science of being, since nothing exists for the subject except these impressions or states, nothing can be known of real being, and the result is scepticism, or subj. idealism, or agnosticism. The other, instead of beginning with a presupposition regarding subj. & object & their relation, takes the facts & endeavors to explain them—that is to show what is necessarily involved in knowledge, and results in the conclusion that subject and object are in organic relation, neither having reality apart from the other. Being is within consciousness. And the result on the side of science of Being is substantial idealism—science as opposed to nescience. Knowing is self-knowing, & all consciousness is conditioned upon self-consciousness. . . .

Have you seen his work on Kant's Critique? His opinions are pretty well developed there.[19]

Partly because of Morris's own genuine devotion to Neo-Hegelianism and partly because the problems troubling Dewey at this time seemed to find solutions in Neo-Hegelianism, he became a quick convert to it. Dewey had come to the Johns Hopkins with a background in intuitionalist philosophy of both the Kantian and Scottish Realist varieties. As an undergraduate he had accepted intuitionalism but with full awareness of its weaknesses, which lay, he believed, in the dualisms it set up between the infinite and the finite, the divine and the human, mind and reality, soul and body, the self and society. These dualisms deeply disturbed him; he had "an intense emotional craving" for a philosophy that would overcome them,[20] a craving intensified by the difficulties he was encountering in his religious experience. Brought up in the tradition of liberal Congregational evangelicalism, he had at first no trouble accepting its teachings; later he found it increasingly difficult to reconcile certain of its doctrines with ideas he felt intellectually entitled to hold.

Neo-Hegelianism, as expounded by Morris, seemed to Dewey to meet his needs. Its conception of reality as an organic unity whose parts are interrelated like those of a biological organism removes the barriers that intuitionalism raises between things; its view that reality is a single organic Life or Mind that differentiates itself into countless finite lives or minds, realizing its own higher Life in and through these finite ones, bridges the gap between the infinite and the finite, the divine and the human.

Finding in Hegelianism the insights for which he had been groping, Dewey experienced a satisfaction that was as emotional as it was intellectual in its overtones. Philosophy, up to this time mostly an "intellectual gymnastic" for him, now became "an immense release," liberating his ideas and feelings from their different compartments and fusing them in a system of thought in which both his mind and heart could find their fulfillment.[21]

Thus involved in Neo-Hegelianism, Dewey's reading was devoted primarily to works by Neo-Hegelians, especially Thomas Hill Green, John and Edward Caird, William Wallace, and others; he judged the movement represented by these men as "at the time the vital and constructive one in philosophy."[22] It was natural, too, that Dewey's writings at this time should expound Neo-Hegelianism to show its superiority over other philosophies.

Dewey's first paper at the Johns Hopkins, inspired by Morris's course in British philosophy, was an examination of the relativity theory of feelings and of this theory's implications for philosophy. This essay is important in a study of Dewey's philosophical development because it reveals how quickly he was won over to Morris's way of thinking. The paper, which he entitled "Knowledge and the Relativity of Feeling," was presented to the Metaphysical Club at the Johns Hopkins on 12 December 1882, just three months after he began his work with Morris.[23] Dewey sent it on 29 December 1882 to W. T. Harris with the following note:

> I send an article on Relativity of Feeling in which I have attempted to apply to one of the phases of Sensationalism the same kind of argument which I used regarding Materialism. If you should like to use in the Journal Spec. Phil. I should be glad to have you. However, I do not wish to crowd you.

The article appeared in the next month's issue.[24]

Following Morris's line of thought in *British Thought and Thinkers*, Dewey argued that it is logically impossible simultaneously to hold the two propositions that feelings (i.e., sensations) are relative and that all knowledge comes from sensations. For, to say that feelings are relative implies the existence of an objective reality which we know absolutely and in reference to which we recognize our feelings as relative. But to hold that all knowledge comes from sensations that are relative implies we cannot know anything absolutely; therefore we can never know that our sense knowledge is relative. For his part, Dewey accepted as true the first proposition, because it is undeniable that sensations, mediated as they are by a nervous system, are relative. But he rejected as false the second proposition. For he found a knowledge not derived from sensation, that is, the knowledge held by a thinking consciousness that experiences simultaneously both the sensations and the objective existence, compares them, and judges the former to be relative. Dewey therefore concluded that the relativity of feelings theory lends support not to sensationalism, subjectivism, or agnosticism as is commonly supposed, but to a theory "which admits the constitutive power of thought, as itself ultimate Being, determining objects." [25]

Dewey's next two papers reflect his growing interest in philosophic method and his conviction that Hegelianism corrects the faults of preceding philosophies. "Philosophic method" is at the heart of any philosophy, because as Dewey used the term, it means a method and criterion for arriving at truth. The first paper, "Hegel and the Theory of Categories," was delivered before the 10 April 1883 meeting of the Metaphysical Club. Because it is not extant, one can only conjecture as to its content. It is safe to assume, however, that it was an appreciative account of Hegel's dialectical method that presents truth as an absolute and harmonious system of concepts arrived at through the union of opposites in a superior synthesis. The second paper was prepared about this same time for presentation to the committee administering graduate fellowships for the academic year 1883–84; it was eventually published in the April 1884 issue of the *Journal of Speculative Philosophy* under the title, "Kant and Philosophic Method." [26]

Dewey believed that Kant started on the right road to a valid philosophical method when he recognized that reason had synthesizing as well as analytic powers, the former enabling it to construct an intelligible world. But an initial error betrays Kant and prevents him from reaching the true philosophical method. Like the rationalists and the empiricists whom he criticizes, Kant makes a "mechanical" separation of subject and object. He postulates, on the one hand, a synthesizing reason, and, on the other, a thing-in-itself lying outside reason. What reason synthesizes, says Kant, is the sense-manifold sent out by the thing-in-itself; what reason knows is the world of appearances or phenomena it has helped to construct. Thus, whatever validity Kant's criterion of truth may possess relates to the world of phenomena, not to the world of real things. Kant's philosophy, therefore, ends in subjectivism, phenomenalism, and agnosticism, falling short of providing a valid method. Kant's doctrine, however, contains the germ of the correct method. "All through his *Critiques*," Dewey wrote, "is woven the notion of an intuitive understanding which is the ultimate criterion of all truth"; and this, it turns out, is the valid criterion.[27] But Kant never develops this theory of an intuitive understanding or "synthetic unity of apperception," as he calls it in his *Critique*. It was left to Hegel to do this to arrive at the "completed Method of Philosophy." [28] This method is "an account of the conceptions or categories of Reason which constitute experience, internal and external, subjective and objective, and an account of them as a system, an organic unity in which each has its own place fixed." [29]

Dewey's fourth paper, written in the fall of 1883 during his second year at the Johns Hopkins, was prompted by a discussion he had had with Torrey on one of their walks together during the preceding summer. The two had discussed the close relation that seemed to exist between the conscious and the unconscious activities of the mind; the more Dewey thought about this the more fundamental it appeared. All our mental activities, he found, including those of our moral nature, seem to be influenced by psychical activities that do not as such come into consciousness. By identifying an unconscious psychical activity with "one that has lost its own particular existence, and has been taken up into the mind i.e. has become one of the functions whereby the mind apperceives," Dewey believed he had solved the problem. But this presupposes the existence of a "permanent identical self-consciousness" which is "continually differentiating itself into 'states' or successive conscio*usnesses*." Thus, the facts uncovered by this study, Dewey found, had led him to "conclusions essentially identical with those of 'transcendentalism.' " Dewey put his ideas together in a paper entitled "The Psychology of Consciousness," which he read to the meeting of the Metaphysical Club held 13 November. The paper was never published, but he described the content in a letter to Torrey four days after the meeting.[30]

Dewey wanted very much to finish his graduate work and get his Ph.D. degree by the end of his second year of study. He had the ever-recurring problem of how to finance his study, but perhaps the dominant reason was his eagerness to get a position teaching philosophy and to settle down to his profession. To complete requirements for his degree, Dewey had to write a doctoral dissertation; to this he set himself. "I am endeavoring to get my Ph.D. this year," he wrote to W. T. Harris, "and my own work is being done largely upon my thesis." [31]

Because Dewey's dissertation was never published and has never been found, the account of it he gave to Harris is particularly interesting. He wrote that the subject of the thesis was "Kant's Psychology":

> that is his philosophy of spirit (so far as he has any), or the subjective side of his theory of knowledge, in which besides giving a general acc't of his theory of Sense, Imagination &c., I hope to be able to point out that he had the conception of Reason or Spirit as the centre and organic unity of the entire sphere of man's experience, and that in so far as he is true to this conception that he is the true founder of modern philosophic method, but that in so far as he was false to it he fell into his own defects, contradictions &c. It is this question of *method* in philosophy which interests me most just at present.[32]

These remarks indicate that the doctoral dissertation covered much the same ground as the earlier essay "Kant and Philosophic Method," reaching very much the same conclusions. Dewey confirmed this in a letter four years later, in 1888, in which he said that "The article [i.e., "Kant and Philosophic Method"] published there [i.e., the *Journal of Speculative Philosophy*] was in somewhat the same line [as the doctoral dissertation] & was presented to obtain the fellowship, but the doctorate thesis . . . has never been published. 'The Psychology of Kant' was its title." [33]

Dewey's concern with philosophic method was matched during the closing months of his graduate study by his interest in the new psychology. When he first began his studies in this field, he wrote to H. A. P. Torrey: "I don't see any very close connection between it & Phil. but I suppose it will furnish grist for the mill, if nothing else." [34] But as his studies in this field expanded, Dewey grew excited about the new psychology and its implications for philosophy. He expressed these thoughts in an essay "The New Psychology," which was presented to the Metaphysical Club at its 11 March 1884 meeting and published the following fall in the *Andover Review*.[35]

In this essay Dewey explained the new psychology in terms of the influences that physiology, biology, and other disciplines had had on it. Study of the physiological conditions of psychical activity has led to the introduction of the experimental method in psychology, supplementing the method of introspection in many fruitful ways. From biology have come the ideas of organism and environment. When the former is adopted and applied to the mental life, psychical activity is viewed as "an organic unitary process developing according to the laws of all life." [36] When the concept of environment is taken into account by psychology, it leads to the awareness that the mind does not develop *in vacuo* but in an organized social life that helps shape and determine it. Thus the new psychology has drawn on the sciences of society, history, abnormal psychology, and other disciplines for data and inspiration.

Dewey continued his account by asserting that the "unity and solidarity of psychical life" that the new psychology insists upon refutes older psychologies that break the mental life up into a medley of isolated atomic sensations and ideas or reduce it to independent autonomous faculties. Moreover, Dewey argued, the logic implied in the new psychology rejects the logic implied in the old psychologies. The new psychology, he said, perhaps with Peirce in mind, "abandons all legal fiction of logical and mathematical analogies and rules" of the old psychologies, and throws itself upon experience, "believing that the mother which has borne it will not betray it." [37] The old psychologies employed a logic by which "that rich and colored experience, never the same in two nations, in two individuals, in two moments of the same life . . . was neatly and carefully dissected, its parts labeled and stowed away in their proper pigeon-holes, the inventory taken, and the whole stamped with the stamp of *un fait accompli.*" The new psychology repudiates such formal schematic logic and replaces it with "the logic of fact, of process, of life." [38]

It is clear from this analysis that Dewey saw an essential identity between the basic concepts of the new psychology—its organicism, its dynamism, its rejection of formalism as a logical model—and those of Neo-Hegelianism; he sensed the problem of bringing these two areas of thought together in some detailed and systematic way.

The two years Dewey spent as a graduate student at the Johns Hopkins contributed much to his intellectual development. They led him to identify himself with Neo-Hegelianism and the new psychology, and they confronted him with the problem of bringing the two together—a problem that was to engage his very best efforts over the next few years and bring him to the attention of the philosophical world. But these years of study did more. The study of Hegel, as Dewey acknowledged later, "left a permanent deposit in my thinking." [39] What this deposit was, he explained in these words:

> Hegel's idea of cultural institutions as an "objective mind" upon which individuals were dependent in the formation of their mental

life fell in with the influence of Comte and of Condorcet and Bacon. The metaphysical idea that an absolute mind is manifested in social institutions dropped out; the idea, upon an empirical basis, of the power exercised by cultural environment in shaping the ideas, beliefs, and intellectual attitudes of individuals remained. It was a factor in producing my belief that the not uncommon assumption in both psychology and philosophy of a ready-made mind over against a physical world as an object has no empirical support. It was a factor in producing my belief that the only possible psychology, as distinct from a biological account of behavior, is a social psychology. With respect to more technically philosophical matters, the Hegelian emphasis upon continuity and the function of conflict persisted on empirical grounds after my earlier confidence in dialectic had given way to scepticism. There was a period extending into my earlier years at Chicago when, in connection with a seminar in Hegel's Logic I tried reinterpreting his categories in terms of "readjustment" and "reconstruction." Gradually I came to realize that what the principles actually stood for could be better understood and stated when completely emancipated from Hegelian garb.[40]

Dewey's abilities were recognized early by George Sylvester Morris. The contributions his young student made to seminar discussions, his written papers, his talks before the Metaphysical Club convinced Morris that Dewey had the potential of an outstanding scholar. Consequently, when someone was sought to teach the undergraduate course in History of Philosophy during the second semester of the academic year, 1882–83, Morris saw to it that Dewey was appointed to the position. The class, which met twice a week, numbered only seven.[41] Dewey was extremely pleased to have, at long last, an opportunity to teach the subject in which he was so interested, but he modestly denied that it was any great honor for him to have received the appointment. "Graduate students in all the depts.," he wrote to Torrey, "assist more or less in the instruction of undergraduates, and as I am the only one making a specialty of the hist. of phil. it was not such a very great honor." [42]

Dewey said of the first course in philosophy he taught in his long career,

The class, of course, is undergraduates. Ueberweg's Hist. is used as the text-book, omitting, of course, a good deal. The object is to give them as much as possible a knowledge of what different phils. have held—as matter of fact, and not critically so that they will have at least a knowledge of some of the questions of phil. and the answers that have been given, and also such a textual knowledge of the theories of different writers, that if they wish to continue the study they will have a good basis in fact. So my work is confined to asking them questions on the text and elucidating it where it needs it. There will only be about 30 recitations on the whole of modern phil. so of course it can't go in very deeply. I have had three recitations so far. Tomorrow we take up Hobbes. It has not only been enjoyable, but promises to be of great advantage in fixing my own knowledge. It will be a fine review for me.[43]

To help finance his second year at the Johns Hopkins Dewey applied in the spring of 1883 for a teaching fellowship, an application that had the hearty support of Morris and other members of the Department of Philosophy. President Gilman, however, had certain misgivings and thought it advisable to get some additional data on Dewey before making the appointment. Consequently, in a letter dated 30 March 1883 to President Buckham, he requested that both Buckham and Torrey send him information concerning Dewey's personal traits. Gilman's letter conveys his impressions of Dewey as a young man:

Mr. J. Dewey, one of your graduates, has been here during the past winter and has made a very favorable impression upon our teachers of philosophy;—& his name has been considered for an appointment. Personally I find him quite reserved,—due perhaps to the fact that our acquaintance has some of the barriers of an official relation; & I have therefore decided to ask you, & through you Professor Torrey, what sort of a character, intellectual, moral, & religious he has sustained. If we invite him to a post as teacher, next year, his instruction will be given to undergraduate students. I have doubted, whether with his recognized mental power, he had enough pedagogic power which is what we are particularly in need of. I shall of course regard any answer you may be so kind as to make as confidential.[44]

The letters Gilman received in reply, written by men who had watched him grow from a child to a mature young man, reveal the kind of person John Dewey was judged to be at this time. President Buckham wrote:

John Dewey has a logical, thorough-going, absolutely independent mind. He is sound and sweet all through—is true and loyal in matters of religion, and without any crotchets, or drawbacks of any kind, so far as I know. He is very reticent, as you see—probably lacks a due amount of self-assertion. This is the only question that would arise in the minds of those who know him—whether he has the amount of dogmatism that a teacher ought to have. I am inclined to think that the confidence in him implied in an appointment would reinforce his own confidence in himself and go far toward overcoming the defect.[45]

Two days later, Torrey wrote in behalf of his young friend and former student:

I have at hand your letter of inquiry concerning Mr. John Dewey addressed to President Buckham. With respect to Mr. Dewey's intellectual ability, I may say that I have never had a pupil in philosophy who has shown more clearness and penetration, as well as original power, and frequent conversations with him upon philosophical subjects since his graduation have led me to form a high opinion of his ability in that direction. Philosophy is his chosen pursuit. From early youth he has manifested a deeply reflective turn of mind, accompanied by the reticence which often attends it. This natural reserve however diminishes considerably on more intimate acquaintance.

Mr. Dewey has always sustained an irreproachable moral character. When quite young he joined the church of which I am a member. Sincerity and depth of conviction rather than emotion have characterized his religious life. He is thoroughly trustworthy in these respects.

In regard to his teaching ability, I have really had no opportunity to judge. I should suppose, however, that in subjects entirely congenial to his natural tastes he would prove a successful teacher. Certainly his pupils could not complain of want of clearness in his instructions. With increased experience and familiarity with his work, I should expect that he would soon acquire practical skill in the art of teaching.

Permit me to say that I have been highly gratified that Mr. Dewey has already been called upon to give instruction temporarily in the philosophical work of the University, and to express my earnest hope that he will fully justify the confidence you have placed in him.[46]

With such backing Dewey was granted a fellowship and listed among the fellows in *The Johns Hopkins University Circular* of 1883–84. His fellowship meant that with fewer financial worries, he could concentrate more fully on his studies and research, despite being called upon occasionally to conduct classes in philosophy.

Social life among students at the Johns Hopkins was markedly different from that on most American campuses. There were no set patterns of student activities such as weekend dances, athletic events, fraternity and sorority parties, homecomings, or hazings. The students had to find their own forms of recreation in the city around them. A modest room over a grocery store served as a social center for members of the university; here students and faculty gathered during off-hours for jollity and good fellowship in the manner of students at German universities.[47] Referring to this side of life at the Johns Hopkins, Dewey later remarked: "The chapter on student life in Baltimore would resemble the famous chapter on snakes in Ireland. There is no student life there. The students are swallowed in the whirl of the great city. The distinctive traditions and customs of the American college are unknown. Were one to ask where college life there centred, he would be pointed to a little club room where students and teachers meet to drink German beer, and sing German songs. There it centres, and there it begins and ends."[48]

What Dewey liked most in the way of recreation was exploring Baltimore, experiencing the sights and sounds of America's sixth largest city, usually with a friend or two and with his brother Davis who had entered the Johns Hopkins a year after Dewey to study economics. After the inhibited life of his childhood and youth, he enjoyed the freedoms of a city where he could go to a theater, drop into a tavern, or miss church with no questions asked. Along with other students he played the part at times of a supernumerary in plays staged in a Baltimore theater. In an interview with Dewey on his ninety-first birthday, a reporter for *The Johns Hopkins News-Letter* found that "there's more of Baltimore than Hopkins that the philosopher-educator remembers sixty-six years later. Ford's theatre brings back memories of a young spear, or message, carrier who would dash on and off stage and then back to school to finish his doctoral thesis on the psychology of Kant." [49]

One of Dewey's last tasks as a graduate student was to take a comprehensive examination for his Ph.D. degree. How well he acquitted himself is revealed in a letter that Morris sent to President Gilman from Ann Arbor, in which he said: "I am delighted to hear that Mr. Dewey's oral examination was so creditable. His name is under serious consideration for a subordinate appointment here." [50]

Morris's recommendation that Dewey be added to the Department of Philosophy staff at the University of Michigan caused no surprise among those who knew them both. Morris was impressed very early with Dewey's potential as a scholar and teacher; he had secretly nourished the hope that Dewey might be appointed at the University of Michigan. He had hinted about the possibility of such an appointment but up to the time he left the Johns Hopkins for Burlington, Dewey had received no further word.

As the weeks passed at home with no offer of a position, Dewey began to wonder whether his decision to abandon secondary school teaching had been wise. Then, in July, he heard from President James B. Angell of the University of Michigan that the university was ready to appoint him an instructor in philosophy at a salary of nine hundred dollars. The letter from Angell was especially cordial since he knew Dewey's parents and remembered Dewey as a little boy from the years when he had been president of the University of Vermont. Dewey was naturally elated with the offer. In his letter to Angell accepting the appointment tendered him, he wrote:

> The notification of appointment to an Instructorship in the Univ. of Mich. was received, and I take pleasure in accepting. I hope my work with you will be of such a character that you may not have to regret the appointment.

While thanking you very much for what you have done to secure me the position, I wish to thank you also for your very kind and friendly words to me personally. I assure you that I appreciate your good wishes, and esteem it an honor to have been remembered by you for so many years.

My parents join with me in expressions of regard, and desire to be remembered to yourself and Mrs. Angell.[51]

With his student years behind him and a position at a distinguished university awaiting him, Dewey was ready to embark on the career that was to bring him worldwide fame and honor.

4. Early University Positions, 1884–1889

THE UNIVERSITY OF MICHIGAN, where Dewey began his duties as instructor in philosophy in September 1884, had already attained considerable prominence among the colleges and universities of America. "In the number of students, quality of instruction, and eminence of men upon her faculties," reads one account, "Michigan stood without a rival beyond the Alleghenies." [1] The student body was not large by present-day standards. During 1885–86, Dewey's second year in residence, it numbered 1,401; by 1893–94, Dewey's last year in Ann Arbor, it had increased to 2,660.[2] The faculty in 1890 had eighty-six full-time members. There were eighteen buildings, including some faculty residences, on the spacious campus grounds just a few blocks from the village business area.

For the pleasant personal relations that prevailed at the university, President James Angell was largely responsible. "To all who taught under him," wrote Dewey's daughter, "Angell remains the ideal college president, one who increased the stature of his institution by fostering a truly democratic atmosphere for students and faculty and encouraging the freedom and individual responsibility that are necessary for creative education." [3]

The situation in the Department of Philosophy was an especially happy one for Dewey. His friendship with Morris, started at the Johns Hopkins when Dewey was a graduate student there, had led to the position he was now entering upon. A year later, in 1885, when Morris was offered the headship of the department, he stated as one of the conditions of accepting that Dewey be put on a permanent basis as his associate in the department.[4] Throughout this first period at Michigan, Dewey and Morris enjoyed "the most intimate and single-minded cooperation." [5] Their association was a major factor in Morris's rejecting an offer to the chair of philosophy at Cornell University in 1885 [6] and one that also made Dewey "quite loathe" to leave Michigan for the University of Minnesota in 1888.[7]

In the university's early years, the teaching of philosophy had been handicapped by the limitations imposed upon it by theology. As at most colleges and universities at the time, the professors of philosophy were mostly clergymen [8] who used philosophy primarily to support a theological position, never examining or questioning its presuppositions. This situation changed in 1881; when Morris was appointed professor of philosophy, he introduced a new spirit of freedom in the teaching of philosophy. Morris was an Hegelian; in his courses he extended the point of view of German idealism to the several fields of philosophic thought. His earlier associates shared Morris's enthusiasm for idealism, adopting this point of view in their courses.

The emphasis on German idealism did not meet with the favor of all students. During the year just prior to Dewey's coming, discontent was expressed in student publications. It was charged that the stress on German idealism caused neglect of "Mill and Spencer and the whole modern scientific school of Philosophy"; further, that this was done "in order to counteract, so far as possible, the growing skepticism and agnosticism among a large class of the best students." [9] The students demanded more instruction in the teachings of Mill and Spencer, especially their philosophy of religion. "What we hold is, in short, that proper instruction is not given on religious subjects in a fair, comprehensible and completely undogmatic way, and based upon data to which all can assent." [10] To this was added that "when young men see the philosophy of these persons, whom they have been taught to respect in science, rather contemptuously left unnoticed, an idea that perhaps it is a disinclination to grapple with them on the part of the professors, is liable to take possession of their minds." [11]

With Dewey as his assistant, Morris revamped the program of studies in the department. Under the new arrangement much more attention was given to empirical and physiological psychology and to British philosophy, especially that of Herbert Spencer. But emphasis remained as before on German philosophy; the point of view adopted was that of Hegel. Even in Dewey's courses in scientific psychology, the interpretation given was in terms of absolute idealism. Hegelianism, as expounded by Morris and Dewey, was generally recognized as the "official" philosophy of the department, so that this division of the university came to be regarded in academic circles at home and abroad as one of the important centers of idealist thought.

The newly worked out schedule of courses assigned to Morris: History of European Philosophy; History of Philosophy in Germany; History of Philosophy in Great Britain; Ethics, Historical and Theoretical; the Philosophy of the State and of History; Aesthetics; and Real Logic, described in the *Calendar* as "the Science of Objective Intelligence, containing the Foundations of the Philosophy of Nature, of Man, and of the Absolute." Morris also conducted a seminar in Hegel's *Logic*. Dewey took over the courses in psychology, offering: Empirical Psychology; Special Topics in Psychology (Physiological, Comparative, and Morbid); Psychology and Philosophy with special reference to the History of Philosophy in Great Britain; Experimental Psychology; Speculative Psychology; and History of Psychology. His courses in philosophy were: Formal Logic; Greek Science and Philosophy; Kant's *Critique of Pure Reason*; the Philosophy of Herbert Spencer; and seminars in Plato's *Republic* and in Kant's Ethics.[12]

During his second year of teaching, Dewey wrote to H. A. P. Torrey, his former professor of philosophy at the University of Vermont, telling of his classes, referring to the one in Plato's *Republic* as "the most interesting class I have had this year so far. . . . There is certainly a great advantage in beginning with those old Greeks. There is a freshness and humanity about them that modern philosophy seems to have succeeded in losing." Dewey added that he was dissatisfied with current textbooks in psychology and was in process of writing one of his own: "Whether I can succeed in bettering the existing text-books, or even in getting it published remains to be seen. I am simply trying, however, to write one with the greatest possible unity of principle, so that without ceasing to be a psychology, it shall be an introduction to philosophy in general."[13]

Dewey was not above publicly calling the attention of students to the offerings in philosophy. When enrollment in the advanced courses in the department proved disappointing, he inserted a notice in the student paper urging students not to confine their course work in philosophy to one of the required elementary courses. "Like all elementary studies, these are mostly 'grinds.' One has to continue his work if he is to derive any particular good from the study. For those who have this work there are several courses in advanced Psychology given by Mr. Dewey and work in the history of philosophy by Prof. Morris, who also offers a course of lectures on 'Ethics' which may be very advantageously taken by those who have just finished Murray's Psychology."[14]

The notice must have borne fruit; in a second letter to Torrey, shortly after the second semester began, Dewey wrote that "the second semester's work began last week, and finds philosophy in a more flourishing condition than the last." He reported that he had 130 students in Logic, "fortunately divided into three sections," each of which he met twice a week. Morris's class in Ethics, he said, numbered 50 and the one in the History of Philosophy about 25. Concerning his advanced courses, Dewey wrote: "I have 10 or 12 in Herbert Spencer's First Principles, and a very nice class of about 20 in a course which I call speculative psychology, discussing philosophical problems from the psychological side." [15]

Because the Hegelianism of Morris and Dewey had a place for traditional Christian concepts, the extension of its point of view to the several courses in philosophy and psychology gave the department a distinctly religious atmosphere that satisfied all but the most orthodox that the religious faith of the students was as safe under Morris and Dewey as it had been under clergymen. The whole department, wrote a faculty colleague in the Latin department, was "pervaded with a spirit of religious belief, unaffected, pure and independent"; the courses given in it, he added, were much more likely to help the student "encounter the skepticism of the age" than were "the more dogmatic lessons inculcated in those institutions which, for particular reasons, feel obliged to advertise the teaching of religion as a specialty." [16]

Morris's religious philosophy was expounded in his highly regarded *Philosophy and Christianity*.[17] In this, he argued that the results of a philosophical study of knowledge point unmistakably to an absolute or final object of knowledge best identified as the God of Christianity. The general trend of the argument is that of "a pietistic, but not dogmatic, orthodoxy, while the perspective is that of absolute idealism, mediated theistically." [18]

Probably because he felt that Morris and such other idealist writers as John and Edward Caird and T. H. Green had sufficiently demonstrated the compatibility of Hegelianism and Christianity, Dewey himself did not undertake this task. But he affirmed with them that Hegelian philosophy "in its broad and essential features is identical with the theological teaching of Christianity," [19] and he reacted rather impatiently to "a tendency in some minds to call every philosophic theory pantheistic which does not offer itself as the baldest deism." [20] But Dewey did enter the lists with other idealist writers to show that the spiritual principle which idealism puts at the core of reality can resist the encroachments of the natural sciences.

One of his first attempts at this was an article entitled "Soul and Body,"[21] in which he declared that religion has nothing to fear from the new physiological psychology despite "the exactest demonstrations of physiology regarding the closest connections of body and soul."[22] Dewey based his claim on facts revealed by the new psychology—the organization and localization of functions in the brain and nervous system. These were not originally in the body, said Dewey; their appearance needs to be explained. He denied the materialist doctrine that they developed automatically and blindly because this doctrine cannot explain why these organizations and localizations so obviously fit the needs and purposes of the mind. The only adequate explanation, Dewey believed, is that they were acquired by the body under "the tuition and care of the soul" and for the sake of ends.[23] Instead of viewing mind and mental processes as mere by-products of the body as the materialist asserts, it is nearer the truth to say that the body in large measure is the product of mind.[24]

A somewhat similar argument appears in "Ethics and Physical Science,"[25] in which Dewey attacked the materialistic interpretation of reality on the ground that it cannot adequately account for man's moral life, for man's ability to entertain moral ends, to make choices, and to view his conduct in the light of an ideal. Materialism claims that the moral evolves from the nonmoral, but this Dewey could not see. He insisted that at least the germ of morality must somehow be present in matter from the first if we are to account for the fully developed moral life that eventually comes. "Granted the germ of morals working from the first, granted that this whole structure of the physical is only the garment with which the ethical has clothed itself, then we can see how the germ shall finally flower in the splendor of the moral life, how the garment shall finally manifest the living form within; but not otherwise."[26] This consideration, Dewey declared, points to a spiritual or religious principle at the heart of reality. "We believe," he wrote, "that the cause of theology and morals is one, and that whatever banishes God from the heart of things, with the same edict excludes the ideal, the ethical, from the life of man."[27]

His course work in psychology enabled Dewey to continue the research that had interested him toward the end of his graduate work at the Johns Hopkins. His studies there, first in Hegelianism, then in the new physiological psychology, had revealed a striking similarity between the two in their use of such concepts as organicism, dynamism, continuity, and anti-formalism.[28] The idea that had occurred to Dewey was to bring the new psychology and Neo-Hegelianism together in a single system of thought without doing violence to either. Now, at Michigan, Dewey made a beginning at this in two articles that appeared in *Mind* in 1886. The first, "The Psychological Standpoint,"[29] argued that since both philosophy and psychology deal with conscious mind and its contents, that is, with experience, the only difference between the two must be one of degree: philosophy is only an expanded or more comprehensive psychology. Philosophy therefore needs no special method or point of view of its own. It needs only to extend the point of view of psychology to have all it requires in the way of method.

This doctrine, Dewey knew, ran counter to that generally held by Neo-Hegelians; therefore in a second article, "Psychology as Philosophic Method,"[30] he addressed himself to them. Idealists, he pointed out, make a sharp distinction between philosophy and psychology. They define philosophy as the science of an absolute self-consciousness that needs a method and procedure all its own to discover the ultimate nature and content of this ultimate self-consciousness; they define psychology as the study of the phenomenal manifestations in finite minds of the Absolute Mind, requiring no methods other than simple empirical ones.[31] Dewey argued the untenability of this position by pointing out that the Absolute Mind and its phenomenal manifestations are one and the same reality viewed from different angles; a single method, that of psychology, is all that is needed. Psychology, he said, is "the ultimate science of reality, because it declares what experience in its totality is; it fixes the worth and meaning of its various elements by showing their development and place within this whole. It is, in short, *philosophic method.*"[32]

The two *Mind* articles brought Dewey to the attention of the philosophical world, stamping him as one of the most original and independent thinkers in America. They also precipitated a skirmish with Shadworth H. Hodgson, an eminent private scholar in London. In an article in *Mind* entitled "Illusory Psychology," Hodgson accused Dewey of "first generalising his own consciousness and making an *ens logicum* of it, and then reconverting it into a really existent consciousness with the attribute of omniscience."[33] By this one stroke, said Hodgson, Dewey substituted psychology for philosophy and made his psychology a largely illusory one.

Despite his preoccupation with teaching, developing his courses, research, and writing, Dewey found time to support campus organizations such as the Philosophical Society, a departmental club founded by Morris in the spring of 1884 just a few months before Dewey arrived.[34] The society was similar to the

Metaphysical Club at the Johns Hopkins to which Morris and Dewey had also belonged; it provided opportunity for the discussion not only of technical problems of philosophy but also of philosophy's bearings on questions in history, literature, politics, science, and religion.[35] Papers read by faculty and students at the monthly meetings were discussed. Dewey was elected to membership at the first meeting of the society after his arrival and gave the principal address of that meeting.[36] His talk, on "Mental Evolution and Its Relation to Psychology," was reported as "without doubt the ablest discussion that has been given in Ann Arbor for some time." [37]

The Students' Christian Association also claimed a large amount of Dewey's attention. This association was one of the most flourishing student organizations, boasting a membership at one time of 294, or over 22 percent of the total student body.[38] It sponsored Sunday morning meetings featuring a talk on some religious topic, usually by a member of the faculty; it made periodic religious surveys of faculty and students; it provided Bible classes for its members; and it published a monthly bulletin. During his first year at the university, Dewey conducted a Bible class of the association, taking as the subject for study "the life of Christ—with special reference to its importance as an historical event." [39] He frequently addressed the Sunday morning meetings, speaking on such topics as "The Obligation to Knowledge of God," "Faith and Doubt," and "The Place of Religious Emotion." [40]

Dewey's religious activities were not confined to those sponsored by the Students' Christian Association. He was also active in Ann Arbor's First Congregational Church, which he joined almost immediately after his arrival in the city.[41] Though faith in democracy and its possibilities was shortly to replace his faith in the Church and its work, at this time Dewey viewed the Church as "the highest product of the interest of man in man," [42] giving it his wholehearted support. He faithfully attended services on Sunday; he conducted a Bible class in "Church History" for students during 1887–88; [43] and he participated in the business meetings of the church.[44]

Dewey's interest in primary and secondary education began during these early years in Michigan. The University of Michigan was an integral part of the state's public school system, but, until 1871, graduates of the state's secondary schools could gain admittance to the university only by passing a formal academic examination on their ability to do university work. In 1871, however, the university decided to admit students with a diploma granted by schools meeting the university's academic requirements. Investigating committees of university administrative and faculty members were sent to high schools that wanted to enter into this arrangement. The committees were charged with determining whether the quality of instruction at a given school and the attainments of its students warranted their being admitted to the university without examination. As one of these investigators, Dewey visited a number of high schools in the state and became interested in what he found there.

Dewey was among the first to sense the need of an organization to study problems of mutual interest to high schools and colleges, and was one of nineteen charter members of the Michigan Schoolmasters' Club when it was founded in 1886.[45] He frequently addressed its meetings, serving as its vice-president in 1887 and 1888.[46]

Because of the close correlation between high-school achievements and grade-school training, Dewey was led quite naturally to a study of the elementary schools. His experience with them convinced him that the methods employed were not in keeping with what psychology teaches about the normal processes of learning in little children. This conviction sent Dewey in search of an educational theory that would reconcile the demands of education, psychology, and philosophy—a search that occupied a major portion of his attention throughout his long philosophical career.

Dewey maintained during these years a deep interest in social affairs but he did not join any social reform movement or enlist in any cause. Rather, he confined his efforts to stating the broad moral and social principles that should undergird society and guide social reform. His essay *The Ethics of Democracy*[47] is a statement of the social liberalism current at the time among English and American idealists. In this, Dewey argued against the individualistic liberalism of the eighteenth century, the notion that society is nothing more than a numerical aggregate of individuals externally related. Society, he maintained, is a social organism; its members are bound together internally by common purposes and ideals. It exists in order to make possible the fullest realization of individual personality, which becomes possible when the individual finds his proper place in the community and freely participates in the larger life of society, as he can most nearly do in a democratic social order. There is an individualism in democracy, Dewey asserted, but it is a moral and not a numerical one. "It is an individualism of freedom, of responsibility, of initiative to and for the ethical ideal, not an individualism of lawlessness."[48]

Dewey came closest to confronting a current controversial

issue when he touched upon industrial democracy. "There is no need to beat about the bush," he wrote, "in saying that democracy is not in reality what it is in name until it is industrial, as well as civil and political." [49] To make democracy industrial, said Dewey, requires that industry be treated as a social function serving the interests of all. But this does not imply socialism; it does not mean "that in some way society, as a whole, to the abolition of all individual initiative and result, is to take charge of all those undertakings which we call economic." It means rather "that all industrial relations are to be regarded as subordinate to human relations, to the law of personality." In the conflict between individualism and socialism, Dewey sided with individualism, believing that the individual initiative and responsibility that are "at the very heart of modern life" should remain there.[50]

The individualism Dewey advocated was not that of an unrestricted laissez-faire. Such an individualism, Dewey recognized, results in evils which no society can tolerate and which must be prevented by law. One function of government is to correct and prevent abuses that appear in the industrial order and to help those victimized by it. Dewey's individualism does not rule out trade unionism; workers have the right to form unions to guarantee themselves a voice in determining the conditions under which they work, a power they lost when the factory system came into being.[51]

Dewey maintained a close friendship during his Michigan years with Henry Carter Adams.[52] The two of them constituted a nucleus of liberal thinkers around whom other liberals at the university rallied. Adams was professor of political economy at the university, but his approach to social problems was more that of the social philosopher than of the technical political economist. Like Dewey, Adams was born in a family of New England, Calvinist background, with a strong, puritan sense of social justice. But unlike Dewey at this time, he made concrete human situations rather than abstract principles the point of departure for his thinking; he never hesitated to deal with specific controversial issues. A talk he gave on labor in New York City during the strike on the Gould railroad system had resulted earlier in his dismissal from Cornell.[53] Adams publicly condemned such evils of laissez-faire as child labor, hazardous working conditions, long work days, low wages, exorbitant profits; he joined the socialists in their attacks on them. But unlike the socialists he had no desire to see industry socialized and brought under minute governmental regulation. This, he believed, would be as tyrannical as the unbridled industrialism it sought to cure. Like Dewey, he was "an advocate of the philosophy of individualism against socialism"; [54] also like Dewey, he stood for a middle course between unrestricted laissez-faire and complete government control. This middle course was an economic order in which individual freedom and initiative would prevail but be curbed by legislation whenever they produced evils that violated basic human rights and offended the public conscience. Adams was a strong champion of trade unions because he was convinced that "combination among workingmen is a necessary step in the re-crystallization of industrial rights and duties." [55]

The important event in Dewey's personal life during these first years in Ann Arbor was his marriage to Harriet Alice Chipman. She had been brought up in Fenton, Michigan, a village some forty miles northwest of Ann Arbor. Her parents had died when she and her sister were very young, and they had been cared for by their maternal grandparents, Frederick and Evalina Riggs. Frederick was a colorful, adventurous type, who had had a rich background of experience both in the West and Midwest; since he had made his way by relying on his own resources and initiative, he expected his granddaughters to do the same. He made light of accepted conventions and traditions, preferring to think his own way through in religion, politics, and social issues. He had had close associations with Indians in the West, and had sided with them in their attempts to get social justice from the white man. The self-reliance, independence of thought, and sensitivity of social conscience that characterized Alice Chipman as a young woman can in substantial measure be traced to influences encountered in her grandparents' home.[56]

Alice Chipman had entered the University of Michigan in the fall of 1882; she was a junior when Dewey began his duties there. She had been graduated from the Baptist Seminary in her home town, then had taught in the nearby village of Flushing before beginning her university work.[57] According to her daughter, "she had a brilliant mind which cut through sham and pretense to the essence of a situation; a sensitive nature combined with indomitable courage and energy, and a loyalty to the intellectual integrity of the individual which made her spend herself with unusual generosity for all those with whom she came in contact." [58] She had a deep interest in philosophy, having taken a number of courses in the department before Dewey arrived. A charter member of the Philosophical Society, she had read a paper at one of its first meetings.[59] During her last two years in college, she took most of the remaining courses available in the Department of Philosophy, including three advanced ones with Dewey: Plato's

Republic; Special Topics in Psychology; and Greek Science and Philosophy.[60]

Alice was twenty-five years of age, a month older than Dewey, when they first met at the boarding house where they both roomed. A friendship developed, culminating in their engagement. But they had to wait till July 1886 for their marriage. Financially it would have been difficult to manage earlier. Alice had just enough money to carry her through two more years of college; as an instructor, Dewey had a salary of only nine hundred dollars,[61] scarcely enough to support a household. By July 1886, the situation had changed: Alice had finished college, and John had been promoted to an assistant professorship at a salary of sixteen hundred dollars.[62] They were married on 28 July in Alice's home town of Fenton; upon their return to Ann Arbor, they lived first at 44 Thompson Street and then at 84 South State Street.[63] Their first child, Frederick Archibald, was born in 1887.

Alice's influence on her husband's intellectual development has been well stated by their daughter:

> Her influence on a young man from conservative Burlington was stimulating and exciting. . . . Awakened by her grandparents to a critical attitude toward social conditions and injustices, she was undoubtedly largely responsible for the early widening of Dewey's philosophic interests from the commentative and classical to the field of contemporary life. Above all, things which had previously been matters of theory acquired through his contact with her a vital and direct human significance. Whatever skill Dewey acquired in so-called "intuitive" judgment of situations and persons he attributes to her. She had a deeply religious nature but had never accepted any church dogma. Her husband acquired from her the belief that a religious attitude was indigenous in natural experience, and that theology and ecclesiastic institutions had benumbed rather than promoted it.[64]

The book on psychology Dewey had been working on appeared in 1887. Since this was his first book, its publication brought him great satisfacton; it also made him a focus of attention in both philosophical and psychological circles. In the *Psychology*, Dewey brought together in a single system the results of the new empirical physiological psychology and the doctrines of philosophical idealism. His procedure was to present in a detailed, systematic way the facts of psychology revealed by the latest scientific studies, then to interpret them in terms of Hegelian idealism. Thus the reader is led to believe that the facts of empirical psychology naturally and inevitably lead over into German metaphysical idealism.

The *Psychology* was praised highly in many quarters. "More

than any other book of the kind in English that I have ever read," commented George S. Morris, "it is a real contribution to self-knowledge." [65] Among the institutions that adopted it as a text were Dewey's alma mater, the University of Vermont, Williams, Brown, Smith, Wellesley, the University of Minnesota, and the University of Kansas.[66] The University of Michigan used it as a text for the next ten years.[67]

The book had its hostile critics, who attacked Dewey's mixing psychological and metaphysical material and allowing the speculative element to determine the meaning of the psychological. "The facts," wrote G. Stanley Hall, Dewey's former professor of psychology at the Johns Hopkins, "are never allowed to speak out plainly for themselves, or left to silence, but are always 'read into' the system which is far more important than they." [68] And in a letter to Croom Robertson, editor of *Mind*, William James wrote:

> Dewey is out with a psychology which I have just received and but one-half read. I felt quite "enthused" at the first glance, hoping for something really fresh; but am sorely disappointed when I come to read. It's no use trying to mediate between the bare miraculous self and the concrete particulars of individual mental lives; and all that Dewey effects by so doing is to take all the edge and definiteness away from the particulars when it falls to their turn to be treated.[69]

But even the book's harshest critics had to admit the skill with which Dewey made the results of the work of Helmholtz, Fechner, Wundt, and other experimental psychologists do service to German idealism. "That the absolute idealism of Hegel could be so cleverly adapted to be 'read into' such a range of facts, new and old," wrote G. Stanley Hall, "is indeed a surprise as great as when geology and zoology are ingeniously subjected to the rubrics of the six days of creation." [70]

The controversy over the *Psychology* was taken up by the students, some of whom sided with the opposition. The following are excerpts from a poem that appeared in a student publication when the controversy was at its height. The poem portrays "Psychology" as an apparition that comes to a man in deep reverie named Dewey, addressing him as follows:

> But first let me say, I'm myself not to blame
> For wearing a mask that should put me to shame.
> But man, daring man, of my folly's the source
> Man,—aspiring to be a Colossus, of course,
> Having one foot in heaven, the other on earth.
> And in lieu of real seeing, his fancy gives birth

To wild speculations, as solid and fair
As water on quicksand, or smoke in the air.
With these fancies he clothed me and called me a science,
And I—proud of the title, lent him alliance.

The apparition then departs, and the man, visibly shaken, mutters to himself:

Boil down your Psychology to the size of *its* soul.[71]

A second book by Dewey followed soon after the first, written at the invitation of George S. Morris who was editing a series of books on German philosophical classics. Dewey was assigned *Leibniz's New Essays concerning the Human Understanding,* finishing it for publication in 1888.[72] Dewey found much in Leibniz that is commendable but attacked the logic that undergirds his system. Leibniz's organicism, dynamism, and theory of continuity seemed to Dewey to accord with what scientific and other experience reveal the world to be. But Dewey believed that the logic Leibniz employs does not adequately account for the world as he conceives it. Leibniz uses formal logic with its principles of identity and contradiction, which lead him to a mode of thought that conceives the world as made up of individual existences, each self-contained, independent, and forever self-identical. And the only way he can bring these together into a single, unified whole is by an externally imposed preestablished harmony. "Leibniz never thought," wrote Dewey, "of investigating the formal logic bequeathed by scholasticism, with a view to determining its adequacy as philosophic method." [73] Had he done so, Dewey believed, he would have abandoned it in favor of a logic of organicism, of life, of process, such as that employed by Hegelianism.

The *Leibniz,* like the *Psychology,* won wide praise. George Trumbull Ladd of Yale characterized it in the *New Englander* as the clearest and most useful member of the series. And James Tufts, while at the University of Chicago, declared: "It is more than a clear historical exposition. It shows an insight into the real questions at issue and a mastery of philosophical principles which attest the maturity of a master who has a well-thought out basis of his own." [74]

Along with other members of the faculty, Dewey was frequently the target of student wit. In a poem entitled "The Clock Rambles," James Rowland Angell, President Angell's son who was a sophomore at the university and later Dewey's valued colleague at the University of Chicago, referred to:

Dewey, with countenance changeless as stone,
Ever recalling the north frigid zone.[75]

Among the definitions given in the "Sophsters New Dictionary" is:

> Dew(e)y.—Adj. Cold, impersonal, psychological, sphinx-like, anomalous and petrifying to flunkers.[76]

Dewey's course in psychology prompted the following:

O what is the matter with yon, lank girl,
  A pale and wild and haggard she,
Oh, don't you know, the old man said,
  She's taking Dewey's Psychology.

Once she was fair to look upon,
  Fair as a morning in June was she,
And now the wreck you see to-day
  Is caused by Dewey's Psychology.

A year had passed, again I strayed
  By the Medic's hall; what did I see
But some whitened bones of a girl who died
  Taking Dewey's Psychology.[77]

Dewey's years at Michigan ended when he was appointed professor of philosophy at the University of Minnesota. His growing reputation as a scholar, his success as a teacher, his simple, friendly manner, and his willingness to participate in the larger life of the university and community had brought him to the favorable attention of administrators at the University of Minnesota. Consequently, when the instructor in philosophy resigned to practice law in Minneapolis, the board of regents on 28 January 1888 unanimously elected Dewey Professor of Mental and Moral Philosophy, his salary to be twenty-four hundred dollars and his duties to begin in the fall of 1888.[78] A letter was sent to Dewey informing him of the board's action and expressing the hope that he would accept the position.

Dewey debated the offer for some time. His reasons for deciding to take the position, despite his many happy associations at the University of Michigan, are stated in his letter to H. A. P. Torrey:

> I have finally accepted the Minnesota position although quite loathe to leave here. Being only one man there, of course there will not be the same chance for advanced work [as] here, nor will I feel that the work is counting for as much there as here where it fits in with other work.

Nor do I suppose that we shall find students there as well prepared, and of course they are not as numerous. But the institution in Minn. is growing rapidly and Pres. Northrop is very ambitious to see it in the front rank. There are some advantages also in a new institution where its policy is still to be shaped, especially for a young man. Then the attractions of a large city like Minneapolis are, I confess, great.[79]

Dewey could have added that the difference in salary was another factor prompting him to go to Minnesota. As assistant professor at Michigan he was earning sixteen hundred dollars a year; as professor of philosophy at Minnesota he would get twenty-four hundred dollars. This fifty per cent increase in pay was not to be overlooked by the father of a young and growing family.

The regents of the University of Michigan accepted Dewey's resignation at their meeting in March 1888, "though with sincere regret that the University is compelled to lose so bright a light from its body of instructors." [80]

When Dewey's appointment was announced, it met with hearty approval in University of Minnesota circles. "The election of Prof. John Dewey, of Michigan University, to the chair of mental and moral philosophy at the University of Minnesota," declared one press account, "is satisfactory to both alumni and students. Although Mr. Dewey is a young man, he has a clearer grasp of philosophic truth than many who have spent a lifetime in its study. His advent to the chair of philosophy at the University will mark the end of the McCosh school and the introduction of a school of philosophy very similar to that introduced by President Porter of Yale." [81] Because Dewey's work both as a scholar and teacher had been highly successful at the University of Michigan, it was said that "Prof. Dewey is a man from whom much may be expected." [82]

The campus of the university to which Dewey went lay on the outskirts of Minneapolis, also bordering on the Mississippi River. Founded in 1851, the university had had a slow start; by 1888 when Dewey began his duties only four buildings had been erected: a main or academic building that housed the university library of some twenty-three thousand bound volumes; an Agricultural College Building; a Military Building; and the College of Mechanic Arts Building.[83] The Dewey family—John, Alice, and their one-year-old son Frederick—lived six or seven blocks from the campus at 925 Fifteenth Avenue, S.E.

Academically, the university was divided into five departments: a College of Science, Literature, and Arts; a College of Mechanic Arts; a College of Agriculture; a Department of Law; and a Department of Medicine.[84] The number of students at the university during the academic year 1888–89 was 781, including 34 graduate students.[85]

Dewey's appointment was in the College of Science, Literature, and Arts. The undergraduate enrollment here during 1888–89 was 414, but of these, 46 were "sub-freshmen," that is, students who had been admitted to the college but who were required because of inadequate high-school preparation to take courses fitting them for regular freshman studies.[86] Dewey's work was entirely with undergraduates of the junior and senior classes. The faculty of the college, including President Northrop, totalled twenty-two. Only three of these had Ph.D. degrees, two had honorary doctorates, and one had a D.D.[87] Thus the appointment of Dewey added greatly to the group's quality.

The academic year for the College of Science, Literature, and Arts, as for the university as a whole, was divided into three terms of approximately twelve weeks each, with courses and credits on a term basis. Course offerings in philosophy for 1888–89 were: Logic, both formal and applied; Psychology, in which Dewey's volume was used as a text; the History of Philosophy, in which were expounded the main ideas of leading philosophers, ancient and modern; Ethics, in which were embraced a brief survey of the history of ethics and an exposition of the principles of theoretical ethics, with their application to practice; and Natural Theology, which included a review of the evidence of God's existence as derived from a study of the constitution of nature and man.[88] These were all one-term courses that met four times a week and carried four hours credit, except the last, which was on a two-hour basis.

Although no record of Dewey's lectures in these courses exists, they probably were much like those delivered in similar courses at Michigan, reflecting his Neo-Hegelian bias. That he did well both as a lecturer and as administrator of his department is shown by a statement in the university monthly in early spring: "Prof. Dewey has made his department one of the most interesting and successful in the institution." [89]

Dewey faithfully attended faculty meetings, soon becoming aware of some pressing problems confronting the university. One of these was the existence of the sub-freshman class. Most members of the faculty felt that the university had undertaken a task which properly belonged to the high schools, that pressure should be put on them to improve the quality of their educational programs, and that the local communities should be urged to provide funds to the schools to do this. Dewey's experiences in a somewhat similar situation in Michigan led him to side with those opposing the sub-freshman arrangement. The result of this agitation was that the class was dropped in 1890.

The faculties of the university were also concerned with such nonacademic needs of the students as housing, health care, and advice on personal problems. As no system of student counseling existed, President Northrop and others believed the time was ripe for such a program. Plans for it began to take shape shortly after Dewey's arrival, suggesting to one historian of the university that Dewey probably played an important part in the endeavor.[90]

Dewey noted the steps being taken to develop the university as a whole; in a letter to Torrey shortly after the beginning of the new year, he wrote: "Our university authorities will ask the coming legislature for $250,000—mostly for buildings. The university has just added law & medical departments; it had mechanical and agricultural schools attached before. The necessity of multiplying new departments will retard the internal development of the university—increase of library, of instructors & courses in the literary dep't—for some time, but no other course seemed open, & it will make a broader foundation in the years to come." [91]

Despite his involvement in university and student affairs, Dewey found time to write. Chief among his published writings was his article entitled "The Philosophy of Thomas Hill Green" which appeared in 1889.[92] Though Dewey was to break with Green a few years later when his thinking began to veer away from traditional Hegelianism, in "The Philosophy of Thomas Hill Green" he was in general agreement with Green's overall philosophy, analyzing it sympathetically. "Upon both sides, the side of philosophic conviction, and the side of political and social life," declared Dewey, "Green is in closest contact with the deepest interests of his times." [93] Dewey attempted to demonstrate this in quite some detail, emphasizing especially the kinship of Green's philosophy of religion with Christianity.

In the previously mentioned letter to Torrey Dewey wrote: "I have just finished making a kind of abstract of my psychology. A gentleman in Toronto Canada, Director of Normal Schools for Ontario & Professor of Pedagogy in the University of Toronto, is writing a book on educational theory and practice and wanted a psychological introduction, and so I have been working in conjunction with him." [94] The outcome of this endeavor was J. A. McLellan's *Applied Psychology* [95] in the preface of which McLellan acknowledged his debt to Dewey. In a number of later printings of the book, however, Dewey's name appears on the title page as coauthor although nothing in the body of the work was changed and the acknowledgement in the preface remained as before.

In her "Note on *Applied Psychology*," Jo Ann Boydston suggests that the change in title page could have been made by the publisher to take advantage of Dewey's prestige or by McLellan himself to acknowledge more generously than before the help he had received from Dewey while writing the book.[96]

Dewey's stay at the University of Minnesota was unexpectedly short. He had been in Minneapolis scarcely six months when word reached him in March 1889 that George S. Morris had died as a result of overexposure while on a fishing trip with his son. Morris's sudden death stunned and saddened the university community in Ann Arbor; it also raised the question of his successor. "Of the irreparable loss that the University has just suffered," the *Chronicle* reported, "we feel totally unable to speak as we ought to speak. . . . It is hard to think that the chair which has been left vacant can ever be filled so ably and so adequately as it has been filled by Professor Morris. Filled it must be, however. Conjectures as to individual men cannot as yet be otherwise than idle and premature. But when the choice shall be made we rest secure in the belief that it will fall upon a man who will fill without reproach a post that the teacher who is dead filled with shining honor." [97]

In casting about for a successor to Morris, it was natural that the administration at Michigan should include Dewey among the top candidates. For, despite his age of only twenty-nine, he had already won wide recognition as a scholar; he had proven his worth as a teacher; he and Morris had held essentially the same views, so that his appointment would insure the continuation of the idealist tradition in the department; and his familiarity with the duties of the post would assure a minimum of the uncertainty and confusion that normally accompany a change in administration.

When rumors began to circulate that Dewey was being seriously considered for the vacant post, the general hope at the University of Minnesota was that he would refuse any offer and stay on. "It is sincerely to be hoped should the position be tendered him," declared one editoral, "he will find it to the best interests of all concerned to remain here." [98]

After considering the several candidates for the position, the Board of Regents of the University of Michigan at its April meeting elected Dewey to the position formerly occupied by Morris at a salary of twenty-two hundred dollars, to begin his duties 1 October 1889.[99]

Having been invited to Ann Arbor in early April for an interview and informed that the position would probably be offered, Dewey and Alice had given the matter much thought, concluding that if an offer came, he should accept it despite the two-hundred dollar decrease in pay. The position at Michigan carried much more prestige than the one at Minnesota; the University of Michigan was growing rapidly and Dewey would have a decisive voice in directing the expansion of the Department of Philosophy; most of his work would be with advanced students, tying in with his own study and research. He recognized that resigning his post at Minnesota after only a year might seem to be letting the university down when it needed him badly, but he was sure that President Northrop would understand his difficult position and would agree that Dewey should go to Michigan.

With his decision made, Dewey was prepared to give an immediate reply to the telegram sent him by President Angell telling of his appointment. His formal letter of acceptance to President Angell and the board of regents declared: "I respectfully acknowledge the honor conferred upon me in electing me to the professorship in philosophy made vacant by the death of Professor Morris, and do hereby accept the same." [100]

He enclosed a personal letter to Angell with the formal one, stating: "Your telegram was rec'd yesterday morning, with thanks for your prompt notification, as well as for the high compliment which I feel that you and the Regents have bestowed upon me. . . . I saw Pres. Northrop yesterday and he was very kind in the matter—as, of course, I had reason to suspect he would be. It was pleasant, however, to see that he fully appreciated my feelings in the matter." [101]

The announcement of Dewey's resignation was greeted with disappointment by faculty and students of the University of Minnesota. Though with them only briefly, he had won their affection and admiration; they wanted him to stay on as a member of the university community. The general feeling was expressed in an editorial in the university monthly:

> It will be learned with regret by all connected with the University that Dr. John Dewey has accepted the chair of Philosophy at the Michigan State University [*sic*]. His loss will be most felt by those who looked forward with a great deal of pleasure to a course under him the coming year, and especially by those whose privilege it has been to receive the benefit of his instruction during the past year.
>
> As a profound thinker and scholar Prof. Dewey stands in the foremost rank, and he is eminently successful as a teacher. He possesses the faculty of making a difficult subject easy and interesting, and his fair, genial treatment has made him loved and respected by all who have come in contact with him. Though we regret to lose him we

heartily congratulate our fortunate sister at Ann Arbor, and wish Prof. Dewey all the success his worth merits." [102]

Academic circles in Ann Arbor were pleased that Dewey was to return to the university; they were confident that he would be a worthy successor to Morris. A statement in the *Chronicle* was typical of the general reaction to Dewey's appointment:

> Prof. John Dewey has consented to take charge of the Chair of Philosophy in the U. of M. The University is to be congratulated. Dr. Dewey may not be as ripe and complete a scholar as his predecessor; but he has already shown a degree of ability that has compelled recognition all over the country, and which must remove all doubt and misgiving as to the future of the Philosophical department. He is still young. His years of activity have hardly commenced. If what he has already done be an earnest of what he is destined to do it will be hard to predict too much from him and for him. We bid him a hearty welcome to his former scenes of labor.[103]

The Board of Regents of the University of Minnesota at its meeting on 1 June 1889 accepted Dewey's resignation, thus officially severing his connection with that institution.[104]

5. The University of Michigan, 1889–1894

UPON RETURNING to the University of Michigan in the summer of 1889, Dewey's first concern as head of the Department of Philosophy was to find an assistant. W. S. Hough, who had followed Dewey as Morris's colleague in the department at Michigan, had left for the University of Minnesota, once again to take a place vacated by Dewey. After considering the candidates for the position, Dewey selected James Hayden Tufts, a native of Massachusetts and the son of a Congregational minister. Tufts, a graduate of Amherst, had also attended the Yale Divinity School where he had received his Bachelor of Divinity degree. Arrangements were made for Fred Newton Scott, newly appointed brilliant young instructor of English and Rhetoric at the university, to give a course in aesthetics in the department.[1]

Dewey turned over to Tufts the courses in psychology and most of the beginning philosophy courses in the department, such as Introduction to Philosophy, Logic, and History of Philosophy. Dewey taught a section of Introduction to Philosophy and advanced courses in Kant's *Critique of Pure Reason*, Hegel's *Logic*, Advanced Psychology, Advanced Logic: The Theory of Scientific Method, Caird's *Critical Philosophy of Kant*, and Hegel's Philosophy of Spirit. He also took over the courses in ethics and social philosophy, fields formerly covered by Morris. Dewey's courses in these were: Ethics, Political Philosophy, Studies in the History of Political Philosophy, and a seminar in Ethical Problems.[2]

Tufts resigned in June 1891 to take advanced work in philosophy at the University of Freiburg, whereupon Dewey appointed George Herbert Mead to take his place. Like Tufts, Mead was born in Massachusetts, the son of a Congregational minister. He had received his A.B. degree from Oberlin College where his father was professor of homiletics in the Theological Seminary;

he had gone to Harvard where he studied under James and Royce. Afterwards, he went to Germany to study at the Universities of Berlin and Leipzig, returning to this country in 1891.

Increased enrollment in philosophy and psychology necessitated the appointment of a second instructor. He was Alfred Henry Lloyd, who had pursued graduate studies at the Universities of Göttingen, Berlin, and Heidelberg and then at Harvard where he received his Ph.D degree. At Harvard, much of his work was done with James and Royce. Lloyd had at one time intended to enter the Congregational ministry, but a growing interest in philosophy had changed his mind.

The division of course work remained much as before. Mead and Lloyd took over the beginning courses in philosophy, psychology, logic, and the history of philosophy, adding, as time allowed, advanced courses suited to their interests. Dewey continued to give the courses and seminars in ethics and social philosophy as well as his Advanced Logic: The Theory of Scientific Method, and Hegel's *Logic*. Like Mead and Lloyd, he gave additional advanced courses along lines of special interest. Among these were a seminar in The Development of Christian Philosophy in the First Four Centuries after Christ, during the first semester of 1892–93 and, beginning in 1891, a course in Advanced Psychology, using as text James's newly published *The Principles of Psychology*,[3] a book that was to be decisive in changing the direction of Dewey's own thinking.[4]

With the course work assigned and classes under way, Dewey's life at the university resumed the routine temporarily interrupted by his year in Minnesota. With Mead and Lloyd, he helped guide the affairs of the Philosophical Society, serving as its president for the next five years and addressing it on such topics as "Philosophical Catharsis," "The Interpretation of Literature," and "Ethics and Politics." [5]

The Students' Christian Association continued to get his help; its leaders considered him "one of our strongest supporters." [6] As before, he gave occasional talks at the association's Sunday morning meetings. One of these, "Christianity and Democracy," is of special importance to the student of Dewey's philosophy as the first clear statement of the fusion in Dewey's thinking of the religious and social motives.[7] At one of the Bible Institutes held on the campus under association sponsorship, Dewey spoke on "The Significance of the Parables," a talk "by many considered to be the best of the institute." [8] Dewey's last public address in Ann Arbor was at the 27 May 1894 meeting of the association. Its subject was "Reconstruction"; [9] the argument clearly foreshadows

Dewey's later widely known book *Reconstruction in Philosophy.*

When the *Inlander,* the student monthly literary magazine, was founded in 1891, Dewey became one of its two faculty advisers, continuing until his departure from Ann Arbor in 1894. During his term of office, Dewey met regularly with the student board of editors, helped plan each issue, and contributed three articles of his own.[10]

His deepening interest in education caused Dewey to renew his membership in the Michigan Schoolmasters' Club, whose meetings he frequently addressed. He also gave talks to other teacher organizations on such topics as "attention," "memory," "imagination," and "thinking."

Upon their return to Ann Arbor the Deweys bought the house at 15 Forest Avenue, in a pleasant neighborhood near the campus, which remained their residence till they left for Chicago.[11] The house was large and commodious, and necessarily so, since the Dewey family was growing. A second child, Evelyn, had been born to them in 1889 in Minneapolis; in 1893 a third child, named Morris after George Sylvester Morris, was born. In addition, Dewey's parents, Archibald and Lucina, came from Burlington to live with them.[12]

Alice's own interest in the learning processes of little children made her quite willing that her husband try out his theories of education on their children, leading to many unconventional situations that caused merriment and comment when outsiders were present. "Old Ann Arborites," according to one report, "still regale one another with tales of how the Dewey methods worked." [13]

The Deweys greatly missed the Morrises with whom they had been on close terms during their first years in Ann Arbor. But a growing friendship with the families of Mead and Lloyd helped compensate for the loss. When Dewey moved to Chicago, he took Mead with him; the two families continued their close association there. "The Meads," wrote Jane Dewey, "remained the closest friends of the Deweys, even after the removal of the Deweys to New York, until their deaths." [14]

Dewey enjoyed informal and friendly contacts with his students; he and Mrs. Dewey frequently entertained them at their home.[15] His students, in turn, admired and respected the scholar in Dewey, who attracted them by his simplicity of manner, his warmth of personality, his gentle sense of humor, and his genuine interest in young people. A student editor wrote the following tribute:

As a man, Prof. Dewey is modest and retiring; but his unassuming, pleasing manner attracts to him many friends. As a teacher, these same characteristics, his easy, earnest and unconscious manner before a class, the utter lack of any spirit of pedantry, and the attitude, as far as desirable, of equality with his students, whom he always treats as intelligent ladies and gentlemen and friends—these characteristics at once make the student feel at home in his class-room, thus putting him in the proper frame of mind for the best work, and win for the teacher the sincere admiration and respect of the students. His methods of instruction are excellent. He is one of the most popular, most satisfactory classroom lecturers in the University. Though he is himself a man of subtle intellect, deep thought, and profound scholarship, and though many of his courses are, by their very nature, deep and heavy, yet his good judgment is ever considerate of these difficulties and of the limited powers of the ordinary student. He wisely puts a much higher premium upon a single attempt at original, intelligent thought than upon the parrot-like repetition of whole volumes of other men's thoughts. Such a thing as either slovenly work, or, on the other hand, a "grind," is entirely unknown in Professor Dewey's classes. One can find at the University few more pleasing instructors or more true and helpful friends than he will find in Dr. John Dewey.[16]

That student life at the university had its seamy side at times was a fact Dewey had to face. For a long time it had been generally known but never openly acknowledged that cheating in the classroom was widely practiced and that little was being done to correct the situation. A symposium under the auspices of the Students' Christian Association brought the issue into the open; faculty members were urged to take the matter up with their classes. Dewey did so, and, as reported in the *Monthly Bulletin*, "spoke about as follows":

During the last year the fact was brought to my attention that a great deal of cheating had been going on in my classes. I have known the course of events more or less thoroughly for the past ten years, and I am aware that practice and public sentiment in the matter of cheating has been continually on the down grade in this University. I acknowledge my share of the responsibility for leaving in the faculty code until recently a rule that treated the matter as a light offense. I admit that the members of the faculty are largely to blame for the low tone of public sentiment on the question, even among good students. But the blame lies most largely with the respectable and upright students who connive at the evil by silence or merry-making. With them primarily rests the responsibility for the present condition of public sentiment. I don't know that I shall change the policy I have so far pursued to any great extent. I shall endeavor not to go to sleep in class, but shall not act as a spy. In any large body of persons, like that in this University, there is always a presupposition by the balance of probabilities that some tricksters and shysters will be found. If there are any such in my classes,—I am glad to say that I do not know

> that there are,—but *if* there are such, any who pursue disreputable methods outside of the class room, I have no objection to their doing the same inside, and I will write them out their credit to get rid of them. But I do object to decent and respectable students, who are upright in other things, resorting to underhand and dishonest methods in the class room. I wish it understood that any who may come to the class room and cheat, I regard with the utmost contempt, not simply officially, but *personally*.[17]

To the student of philosophy, the most interesting aspect of Dewey's life at this time is the intellectual one. During his second period at Michigan, Dewey's thinking began to take a new direction, one that led gradually away from Hegelianism toward the instrumentalism for which he later became so well known. The shift was brought about by the increasing dominance of functional psychology and evolutionary biology in his thinking, forcing upon him the idea of a total organism in an environment, actively engaged in adjusting to it. James's *Psychology* underscored this general notion, expounding a theory of mind that profoundly affected Dewey's own thought. Mind, according to James, is not something apart from nature, viewing it from the outside, but is the objective, conscious process by which the organism and its environment become integrated. James's thesis is that organism and environment mutually determine each other, that thinking is simply a function of the interaction between the two, like breathing and walking. It was James's objective, biological conception of mind, said Dewey, which "worked its way more and more into all my ideas and acted as a ferment to transform old beliefs."[18]

Functional psychology and evolutionary biology had an impact on the thinking of Mead and Lloyd also, leading them in the direction of pragmatic philosophy.[19] Mead's courses in psychology focused on the total organism adjusting to an environment, and treated mental processes as functions of the interaction between the two.[20] His course in "The Philosophy of Evolution" sought to determine the bearings of evolution on scientific psychology, opening avenues of thought that were to lead to original and valuable contributions to pragmatist philosophy. Dewey found Mead stimulating and helpful, so that, as Jane Dewey has remarked, "from the nineties on, the influence of Mead ranked with that of James."[21]

Lloyd's ideas were later elaborated in his *Dynamic Idealism*, which stresses the active, creative individual in interaction with its environment, declaring that "ideas are plans, and consciousness is always a planning."[22] Lloyd shared Dewey's deep interest in education; he believed its most pressing need was to "find some way of applying in its methods the irrefutable fact that real knowledge is born and bred with action, interest being only in what one is doing, and ideas being only plans of the existing activity." [23] Lloyd adopted an idealistic interpretation of the universe, but his idealism, he insisted, was "dynamic," not the "formal" idealism of the German idealists. The points of agreement between Lloyd and Dewey are so numerous and obvious as to point unmistakably to their influence on each other.

Dewey's own thinking at this time is revealed in several articles on logic, ethics, and other topics, and in two short books on ethics. The first of these was *Outlines of a Critical Theory of Ethics* (1891),[24] which grew out of Dewey's undergraduate course in ethics. It was used as a text in his classes, but was also intended to be "an independent contribution to ethical science." [25] Though relying heavily on the ethical teachings of such idealists as Green, Bradley, and Caird, the book's characteristic feature is its "analysis of individuality into function including capacity and environment," [26] and its working out the implications of this for ethical theory. Apparently, few reviewers sensed the significance of what Dewey was doing, for, in a letter to William James, Dewey said that, so far as he could tell, James was "the first man to see the point" of his *Outlines.* In the same letter he remarked that he wished James's article "The Moral Philosopher and the Moral Life" could have appeared before he wrote his *Outlines* because there was much in it from which he could have profited.[27]

The second book was *The Study of Ethics: A Syllabus,*[28] written to take the place of the *Outlines* when the edition of that was exhausted. This book, as Dewey explained in a prefatory note, was "in no sense a second edition of the previous book" but rather "a thorough psychological examination of the process of active experience, and a derivation from this analysis of the chicf ethical types and crises—a task, so far as I know, not previously attempted." [29]

In the two books and in the several articles, the ferment at work in Dewey's thinking is striking. The role of intelligence becomes predominantly practical; its function is to guide the individual's attempt to adjust to its physical, social, and cultural environment. Intelligence comes into play when there is a conflict of ends needing to be mediated. Impulse and habit cannot do this, so reflection is called on. Reflection involves postponement, delay, and the conscious weighing and balancing of the consequences attending alternative ways of acting. In Dewey's terms, reflection is "a process of tentative action; we 'try on' one or other of the ends, imagining ourselves actually doing them, going, indeed, in this make-believe action just as far as we can without actually doing them."[30] Ideas now become working hypotheses or plans with which the individual hopes to solve the problem confronting him; their verification consists in putting them into action and noting their "ability to *work*, to organize 'facts'."[31] Logic becomes the study of the thought processes involved in learning through problem solving; since such processes are displayed at their best in the scientific enterprise, logic for Dewey becomes the study of the mental activities involved in acquiring scientific knowledge.[32]

The role of intelligence in the moral life is similarly practical. Moral goals, motives, ideals are determined not by reference to some absolute, transcendent Self or Personality[33] but in terms of individual needs, wants, capacities, and the conditions under which these must be fulfilled. The moral end is self-realizaton, not in T. H. Green's sense of "filling in the blank scheme of some undefined, purely general self,"[34] but in the concrete sense of "the performance by a person of his specific function, this function consisting in an activity which realizes wants and powers with reference to their peculiar surroundings."[35] Moral ideals are not abstract principles transcending experience,[36] but are "the *working hypotheses* of action,"[37] playing the same role in the moral life as the working hypotheses of science do in scientific experience.[38] Social institutions are not so much man's imperfect attempts to embody in human relations the social ideal of a Universal Mind or Spirit[39] as they are "organized modes of action, on the basis of the wants and interests which unite men. . . . They are *practical*, existing for the sake of, and by means of the will—as execution of ideas which have interest."[40]

Despite the undeniably pragmatic slant of his thinking, Dewey was at this time still a metaphysical idealist. Although he focused on the active, dynamic individual adjusting to his environment, he believed that this could best be accounted for by an idealist metaphysics, in terms of an Absolute Mind manifesting itself as a rationally structured universe. Dewey tied his pragmatism and idealism together by asserting that the only way the individual can acquire knowledge of Reality, or Truth, is through action and experiment. Nowhere is this better expressed than in the essay, "Christianity and Democracy,"[41] where Dewey declared that "beyond all other means of appropriating truth, beyond all other organs of apprehension, is man's own action. Man interprets the Universe in which he lives in terms of his own action at the given time. . . . In final analysis, man's own action, his own life movement, is the only organ he has for receiving and appropriating truth."[42] Dewey called his point of view "experimental idealism," [43] which accurately states his position. As a close associate of Dewey's at the time wrote: "To call Prof. Dewey an Hegelian . . . would be, for some senses of the term, unfair, for others, preposterous. One may have a very lively sense of the tremendous value for us to-day that lies in understanding the significance of the philosophical movement of which Kant was the *terminus a quo* and Hegel the *terminus ad quem*, without ceding for an instant one's birthright as a child of the 19th Century." [44]

The belief that science ought to be an organizing and integrating factor in society became a leading one in Dewey's social philosophy. Comte had originally planted this notion in his mind; [45] Dewey's deepening interest in science and practical social affairs prompted him to explore the matter further. He called attention to the fact that despite the vast increase in scientific knowledge and techniques, little use is made of them in human affairs. Among the factors responsible, he believed, were the lack of social organization among scientists, the specialization and abstract nature of their research, and the lack of confidence—among scientists and people generally—in the usefulness of applying science and its methods to the solution of human problems.[46] "*The* duty of the present," wrote Dewey, "is the socializing of intelligence—the realizing of its bearing upon social practice." [47]

Renan had advanced a similar idea some years before in his book, *The Future of Science,* in which he had depicted a social future for science, a future in which it would operate as a "social motor," giving guidance in the ordering of human affairs. Some forty years later Renan partially retracted this faith, discouraged by the failure of science to get to the masses. Though not underestimating the difficulties involved,[48] Dewey believed that because man's interests are "finally and prevailingly practical," science will eventually prevail. "I cannot but think," he wrote, "that the Renan of '48 was wiser than he of '90." [49] Dewey retained this faith to the end of his life never ceasing to urge men to adopt the knowledge and methods of science in solving their human problems. "Great as have been the social changes of the last century," he wrote in his seventies, "they are not to be compared with those which will emerge when our faith in scientific method is made manifest in social works." [50]

A friendship with Franklin Ford gave Dewey an opportunity to put his faith to a practical test.[51] Ford was a newspaperman who was dissatisfied with the way the newspapers were informing the public. They presented vast numbers of unrelated facts as news, making no attempt to relate facts to each other or to discover and interpret deeper social trends of which the facts were merely symptoms. Consequently, the people remained unenlightened, without a basis for intelligent social action. What was needed, Ford insisted, was a paper that would make inquiry and the sale of truth its business, so organizing and socializing intelligence as to make enlightenend social action possible. The paper would defer to no class interest but would be "the organ of the whole." [52] "The war cry of a false socialism," he declared, "is heard on every hand. . . . But the road to social union lies through the organization, the socializing, of intelligence." [53]

Dewey was impressed by Ford's ideas about the socializing of intelligence, incorporating some of them in his ethical theory in the *Outlines*.[54] He was also impressed by Ford's argument concerning the need for a new kind of newspaper; he agreed to join him in a novel journalistic venture. The two proposed in the spring of 1892 to bring out a periodical called "Thought News" under Dewey's direction. The main object of the paper, according to its sponsors, was "to use philosophic ideas in interpreting typical phases of current life." The paper would be designed to appeal not so much to the professional student of philosophy as to "the man interested in getting hold of superior tools for reading life." [55] In an interview with a *Detroit Tribune* reporter, Dewey disavowed any intention to revolutionize journalism. The object of "Thought News," he declared, was "not to introduce a new idea into journalism at large, but to show that philosophy has some use. . . . Instead of trying to change the newspaper business by introducing philosophy into it, the idea is to transform philosophy somewhat by introducing a little newspaper business into it." [56]

As was to be expected, the proposal aroused considerable interest in the university community as well as among newspapermen. The Ann Arbor correspondent of the *Detroit Tribune*, reporting on the venture, declared that since it was something new and experimental, it merited careful watching. But he could not resist adding facetiously that in Ann Arbor it was "generally understood that . . . Mr. Dewey proposes to get out an 'extra' every time he has a new thought." [57]

No issue of "Thought News" ever appeared. Referring to the venture in later years, Dewey remarked: "No issue was made; it was an over-enthusiastic project for which we had not the means nor the time—and doubtless not the ability to carry through. In other words . . . the *idea* was advanced for those days, but it was too advanced for the maturity of those who had the idea in mind." [58]

Though Dewey resumed his connections with the First Congregational Church in Ann Arbor and remained active in it,[59] his talks and writings made it obvious that social interests were absorbing his religious interests, that concern with democracy was replacing his concern with the Church. He now defined Christianity as essentially a religion of revelation designed to reveal God or Truth; for it is Truth, according to Jesus, that sets men free: "free negatively, free from sin, free positively, free to live his own life, free to express himself." [60] The truth Jesus had in mind, however, that Christianity seeks to reveal, is not some fixed, esoteric, special set of truths labeled religious, but is Truth itself—Truth universal and one and continually unfolding itself to man. For truth to function and make men free it must be appropriated not only by the individual but by men generally; it must become "the Commonwealth, the Republic, the public affair." [61] When truth becomes the common possession and inspiration of men, they become spiritually united and constitute the brotherhood of man, what Jesus called the Kingdom of God.

The discovery of truth and its dissemination among men require a suitable form of social order, an order in which truth has "a chance to show itself, a chance to well up from the depths," and to be communicated to all.[62] Such conditions, said Dewey, most nearly prevail in a democratic society, for democracy means "the breaking down of the barriers which hold truth from finding expression" and "the securing of conditions which give truth its movement, its complete distribution or service." [63]

Democracy, therefore, rather than the Church taken by itself, is "the means by which the revelation of truth is carried on." [64] The Church "needs to see that it can claim no longer to be the sole, or even the preëminent representative in the cause of righteousness and good-will on earth; that partly through, and partly without, its own activities, the ideal which at the outset it represented has now become a common fact of life; so that its present duty is to take its place as one among the various forces of social life, and to co-operate with them on an equal basis for the furtherance of the common end." [65] Speaking to a group of students planning to enter the ministry, Dewey declared: "The next religious prophet who will have a permanent and real influence on men's lives will be the man who succeeds in pointing out the religious meaning of democracy, the ultimate religious value to be found in the normal flow of life itself." [66]

Democracy in all its phases—political, economic, social, cultural—came to claim Dewey's strongest allegiance and to command his deepest loyalties; interest in social aid and social reform groups began to replace his interest in the Church.[67] Thus it is not surprising that Dewey's formal connection with organized religion ended when he left Ann Arbor. A few years after settling in Chicago, he withdrew his membership from the church in Ann Arbor and did not ask for a letter of transferral to a church in Chicago. "Dismissed without letter" is the last notation under Dewey's name in the records of the Congregational Church in Ann Arbor.[68]

Dewey's years at the University of Michigan were drawing to a close. President William Rainey Harper of the newly founded University of Chicago had gathered together a group of brilliant men to head the several departments. He was, however, still in search of a man to direct the university's Department of Philosophy when Dewey was called to his attention. James H. Tufts, now a member of the department at Chicago, especially urged the appointment of Dewey to the post. In a memorandum to Harper, Tufts called attention to Dewey's accomplishments as a scholar, his ability as a teacher, and his characteristics as a man: "simple, modest, utterly devoid of any affectation or self-consciousness" and "withal a delightful man to work with." Also "a producer himself," wrote Tufts, "he knows how to guide other men into fruitful lines of research." [69] Harper, himself adept at recognizing able men, was quickly won over; early in 1894 he offered Dewey the head professorship of philosophy.

The post attracted Dewey for several reasons, among which, as he wrote to Harper, were "the chance to build up the department of philosophy, to associate with men whose main interest is in advanced research, the opportunity to devote myself to that kind of work, the living in Chicago." [70] In addition, the inclusion of psychology and pedagogy in the Department of Philosophy would provide an opportunity to unite the three disciplines, giving pedagogy a solid grounding in psychology and philosophy—a task that he had long considered urgent.

But Dewey was dissatisfied with Harper's offer of four thousand dollars as annual salary. Such an amount, Dewey wrote to Harper, was scarcely enough to provide "an adequate basis for living as we should want to live (and as the University would want us to live) in Chicago." Dewey suggested a salary of five thousand dollars, declaring that, if he could be assured of this, he would "accept with pleasure; and come to Chicago in condition to throw my best powers into helping strengthen the University through its philosophical department." [71] Harper's reply was that, though he could not now guarantee such a salary, he would work faithfully toward it for the very near future. Dewey thereupon accepted the position "in the expectation of having the full salary in due season." [72]

When President Harper announced Dewey's appointment at the Spring Convocation of the University of Chicago, the reaction was highly favorable. The *University of Chicago Weekly* said: "The announcement of Prof. Dewey's appointment will be received with pleasure by every person who has the interest of the University of Chicago at heart. Prof. Dewey brings to Chicago a reputation for scholarship of which any man might well be proud." [73] The *Weekly's* editorial comment was: "The appointment of Professor John Dewey of Michigan, to the chair of philosophy and the head professorship of the department of philosophy, is another of the series of brilliant moves the University has made. He is among the foremost thinkers in ethics and metaphysics. He is a brilliant writer and his work on psychology is famous. Then he is a young man. As the philosopher grows in years he gains in wisdom. His best work may be expected yet to come. But the world knows his name already and if we are proud of the reputation of our faculty we are proud of the association of a scholar who enhances and brightens that reputation greatly." [74]

At the University of Michigan there was regret the university was losing so eminent and popular a member of its faculty, mingled with satisfaction that Dewey was to have a broader and more challenging field for the exercise of his talents. The *Monthly Bulletin* of the Students' Christian Association summed up the general feeling:

> The University will lose a great deal by the withdrawal of Prof. Dewey from the faculty. Although he goes to accept a position as head of the department of philosophy in Chicago University, we are loath to lose him. But perhaps he will find a wider field of usefulness in his new position. At any rate his opportunities for study will be much better in the Western metropolis than they would be here. Prof. Dewey's high standing as a philosopher and his practical sense and lively interest in social problems combine to promise for him a bright future, and we congratulate Chicago University on her good fortune in securing his services. His place will be hard to fill at Ann Arbor, but the best wishes and the highest hopes of his Michigan students will follow him in his widening career.[75]

Dewey's resignation was accepted by the board of regents at one of its spring meetings,[76] thus closing Dewey's years at the University of Michigan. The University of Chicago to which he went was to be the scene of still greater achievements, but also the place where he would experience some of his deepest frustrations.

6. The University of Chicago, 1894–1904: I

THE UNIVERSITY OF CHICAGO, only four years old when Dewey arrived, had already attained high standing among the universities of the country, chiefly because it had set out to be not simply another college but a university like those of Europe and like the Johns Hopkins and Clark universities in this country. The graduate schools of the university were to be stressed, with a large part of the faculty devoting itself exclusively to graduate instruction and research. The type of faculty member the university looked for "must be a teacher, but first and foremost he must be a scholar, in love with learning, with a passion for research, an investigator who could produce, and, if what he produced was worthy, would wish to publish." [1] In the four years since its founding, the university had assembled one of the most outstanding faculties in the country, including: T. C. Chamberlin in astronomy, Rolin D. Salisbury in geology, Albert Michelson in physics, Jacques Loeb in biology, J. M. Coulter in botany, Thorstein Veblen in political economy, Albion Small in sociology, Paul Shorey in Greek, J. H. Breasted in Egyptology, and R. G. Moulton in English.

President Harper was in large measure responsible for the university's early successes. "Those massive buildings, millions of money, thousands of scholars and scores of teachers," wrote one of his admirers, "are a monument to the foresight, nerve and ceaseless activity of W. R. Harper, a veritable Napoleon in the educational field." [2] Born 26 July 1856, Harper was three years older than Dewey and equally precocious. He received an A.B. degree from Muskingum College at fourteen; he entered Yale as a graduate student when he was seventeen, receiving his Ph.D. there at the age of nineteen. He began his career teaching Hebrew at the Baptist Union Theological Seminary in Chicago, moving to Yale in 1886. Harper's views, expressed in his extensive writings on theological matters had prompted an attack in 1888 on his orthodoxy. He weathered that storm, however, continuing throughout his life to be a staunch defender of liberal theological thought. Harper had tremendous vitality and enthusiasm; these qualities, along with his scholarship, led to his appointment as first president of the university when it was founded in 1890. Harper and Dewey were to have close associations on the administrative level; though many of these were pleasant and cordial, others turned out to be not so harmonious, leading eventually to Dewey's resignation from the university.

Harper was particularly concerned that a strong department of philosophy be established at the university, but up to the time of Dewey's appointment he had not succeeded in getting an outstanding scholar to head the department. George Herbert Palmer, who had been offered the position, preferred to remain at Harvard, where with James, Royce, Santayana, and Münsterberg, he helped direct the Department of Philosophy during its most notable years. Jacob Gould Schurman, professor of philosophy at Cornell, had also been tendered the post but declined, to become president of Cornell in 1892. E. Benjamin Andrews, the third person approached, did not care to give up his newly acquired presidency of Brown University.[3] Charles S. Peirce was also considered for the position, a plan that was dropped when George Herbert Palmer strongly discouraged the idea.[4]

Upon his arrival in Chicago in July 1894, Dewey immediately took steps to build up the Department of Philosophy, which included psychology and pedagogy. Since the opening of classes at the university in October 1892, only two regular appointments had been made in the department: Charles A. Strong in psychology and James H. Tufts in philosophy. The terms of two docents, teaching fellows who had helped in the department, had expired by the time Dewey arrived.

Dewey first appointed two men whom he had known for some time and whose ability he respected. The first was George Herbert Mead who had been Dewey's colleague at the University of Michigan since 1891. The second was James R. Angell who had taken undergraduate work with Dewey and Mead at the University of Michigan where he had been introduced to functional psychology. Angell had gone to the Universities of Berlin and Halle for graduate work in psychology; upon his return to this country he was appointed assistant professor of psychology at the University of Minnesota, from which post Dewey called him.

Two teaching fellows were selected for the academic year 1894–95—Addison W. Moore and Edward Scribner Ames, both graduate students who stayed on to get their doctorates in the department. Each was eventually made a regular member of the department—Moore in the fall of 1895, and Ames in 1900 when he returned to Chicago from a professorship in philosophy and pedagogy at Butler University.

Numerous temporary appointments were made in the department during the decade Dewey was its head, but the regular staff became stabilized as Dewey, Tufts, Mead, Angell, Moore, and Ames.[5] These men were all young—Dewey, the oldest, was not quite thirty-five; Tufts and Mead were in their early thirties; Moore and Ames in their mid-twenties.

With its enlarged corps of instructors, the department was able to establish additional courses in philosophy and psychology on both the undergraduate and graduate levels, thus making available a more rounded and complete program of work for students entering these fields.

Dewey also set about to strengthen the position of pedagogy at the university and to tie it in more effectively with philosophy and psychology.[6] He was particularly interested in doing this because his contacts with the elementary and secondary schools in Michigan had convinced him that much current educational practice was at variance with what psychology taught about learning processes.

Harper also had a deep interest in education, which he showed by serving on the Chicago Board of Education, by trying to bring the university into closer and more fruitful relations with the elementary and secondary schools of the city and state, and by encouraging organizations of teachers and educators to hold their professional meetings on the university campus. Despite this interest, Harper had done little to improve the standing of pedagogy at the university. Only two courses in the field had been offered since the university opened, one in the history and the other in the theory of education. In 1892 Harper had appointed Julia E. Bulkley as associate professor of pedagogy, but she had immediately been given a three-year leave of absence to take advanced work in pedagogy at the University of Zurich. In Dewey, Harper believed he had a person who could supply the leadership and scholarship necessary to raise pedagogy to the position it ought to have.

Dewey was convinced that if pedagogy were to get the status it deserved in the university, it should be a separate department. Such a department, he believed, should, first of all, train students to become specialists in education: professors of pedagogy, superintendents, supervisors of teacher normal schools; second, it should undertake a program of "pedagogical discovery and experimentation."[7] Since experimentation requires a laboratory, Dewey said that a department of pedagogy should have its own particular kind of laboratory—a school in which new educational theories and practices could be tried and their validity tested.[8] Also included in Dewey's early plans was a "Pedagogical Museum" to exhibit the latest texts, reference books, mechanical appliances, and other things of interest and value to teachers of the primary and intermediate grades.[9]

Dewey's proposals concerning pedagogy were heartily endorsed by Harper and approved by the Board of Trustees. In another action, upon Harper's recommendation, the trustees appointed Dewey head of the new department, retaining him as head of the department of philosophy.

As an added inducement for Dewey to come to Chicago, Harper had promised him an extra three-months vacation so that he could, if he wished, have three successive quarters away from the university. "It was the prospect of getting nine mos. vacation all at once," Dewey had written Harper, "that made me willing to take $4000 the first year."[10] While still in Ann Arbor, the Deweys had planned an extended tour of Europe; Mrs. Dewey and their three small children, Frederick, Evelyn, and Morris, left in May and Dewey was to join them the following January.[11] He was in residence at the university during the summer and fall quarters of 1894 to take care of the more immediate and urgent problems of his new position, then joined his family as planned.

The five proceeded together on their European travels. All went well till the family reached Italy. Here Morris, the youngest child, became ill and died. "His death of diphtheria in Milan, Italy at the age of two and a half," wrote Jane Dewey, "was a blow from which neither of his parents ever fully recovered."[12]

Upon their return to this country late in the summer of 1895, the Deweys took for a while an apartment in the Del Prado Hotel, located near the university on the Midway Plaisance at Monroe Avenue (now Kenwood Avenue), a favorite residence for university personnel.[13] After this they lived at different places in the vicinity of the university,[14] each a good-sized house or apartment because of the space needs of the growing Dewey family.

The Deweys had good reason to be pleased with their Chicago surroundings. The greater Hyde Park area where they lived was noted for its extended lakeshore, its parks, its beautiful residential areas, and the quality of its people. Not least among the physical attractions was the university campus itself. Largely because of President Harper's persuasive abilities, wealthy Chicagoans, including such well-known families as the Swifts, Fields, McCormicks, Kents, and Ryersons contributed generously to the university's support. The university's chief benefactor, however, was John D. Rockefeller who, along with the American Baptist Education Society, was mainly responsible for founding the university. With Rockefeller's help, the university purchased land facing south along the spacious Midway Plaisance, erecting most of the handsome Gothic buildings that graced the campus. Rockefeller's gifts by 1910 totalled almost thirty-five million dollars, one of the largest amounts ever given to an educational institution up to this time.[15] With good reason the students of the university sang:

"John D. Rockefeller, wonderful man is he,
Gives all his spare change to the U. of C.
He keeps the ball a-rolling
In our great 'Varsity,
He pays Doctor Harper to help us grow sharper,
To the glory of U. of C." [16]

The university's educational opportunities, especially for graduate study, attracted students in ever increasing numbers. These came at first mostly from Chicago and the Midwest, but as the university's fame spread, students arrived from all over the country. During its first year of operation (1892–93), student enrollment was 540, including 217 graduate students. During Dewey's last year at the university, the student body totalled 3,548, of whom 1,068 were graduate students.[17] The faculty underwent a similar increase. In 1892, the teaching staff, including that of the South Side Academy, numbered 103; by 1902 it had increased to 280.[18]

The Department of Philosophy also flourished. The number of courses in philosophy increased from fourteen in 1893–94 to thirty-two in 1899–1900; the number of offerings in psychology grew from two to twelve. A rough division of labor settled in among the staff, except for Dewey, whose interest continued to range the entire fields of philosophy, psychology, and education. Tufts concerned himself mostly with ethics, social philosophy, and aesthetics; Mead with the philosophy of mind and social psychology; Moore with logic and theory of knowledge; Ames with the psychology and philosophy of religion; and Angell with functional and experimental psychology.

The department sponsored a Philosophical Club that met biweekly for the "presentation of original papers, reports of articles in journals, and discussion." [19] Dewey served as its president during 1895–96. On 12 February 1904, the department, like departments of philosophy at many other colleges and universities, celebrated the centenary of the death of Immanuel Kant. Dewey spoke at the occasion on "Kant's revolutionary philosophic method and of his great achievement in connecting the whole body of earlier speculation with his own thought." [20]

The extent of Dewey's interest in philosophy was partly reflected in the courses he gave. His continued interest in Hegelianism is indicated by the repetition of his seminar in the Philosophy of Hegel each year from 1894 to 1899, when a year's course in The Theory of Logic took its place. His preoccupation with the theories of the great absolute idealists of his day showed in such courses as: Introduction to Contemporary Metaphysical Thought, in which were used such texts as Bradley's *Appearance and Reality* and Edward Caird's *Metaphysics*; a seminar in Contemporary Idealism, which compared the points of view of Green, Bradley, and Royce; and a Seminar in Philosophic Method, described as an "examination of the logical presuppositions of contemporary philosophy." His concern with moral and social philosophy manifested itself in: the Logic of Ethics; the Philosophy of Ethics; the History of Political Ethics; Nineteenth-Century Ethical Thought; the Sociology of Ethics; the Development of English Utilitarianism; and Contemporary Theories Regarding Ethical Relations of the Individual and Society.[21]

Dewey's kindly disposition toward the students in the department made him well liked; his scholarship elicited their admiration and respect. Perhaps because of this, students felt free to poke fun at him. In one instance an anecdote tells of a girl student who argued with her instructor in psychology and "sought to prove, in the light of her own investigations, the absurdity of Dewey's theories." [22] A more serious account was given by E. S. Ames, the first student to receive a Ph.D. degree from the department:

My first real contact with John Dewey was on a very hot September afternoon in 1895 when I faced him, James Rowland Angell, and other professors to take the oral examination for the Ph.D. degree in philosophy. Professor Dewey was just entering upon his engagement as head of the department of philosophy. He was then thirty-five. He had been on vacation in Europe for a year before beginning his work at Chicago. He was of medium height and weight, with heavy brown hair and mustache, and he wore glasses. His manner was deliberate, kindly, and marked by a thoughtful, conversational, questioning attitude. This questioning attitude has always seemed to me an interesting characteristic. Even when lecturing, he was still inquiring, as if weighing his words and ready to make any qualifications which the current of his thought might suggest. This is a provocative and encouraging trait, for it at once elicits intellectual co-operation on the part of the hearers and invites a sense of participation in reflection upon the problem under consideration."[23]

Though the department became widely known for the abundance of its course offerings as well as the quality of its instruction, it was through the published research of its members, especially of Dewey, that the department acquired its fame. This research had begun at the University of Michigan where Dewey, Tufts, and Mead were colleagues and Angell an undergraduate student. Deeply influenced by Darwinian biology and the functional psychology of William James, these men had undertaken to work out the implications of these for philosophy and psychology, and, in Dewey's case, for education also. Now at Chicago, their number agumented by Moore, Ames, and some graduate fellows, they continued the research, each man grappling with the problems that touched his particular interest, but cooperating with and learning from the others. Dewey's profit from these associations with his colleagues is mentioned in a letter to James. "For a number of years," he said, "I have funded for my own intellectual capital more of the ideas of other people—students and colleagues—than I can tell, and Moore has given at least as much as he has received."[24] In another statement, he acknowledged "personal indebtedness to his present colleagues" and singled out George H. Mead for special mention.[25]

Dewey's published work during his first five years at the University of Chicago gave no hint of his coming break with the "experimental idealism"[26] developed during his last years at Michigan, which he believed successfully combined the basic concepts of Hegelianism with those of evolutionary biology and functional psychology.[27] Dewey's early Chicago publications included his two books, *The Psychology of Number*, in collaboration with James A. McLellan, and *The School and Society*, as well as articles in professional journals of philosophy, psychology, and education.[28] In all these appears Dewey's characteristic attack on dualisms and external or mechanical relations and his insistence on organicism, functionalism, continuity, growth, conflict and adjustment—concepts which can be understood and interpreted as well in terms of a Hegelian metaphysics as in terms of an evolutionary and functional science.

His studies in logical theory eventually led Dewey to abandon his Hegelianism. He related that "there was a period extending into my earlier years at Chicago when, in connection with a seminar in Hegel's Logic, I tried reinterpreting his categories in terms of 'readjustment' and 'reconstruction.' Gradually I came to realize that what the principles actually stood for could be better understood and stated when completely emancipated from Hegelian garb." [29]

The first published indication of Dewey's impending break with Hegelian logic and metaphysics appeared in 1900 in his article entitled "Some Stages of Logical Thought," [30] in which for the first time he criticized transcendental logic. Following Peirce in identifying thought with the "doubt-inquiry process," Dewey surveyed the several historical stages of logical thought and judged science to be its highest and final stage. He also found that up to this time there had been no adequate theory of the logic employed in the scientific enterprise. Aristotelian, empirical, and transcendental logic all claim to give an adequate theory of scientific thinking, but, as Dewey pointed out, they each fail for one reason or another to do this. Transcendental logic, for example, holds "that our logical processes are simply the reading off or coming to consciousness of the inherently rational structure already possessed by the universe in virtue of the presence within it of this pervasive and constitutive action of thought." [31] But such a logic, Dewey argued, has no place for the kind of practical doubt and inquiry that characterize science. The great need, he concluded, is for a logic in which "all the distinctions and terms of thought—judgment, concept, inference, subject, predicate and copula of judgment, etc. *ad infinitum*—shall be interpreted simply and entirely as distinctive functions or divisions of labor within the doubt-inquiry process." [32]

The beginnings of such a logic appeared three years later in *Studies in Logical Theory* by Dewey and seven of his associates. This volume was the culmination of several years of study in logical theory by Dewey and the other authors. All the writers agreed on "the intimate connections of logical theory with functional psychology"; [33] all acknowledged "a pre-eminent obligation . . . to William James, of Harvard University, who, we hope, will accept this acknowledgment and this book as unworthy tokens of a regard and an admiration that are coequal." [34]

Dewey contributed to the volume four essays under the general title "Thought and its Subject-Matter." These essays discussed the general problem of logical theory; the antecedents of thought; the datum of thinking; and the content and object of thought. Because the essays are the first extended statement of Dewey's new instrumental logic, they are particularly significant in the history of philosophical thought.

Throughout his exposition, Dewey used the logical theories of Lotze and transcendentalism as foils for his own doctrine. He characterized these logics as "epistemological" because for them the main problem of logical theory is to explain "the eternal nature of thought and its eternal validity in relation to an eternal reality." [35] Both theories teach that the function of thought is to represent reality and that the truth of an idea depends upon how faithfully it does this.

Dewey examined the arguments of Lotze and of transcendentalism in masterly detail; he found that, though they begin with fundamentally different metaphysical and epistemological premises, both eventually end up with the same insoluble problem, namely, "the reference of thought-activity to a wholly indeterminate unrationalized, independent, prior existence." [36] Neither theory is able to explain, within its own framework, how thought and reality coalesce to result in a knowable universe.

Dewey argued that the way out of the difficulties encountered by Lotze and transcendentalism is to abandon the notion that there is a "thought in general" whose function is to represent a "reality in general" [37] and to recognize that thought is always a specific affair aimed at overcoming a specific problem arising in experience. Dewey called his logic an "instrumental type of logic" [38] because for it an idea is simply a plan of action designed to solve a specific problem; its truth depends not upon its correspondence to some prior reality but upon "its functional or instrumental use in effecting the transition from a relatively conflicting experience to a relatively integrated one." [39]

When reality is "defined in terms of experience" [40] and thought is viewed as a doubt-inquiry process within this experience, said Dewey, the distinction between fact and idea, datum and ideatum, existence and meaning is seen to be functional, not ontological or metaphysical. "In the logical process, the datum is not just real existence, and the idea mere psychical unreality." [41] Rather, both are parts of the same conflicting experience and therefore have the same real or ontological status. Their only difference is a functional one, in that an item of experience which functions as an idea in one set of circumstances may function as a fact in another type of situation. "In other words," said Dewey, "datum and ideatum are divisions of labor, co-operative instrumentalities, for economic dealing with the problem of the maintenance of the integrity of experience." [42] And what is true of datum and ideatum is true also of the other factors involved in the logical process—judgment, concept, inference, subject, predicate, etc.—all are to be explained as functions or divisions of labor in the doubt-inquiry process taking place within experience.

Studies in Logical Theory aroused little critical comment at the time of its appearance. It might have gone largely unnoticed had it not been accorded a warm and enthusiastic reception by William James. "It rejoices me greatly," James wrote to Dewey, "that your School (I mean your philosophic school) at the University of Chicago is, after this long gestation, bringing its fruits to birth in a way that will demonstrate its great unity and vitality, and be a revelation to many people, of American scholarship." [43] In his review of the book a short time later, James said that "Professor John Dewey, and at least ten of his disciples, have collectively put into the world a statement, homogeneous in spite of so many coöperating minds, of a view of the world, both theoretical and practical, which is so simple, massive, and positive that, in spite of the fact that many parts of it yet need to be worked out, it deserves the title of a new system of philosophy." [44] James predicted for it a great future, declaring it "certainly something of which Americans may be proud." [45]

Dewey was pleased with James's comments. In a letter, he told James, "I need hardly say what I have said before, such approval as you feel drawn to give means more to us than that of anybody else. None the less as far as I am concerned I have simply been rendering back in logical vocabulary what was already your own." [46]

In England, F. C. S. Schiller, the noted English pragmatist and humanist, welcomed the book with an enthusiasm second only to that of James. James had previously called Schiller's attention to the work being done by Dewey's department, saying that "it appears now that, under Dewey's inspiration, they have at Chicago a flourishing school of radical empiricism of which I for one have been entirely ignorant . . . though I could discern that Dewey himself was laboring with a big freight, towards the light." [47] After he had read the *Studies*, James again wrote to Schiller that "it is splendid stuff, and Dewey is a hero. A real school and real thought. At Harvard we have plenty of thought, but not school. At Yale and Cornell, the other way about." [48]

Schiller in his review found the book "a weighty contribution to current logical controversy" and its argument analogous to that of James's pragmatism. "So close indeed is this parallel and so undesigned the coincidence," wrote Schiller, "that no one who fully realises the importance of this movement can fail to be reminded of the double discovery of Natural Selection by Darwin and by Wallace." [49] Schiller declared in another place that Dewey deals a deadly blow to absolute idealism by "his admirable proof of the superfluity of an absolute truth-to-be-*copied*, existing alongside of the human truth which is *made* by our efforts." [50]

Charles S. Peirce, who had taught Dewey logic at the Johns Hopkins, wrote in his review that the volume reflected "an impressive decade's work" on the part of Dewey and his colleagues, affording "conclusive proof" of the service Dewey was rendering his department. Peirce approved Dewey's effort to make mind continuous with experience, and logic "a natural history of thought"; he wished the Chicago School "godspeed in their enterprise of discovery." But Peirce wondered whether Dewey was "as radically opposed to the German school" as he supposed. "We must confess," wrote Peirce, "that had he not put so much emphasis upon it, we should hardly have deemed the point of difference so important." [51]

Not all comments about the new instrumentalism were as favorable as those of James and Schiller. Some criticized Dewey's identification of reality and experience as running counter to the commonsense belief that a real world, which exists prior to anyone's experience of it, stands authoritatively over against one's ideas and gives them their truth. By refusing to admit the existence of a reality independent of experience, these critics asserted, Dewey may have avoided the problems attending a dualistic theory of knowledge but only by making "the riddles of existence rather simpler than the facts warrant." [52]

Some criticized Dewey's commitment to the "reigning biological categories" as leading him to narrow unduly the nature and function of thought. The biological orientation of Dewey's philosophy, these critics declared, caused him to overlook that, in addition to its practical and instrumental function, thought may also have a purely cognitive, contemplative, or aesthetic end as attested by philosophy, art, and religion.[53]

Still others wondered how thought can arrive at universal and necessary truths when, as Dewey argued, logical processes are inextricably tied in with psychological ones. "If in the end," wrote F. H. Bradley, "there is to be no such thing as independent thought, thought, that is, which in its actual exercise takes no account of the psychological situation, I am myself in the end led inevitably to scepticism. And on this point I have so far failed to gain any assistance from Prof. Dewey." [54]

These pertinent and sound criticisms Dewey could not well ignore. Consequently, during the coming years at Columbia University, he devoted a large amount of his time to clarifying and developing his doctrine, attempting to answer his critics.

Paralleling his work in philosophy and equally noteworthy were Dewey's efforts in education. The Department of Pedagogy was opened as an independent unit of the university in the fall of

1895 after Dewey had returned from Europe and Julia E. Bulkley had come back from her studies in Switzerland. Dewey and Mrs. Bulkley carried the major portion of the teaching load during the early years of the department but other instructors were added as the need arose. Among those appointed over the next few years were Nathaniel Butler, Fred Warren Smedley, Ella Flagg Young, and George H. Locke. Of these, Ella Flagg Young was the most highly regarded by Dewey. At the time of her appointment in 1900, she was fifty-five years old, with over twenty-five years of experience in the public schools of Chicago, both as teacher and administrator; she had served as District Superintendent of Schools in Chicago during 1887–99. According to his daughter, Dewey regarded Ella Flagg Young as "the wisest person in school matters with whom he has come in contact in any way. . . . Contact with her supplemented Dewey's educational ideas where he lacked experience in matters of practical administration, crystallizing his ideas of democracy in the school and, by extension, in life." [55]

The schedule of courses in the department for the years 1895–96 and 1896–97 reflected the new era in the study of pedagogy at the university. Courses in General Pedagogy, Pestalozzi and Herbart, Development of English Pedagogy, General Principles of Pedagogy, and a Seminar in Pedagogy were given by Mrs. Bulkley. Introductory courses in psychology, logic, and ethics, required of all students in pedagogy, were given by Mead, Angell, and Moore. Because of other pressing matters, Dewey did not give a course in pedagogy during 1895–96, but thereafter offered a wide range, including: Educational Psychology, Philosophy of Education, Educational Methodology, Evolution of Educational Theory, Elementary Education, Logical Methods in Relation to Education, and the Evolution of the Curriculum in the Fifteenth to the Seventeenth Centuries "with reference to general social and intellectual conditions." [56] As additional appointments to the staff were made, the number of courses increased so that by 1900 there were twenty-three.

Among matters confronting Dewey in the fall of 1895 were those connected with the opening of the University Elementary School, the name given to the experimental school of the Department of Pedagogy.[57] By late autumn these had been sufficiently settled to allow the school to open in January 1896.

A contemporary account describes the opening session of the school that was to win such a prominent place among the new schools of the country:

The primary school connected with the pedagogical department of the University opened Monday morning with twelve children in attendance, and twice that number of parents and visitors. The building, No. 389 Fifty-seventh street, is a new house; has large windows, sunny rooms, and is surrounded by a playground. The work of the first morning began with a song, followed by a survey of the premises to test the knowledge of the children regarding the use of garden, kitchen, etc., as well as their powers of observations. They were then seated at tables and provided with cardboard. At the end of the morning each child had completed a paper box for pencils and other materials. A story was told by one of the children, and physical exercise concluded the program.[58]

During the six and a half years of its existence, the school experienced an impressive growth in number of students and teaching staff. It opened with sixteen regularly enrolled pupils and two teachers. By 1902 it had one hundred and forty pupils and twenty-three instructors plus some graduate assistants from the Department of Pedagogy. In addition, representatives from other departments of the university frequently gave talks on their specialties to the children.[59]

The Department of Pedagogy extended its efforts beyond the classroom and the experimental school. It sponsored round-table discussions for teachers in the Chicago area;[60] it invited prominent educators to the campus to speak on topics of pedagogical interest; and it collaborated with the university in bringing numerous city, state, and national educational organizations to the campus for their meetings. It arranged a celebration of the 150th anniversary of the birth of Pestalozzi in January 1896[61] and in May of the same year commemorated the 100th anniversary of the birth of Horace Mann.[62]

The department had a Pedagogical Club whose meetings were devoted to reading and discussing original papers by faculty and graduate students, to book reviews, and to reports of current events in the educational world. Dewey regularly attended the meetings of the club, and also presented papers on such topics as "The University School,"[63] "Education and Power of Control,"[64] and "Psychology and Education."[65]

These early efforts of the university and of the Department of Pedagogy to advance the cause of education were deeply appreciated by those actively engaged in education, leading one group of summer quarter students to pass formal resolutions including one referring to Dewey and his work:

WHEREAS, The University of Chicago has from the beginning of its career recognized the fact that a pedagogical department is one of the essential features of a great modern university, and has in accordance with this idea undertaken to build up a strong faculty in said department, and

WHEREAS, The University has freely opened its doors during the Summer Quarter to the teachers of the country, thus enabling them to take advantage of the instruction given in the University.

Therefore, be it Resolved, That we, who in some measure, at least, represent the teaching force of the country in its various departments from kindergarten to university, express to those in authority our hearty approval and appreciation of all serious attempts thus far made in the direction before mentioned.

We furthermore express the hope that what has thus far been accomplished may prove to be but a milestone in the University's career of usefulness in its department of Pedagogy.

Further, be it Resolved, That we, the members of Head Professor Dewey's class in Educational Psychology, express to him our most hearty and unqualified appreciation of the masterly lectures he has delivered before us during the past term—lectures at once so simple and clear as to be within the comprehension of the novice, and so profound and fundamental as to be of the highest value to the educational expert.

We also express the hope that the teachers of the country may have frequent opportunities to profit by Dr. Dewey's clear and profound insight into the educational problems of the day.[66]

Another milestone in the university's pedagogical program was reached in 1901 when the Chicago Institute merged with the university. The Chicago Institute was founded in 1899 and endowed with a million dollars by Mrs. Emmons Blaine, daughter of Cyrus McCormick, founder of the International Harvester Company. The institute was established to provide a school where Colonel Francis W. Parker and his staff could work out their progressive ideas on education and teacher training without the constant interference of politically minded and conservative school commissioners—an interference they had continually to contend with while working for the publicly controlled Chicago Normal School. The institute had one year of successful operation during 1900–1901, but because of building strikes had erected no building. Negotiations carried on during the spring of 1901 resulted in the incorporation of the Chicago Institute, including its kindergarten and elementary practice school, in the University of Chicago. This new division of the university was called the School of Education; Colonel Parker was made its director and put also in charge of its elementary teachers training program.[67] Wilbur S. Jackman, long associated with Parker as a teacher of natural science, was appointed dean of the school.

The Department of Pedagogy under Dewey was left standing, with its name changed to the Department of Education. It continued as before to give both undergraduate and graduate courses to students interested in becoming educational specialists, also operating as before its elementary laboratory school. Two secondary schools, the Chicago Manual Training School and the South Side Academy, were also incorporated in the university at this time under the direction of Dewey and the Department of Education.[68]

The continuance of the Dewey experimental school was approved, but not without a struggle. Harper and the trustees favored consolidation of the Dewey and Parker elementary schools, primarily for financial reasons; only after parents, patrons of the Dewey School, and prominent educators throughout the country urged that the school be permitted to stand, did the trustees agree to allow the school to continue. However, this was to be on a year-to-year basis and only if the money needed to run the school was guaranteed annually in advance.[69]

As the school year 1901–2 wore on, Colonel Parker's health began to fail. In February he was ordered by his doctor to go south for rest and recuperation. His condition grew worse, however, and on 2 March 1902, he died. Parker's death was a serious loss to the university, necessitating the appointment of a new head of the School of Education. After considerable discussion and numerous interviews, in May the trustees of the former Chicago Institute nominated Dewey for the position. The trustees of the university endorsed the nomination and appointed Dewey the new director.[70]

Dewey accepted the position primarily because he felt that the pioneering work in education at the university should go on. Training elementary school teachers after Parker's method, providing programs for specialists, carrying on experiments in education in the laboratory school, and supplying training in the manual arts were efforts he judged ought to be continued.[71] But Dewey was "deeply conscious of the difficulties of the task," mentioning "the frequent demands I may have to make upon the sympathetic judgment and assistance of others."[72]

With the educational program now under a single head, Harper and the trustees believed that a simpler organization was in order. With Dewey's concurrence they abolished the Department of Education as a separate unit of the university, putting its undergraduate work in the School of Education and its graduate work in the Department of Philosophy. The Chicago Manual Training School and the South Side Academy were combined as the Secondary School of the School of Education. The two elementary schools—the Parker practice school and the Dewey laboratory school—continued as independent units within the School of Education for the academic year 1902–3, but were merged in the fall of 1903 and operated as a single school under Mrs. Dewey's principalship during 1903–4, Dewey's last year at the university.

The several teaching staffs were consolidated. The faculties of the School of Education, the former Department of Education, the South Side Academy, the Chicago Manual Training School, and the Laboratory School were brought together into a single faculty as a single administrative body under Dewey.[73]

The University of Chicago's program in education at this time was generally considered the most rounded and comprehensive in the country. Dewey himself wrote of it that it "incarnates in itself all the elements which constitute the theoretical educational problems of the present. I mean we have right here in concrete, actual institutional form all the factors which any writer on education of the present day would lay down as involved in the problem of education." [74]

Except for Dewey's writings, the publications of the members of the School of Education did not match those of the members of the Department of Philosophy.[75] Ella Flagg Young wrote a series of monographs that were included in the University of Chicago Contributions to Education; [76] other members of the School of Education wrote occasional articles and reports. The *Elementary School Teacher*, formerly published by the Chicago Institute, was taken over by the School of Education, with members of the faculty contributing occasionally. Dewey's writings on education, however, were numerous and covered a variety of topics. Because of their originality and significance, they brought recognition not only to their author but also to the school of which he was head.

Dewey's publications reflect the situation in the educational world at this time. During the latter half of the nineteenth and the early twentieth centuries, educators made widespread efforts to replace conventional education emphasizing textbook and teacher with an education centering in the interests and activities of the child. Theories of education and studies in child psychology appeared in support of the "New Education"; in many parts of the country schools were established where new ideas and methods were tried out, schools that Dewey referred to as "educational 'experiment stations' " and as "the outposts of educational progress" in this country.[77]

Prominent in the movement were Herbartians such as Charles De Garmo of Cornell University, Charles A. McMurry of the Illinois State Normal School, and Frank M. McMurry of Teachers College, Columbia. These men, through their wide influence, were instrumental in entrenching Herbartianism in most of the teacher training schools of the country. In the classroom, "Every good teacher was supposed to have a lesson plan for each class period, and the five formal steps were very much in evidence." [78]

The followers of Froebel made their influence felt in this country through the kindergarten and manual training movements. One of the important figures in this connection was Colonel Francis W. Parker, who was so taken by the kindergarten that he applied its methods to all the grades, first in the public schools of Quincy, Massachusetts, and later, in 1883, in the Cook County Normal School in Chicago where Dewey first met him. Dewey's judgment, expressed some years later, was that "Colonel Francis W. Parker, more nearly than any one other person, was the father of the progressive educational movement." [79] Dewey was deeply influenced by the Froebelian movement; he acknowledged that his laboratory school attempted throughout all grades "to carry into effect certain principles which Froebel was perhaps the first consciously to set forth." [80]

Conservatism in education was best represented at this time by W. T. Harris, who, as founder and editor of the *Journal of Speculative Philosophy*, had encouraged Dewey to make philosophy his career. Harris served as United States Commissioner of Education from 1889–1906, exerting great influence in this capacity. Harris's Hegelianism led him to stress traditional moral and spiritual values in the education of the child at a time when these were in danger of being neglected in favor of the sciences. This emphasis won for Harris a wide popularity; it was said of him that he "was quoted more frequently and with more approval by educational journals and by public-school teachers than any other American—not even excepting Horace Mann." [81]

In child psychology, G. Stanley Hall, Dewey's former professor of psychology at the Johns Hopkins, and Edward Lee Thorndike were the outstanding figures. Hall began his pioneering studies in the 1880s, and in 1904 published his *Adolescence*, a landmark in the scientific study of the child. Thorndike's initial interest was the learning process of animals, but upon his appointment as instructor in psychology at Teachers College in 1899, he shifted his interest and applied the techniques worked out in his study of animals to the learning processes of children. His *Educational Psychology*, published in 1903, was another milestone in child psychology.

Dewey contributed to the new education by bringing the insights of functional psychology and of his own instrumentalist theory of knowledge to bear on educational theory, testing the resulting ideas in his laboratory school.[82] Dewey's soberly scientific approach thus avoided the metaphysical and romantic approaches that characterized much of the thinking of his contemporaries in the Herbartian, Froebelian, and Hegelian camps. The scientific approach, coupled with his modest, nonaggressive personality, cost Dewey a certain amount of popularity at the time, especially since the romantic wing of the new educational movement was represented by such powerful and magnetic personalities as Colonel Parker, Harris and Hall. But, in the years ahead, Dewey's influence grew and spread while that of his contemporaries receded, so that eventually Dewey became the acknowledged leader among American educational philosophers.

The following account vividly contrasts the platform manners of Dewey and Parker:

> It was my privilege recently to be present at the last one of a series of lectures on psychology by Dr. Dewey. . . . His course of lectures was delivered at the Cook County Normal School. If one had been deaf, the interest in watching the "personnel" of the two famous men, Dr. Dewey and Col. Parker, the psychologist whose fame is not confined to his own country, would have been enough to repay one for coming. Dr. Dewey is one of the quietest and most modest appearing men imaginable. He appears like a gentle young man who is studious and willing to learn. To see him on the platform in his gray sack coat, drooping moustache, hair parted in the middle and his "excuse me for intruding" air, as opposed to Col. Parker, with his massive bald head, his impressive and aggressive personality and his "you had better not get in my way" air one would never dream that the quiet man with his level eyebrows and pleasant gentle voice was the lion, and the great Colonel Parker was the lamb.
>
> Such, however, is the case. Col. Parker sits at one side of the platform, listening, often with closed eyes, as is his wont, to the agreeable voice of Dr. Dewey, as he quietly utters those radical ideas which simply remove the bottom from all existing forms of educational effort, excepting those scattered instances, here and there, of those who are applying the right methods, or those who, natural teachers, apply them unconsciously. Col. Parker, in his aggressively earnest way, has been lustily pounding for years, on the same thing. Dr. Dewey does not pound. He quietly loosens the hoops, and the bottom insensibly vanishes.
>
> Dr. Dewey is worshipped by his hearers. There is a charm about his personality which is simply irresistible. He is as simple in his language as in his manner, and the ease with which even the great unwashed can comprehend the principles he lays down, is proof of his grandeur.
>
> At the close of the lecture—which in itself is artistic, for instead of sending off a literary sky-rocket at the end, he simply turns away from the board and melts into the nearest chair—one of the bright girls of the training-class stepped up and handed him a beautiful bouquet of pink and white carnations. . . .
>
> He rose, and true to his nature, uttered just the right thing, in

about six words, thanking his listeners for the stimulus they had furnished him, which was all a man could desire.

Col. Parker then arose, and in an unnaturally tame voice, which indicated to those who know him best a mighty surging torrent of emotion within, said: "Ladies and gentlemen, if what Dr. Dewey has been telling you is true, the millions upon millions which are expended upon our public school system is not only spent in the wrong way, but we are dulling bright intellects and doing incalculable harm to the future generations." [83]

Dewey showed the bearings of the new psychology and of his instrumentalist theory of knowledge on educational thought and practice in his two small books, *The School and Society* and *The Child and the Curriculum*, and in numerous articles. Among the more significant of these are: "The Results of Child-Study Applied to Education," "Interest in Relation to Training of the Will," "The Reflex Arc Concept in Psychology," "Ethical Principles underlying Education," "Principles of Mental Development as Illustrated in Early Infancy," "Psychology and Social Practice," and "The Place of Manual Training in the Elementary Course of Study." [84]

His biological and functional psychology led Dewey to stress first that the child is from the beginning an active, dynamic being with impulses, interests, and activities of his own and that therefore there is no need for the teacher to "induce," "draw out," or "develop" any. "The work of the educator, whether parent or teacher," declared Dewey, "consists solely in ascertaining, and in connecting with, these activities, furnishing them appropriate opportunities and conditions." [85] "Through direction, through organized use," he continued, "they tend toward valuable results, instead of scattering or being left to merely impulsive expression." [86]

Moreover, functional psychology holds that learning comes as a by-product of these activities. Unlike the older educational psychology which believed that ideas exist prior to and apart from activity, the new psychology teaches "that ideas arise as the definition of activity, and serve to direct that activity in new expressions." [87] It teaches "that a motor factor is so closely bound up with the entire mental development that the latter cannot be intelligently discussed apart from the former." [88] Thus, in the ideal school, said Dewey, the activities or life of the child become the all-controlling aim. "All the media necessary to further the growth of the child center there. Learning?—certainly, but living primarily, and learning through and in relation to this living." [89]

Functional psychology teaches further that living and learning are essentially social matters. It considers mind "a function of social life—as not capable of operating or developing by itself, but as requiring continual stimulus from social agencies, and finding its nutrition in social supplies." [90] It follows that the school must be organized along social rather than individual lines, that children must be given opportunity to engage in group activities centering in some interest and challenging their abilities. Through the free give-and-take of such shared experience, the child's mind escapes the narrow confines of its private life, entering into the larger life of his fellows where it finds the stimulus and sustenance necessary for highest and fullest development.

The school organized as a "miniature community" [91] also supplies opportunity for the development of the moral and social attitudes so necessary for life in a democratic society. Dewey believed that it is as futile to try to develop these attitudes apart from actual social living as to try to develop skill in swimming outside of water. "The only way to prepare for social life," he insisted, "is to engage in social life. To form habits of social usefulness and serviceableness apart from any direct social need and motive, and apart from any existing social situation, is, to the letter, teaching the child to swim by going through motions outside of the water." [92]

Dewey's instrumentalist theory of knowledge led him to stress the problematic situation in the learning process. "No one seriously questions," he wrote, "that, with an adult, power and control are obtained through realization of personal ends and problems, through personal selection of means and materials which are relevant, and through personal adaptation and application of what is thus selected, together with whatever of experimentation and of testing is involved in this effort." [93]

But in the school we deny the child every one of these conditions that we recognize as necessary for effective learning in the adult.

> With the adult we unquestioningly assume that an attitude of personal inquiry, based upon the possession of a problem which interests and absorbs, is a necessary precondition for mental growth. With the child we assume that the precondition is rather the willing disposition which makes him ready to submit to any problem and material presented from without. Alertness is our ideal in one case; docility in the other. With the one we assume that power of attention develops in dealing with problems which make a personal appeal, and through personal responsibility for determining what is relevant. With the other we provide next to no opportunities for the evolution of problems out of immediate experience, and allow next to no free mental play for selecting, assorting, and adopting the experiences and ideas that make for their solution.[94]

Recognizing that the child and the adult learn in identical ways, said Dewey, would compel the educator to adopt radically new methods in the classroom. The teacher would arrange for the child to be involved in meaningful, concrete, problematic situations of absorbing interest to him; he would encourage the child to think creatively and independently in solving a problem; he would allow the child to test his ideas in actual practice and to profit from this experience. Under such conditions, education becomes "a continuing reconstruction of experience." [95] The test of a pupil's progress would be not the amount of factual material his mind has assimilated, but his increasing ability to meet novel situations through habits of intelligent response.

Dewey's educational philosophy maintains that when the interests and activities of the child are made the starting points in education, when the school is organized as an embryonic society, and when problematic situations of interest to the child are the base of the child's educational life, numerous problems that have traditionally troubled the educator largely disappear.

For one thing, the dualism traditionally existing between life in the school and life outside the school is eliminated, for life in the school is now simply a continuation in a more formal, controlled, and organized way of the informal, relatively uncontrolled and unorganized life outside the school.[96]

The dualism between the child and the curriculum in large measure vanishes, for the child's present interests and those represented by the curriculum are viewed as two limits to one and the same process: "The facts and truths that enter into the child's present experience, and those contained in the subject-matter of studies, are the initial and final terms of one reality. To oppose one to the other is to oppose the infancy and maturity of the same growing life." [97]

The problem of the correlation of subject matter largely dissolves because the child in his ordinary activities has no need of any plan or principle to correlate his activities. "The things that occupy him," said Dewey, "are held together by the unity of the personal and social interests which his life carries along." [98]

The opposition between the individual and social aims of education disappears because the school starts with and respects the child's individual and unique abilities, interests, and activities, but it directs these in ways that will fit them in with social needs and requirements. The school seeks the fulfillment of the child, but this fulfillment must be that of the socialized individual who finds his happiness and well-being in harmonious association with others.[99]

The problem of discipline is largely taken care of because the activities children are engaged in can be depended upon to develop discipline, "that deeper and infinitely wider discipline that comes from having a part to do in constructive work, in contributing to a result which, social in spirit, is none the less obvious and tangible in form—and hence in a form with reference to which responsibility may be exacted and accurate judgment passed." [100]

When Dewey came to apply and test in his laboratory school his new ideas on education, his problem, as he conceived it, was "to discover in administration, selection of subject-matter, methods of learning, teaching, and discipline, how a school could become a coöperative community while developing in individuals their own capacities and satisfying their own needs." [101] The plan he adopted was to make occupations such as cooking, weaving, sewing, carpentry, and metal-work, the ground experience of the education of the child.

In *The School and Society*, Dewey explained why he did this. For one thing, when occupations are conceived as "methods of life" and not as "distinct studies," [102] they call out and develop not only the child's intellectual abilities but his imaginative, emotional, creative, and social capacities as well. Moreover, when studied in their factual and historical contexts, occupations provide natural avenues to the study of science, geography, and the history of human cultures. "You can concentrate the history of all mankind," Dewey explained, "into the evolution of the flax, cotton, and wool fibers into clothing." [103] Also, occupations open up ways for effective instruction in the symbols and tools of learning—reading, writing, spelling, and arithmetic—which can be related to the demands of the activity the child is engaged in and so can be made more vital and significant to him.

Dewey also maintained that an education centering in occupations helps to compensate for the educational losses resulting from the changes in industrial organization. The Industrial Revolution, he pointed out, has destroyed the old household and neighborhood industries among which children once lived and learned. The child brought up in an urbanized, industrialized community no longer has opportunities to observe or to participate in the economic and industrial life around him, thus missing the very real educational experiences that former generations of children had.[104]

"The great thing to keep in mind, then, regarding the introduction into the school of various forms of active occupation," Dewey concluded, "is that through them the entire spirit of the school is renewed. It has a chance to affiliate itself with life, to become the child's habitat, where he learns through directed living; instead of being only a place to learn lessons having an abstract and remote reference to some possible living to be done in the future. It gets a chance to be a miniature community, an embryonic society. This is the fundamental fact, and from this arise continuous and orderly sources of instruction." [105]

The methods adopted in the Dewey school created conditions quite different from those found in the conventional school, as indicated by these excerpts from an eye-witness account:

> The visitor is impressed, first of all, with the freedom and unconstraint everywhere manifest. He sees clusters of children here and there in the different rooms, gathered about an older person, all talking familiarly together about something which seems to be extremely interesting. He thinks at first that he must have stumbled into a very big family, where every one is having the happiest kind of a time.
>
> Except in the assembly room and the library, there are no desks or stationary chairs; and when a class is called the eight or ten children who compose it do not sit or stand in a stiff row before the teacher, but they draw up their low chairs and gather around her just as they please, just as they would if they were at home and she was telling them a story. If they wish to ease their restless limbs by wriggling about, they are at perfect liberty to do so; they may change their places if they do it quietly; and, indeed, if one in the exuberance of his enthusiasm over some exciting point in the discussion should jump out of his chair and execute an ecstatic little hop or skip, I do not think the rebuke would be very severe. They may talk to each other in the classes and elsewhere, and discussions over difficult questions are often lively. There is freedom from constraint, and yet the liberty is never allowed to degenerate into license.[106]

Though *The School and Society* got little critical attention when it first appeared in 1899,[107] it was well received by leaders in education, teachers, and the interested lay public. Originally delivered as lectures before audiences of parents and patrons of the school, the book was written in a simple and easily understood style; almost immediately it became a best seller. It went through seven printings in the next ten years, eventually being translated into every important foreign language.

Besides spreading Dewey's ideas on education to a wider public, *The School and Society* brought the University Elementary School to the attention of educators throughout the country. "More eyes are now fixed upon the university elementary school at Chicago," declared B. A. Hinsdale, professor of pedagogy at the University of Michigan, "than upon any other elementary school in the country, or probably in the world—eyes watching to see the outcome of the interesting experiment." [108]

7. The University of Chicago, 1894–1904: II

DEWEY'S reputation in philosophical, psychological, and educational circles brought him many invitations to lecture at other institutions of higher learning; he kept busy meeting these engagements. In July 1896, for example, he headed the departments of psychology and pedagogy at the Summer Institute of Martha's Vineyard,[1] and in August delivered two lectures on "Imagination in Education" at Chautauqua.[2] During the summer of 1901, he gave courses at the University of California in Berkeley and at Brigham Young Academy,[3] and in the spring of 1904 gave six lectures on "Problems of Knowledge" at Columbia University as well as three lectures on "Moral Education" at the Brooklyn Institute.[4]

Dewey was also in demand as a speaker at professional meetings of philosophers, psychologists, and educators. In the spring of 1896 he spoke at the first annual meeting of the North Central Association of Colleges and Secondary Schools.[5] He was elected president of the American Psychological Association for the year 1899–1900, giving as his presidential address, "Psychology and Social Practice"; later, in December 1901, he addressed the association on "Interpretation of Savage Mind."[6] Dewey was an active member of the American Philosophical Association, of which he became president in 1905; he was a member of the Illinois Society for Child-Study and of the National Herbart Society, frequently addressing meetings of both these organizations.

With so much time taken by off-campus engagements, Dewey could not participate in on-campus activities as much as he might have wished. Nevertheless, like other members of the faculty, he took his turn speaking at the afternoon lecture series the university provided for the students. The most outstanding of Dewey's talks on these occasions were two he delivered in the summer of 1897. Entitled "Evolution and Ethics," these created quite a stir because in them Dewey defended evolution and attacked the dualism between the cosmic and ethical processes that T. H. Huxley had set up in his Romanes Lecture of 1893. Dewey argued that the ethical has its roots in the cosmic and is continuous with it.[7]

There is no record of Dewey's having spoken, as did many other faculty members, at the university chapel services held for a time each noon on the campus. Indeed, during his Chicago years and thereafter, Dewey disassociated himself more and more from organized religion, devoting his energies instead to educational and social affairs. He did not join the Hyde Park Congregational Church upon surrendering his membership in the Congregational Church in Ann Arbor, nor did he require that his children do so. When his mother, a loyal and pious Congregationalist, remonstrated, declaring that the children ought to be sent to Sunday School, Dewey's reply was that in his youth he had gone to Sunday School enough to make up for his children's failure to do so.

Dewey attended meetings of the University Senate irregularly, being present at but eleven of the nineteen held during his years at Chicago. However, he made his voice heard when he was present. He was one of two opposed to the establishment of a separate school of commerce and political science; [8] he moved to waive the requirement of Latin for graduation from the Senior College; [9] he proposed "a modification of the requirements respecting history in the undergraduate course"; [10] and he voted in favor of requiring one unit of science for admission to the Junior College.[11]

Except for the philosophical and pedagogical clubs, Dewey did not have the close association with student organizations that he had had at the University of Michigan. He twice addressed the students of the Graduate School of Arts, Literature, and Science at their monthly meetings, once on "Psychology as a University Study" and once on "Responsibilities in the Use of Mind." [12] He spoke once at the Sunday evening religious services sponsored by the Christian Union, choosing as his topic "Psychology and Religion," [13] but there is no record of his having conducted one of the Christian Union's Bible study classes or having spoken at any of the student conferences on religion held on the campus. Similarly, no record indicates that Dewey had any close connection with the University of Chicago Settlement, organized in 1894 by a committee of faculty and student members of the Christian Union to serve as an outlet for student and faculty social and philanthropic endeavors. Dewey's efforts in these areas seem to have been confined to Hull House.

Dewey shared with other members of the university community a deep interest in attacks on the university made by outside groups because of the teachings of some of its faculty. Conservative religious groups attacked members of the university's Divinity School because of their "higher criticism" of the Bible, while conservative business interests attacked members of the social science departments because of their alleged radicalism. These attacks raised the question of academic freedom, stirring up much discussion at the university and in the press.

Rockefeller interests, especially, were suspected in many quarters of attempting to influence instruction at the university and of forcing Edward W. Bemis to resign in 1895 from the Department of Political Economy because of his outspoken liberalism. The press gave the Bemis case wide publicity. "Even the various 'heresy trials' that have occurred from time to time of late at our theological institutions," declared the editor of the *Boston Herald*, "have not raised such a general storm of indignation in the press of the country as the persecution of Prof. Bemis at Chicago University for opinion's sake. Mr. Rockefeller is reported to have said, in substance, at the time that Prof. Bemis's attitude toward monopolies was brought to his notice, that he did not give his money for any such purpose, and he did not propose to have any such teachings permitted." [14] "As the case now stands," declared another writer, "the only conclusion the public can draw is that political economy and social science must be taught in that university in ways that are agreeable to the corporate influences that endowed it." [15]

The reply of the university authorities to such attacks was that "the University of Chicago from its inception adhered to the policy of allowing its members perfect freedom not only in holding but in publishing their ideas in whatever manner they chose, provided such ideas did not contemplate the subversion of all social order. . . . As to the declaration that the Department of Economics is conducted in the interest of the Standard Oil Trust and Mr. Rockefeller, nothing could strike wider of the mark." [16]

Dewey stated his views on this matter in an article entitled "Academic Freedom," [17] in which he tended to discount any growing threat to academic freedom in nonsectarian universities. He declared that the widening spirit of scientific inquiry, the increasing unity among university faculties, the pressure of public opinion, and the alertness of the press to infringements of speech and communication were decreasing the possibilities of attacks on academic freedom. As for wealthy benefactors, Dewey believed that "the man with money hardly dare directly interfere with freedom of inquiry, even if he wished to; and no respectable university administration would have the courage, even if it were willing, to defy the combined condemnation of other universities and of the general public." [18] Where individual faculty members had been under attack, wrote Dewey, it was frequently more because of the manner in which they presented their views than because of the views themselves. "Lack of reverence for the things that mean much to humanity, joined with a craving for public notoriety, may induce a man to pose as a martyr to truth when in reality he is a victim of his own lack of mental and moral poise." [19]

Dewey would hardly have been so optimistic had he been aware of the numerous letters President Harper received from Frederick T. Gates, Rockefeller's private secretary. These letters reveal that Gates was very much on the alert for anything said by liberal faculty members that might cast reflection on his employer or that ran counter to conservative social thought. In one letter Gates asked President Harper whether "you can yourself afford to appear in this magazine" now that it has become "a byword and a laughing stock" as a result of its opening its columns to articles attacking the Standard Oil Company.[20]

Dewey belonged to the Civic Federation of Chicago whose membership included many of the university faculty and several of the city's most prominent citizens. The federation, through its several committees, made studies of the political, educational, moral, philanthropic, and public health aspects of the city's life, offered recommendations, and urged voters to support candidates committed to liberal programs of reform.

Of particular concern to Dewey were Chicago's public schools which had been allowed to deteriorate to the point where the situation had become a national scandal.[21] He joined with other public-spirited citizens to bring about reform; when the city was offered as a gift the Cook County Normal School for the professional training of the city's teachers, Dewey wrote a letter to the press urging the Board of Education to accept the school. "I do not believe there is a single step," he declared, "which would do as much for the Chicago schools." He also pledged his own efforts as head of the Department of Pedagogy "to any and every cooperation possible to helping the public schools of Chicago through the instrumentality of a training school." [22] Throughout his years in Chicago, Dewey worked hard to bring the elementary and secondary schools of the city into closer, more effective association with the university so as to raise standards and instill in the teachers a sense of professional pride.

Dewey was absorbed by the problems growing out of the

city's economic and industrial life—an interest he had had since his undergraduate days at the University of Vermont.[23] These problems were particularly urgent in Chicago because of the bitterness and violence attending the workers' struggle for higher wages and greater security. Mass demonstrations, strikes, roaming mobs, violence such as erupted during the Haymarket Riot in May 1886, and melodramatic newspaper headlines were common in Chicago during the hard times of the 1870s and 1880s, prompting Marshall Field to recommend that "a standing army be constantly on the alert to put down such demonstrations." [24] When Dewey arrived in Chicago in the summer of 1894, the strike of the American Railway Union under Eugene V. Debs and strikes by unions in sympathy with the railroad workers were taking place.

Opponents of the existing social order found Chicago a fertile field for their ideas, making the city a center of radical social thought. Communists, socialists, anarchists competed to spread their ideas and win converts.

Dewey belonged to the group of liberal thinkers on the University of Chicago faculty at this time—men such as Albion Small and W. I. Thomas of the Department of Sociology; Edward W. Bemis and Thorstein Veblen of the Department of Political Economy; Frederick Starr in Anthropology; and Tufts, Mead, Moore, and Angell of Dewey's own department.

These men were infected by what Albion Small called the "Spirit of the New Humanity," manifested in

> the growing popular and scientific belief that the elements of human welfare are knowable and controllable. . . . We no longer believe that the evils of life are chiefly necessary evils. We believe that the conditions of life can be so understood as to reduce social failures to the status of risks against which society can ultimately insure its members as systematically as we now insure against death, or fire, or crop failure, or faulty titles, or breaches of trust.[25]

The Chicago group did not believe in drastic cures for society's ills. They were not extremists of the Marxist, Lassallian, or anarchist type. They believed in the existing capitalist order, but taught that it should be controlled or modified so as to eliminate or lessen the evils and abuses which attend an unrestricted laissez-faire economy. They recognized the danger of giant monopolies, urging their regulation by government. They supported labor unions because these gave the working masses a stronger voice in determining the conditions under which they worked. They favored, under certain conditions, municipal ownership of such public utilities as street railways, gas, water, and electricity. They were opposed to violence and lawlessness in the settling of labor disputes and to strikes that forced others to be idle, declaring that anyone who defended these practices "would find no sympathy with such views in any department of the University of Chicago." [26]

Dewey shared these views; he had stated many of the same notions while at the University of Michigan.[27] But he did not expand these ideas nor touch upon any of the explosive issues of the day in any published article while at Chicago. Nothing among Dewey's writings at this time is analogous to Thorstein Veblen's *The Theory of the Leisure Class,* Charles Zueblin's *American Municipal Progress,* or to articles by Albion Small, Edward W. Bemis, and W. I. Thomas which discuss vital and controversial issues. The closest Dewey came to a published statement about a social issue was his remark that the school is "the primary and most effective instrument of social progress and reform" and that "through education society can formulate its own purposes, can organize its own means and resources, and thus shape itself into definiteness and economy in the direction in which it wishes to move." [28]

But though Dewey's writings did not discuss pressing social problems, his lectures in such courses as Contemporary Theories Regarding Ethical Relations of the Individual and Society and The Sociology of Ethics did. Certainly the talks he gave and the discussions he led at Hull House were in large measure concerned with social matters, stamping him a social liberal. "Years ago," declared Jane Addams, "before trade unions had proved their social utility and when it was scarcely respectable to be identified with them, John Dewey made it easier for them and for all their Chicago friends." [29]

Dewey had close relations with Hull House, founded in 1889 by Jane Addams, by all odds the most famous of the many social settlements in large cities at this time. He was on its first board of trustees, and "unlike many trustees, he actually worked on the job." [30] Dewey conducted courses, gave talks, led discussions; one year, on midwinter Sunday afternoons, he presided over the Plato Club, whose debates were "an epitome of all discussions held on social questions in the nineties." [31]

Jane Addams and her staff, which included such outstanding women as Ellen G. Starr, Julia Lathrop, Florence Kelley, and Alice Hamilton, were militant social workers who did not hesitate to enter the arena of local politics. They spoke at neighborhood political rallies, marched in parades, and vigorously supported candidates committed to social reform. They made studies of the evils that infected slum neighborhoods and publicized their findings. "In 1893, after an investigation of the sweating system by one of her co-workers [Florence Kelley], the Illinois Legislature was prodded by Governor Altgeld into passing what Henry Lloyd called 'the best anti-sweatshop law of any civilized community.' "[32]

Hull House was a popular meeting place for people of diverse social views. Here, in the evenings and on Sundays, liberals, socialists, communists, anarchists, and others met to exchange ideas. Here came Henry Demarest Lloyd whose article, "Story of a Great Monopoly,"[33] attacking the practices of the Standard Oil Company, was a turning point in the social history of America. Here came also followers of Henry George, members of the Chicago Single Tax Club, to debate the merits of George's single tax theory as expounded in his *Progress and Poverty*, a book which Dewey said had "a wider distribution than almost all other books on political economy put together" and whose author Dewey judged to be "one of the world's great social philosophers, certainly the greatest which this country has produced."[34] Members of the editorial staff of the *Chicago Commons*, liberal mouthpiece of social workers, were also frequent visitors. The *Commons* often contained blistering attacks on corrupt politicians, arrogant monopolists, sweatshops, and slums. To these writers, "the 'anarchist' whom we need to fear in these days is the man who tramples underfoot the rights of his fellow-men, who by the power of wealth forces his will upon the people in spite of their protesting helplessness. Such a man, be he never so high in church or state or society, is to be feared and dreaded—and restrained."[35]

Dewey owed much to the influences he encountered at Hull House. His contacts with people with more radical and extreme views than his deepened and sharpened his own ideas. Jane Addams's faith in the common man and her conviction "that the simple, the 'humble' peoples of the earth are those in whom primitive impulses of friendly affection are the least spoiled, the most spontaneous"[36] reinforced Dewey's own "faith in democracy as a guiding force in education."[37] The fighting qualities in Jane Addams and her coworkers undoubtedly sparked the same qualities in Dewey's nature so that as the years passed he increasingly left the classroom and study to enter the world of practical affairs to fight for the causes he judged important.

Dewey's family life surrounded him with the warmth and affection he needed. He and Mrs. Dewey were drawn closely together not only by common family interests and responsibilities but also by shared intellectual and professional pursuits. Alice Dewey's keen intellect enabled her to keep abreast of her husband's research activities; she always awaited the published results with eagerness. She helped Dewey set up the laboratory school and, as time permitted, also taught and supervised in it. "The clear and experienced intelligence of my wife," wrote Dewey in one of his references to the school, "is wrought everywhere into its texture." [38]

As both Alice and John Dewey were extremely fond of children, they enjoyed their large family. One son and two daughters were born during their Chicago years: Gordon Chipman, Lucy Alice, and Jane Mary. These children, together with Frederick and Evelyn, made a good-sized group, enlivening the life of the family. Unlike William James who complained that he found "the cares of a nursing father to be very different from those of a bachelor. Farewell the tranquil mind," [39] Dewey's temperament enabled him to take on the responsibilities of parenthood with relative ease. The noises and disturbances that James found so unsettling left Dewey unruffled. "As a logician," wrote Max Eastman, "Dewey is at his best with one child climbing up his pants leg and another fishing in his inkwell." [40]

The Deweys' social life centered in the university community. Among the faculty, the Meads, Tufts, Moores, Angells, and Smalls were their good friends. Of these, the Meads were the closest to the Deweys.[41] Not only were the two families personally congenial but the Meads took also a deep interest in the Dewey School, giving it financial as well as moral support. When *The School and Society* was being prepared for publication, the Meads put on the finishing touches—a mode of authorship, Dewey wrote, "which I recommend to others fortunate enough to possess such friends." [42]

The Deweys also developed deep attachments to Jane Addams and the members of her staff—their daughter Jane Mary was named after Jane Addams and her close friend, Mary Smith. When Gordon Dewey died while the family was abroad, Jane Addams arranged a memorial service at Hull House at which she gave the principal address.[43] Close association between Dewey and Jane Addams was cut off when the Deweys left Chicago, but, wrote Jane Dewey, "there was never a breach in their mutual esteem and affection." [44]

During the summer months the family continued to go, as they had while at Michigan, to their cottage in Hurricane, New York, in the Adirondacks. Their cabin was just across a brook from "Glenmore," the camp and summer school Thomas Davidson had established in 1889 on East Hill. Davidson, himself a scholar and writer of note, a close friend of William James, patterned Glenmore after the famous Concord School of Philosophy in

Massachusetts. The school attracted a scholarly clientele, mostly from the faculties of colleges in the East and Midwest; here Dewey had close personal contacts with such men as William James, W. T. Harris, and Felix Adler.

During most of their Chicago years, John and Alice Dewey felt keenly the financial burden of a growing family in a big city. Beginning in 1895, John's salary as head of the Departments of Philosophy and Pedagogy remained fixed at $5,000. To this was added the $500 Alice received as a part-time teacher in the University Elementary School. With limited income the family had to watch expenditures, foregoing some of the things they would have liked. As late as 1900, the Deweys had no telephone in their home, but relied on the people in a neighborhood drugstore to relay calls to them. On one occasion, Dewey failed to get an important message from Mrs. Blaine, because, as he explained to her, "the telephone people at the drugstore referred to are not very reliable."[45] When Frederick, the oldest child, expressed a desire for a bicycle, the proposal precipitated a "family crisis," with the family debating the matter long and hard before deciding to get him one. Since the family could not often afford the more expensive forms of recreation such as theater, opera, and concerts, they contented themselves with visits to the several parks and museums for which Chicago was noted.[46]

The family's fortunes improved considerably in 1901 with Dewey's appointment at an additional salary of $2,000 as supervisor of the South Side Academy and the Chicago Manual Training School when the two institutions were incorporated in the university.[47] In 1902, upon the death of Colonel Parker, Dewey became director of the School of Education at a salary of $2,500, making his total salary from the university $7,500.[48] The family income was further increased when Mrs. Dewey was made principal of the University Elementary School in 1901 at a salary of $1,250.[49] In 1903, when she became principal of the combined Dewey and Parker schools, her salary was put at $2,500.[50] These favorable turns in their finances enabled the Deweys to move to more commodious quarters at 6016 Jackson Park Boulevard (now Stoney Island Avenue) and to plan to take the family to Europe for an extended stay.

Incorporation of the Chicago Institute in the University of Chicago caused general rejoicing. Those connected with the institute were pleased because it became an integral part of a great university with all its prestige and resources. President Harper, the trustees, Dewey, and others at the university were happy because in the highly endowed institute they saw the means for expanding and enriching the university's work in primary and secondary education. Shortly after the merger was announced, the university gave a reception in honor of Mrs. Blaine and the faculty of the Chicago Institute. In the receiving line with President Harper and Miss Marion Talbot, dean of women, were Mrs. Blaine, Colonel Parker, and Dewey. Among those invited were the faculty and trustees of the two secondary schools that united with the university, representatives from all the departments of the university, the trustees of the university, and noted educators in and around Chicago. "As the hall filled with the guests and they mingled like one big happy family in the educational household," reads one account, "Dr. Harper's face beamed with satisfaction and Mrs. Blaine appeared radiantly happy." [51] This pleasant situation did not last.[52] Complications arising from the merger gave rise to numerous misunderstandings and to a certain amount of jockeying for position. As a result of the consolidation, two separate and quite distinct divisions had been set up to carry on the pedagogical work of the university—the School of Education including its practice school under Parker, and the Department of Education with the laboratory school under Dewey. Each unit was staffed by a faculty that had deep loyalty to its own organization and to the man who headed it; each wanted to make sure the merger did not work to the disadvantage of its special program.

Against this background, Dewey and Wilbur S. Jackman were soon at odds. Their difference began when, during the summer just after the merger, Jackman sent circulars and application forms to parents calling attention to the "University Elementary School" connected with the new School of Education, informing them that the school was now ready to receive applications. Dewey objected that Jackman should not have referred to the Parker practice school as the "University Elementary School" because this was the name by which the Dewey school had been continuously known for a number of years and parents would be uncertain as to which school was meant. Since such confusion might result in a decrease in enrollment in the Dewey school with a subsequent loss in much needed tuition, points on which Dewey was particularly sensitive, he asked Harper to instruct Jackman not to use the name. Also in his letter to Harper, Dewey cited an instance in which a parent who asked for an application form of the Dewey school was given the form of the Parker school with the comment that the schools were "exactly the same." "I need not say," wrote Dewey "that we have appreciated the inevitable embarrassments growing out of the situation itself, and endeavored to lessen them by a spirit of comity & straightforwardness. We shall continue in that spirit, but it is obvious that I shall not stand by and see an educational enterprise with which my name & professional reputation are bound up put at a factitious disadvantage." [53]

Dewey was further irked when the bulletin of the School of Education came from the press. In a letter to Jackman, Dewey pointed out that the bulletin had failed to include his own name and that of other members of the Department of Education on the list of the School's faculty who "had officially received and accepted appointments." [54]

Dewey wrote further that Jackman should not have used the term "graduate work" in referring to School of Education courses, because the courses were not graduate in the university's sense of the term. The only courses in education recognized by the university as on the graduate level, Dewey implied, were those given in the Department of Education. Finally, Dewey called Jackman's attention to a rumor that someone on his staff had "advised a summer school student to take work with you rather than in the university department because your work was 'correlated' while ours was not." [55] To Dewey it seemed that Jackman and some of his staff were not above advancing the fortunes of the School of Education and its practice school at the expense of the Department of Education and its laboratory school. To Jackman it appeared that Dewey was oversensitive in matters relating to his department and laboratory school, attributing bad motives where none existed.

More unpleasantness set in when Dewey took up duties as director of the School of Education in the summer following Parker's death. Dewey allowed Jackman and the faculty of the School of Education to continue as before with the routine mechanics of administration, but in matters of broad policy he mostly ignored Jackman and the faculty, turning for help and advice to people he had known for some time and whose judgment he respected—people like Mrs. Dewey, Ella Flagg Young, and the Misses Zonia Baber and Emily R. Rice, long associated as teachers with Parker's practice school. Dewey was inclined to do this because of his own limited experience in school administration and because the pressure of other duties, including research, prevented his spending time in his School of Education office. Jackman and the older, more influential members of the former Chicago Institute faculty were piqued at Dewey's almost totally ignoring them; they felt that they, after all, had over the years been most closely associated with Parker and his work, helping bring the school to its present standing.

In the course of the school year 1902–3, Jackman again displeased Dewey, this time by using Dewey's name without permission on an announcement calling a meeting of the parents' association. Dewey was incensed at this; in a letter he warned Jackman: "If such a matter ever occurs again, I shall take it upon myself to print and send to everyone concerned a statement that an unauthorized use has been made of my name." [56] Jackman was equally incensed that Dewey made so much of the matter, replying: "In general I would deprecate a policy of administration and control by threats or force and I should dislike to feel that my mode of administration requires me to be subject to either. . . . Irritating mistakes will occur—not more annoying to you than to me, but I should like to have you feel that they are mistakes to be remedied rather than offenses to be punished." [57]

Early in the spring of 1903, Dewey let it be known he favored consolidating the Parker and Dewey elementary schools. When this proposal was first made by Harper and the trustees in the spring of 1901 at the time the Chicago Institute was being joined with the university, Dewey had vigorously opposed it, fearing that the laboratory school would be absorbed in the larger, well-endowed Parker school. Now, in the seat of administration where he could prevent that, Dewey urged the merger of the two schools for the same reasons advanced earlier by Harper: he could not do justice to both schools, the existence of two elementary schools at the university created confusion in the minds of parents, and consolidation would greatly reduce costs.[58]

The faculty of the School of Education greeted the proposal with mixed feelings. On the one hand, they favored union of the two schools, for the reasons Dewey gave; on the other hand, they were somewhat fearful that by the merger some of them would lose their jobs.[59] Strong opposition to the plan arose, however, when it was learned that Dewey had formally recommended to President Harper that Mrs. Dewey be made principal of the combined schools.

Faculty opposition to Mrs. Dewey stemmed from her past criticisms of many things done in the Parker school,[60] and her quickness to dismiss teachers she judged incompetent.[61] They also believed that the consolidation would cause the Parker school to lose its distinctive character and become "Mr. and Mrs. Dewey's school." [62] Many of the faculty of the School of Education threatened to resign if Mrs. Dewey's appointment went through.[63]

When Mrs. Blaine, acting as intermediary in the dispute, told Dewey of the feeling against Mrs. Dewey, he reacted with disappointment and chagrin. Had he known of this opposition, he told

Mrs. Blaine, he would never have recommended Mrs. Dewey for the post.[64] He was particularly irked with Miss Rice because she had been present as adviser with himself and Ella Flagg Young when Mrs. Dewey was being considered for the post and had voiced no objection.[65]

As a result of Miss Rice's failure to speak out, Dewey found himself in this predicament: if he rescinded the nomination of Mrs. Dewey, it would seem he had made it hastily or without serious intention; if he stuck by the nomination, he would seem to be making "an arbitrary use of authority" or ignoring "the intrinsic morals of the situation." [66] He decided the matter had developed to such a degree he could retain "an ordinary and decent self respect" only by maintaining his nomination of Mrs. Dewey.[67]

Jackman, in the meantime, judged events in the School of Education to have reached an "acute stage"; he called the situation to Harper's attention. In a sixteen-page typewritten letter to President Harper setting forth the grievances he and his faculty had against Dewey, he suggested ways to remedy the situation. Jackman charged that Dewey was rarely present at meetings of parents of the children attending the Parker school, thus impairing its public relations; Dewey took little personal interest in the students enrolled in the School of Education, and the students felt this keenly; though Dewey claimed "to stand for Democracy and for faculty control," [68] he did not call enough faculty meetings where the faculty could discuss matters of broad policy and make their wishes known; Dewey rarely consulted his dean but instead solemnly deferred "to the point of ludicrousness" to other advisers; Dewey's administration of the school was "not without some prejudice" in that the chairmanships of important committees were given to people close to Dewey; and, finally, Dewey's plan for consolidating the two schools was so "poorly matured and partially expressed" as to cause loss of confidence in his leadership. People were "waiting to see Col. Parker's Faculty scattered like autumn leaves." [69]

Jackman's suggestions for correcting the situation were that the school must be freed from "the curbstone politics of cliques"; that more frequent faculty meetings should be arranged; the director must adopt a more sympathetic attitude toward the faculty, students, and work of the School of Education—"the present glacial epoch" must be brought to a speedy end; there must be "no dismissal of those teachers who have been from the beginning identified with the school,"—to dismiss any of these would "certainly stir up outside influences"; and the principalship of the consolidated elementary schools should not be a "family affair" but filled by a man able and strong enough to bring the several factions of teachers together in harmonious and effective relations.[70]

These developments put President Harper in a difficult position. He did not want to offend Dewey and Mrs. Dewey by refusing to appoint her. On the other hand, he did not want to offend the faculty of the School of Education, risking wholesale resignations by making the appointment. The compromise plan he worked out provided that teachers in the School of Education who lacked permanent tenure would be given three-year contracts to insure against sudden dismissal; at the same time Mrs. Dewey would be appointed principal with the understanding that because the appointment was contrary to university policy of not employing husband and wife in the same department, it would be temporary.

When President Harper presented his plan to Mrs. Blaine and the trustees of the Chicago Institute they agreed to it, provided it was clearly understood that Mrs. Dewey's appointment was provisional only.[71] When she communicated this action to President Harper, Mrs. Blaine strongly recommended that, to avoid future misunderstandings, Harper put in writing to Dewey the temporary character of Mrs. Dewey's appointment.[72] But in talking with Dewey to get his approval of the compromise, Harper failed to make clear the temporary nature of the appointment, thus leaving the door open to precisely the kind of misunderstanding Mrs. Blaine had hoped to avoid.

The compromise agreement settled matters for a time; the school year 1903–4 began on a note of cautious optimism. No evidence has been found about Mrs. Dewey's work as principal or about the faculty's reactions to her presence. But as the school year progressed, President Harper felt compelled by the terms of the compromise to make clear to Dewey that Mrs. Dewey's appointment was contrary to university policy and that she was to be principal for only one year. Accordingly Harper wrote Dewey in February suggesting that they get together for "a full and complete survey of the entire situation."[73]

But Harper was in the hospital for a brief period; then Dewey's out-of-town commitments caused postponements of the meeting, so that some weeks elapsed before Harper and Dewey got together. In the meantime, shortly after his release from the hospital, during one of Dewey's absences from the city, Harper had an interview with Mrs. Dewey. He explained to her that it had been agreed between him and Dewey that her appointment was to be for no more than a year. Dewey, not having understood her appointment in this way, had not told Mrs. Dewey; she was taken aback by Harper's statement and deeply embarrassed.

Upon Dewey's return to Chicago, husband and wife reviewed the entire situation in the School of Education; they concluded that their years of usefulness in its behalf had come to an end and that they should both resign. Accordingly, on 5 April, Mrs. Dewey sent a letter to this effect to President Harper; one day later Dewey did the same. Then, judging it best that the family sever all connections with the university, Dewey also sent Harper a letter of resignation from the Department of Philosophy.

Harper was not prepared for such a sudden and drastic turn of events. He truly believed he had made it clear to Dewey that since Mrs. Dewey's appointment was contrary to university policy it could therefore be for one year at most. He was genuinely surprised to find that Dewey had not understood Mrs. Dewey's appointment in these terms.

Harper felt that most of the difficulties between himself and Dewey were due to misunderstandings. Thinking they could be cleared up by open discussion, Harper wrote Dewey:

> It certainly is incumbent upon us as men standing for scientific work to have fully in mind all the data before reaching a final conclusion. In view of this I shall not present to the trustees to-morrow the resignations which are in my hands, and I shall hope that on Wednesday we may have the opportunity for a fuller consideration of the whole matter than we have yet been able to have.[74]

Harper and Dewey met to discuss matters on at least two subsequent occasions but made no progress in straightening out their differences. Consequently, Harper decided to accept the resignations; he wrote Dewey stressing again that Dewey surely must have understood Mrs. Dewey's appointment to be for only one year and expressing "regret that my effort to make this matter clear was unsuccessful."[75] Harper concluded his letter: "In recommending the acceptance of your resignation, I wish to express to you most heartily the appreciation of the University for the splendid work you have performed in these years of its early history, and also to assure you of the peculiar satisfaction which I have enjoyed in co-operating with you in many interesting lines of work."[76]

Harper wrote also to Mrs. Dewey, emphasizing that he could not understand "how Mr. Dewey could have failed to appreciate the point as brought forward in our conference last spring" that her appointment was to be for no more than one year.[77] He closed with a statement of his "sincere appreciation of the earnest and laborious work you have done in connection with the Laboratory School and the elementary work of the School of Education. Your work has been characterized by a true spirit of devotion." [78]

Dewey was considerably annoyed by Harper's letters to him and Mrs. Dewey because they implied that Dewey's sole or chief reason for resigning was that he could not have his way about Mrs. Dewey's appointment, whereas the truth was that this factor had not entered at all into their decision to resign. He wrote to Harper:

> As you are aware, the construction you put by statement and by implications of context upon my resignation in your letters of April 30th do not represent my own reasons for resigning—a point upon which I am presumably the better informed.
>
> In presenting my resignation to the Board of Trustees, and in recommending its acceptance, I request that you make it clear to the Board that the question of the alleged failure to reappoint Mrs. Dewey as Principal of the Elementary School is in no sense the cause of my resignation, and that this question had never been discussed between us till after our resignations were in your hands. Your willingness to embarrass and hamper my work as Director by making use of the fact that Mrs. Dewey was Principal is but one incident in the history of years.[79]

Dewey's letter resigning his posts in Philosophy gave no reason for his action; [80] as for the School of Education, he said simply, "Since the administrative or external side of the work which I undertook in assuming the Directorship of the School of Education has now been accomplished, and since the conditions as you outline them are not favorable to development on the educational side, I hereby present my resignation as Director of the School of Education, the same to take effect July 1st, 1904." [81] But in a letter to W. T. Harris informing him of his resignation, Dewey indicated in a general way why he resigned. "It is a long story," he wrote Harris, "with which I will not trouble you. But the gist of it is simply that I found I could not work harmoniously under the conditions which the President's methods of conducting affairs created and imposed. So it seemed to be due both him and myself that I should transfer my activities elsewhere. I resigned, however, without having anything in view." [82] And in another letter to Harris three days later, Dewey made the surprising statement: "I am still not entirely sure that I wish to devote myself permanently to philosophical rather than to administrative work, and I may come back to you some time with a request for advice." [83] President Harper submitted the resignations of Dewey and Mrs. Dewey to the trustees on 2 May 1904; "after full consideration the resignations were accepted" and the secretary instructed "to express to Mr. Dewey for the trustees their great appreciation of the services he has rendered to the University and the cause of education." [84] Though Dewey's active connection with the university ended in June 1904, with the close of the spring quarter, his official connection continued til 1 January 1905.[85]

Dewey's resignation was a shock to the University of Chicago community and other university circles. President Harper expressed the "surprise and great regret" of the university in Dewey's going; [86] Professor Angell spoke of "the depressing influence of Mr. Dewey's departure" on the Department of Philosophy, urging that this be offset by "every possible evidence of vigor and vitality." [87] W. T. Harris's reaction was typical of that of educators generally. Writing to Dewey he declared: "I am of course very much astonished. I do not think it possible that the President of Chicago University can be persuaded to accept your resignation, but if you force it on him by accepting another call he cannot help himself." [88]

It was not easy for the Deweys to sever connections with the university. Dewey regretted leaving the Department of Philosophy and breaking the ties that had held him so closely to the members of the department. Also, both he and Mrs. Dewey disliked abandoning the laboratory school with its loyal corps of teachers—a school they had labored to establish and bring to its present level of attainment. Finally, they would miss the warm friendships they had developed over the years both at the university and in the city at large. Mrs. Dewey expressed their feelings in a letter to W. T. Harris: "It is a very hard pull to tear up our roots here, but the situation seems so obviously to demand this step that we could not any longer balance considerations." [89]

Shortly after Dewey completed the work of the spring quarter, the family left for an extended stay in Europe. As on their first trip to Europe ten years earlier, tragedy again struck the family. The Deweys' eight-year-old son Gordon contracted typhoid fever while the family was enroute to Liverpool. After a seeming recovery in a Liverpool hospital, he went with the family on a short trip to Ireland where he suffered a relapse and died. Gordon's death was a severe blow to the entire family, but to Mrs. Dewey the shock was such "that she never fully recovered her former energy." [90] Despite this tragedy, the Deweys took the children to the continent as planned. While in Italy, John and Alice Dewey adopted an Italian boy, Sabino, of approximately the same age as Gordon. Sabino fitted into the Dewey family immediately and became a beloved member of the group.

8. Columbia University, 1905–1914

WHEN DEWEY sent his letter of resignation to President Harper on 5 April 1904, he had no position elsewhere. But he was not particularly worried; his scholarly achievements and his standing in the teaching profession made him confident he would find a position to his liking. And that was how matters eventually worked out.

Because Columbia University was expanding rapidly at this time, Dewey thought a place in the Department of Philosophy and Psychology might be available to him there. Consequently, a few days after his resignation, he sent a letter of inquiry to the department chairman James M. Cattell, a friend from graduate days at the Johns Hopkins. Dewey knew that Cattell would tell him frankly what his chances were of getting a job at Columbia.

Dewey learned from Cattell that no position was then open. Cattell added, however, that he very much wanted Dewey to join the department and would consult President Butler of the university to see if this could be arranged.[1] Butler, himself trained in philosophy and former head of the department, was as desirous of getting Dewey as was Cattell. Butler, however, could not definitely promise Dewey a job until money was obtained to finance it. Butler instructed Cattell to "keep in touch with Dewey, while I am in search of the funds," adding that he was "somewhat hopeful" he could get them.[2]

Cattell was sure other high-ranking institutions would be after Dewey once it became known that he was leaving Chicago; he reminded Butler that speed in the negotiations with Dewey was of utmost importance. "I do not of course know," he wrote, "what they would do at Harvard. . . . At all events if they do not call Dewey and we do, they will lose their philosophical position. I fancy Yale or Pennsylvania would gladly take him. They could not compete with us, but if we let him go to New Haven or Philadelphia it would be a serious matter." [3]

Butler succeeded in getting $20,000 from an anonymous donor to finance a new chair in philosophy; [4] he immediately wired Dewey asking if he would accept a professorship of philosophy at a salary of $5,000 if the trustees offered it.[5] Upon receiving Dewey's reply that he would, Butler, following university procedure, presented the matter to the Committee on Education, a committee of trustees charged with overseeing appointments.

The committee readily agreed that Dewey should be given an offer, so recommending at the next meeting of the trustees. In their statement the committee declared that "Professor Dewey is one of the two or three most distinguished students and teachers of philosophy now living" and that if he were to join the Department of Philosophy and Psychology it would without doubt be "the most effective and the most distinguished to be found in any university in the world." The committee emphasized that they regarded the step they were recommending "as of much more than ordinary importance." [6]

Following the committee's recommendation, the trustees voted to hire Dewey at an annual salary of $5,000, to start on 1 February 1905 with the opening of the second semester.[7] The appointment was publicly announced on 2 May 1904; by a previous arrangement with President Butler, President Harper on the same day announced Dewey's resignation from his posts at the University of Chicago. Dewey's new appointment carried with it seats in the Faculty of Columbia College, the Faculty of Philosophy, one of the three graduate faculties at the university [8] and, "upon the request of the Faculty and Trustees of Teachers College," a seat in the Faculty of Teachers College.[9]

Dewey was pleased with this turn of events. As he wrote from Chicago to a Teachers College faculty member who had welcomed him to Columbia, "I assure you while it is a good deal of a wrench for me to cut off my intimate personal and educational ties here, I am looking forward with very great pleasure to taking up the work at Columbia, which I expect to begin February 1st." [10]

When Dewey began his duties at Columbia, he became affiliated with an institution in process of becoming one of the nation's great universities. Founded in 1754 as King's College, it had remained a relatively small institution during its first century and a quarter, serving primarily the undergraduate needs of the youth of New York City's more prominent families. Upon the accession of Seth Low to the presidency in 1889, the college and the four loosely attached professional schools—the School of Medicine, the School of Law, the School of Mines, and the School of Architecture—were organized along university lines and brought into a closer administrative unity. Also during Low's administration, the university moved from its crowded quarters at 49th Street and Madison Avenue to a new campus on Morningside Heights. Here, it was thought, "the great open spaces, the remoteness from the busier parts of the town" would contribute to a more congenial and effective academic life.[11] Accordingly, buildings were constructed on Morningside Heights; on 4 October 1897, less than eight years before Dewey arrived, the university opened its doors to students on the new site.

Low resigned the presidency of the university in 1901 to become mayor of New York City. Nicholas Murray Butler was thereupon appointed acting president, becoming president on 6 January 1902. Under Butler's leadership, the university's program of studies, especially on the graduate and professional levels, was expanded and improved to become eventually one of the best in the nation. At the same time, the number of students and faculty increased till Columbia ranked as one of the country's largest institutions of higher learning. The university's location was an important factor in this development. "Columbia is what she is," wrote one of her historians, "because she is Columbia University *in the City of New York*. Her growth has been a function of the growth of the city, and it is to the city that she owes and is trying to pay her chief debt." [12]

The university's rapid growth in student body and faculty is seen in the statistics for these years. In 1905, when Dewey arrived, the number of students in all divisions of the university totaled 4,981, mostly from New York City and its environs.[13] Twenty-five years later this number had increased to 38,230 students drawn from all quarters of the world.[14] Similarly, the teaching and research staffs increased from 523 in 1905 [15] to 1,794 in 1930.[16] Thus during the period of Dewey's most active association with the university, it changed rapidly from the small provincial institution it formerly had been to the large metropolitan, cosmopolitan university it has since remained.

With its change to university status and because of the attractive salaries it could offer to key men,[17] Columbia was able to add to its several departments an unusually large number of outstanding teachers and scholars. Among these were John W. Burgess and Charles Beard in political science; Henry R. Seager, E. R. A. Seligman, Vladimir Simkhovitch, and Wesley Mitchell in economics; Robert M. MacIver in sociology; James Harvey Robinson, William A. Dunning, and James Thomas Shotwell in history;

Franz Boas in anthropology; James M. Cattell, C. A. Strong, and R. S. Woodworth in psychology; F. J. E. Woodbridge, Felix Adler, William P. Montague, George Stuart Fullerton, and Wendell T. Bush in philosophy.[18]

Under Woodbridge, Adler, Montague, Bush, and Dewey the Department of Philosophy[19] at Columbia flourished, winning preeminence among the departments of philosophy in the country. Many considered it on a level with the famous Harvard department of the 1890s, which included such men as William James, Josiah Royce, George Herbert Palmer, George Santayana, and Hugo Münsterberg. In 1911 John Jacob Coss came as an assistant to the department; after 1918, a number of younger scholars, all trained at Columbia, were added to the permanent staff. These included Herbert W. Schneider, J. H. Randall, Jr., Irwin Edman, Horace L. Friess, and somewhat later, in 1931, Ernest Nagel. These men, who became known in academic circles as "the younger school of Columbia philosophers,"[20] did much to carry on the work established by Dewey and Woodbridge in the Graduate Faculty.

The administration of the department was for many years in the hands of Woodbridge, who had been called to Columbia to organize an effective program of graduate study in philosophy. Woodbridge was highly successful in this task; he was the main factor in getting the department under way and making it a major center of graduate instruction and research in philosophy. After Woodbridge, Coss took over the administration of the department. Among his achievements was a program of Honors Work in philosophy in which qualified undergraduates were allowed to take graduate work in philosophy without the usual prerequisite courses.

After his unusually heavy administrative load at the University of Chicago, Dewey was content to leave the administrative duties of the department to others, confining his efforts to teaching, thesis supervision, and research. He was executive head of the department for two years beginning 1 July 1909[21] and again in 1917, but in general he preferred that others take over. He was, of course, always consulted on matters of major importance to the department such as permanent appointments and basic policy changes; for the rest he avoided involvement in administrative detail. Dewey did not hesitate, however, to speak his mind on matters he believed called for comment. He deplored, for example, the great amount of time set aside for registering students before the beginning of each semester. In a letter to Woodbridge he remarked that "it is entirely against the life of reason to encourage the university & the students in the present absurd system of dragging registration through a week when it could all be done in one day." [22]

Association with the members of the faculty at Columbia contributed greatly to the development of Dewey's thought. Unlike the situation at Chicago where his colleagues in philosophy and psychology were all pragmatists cooperatively engaged in establishing the leading ideas of the Chicago School's version of instrumentalism, the members of the department at Columbia were men of diverse philosophical views who created an intellectual climate in which, as Dewey later recalled, he found "a new challenge and a new stimulus." [23]

Woodbridge, who was eight years younger than Dewey, had originally planned to become a clergyman in the Episcopal Church. After Amherst College and three years of study at Union Theological Seminary, his interests changed; in 1892, he went to the University of Berlin where he studied philosophy under Friedrich Paulsen. Returning to this country in 1894, he accepted a position teaching philosophy at the University of Minnesota, where he remained till 1902 when President Butler called him to Columbia. Woodbridge worked out a version of Aristotelianism which replaced the Aristotelian categories of matter and form with the newer categories of structure and activity while retaining Aristotle's notion of a natural teleology.[24] Woodbridge shared Dewey's belief in naturalism, pluralism, and empiricism but he could not entirely accept the pragmatic theory of mind and knowledge, his position in this respect being closer to realism than to pragmatism. There is, he said, an object antecedent to our knowing and to which knowledge must accommodate itself if it is to work. The nature of this object and the way it behaves need not await the outcome of inquiry to be real and intelligible. "I have, consequently," he remarked, "often called myself a realist, and one of a very naïve sort." [25]

Dewey wrote that during his earlier years at Columbia he had "many conversations" with Woodbridge and "learned a lot from him." [26] Among other things, Dewey learned the possibility of a strictly empirical, analytic metaphysics—a metaphysics that, in Woodbridge's words, "takes things as they are, in all their obvious plurality, and never supposes that they can be reduced to ultimates from which they sprang by miracle or evolution." [27] Jane Dewey, describing Woodbridge's influence on her father, remarked that their agreements and disagreements were such as "to make their intellectual association of peculiar importance in further developing Dewey's thought." [28]

Adler, born in Germany in 1851, was as much older than Dewey as Woodbridge was younger. Adler came to this country at the age of six, the family settling in New York City where his father had a distinguished career as a Reform rabbi. Though Adler had first planned to become a rabbi, he abandoned this idea upon finishing his graduate studies at the University of Heidelberg, becoming instead the leader of the New York Society for Ethical Culture, which he helped found in 1876. Besides his work with that society, Adler served on numerous city, state, and national commissions concerned with social reforms. He wrote extensively on religious, educational, moral, social, and political issues; it was this activity that brought him to the attention of the academic world. In 1902 Columbia invited him to become professor of social and political ethics, a position created especially for him in which he remained till his death in 1933.

Adler was deeply impressed by the possibility of a free and universal religion of right and duty as advocated by Kant. He found much that was helpful in the doctrines of the idealists, especially transcendentalists like Emerson. Adler felt, however, that Kant's ethics and Emerson's political views were much too individualistic and needed tempering by considerations of the social whole. Accordingly, one of his major intellectual endeavors was to socialize Kant's moral idealism within a framework more explicitly democratic than that of Kant. Adler believed that his doctrine of an "ethical manifold" did this, for his manifold is a communion of individuals, each a unique moral entity. At the same time it has the unity of a whole as it is a community of moral agents each intent on developing his own uniqueness by helping others to bring out their potential uniqueness.[29] In his social philosophy, Adler, like Dewey, rejected the notion of a strongly centralized government, advocating instead collective reform movements operating within a pluralistic, functionally organized democratic society.

Since Adler's off-campus duties prevented him from spending much time at the university, he and Dewey failed to develop the close ties that each would have welcomed and from which each could have profited. Nevertheless, Adler was one of the contributors to the collection of essays published in commemoration of Dewey's seventieth birthday,[30] and Dewey delivered the main address in honor of Adler to the New York society on 24 October 1938[31] at the commemoration of the sixtieth anniversary of the Ethical Culture Schools.

Montague was educated at Harvard, receiving his Ph.D. degree there in 1898. After teaching five years at Radcliffe and Harvard, he was appointed lecturer in philosophy at Barnard College in 1903; four years later he became a member of the graduate faculty of Columbia. Montague had an abiding interest in speculative philosophy. He believed that the main function of philosophy was to supply a meaningful interpretation of the universe and of man's place in it. His own position, which he called "animistic materialism," held that every item of existence could be explained in terms of physics. Thus he conceived consciousness as a kind of potential energy; biological variation and heredity were declared to be the result of physical stresses and strains within protoplasm. Montague was a leader in the new realist movement among philosophers, collaborating with five others in writing "The Program and First Principles of Six Realists,"[32] later expanded by the authors into the volume *The New Realism.*[33] For Montague, as for other realists, the truth of an idea consists in its correspondence with reality and this "*antedates* the process by which it is verified (or refuted)."[34] Montague thus rejected the Deweyan doctrine that truth is the outcome of processes of verification. Montague took an active interest in social problems; during the depression of the 1930s, he urged the establishment of special communities for those out of work as the solution to the unemployment problem. Montague's concern for the underprivileged and for the victims of economic dislocations found a warm response in Dewey's own thinking so that, as Jane Dewey remarked, "Montague and Dewey came closer together in their ideas on social subjects than upon technical philosophical ones."[35]

Bush took his graduate work at Harvard and Columbia, receiving his Ph.D. degree from the latter in 1905. He was appointed lecturer in philosophy at Columbia in 1905 and professor of philosophy in 1928. From 1906 on, he shared with Woodbridge the responsibility of editing the *Journal of Philosophy.* While at Harvard, Bush studied under James and Santayana, whose influence is marked in his thought. From James he acquired a penchant for the empirical, scientific, "clinical" approach to the problems of philosophy; from Santayana he absorbed a deep interest in the religious and aesthetic aspects of culture. Bush's frequent contributions to the *Journal of Philosophy* were notable for their freshness, penetrating analysis, and lively expression. He shared Dewey's functional theory of knowledge while emphasizing its anthropological context. Persons close to both knew how much Bush and Dewey enjoyed each other and how the "sympathetic but penetrating criticisms of Bush" helped Dewey to appreciate the relevance of his ideas to nontechnical issues and aspects of human cultures.[36]

Among colleagues outside the Department of Philosophy who had a marked influence on Dewey's thinking was Franz Boas, whose reputation in anthropology rivaled that of Dewey in philosophy. Boas, partly through Bush, helped Dewey see that a sound philosophy of experience could not restrict itself within the confines set by biology and psychology but had to include also institutional and cultural factors, which play a role as decisive in determining what experience is and will be as do the factors usually emphasized in theories in knowledge. Hegel, as already noted, had earlier introduced Dewey to very similar notions; now Boas and other anthropologists, including Ruth Benedict at Columbia, helped guide Dewey's thinking further toward the cultural anthropology that was to be such an important feature of his later philosophy.

Others influencing Dewey were the university's distinguished social scientists, who learned much in turn from Dewey. Such men as Charles Beard, James Harvey Robinson, James Shotwell, Robert M. MacIver, Wesley Mitchell, and Rexford Guy Tugwell all entertained a liberal social outlook that found expression in their numerous articles and books on political, economic, social, and historical topics. Contact with the ideas of these men helped Dewey relate the broad principles of his own liberal social philosophy to the more concrete and particularized ideas of his social science colleagues. The social scientists, finding in Dewey's writings the general philosophical principles implicit in their own thinking, readily accepted him as their philosophical spokesman.[37]

The courses Dewey gave during his first decade at Columbia stemmed from his prevailing interests.[38] His concern with instrumental logic led to such courses as The Logic of Experience, Advanced Logic, and Types of Logical Theory. His interest in developing a philosophy of experience prompted courses in Theories of Experience, and Analysis of Experience. His desire to extend the method of scientific inquiry to moral problems gave rise to the course in The Logic of Ethics; his conviction that a sound moral theory must rest on a functional and biological psychology found expression in the course entitled Psychological Ethics. Dewey's interest in political, economic, and social theory was reflected in the course Moral and Political Philosophy. He continued to give courses along these general lines under these same titles throughout his teaching career at Columbia, varying their content as his own thinking changed.

Dewey began his researches at Columbia during a period of lively philosophical debate. The old, established, post-Kantian idealisms that had dominated the philosophical world in Europe and America during the last quarter of the nineteenth century were being challenged in the early 1900s by new and vigorous schools of realism and pragmatism. So many-sided and intense were the discussions and so numerous the participants that one observer was led to remark that "even in the palmiest days of the Grecian culture, or of idealism in the German universities, the numbers engaged—whether of individuals or schools—were presumably not so great as now, nor was the mutual clearing-up of ideas which discussion affords so eagerly sought. And certainly never was controversy so keen." [39]

As one of the key figures, Dewey was deeply involved in the discussions; his articles at this time reflect the more important issues debated and the polemic character of many of the discussions. Between 1905 and 1914 Dewey wrote more than thirty major articles expounding and clarifying his ideas and defending them against his critics.[40] The *Journal of Philosophy*, founded in 1904 by Bush, Woodbridge, and Cattell and published at Columbia under the editorships of Woodbridge and Bush, was a convenient vehicle for Dewey's writings; most of his essays at this time appeared in the *Journal*.

Because many of his ideas were subtle, and because they were difficult and ambiguous expressed in traditional terms, Dewey's writings were constantly misunderstood. These misunderstandings led to charges and countercharges, claims and disclaimers, open letters and replies, rejoinders and reassertions between Dewey and his critics. That Dewey profited from these exchanges is shown in his statement about this period of his development: "But I gladly admit that my philosophic views did not develop in a vacuum and that I took seriously philosophic doctrines that were current. Undoubtedly, study of the problems they presented played a part in the development of my own philosophic method and doctrines. For I felt myself under an obligation to develop my personal intellectual predilections in a way that took cognizance of strong points in other teachings while trying to avoid what appeared to me to be their weak points." [41]

One doctrine Dewey sought especially to clarify and establish was that reality is to be identified with experience; he gave it a number of statements that left his readers considerably confused. A few months after his arrival at Columbia, he declared in "The Postulate of Immediate Empiricism" [42] that "immediate empiricism postulates that things—anything, everything in the ordinary or non-technical use of the term 'thing'—are what they are experienced as. Hence, if one wishes to describe anything truly, his task is to tell what it is experienced as being." Thus, a horse may be described from the point of view of a horse-trader, a jockey, a family man who wants a "safe driver," a zoologist, or a paleontologist. "If these accounts turn out different in some respects, as well as congruous in others, this is no reason for assuming the content of one to be exclusively 'real,' and that of others to be 'phenomenal." They are all equally real, Dewey insisted, and, if a comparison is to be made, it should be "not between *a* Reality, and various approximations to, or phenomenal representations of Reality, but between different reals of experience." [43]

Dewey stressed this last point because some among the idealists and realists alike believed that things are only and exclusively what they are reflectively or scientifically *known* to be, that the things present in noncognitive experience are merely the appearances or phenomenal manifestations of what is more truly or genuinely real. This claim is one phase of what Dewey called the "intellectualistic fallacy," a fallacy, he said, that has been the source of innumerable philosophical difficulties.[44] For, "the universe at large being divided into the real and the unreal, the objective and the subjective, being and appearance, absolute and phenomenal, gives rise inevitably to all sorts of problems as to how these antithetical things get on together; there being none of the specific tests that condition common-sense knowing and science, these inquiries may proceed indefinitely." [45]

Of course things are what scientists and other knowers find them to be, said Dewey, but they are much more than this. They are also what our sensitive, emotional, aesthetical, and volitional natures experience them to be—pleasurable or painful, satisfying or frustrating, friendly or hostile, safe or hazardous. These features are just as much characteristic of things as are the structural, quantitative, and relational aspects disclosed by knowing experience. "Why, putting it mildly," asked Dewey, "should what gives tragedy, comedy, and poignancy to life, be excluded from things? Doubtless, what we call life, what we take to be genuinely vital, is not all of things. But it is a part of things; and is that part which counts most with the philosopher—unless he has quite parted with his ancient dignity of lover of wisdom." [46]

Reality, thus described, seemed to many of Dewey's readers something subjective, mental, and relative to the interests and ideosyncrasies of the individual; his philosophy was generally characterized by his opponents as "a thoroughgoing idealism, and a subjective idealism at that." [47] Dewey agreed that if experience is taken to be what Hume took it to be, "made up of states of mind, of sensations and ideas," [48] the characterization would hold.

But this view of experience, Dewey declared, is no longer tenable in the light of what biology teaches. Biology reveals an organism occupying an environment, interacting with and adjusting to it. These interactions are the stuff out of which life itself is made; they are what constitute experience. Experience is "a matter of functions and habits, of active adjustments and re-adjustments, of co-ordinations and activities, rather than of states of consciousness," [49] and is as objective and external, as open to public examination as any realist could require.

But if reality is identified with experience and experience is conceived as the interaction of organisms and environment, it follows that reality exists only where organisms with relatively advanced nervous systems are present. And this, said Dewey's critics, runs counter to both common sense and science. If science, for example, is correct, this earth existed long before conscious organisms appeared on it; therefore there was a time when there was a reality but no experience.

Dewey recognized the problem these considerations posed for him; in an article entitled "Reality as Experience," [50] he himself asked: "Must we not, then, either give up the identification of the two conceptions [reality and experience], or else admit we are denying and sophisticating the plain facts of knowledge?" [51] Dewey believed there is a sense in which reality can be identified with experience. In the article cited, he undertook to explain what this sense is. But his statements tended to confuse rather than enlighten his readers. In one place he spoke of this prior reality not as experience but as "at any and every point on its way to experience," declaring that "so viewed, the question of reality *versus* experience turns out to be only the question of an earlier version of reality against a later version." [52] He also referred to this prior reality as a "non-contemporaneously experienced earlier reality" which cannot be chopped off from "later experience." [53] Also he argued that this prior reality has its nature only partially fulfilled by being scientifically known; it needs to be made a part of "an inclusive, vital, direct experience" in order for its nature to be more fully realized.[54]

These statements were typical; the confusion they caused for one of Dewey's readers is reflected in his comment:

> Professor Dewey claims [in "Pure Experience and Reality: A Disclaimer"] [55] that, in the article ["Reality as Experience"] [56] which I examined, he repeatedly referred to reality prior to experience, and that he spoke of such reality as the condition of the subsequent experience. This is true: I saw the words. But when I tried to get any meaning out of them, the "past" reality became for me a present one, for

Professor Dewey's past realities have a way of *now* undergoing *past* changes every time they are differently experienced. A thing which now changes I cannot bring myself to experience as a past reality. A leopard which died in Jeremiah's day and yet now manages to change the spots it had during the Exile, seems to me not so much a creature of the past as an interesting monstrosity of the present.[57]

A few years after "Reality as Experience," Dewey's *Influence of Darwin* appeared; included among its collected essays was the earlier "The Postulate of Immediate Empiricism," in which Dewey had declared that things are what they are experienced as. Because of the misunderstandings arising originally from this article, Dewey appended a long note designed to clarify his position. In this note he made two statements about his theory of reality and experience. One of these is that he did not mean by "immediate experience" some "aboriginal stuff out of which things are evolved." Rather he used the term to point out "the necessity of employing in philosophy the direct descriptive method that has now made its way in all the natural sciences." That is, the real significance of the principle of immediate experience is that it indicates a method of philosophical analysis, not a metaphysics as to the ultimate nature of things.[58] Dewey's other statement is that things can and do exist "temporally prior to human experiencing of them." In fact, most things we experience, he said, we experience "*as* temporally prior to our experiencing of them." It is important to understand what is involved in experiencing a thing as belonging to the past.[59]

Despite his attempts at clarification, Dewey's critics complained that they found his ideas obscure and difficult to grasp. Dewey was not insensitive to the complaints of his readers; in the years immediately ahead, he undertook to explain still further what he meant by such terms as "existence," "reality," "nature," "environment," and "experience," restating his philosophy in a way that would more satisfactorily clarify his position. These attempts culminated in 1925 with the publication of *Experience and Nature*,[60] the book generally recognized as Dewey's *magnum opus*.

Dewey was also concerned during these years with clarifying and defending his theory of knowledge. His position was that thinking or reflection is inquiry and that all the factors involved in the thinking or knowing process must be viewed and interpreted within the context of inquiry.

His view contrasts sharply with the traditional or intellectualist theory of knowledge of idealists and realists alike, which holds that the knowing process aims at a knowledge that copies or reproduces in consciousness a preexisting, ready-made reality and is true according to how faithfully it does this. The knowing process, it maintains, involves, on the one hand, a mind or knower intent on knowing, and, on the other hand, a ready-made fixed world waiting to be known; knower and world each have a separate and different kind of existence. It declares that the task of theory of knowledge is to discover the universal forms and principles of thought, showing how these hold good for reality at large irrespective of any difference in the objects. "Passionless imperturbability, absolute detachment, complete subjection to a ready-made and finished reality—physical it may be, mental it may be, logical it may be—is its professed ideal." [61] Traditional epistemology has a place for inquiry but a very subordinate one. It holds that inquiry "is concerned with methods of investigation which obviate defects in the relationship of thought at large to reality at large, as these present themselves under the limitations of human experience. It deals merely with hindrances, and with devices for overcoming them; it is directed by considerations of utility." [62]

Dewey rejected the traditional view of the knowing relation because so far as an empirical philosophy can determine, there is no knower in general seeking to know a world in general. Such a view of the knowing process, Dewey declared, sets up an artificial knowing situation and a problem of knowledge whose solution is impossible "in virtue of the very terms in which it is stated." [63] All that an empirical philosophy can discover in regard to the knowing process is particular individuals confronting specific problems, attempting to solve them by a process of inquiry. These inquiries enter into every area of life, into every aspect of every area. They comprise the practical deliberations of the ordinary person in his everyday life as well as the research activities of the man of science. Since they are objectively there, they can be studied as other processes in nature can be studied; the results of the analysis can be empirically tested. Thus, differences in theory of knowledge that separate pragmatists and nonpragmatists concern "matters of fact, and not matters to be decided by assumption, definition, and deduction." [64]

When an act of reflection or inquiry is examined, said Dewey, it will always be found to have this general pattern or structure: there will always be a felt difficulty or problem; there will be observation aimed at clarifying or defining more precisely the nature of the problem; there will be a suggestion, hypothesis, or idea as to a possible solution of the problem; there will be a rational elaboration of the hypothesis to determine its implications for action; and there will always be further observation or experiment to test whether the actual results or facts correspond to the rationally deduced ones. A theory of inquiry must explain each of these factors and show how they cooperate to produce valid knowledge.

Dewey particularly stressed the nature and role of "idea" and "fact" in the knowing process and the type of "correspondence" required if the idea is to be considered true. He emphasized these points because "it was precisely the lack of an adequate and generally accepted theory of the nature of fact and idea, and of the kind of agreement or correspondence between them which constitutes the truth of the idea, that led to the development of a functionalist theory of logic."[65] And, he said, "the way in which the functional logician has been turned upon by both idealist and realist is suggestive of the way in which the outsider who intervenes in a family jar is proverbially treated by both husband and wife, who manifest their complete unity by berating the third party."[66]

When ideas are examined within the framework of inquiry, said Dewey, they are found to be beliefs, conjectures, guesses, working hypotheses, plans of action designed to overcome the difficulty that started the inquiry. So long as life moves smoothly and agreeably, people do not think or entertain ideas. They act, live, enjoy. Only when their experience is interrupted and they are faced with a situation that is uncertain, confused, or troublesome do they concern themselves with the means of overcoming the troublesome situation and transforming it into a satisfactory one. And the means they employ are ideas or concepts that take the form of working hypotheses or plans of action. These are the tools or instruments by which they hope to construct a new, more meaningful situation in which the problem is solved and experience is again integrated. Ideas thus have a reconstructive function. Nowhere do we find them functioning as static copies of a fixed, ready-made, preexisting reality as the intellectualist maintains.

The pragmatic theory of knowledge, said Dewey, claims "to mediate between realistic and idealistic theories of knowledge." It is realistic in that "it holds to reality, prior to cognitive operations and not constructed by these operations, to which knowing, in order to be successful, must adapt itself." But it also maintains that the object as eventually known is not a literal copy of this prior reality but is a construct of the knowing process; by manipulating and experimenting with the prior, dubious reality, the agent transforms it into an object that is more meaningful and assured. "Hence it claims to recognize and include the verifiable facts as to the rôle of thought in the world which have given rise to the idealistic exaggeration."[67]

Dewey's intellectualist critics quite agreed with him that an individual confronted with a problematic situation needs a plan of action to lead him out of it. They agreed also that the plan, when put into operation, may be successful or unsuccessful. But they disagreed strongly with Dewey's claim that a plan of action is an idea. A plan of action, they insisted, is not an idea; an idea is a judgment—a judgment about something—and therefore always a matter of truth and falsity. A plan of action, on the other hand, is a program for doing something; when put to work, it may turn out to be successful or unsuccessful, but never true or false. According to one of Dewey's intellectualist critics: "When he [the intellectualist] says an 'idea' is true he uses the word in quite a different sense—namely, as meaning a *judgment.* To him an idea which is not a judgment, but is a mere image, or plan, or formula, may lead in what direction it likes, it may be useful, successful, satisfactory, or their opposites, it may have any function you will, but it is not in the category of things that can be either true or false. . . . The usefulness of a plan of action depends, of course, upon its being used. A judgment, on the other hand, may be useful and good, but that is not what makes it true. A judgment is one thing; a plan of action quite another." [68] And the writer goes on to say, "It is no wonder, then, that using the word 'idea' in such radically different senses, the intellectualist and the pragmatist should often misunderstand each other and fight as those who beat the air." [69]

Dewey rejected this distinction between idea and plan of action because to him inquiry is itself a process of judging; the plan of action that grows out of it is itself a judgment. In inquiry, as in a case of judging, something is at issue, something at stake, something uncertain that needs to be decided. There is the calling in of witnesses—the facts and data that supply information relevant to reaching a decision; there is the process of comparing, weighing, and interpreting the evidence; and finally there is the decision or judgment—a practical judgment, held hypothetically, in anticipation of action—that the case is so and so.[70] And this judgment, when acted upon, can be called true or false if these terms are defined as suggested by an empirical study of the knowing process, that is, in terms of its success or failure in solving the problem. Dewey argued that his functional or experimental logic is as much a logic of judgment as the logic of his intellectualist opponents. His logic differs from theirs, he said, in being taken out of the realm of assumptions, abstractions, and definitions and made to apply to the concrete and practical judgments that the ordinary person and the scientist are constantly called upon to make.

Within the context of inquiry, it is obvious that the "fact" to which an idea, as plan of action, refers is the consequences it hopes to bring about. Literally, as Dewey pointed out, the term "fact" refers to something done, accomplished, secured; it has an element of assurance and conviction. It is, therefore, the logical antithesis of idea, guess, hypothesis.[71] In a sense, then, the "fact" or "object" *transcends* the idea just as traditional epistemology maintains. But this transcendence is a practical transcendence, not the ontological one that intellectualist theories of knowledge claim. The fact transcends or lies beyond the idea in the same way as the achieved consequences of a plan lie beyond the plan before it is put into operation. There is a sense, too, in which the "fact" is represented by the idea just as orthodox theory of knowledge holds. But this representation is a practical one, not the pictorial or copy one of the intellectualists. Ideas represent facts, said Dewey, "in the sense in which a signature, for legal purposes, represents a real person in a contract. . . . They are symbols, in short, and are known and used as such."[72]

When the "idea" is taken as a plan of action and the "fact" is regarded as the consequences of the plan put to work, at hand is a solution to the problem that has always troubled traditional epistemologies: how idea and fact come together so as to result in valid knowledge. From the point of view of functional logic, the passage from idea to fact is effected not by some mysterious or miraculous epistemological leap from one ontological realm to another as in traditional theories of knowledge, but through action. The idea as plan of action, if put to work and if successful, *is* the new concrete, factual situation it aimed to bring about; it is recognized as such. In every instance involving idea and fact, said Dewey, the relation in question is "that of an agent to its act, not that of one of the two terms of knowledge to the other term."[73] Nowhere in all this do we find the "fact" functioning as a fixed, ready-made reality waiting to be copied or reproduced in consciousness as traditional epistemologies argue.

The nature of the "correspondence" between a true idea and its fact or object should now be evident. Viewed within the framework of inquiry, the agreement involved is between the anticipated consequences implicit in the plan of action and the consequences actually brought about when the plan is put into operation. "The agreement, correspondence," said Dewey, "is between purpose, plan, and its own execution, fulfillment."[74] Like James,

Dewey argued that truth *happens* to an idea. An idea *becomes* true when it leads *truly*, that is, successfully, to its desired goal. Dewey stressed the active, dynamic, adverbial nature of truth, declaring that "it would be a great gain for logic and epistemology, if we would always translate the noun 'truth' back into the adjective 'true,' and this back into the adverb 'truly'." [75]

In contrast to the pragmatic theory of truth, the intellectualist theory makes truth or correspondence a static quality which inheres in the idea as idea; it argues that truth has no necessary connection with its verification. If the idea corresponds to the reality to which it refers, it is *ipso facto* true regardless of whether this truth is ever verified. One reason Dewey objected to this doctrine is that when truth and verification are kept apart, the nature of the agreement between an idea and its object is left uncertain. Situations involving correspondence are so varied that, in order to know what the term means in any particular case, the agreement intended must be spelled out. A map is supposed to correspond to the territory it covers, a photograph is said to correspond to the person of whom it is a photograph, the figures in an auditor's statement are said to agree with the actual financial status of the company audited, the vocal rendering of a song is said to correspond to the notes in the songbook. This kind of spelling out is necessary for correspondence to become meaningful. But traditional epistemology does not do this. It contents itself, said Dewey, with taking correspondence as a "Relation at Large" just as it takes the knower to be a "Knower at Large," and the reality to be known as the "World at Large." In traditional epistemology, correspondence remains "an ultimate and unanalyzable mystery, to be defined by iteration," [76] "some mysterious static correspondence," [77] " 'a static inert relation', which is so ultimate that of it nothing more can be said." [78] But in the functional theory of knowledge the correspondence in question is always given a detailed and concrete explanation in terms of consequences anticipated and consequences actually attained when the idea is acted upon. The correspondence involved in map, photograph, auditor's figures, vocal rendering can be specifically and concretely defined when a plan of action is introduced for each of them and the intended consequences set over against the actual ones.

When intellectualists argue that truth exists prior to verification, completely independent of it, they use such examples as the rotation of the planets around the sun and the existence long ago of a Carboniferous Age, arguing that these facts would have been true even though no one had ever verified them. Dewey's reply was that these examples refer not to truths but to realities, occurrences, events; as such they are no more true or false than they are moral or immoral.[79] They simply are; it makes no sense to say that they are true or false. Truth and falsity apply only to ideas, beliefs, judgments. So far as realities or events are concerned, "some conviction, some belief, some judgment with reference to them is necessary to introduce the category of truth and falsity." [80] Realists and idealists initially know and accept this, said Dewey. But, then, unknowingly it seems, they shift their position and identify "the bare existence or event with truth," [81] believing that they have demonstrated that truth is prior to verification when actually, only the event is.

When the instrumentalist argues that the truth of an idea lies in its success, opponents usually reply that the success of an idea grows out of its being antecedently true. It is because of the idea's prior truth or correspondence with reality in the intellectualist's sense that the idea works in the pragmatist's sense. Dewey's rejoinder was that "if one remembers that what the experimentalist means is that the effective working of an idea and its truth are one and the same thing—this working being neither the cause nor the evidence of truth but its nature—it is hard to see the point of this statement." [82]

Dewey's theory of knowledge also undertakes to give an empirical and naturalistic account of what he called "the machinery of universals, axioms, *a priori* truths, etc." [83] Traditional rationalism has always regarded these as innate, intuitive, or, like Kant and the post-Kantians, as *a priori*, transcendental categories of the mind to which the material of knowledge must adjust if valid—that is, if universal and necessary knowledge is to result. But rationalism has never been able to explain the precise mechanism by which the material of knowledge—sensations, feelings, images, etc.—and the *a priori* forms of thought get together so as to yield valid knowledge. Traditional empiricism has always viewed these principles and axioms as originating in experience, as being generalizations or summaries of how men have thought in the past. But empiricism has never been able to explain why these principles or forms of thought should hold equally well for future thought.

Dewey argued that when axioms, principles, *a priori* truths are examined within the context of inquiry, they are found to function as the principles or rules of procedure by which men carry on the more distinctly "mental" phases of the inquiry process. They guide men in weighing, comparing, and classifying data, in inferring hypotheses, and in working out the bearings or implications for action of the suggested hypothesis. These principles, rules, canons of investigation, Dewey declared, have evolved in the course of past inquiries, becoming established ways of human thinking because they have proved helpful in past inquiries and give promise of being equally useful in present and future inquiries that retain the same general pattern. "Their value," said Dewey, "is teleological and experimental, not fixedly ontological." [84] When certain of these principles are referred to as "eternal" truths, this "does not indicate a property inherent in the idea as intellectualised existence, but denotes a property of use and employment." [85] The reason that knowledge resulting from reflection and experimental inquiry has the universality and necessity generally associated with valid knowledge is that the process of inquiry that produces such knowledge is strictly controlled and systematized by principles and rules of procedure adopted by thinkers and experimenters everywhere.

Historic rationalism is correct, said Dewey, in regarding these axioms and principles as *a priori,* for they do precede any subsequent inquiry. But it is in error when it views these principles as *a priori* in some ontological, transcendental sense instead of as rules of procedure that are *a priori* only in a practical sense. Similarly, traditional empiricism is correct in recognizing these axioms and rules as originating in past thought experiences. But it errs in viewing these principles as simple recordings or summaries of past experiences rather than as rules of procedure with relevance for future inquiries.

Inquiry always starts with observation, to define more precisely the nature of the problem to be dealt with; it also ends with observation, to test the validity of the hypothetically held idea. Dewey's theory of inquiry therefore includes an account of such observational material as sensations, perceptions, feelings, images, etc., and their role in inquiry.

Because it viewed the individual as primarily a knower, believing that "being in consciousness is always presence for or in knowledge," [86] traditional intellectualism has regarded immediate experience as instances of knowing. The knowledge these give may not be as valid as that resulting from the more reflective and perfected forms of the knowing process, or it may relate only to the appearance or phenomenal manifestation of things or to a realm of subsistence, but in every case an immediate experience is a knowing experience that in some way or other reflects reality. As one idealist remarked: "For the idealist, experience is always a complex of the immediately perceived and the mediately conceived, and that no matter how far one goes down the scale for his starting-point. . . . Not that he denies immediacy, but that he affirms mediation to be equally fundamental. Nowhere in experience does he find sheer immediacy. . . . The facts of experience are one and all, and from first to last, tainted with mediation." [87]

Since Dewey had held the identical doctrine during his Hegelian days, his repudiation of it is the more interesting. Dewey's rejection of the doctrine grew out of his conviction that the knowing process must be limited to the inquiry process and that knowledge is to be exclusively identified with the outcome of inquiry. Such knowledge seizes upon the structural, quantitative, and relational aspects of things, giving the power to predict and control. Sensations, perceptions, feelings, and images taken by themselves obviously do not do this; they therefore cannot be viewed as instances of knowing. They are, rather, cases of having, undergoing, enjoying, enduring—"simply natural events having, in themselves (apart from a *use* that may be made of them), no more knowledge status or worth than, say, a shower or a fever." [88]

For an immediate experience to have any cognitive value, said Dewey, it must play a role within inquiry. When viewed within the context of inquiry, such immediate experiences as sensations, perceptions, feelings, and images are found to function as stimuli, guides, signs, checks, controls. A smell, for example, taken by itself and apart from inquiry, has no cognitive standing. It is simply an event, occurrence, happening. But when it is taken as a sign that a rose is near, when at the same time, perhaps, it stimulates inquiry to test whether this is so, the smell functions cognitively. When logically considered, "such distinctions as sensation, image, etc., mark instruments and crises in the development of controlled judgment, *i. e.*, of inferential conclusions." [89] When viewed practically, "the undoubted facts which go by the name of sensation, perception, image, emotion, concept, would be interpreted to mean peculiar (*i. e.*, specifically qualitative) epochs, phases, and crises in the scheme of behavior." [90]

Summing up the issue between traditional or intellectualist and instrumentalist theories of knowledge, Dewey asked: "Is the theory of knowledge to be epistemological or logical? Is it to be concerned with the nature of knowledge and of truth in general, that is, with conceptions which are totally irrelevant to the methods and tests by which particular knowledges are effected and particular truths tested? Or is the theory of knowledge to be a generalized statement of particular instances of knowing, and the theory of truth a generalized statement of particular instances of 'trues'?" [91]

In addition to many articles and two monographs on educational topics, Dewey brought out three books during his first ten years at Columbia. These were: *Ethics*,[92] a textbook he wrote in collaboration with his former colleague at the University of Chicago, James H. Tufts; *The Influence of Darwin on Philosophy and Other Essays in Contemporary Thought*,[93] and *How We Think*.[94] Since *How We Think* is oriented to education, it is discussed later in connection with Dewey's work at Teachers College.

The Influence of Darwin on Philosophy and Other Essays in Contemporary Thought was, as the title suggests, a collection of articles of which all but one had been previously published.[95] Since the doctrines contained in the book had already been widely debated, the reviews and comments that greeted the volume's appearance were brief, with criticism running along partisan philosophical lines.

The *Ethics* stirred considerably more attention. As the authors explained in the preface, the significance of the book "lies in its effort to awaken a vital conviction of the genuine reality of moral problems and the value of reflective thought in dealing with them." [96] The text was divided into three parts. The first, entitled "Beginnings and Growth of Morality," was written by Tufts. Its primary aim was to make the student aware of the dynamic and changing character of the moral life. The second part, named "Theory of the Moral Life," was written by Dewey. Its purpose was to provide the student with the intellectual perspective and tools with which to make independent and enlightened moral judgments. The third division was called "The World in Action"; it undertook to bring moral theory and judgment to bear on pressing political, economic, and social problems. Dewey contributed two of the seven chapters in this section, one entitled "Social Organization and the Individual," and the other "Civil Society and the Political State."

The Dewey and Tufts *Ethics* was not the first book to deal with the genesis and history of the moral life, nor was it the first to examine political, economic, and social problems from the point of view of morality. But *Ethics* was the first textbook to combine with the historical and theoretical treatment of ethics a discussion of current social problems. This feature was probably the main reason for the book's very favorable reception. "If this is not the ideal text-book in ethics for which we have been waiting so many years," wrote one reviewer, "it is, at least, a very good substitute for it." [97] The reviewer saw in the *Ethics* "the first of a new type of texts," one that would mark "the end of the abstract, speculative treatises and the beginning of the positive studies of established human values."[98] Another reviewer believed the book "promises to be the foremost text-book of ethics for the next decade."[99] Others, however, thought the authors' genetic, empirical, naturalistic approach was unfortunate because it failed to do justice to the mystical elements in the ideally good life. "And it is conceivable, even from the point of view of mere theory," wrote one critic, "that Professors Dewey and Tufts would have done more alike for ethics and for American students, if they had stood somewhat more above the economic struggle of to-day than they have done, and surveyed it all from a really higher standpoint."[100]

Dewey's connections with Teachers College during his first ten years at Columbia were not as close and numerous as those with the Department of Philosophy and Psychology. He gave a course or two in the college each year and occasionally attended a meeting of its faculty. He took a lively interest in the schools affiliated with Teachers College, familiarizing himself with the work done in them. The college's kindergarten under the direction of Patty Smith Hill caught his attention; this was one of the schools described in his and his daughter Evelyn's *Schools of To-morrow*.[101] The Horace Mann School for Boys and the Horace Mann School for Girls, both observation and practice schools for teacher training at the college, were sources of continued interest to him; after the Lincoln School was taken over by Teachers College in 1917 as a laboratory school for "scientific experimentation and constructive work in the reorganization of elementary and secondary education,"[102] Dewey followed its work closely. Despite these several interests, however, his major effort was devoted to philosophy, since he felt the more immediate and basic challenge to his thought lay here rather than in education. But as his work in Teachers College continued and expanded[103] and his associations with colleagues and students became more firmly established, the impact of his thinking on the college grew till eventually his name and that of the college were inextricably linked in the minds of professional educators everywhere.

Teachers College had reached a position of eminence among its sister colleges in the nation some years before Dewey arrived. Educators had for some time recognized it as the home of liberal educational thought in America, the center of pioneer work in educational practice. Among its faculty when Dewey joined it were: James Earl Russell, who as dean of the college did much to advance the professional training of teachers in this country; Paul Monroe, one of the first historians of American education; Edward Lee Thorndike, a pioneer in experimental educational psychology; Frank McMurry, who had abandoned his earlier Herbartianism in favor of an educational philosophy based on the work of Dewey and Thorndike; Charles R. Richards, one of the first to explore the possibilities of industrial education and founder of the National Society for the Promotion of Industrial Education; and Patty Smith Hill, whose work with the kindergarten was winning wide acclaim. William Heard Kilpatrick, who brought Dewey's philosophy of education to a whole generation of students during his long and distinguished career at the college, joined its faculty in 1913. Harold Rugg, George S. Counts, and John L. Childs became members of the faculty in the 1920s, contributing greatly to its prestige. So rapidly did the fame of the college spread that during the first two decades (1897–1917) of Russell's administration enrollment grew from 450 to 2,500 students drawn from practically all parts of the world.

Among the courses Dewey taught were: Logic and Educational Problems; Ethics and Educational Problems; Social Life and the School Curriculum; and a seminar in Historical Relations of Philosophy and Education. He also collaborated for a time with Kilpatrick in a seminar in Philosophy of Education.

If Dewey's contributions to *A Cyclopedia of Education* [104] are excepted, his publications in education during his first ten years at Columbia were not nearly as numerous as those in philosophy. He wrote some half-dozen articles on topics such as "The Bearings of Pragmatism on Education," "Teaching that Does Not Educate," "Is Co-education Injurious to Girls?" "Reasoning in Early Childhood," and a "Report on the Fairhope [Alabama] Experiment in Organic Education." [105] He also published two monographs. One of these was *Moral Principles in Education,*[106] a slightly elaborated version of the article "Ethical Principles underlying Education" published some years before in the *Third Yearbook* [107] of the National Herbart Society. The other was *Interest and Effort in Education,*[108] an extended treatment of the topic which he had previously dealt with in his *Interest in Relation to Training of the Will,* which had appeared as the *Second Supplement to the First Herbart Yearbook.*[109]

The *Cyclopedia of Education* was a five-volume work published during 1911–13. Edited by Paul Monroe of Teachers College, it included a wide variety of articles intended to supply background and insight to students of education. Dewey made eleven contributions to the first volume, thirty-nine to the second, twenty-three to the third, twenty-two to the fourth, and twenty-five to the fifth. Ranging in length from one or two paragraphs to two or more columns, they covered a variety of topics in philosophy, psychology, and education. Wherever the subject matter allowed,

Dewey undertook to show the topic's bearing on educational theory and practice. In his article, "Evolution: The Philosophical Concepts," for example, he pointed out the impact of the idea of evolution on educational philosophy, referring the reader to his articles on Adaptation, Adjustment, Conflict, Control, Environment, Function, Heredity, Stimulus and Response for additional "concrete applications of evolutionary philosophy to educational concepts." [110]

Except for the monograph *Interest and Effort in Education*, by far the most influential of Dewey's writings on education at this time was the little volume, *How We Think*. Though the book contained nothing new on Dewey's educational philosophy, it presented this philosophy in a novel way. Designed primarily as an aid to teachers, it was written in a simple, nontechnical style, making extensive use of illustrations from classroom and everyday experience. The book's underlying conviction is that because the learning process is the thinking process, if the child is to learn it must be taught to think. Since, for Dewey, thinking at its best is exemplified in the scientist's attitudes of mind and habits of thought, the aim of education on its intellectual side should be to develop in the child the traits of mind characteristic of the scientist's mind.[111] This aim, Dewey argued, is not as farfetched as it might initially seem. For, as he pointed out, "the native and unspoiled attitude of childhood, marked by ardent curiosity, fertile imagination, and love of experimental inquiry, is near, very near, to the attitude of the scientific mind." [112] The educator's task, then, is to help the child develop, discipline, and systematize these tendencies to make them approximate attitudes and procedures of the scientifically minded person. *How We Think* is aimed at helping the teacher do this. Perhaps the best known section of the book is its famous sixth chapter which analyzes a complete act of reflective thought, distinguishing within it the well-known five steps: a felt difficulty, its location and definition, the suggestion of a possible solution, the mental elaboration of the suggestion, and further observation or experimentation leading to acceptance or rejection of the proposed solution.

How We Think had a very warm reception. Concerning its general argument, most critics agreed that the book was "not only an excellent exposition of the principles of thinking and of the best methods for developing the reasoning power but also a searching critique of certain present day defects in educational aims and systems." As for its style, most readers found the book written in a manner "warmly commendable for its simplicity, lucidity, and directness." [113] One reviewer, however, believed that

Dewey's "desire to write down to the level of the reader is so marked that much criticism might be directed at a number of the illustrative examples." [114] The following appraisal probably best sums up the general reaction: "In this book Professor Dewey renders an important service to educational theory and to philosophy. It is that rare kind of book in which simplicity is the outcome of seasoned scholarship in diverse fields. Logical, psychological, and educational theory are made to contribute to a work which is intelligible to the layman. . . . Teachers of all kinds will find the book a source of stimulus and enlightenment, and they will doubtless give to it the cordial welcome which it so eminently deserves." [115]

How We Think almost immediately became a classic in educational literature with a profound influence on educational practice, particularly on the kindergarten and elementary school levels. As William H. Kilpatrick pointed out, in *How We Think*, especially in its analysis of an act of thought, "American education discovered, so to speak, 'the problem approach' as a teaching device." [116] With this discovery, first the more progressive schools of the country and then others abandoned teaching methods based on the five formal steps (preparation, presentation, association, generalization, and application) of the prevailing Herbartianism, adopting instead methods based on Dewey's five steps.[117]

The high respect in which his professional colleagues held Dewey led to their electing him to positions of honor. While still at Chicago, his work in psychology had resulted in his being chosen president of the American Psychological Association for 1899. Now, at Columbia, his colleagues in the American Philosophical Association bestowed a similar honor. At the association's fourth annual meeting, held at the University of Pennsylvania in December 1904, members elected him president for the year 1905.[118] In 1909, Dewey was elected a vice-president of the American Association for the Advancement of Science, having previously served as chairman of the Council of Section L (Education) of the association. At Chicago, in 1904, he had been granted the LL.D. degree from the University of Wisconsin, the first of many honorary degrees he was to receive. In 1910, he was awarded the LL.D. degree by his alma mater, the University of Vermont; in 1913, the University of Michigan bestowed the same degree.

Though deeply engrossed in the technical and theoretical problems of philosophy and education, Dewey did not allow this to cut him off from the world of affairs. Very much alive to movements he judged important, he never hesitated to express himself on them. He was also ready to support actively causes he judged significant that he thought might benefit by his help. Dewey was especially alert to proposals affecting the public schools of the nation; he could usually be found in the forefront of those debating these issues.

One such issue in the early 1900s was the proposal that industrial education be provided for children leaving school at twelve or fourteen. The need for this education was manifest in the glaring unfitness of such boys and girls for the work into which nearly all of them went. Not being able to hold their jobs, they drifted from place to place where they learned nothing and where advance became impossible. Educators, social workers, parents, employers, and organizations such as the National Society for the Promotion of Industrial Education had long advocated vocational education for these children; more recently some state legislatures had taken up the matter. Dewey, having long recognized the need of industrial education, was one of its strongest supporters.

Almost from the first, however, the basic question was whether the new education should be an integral part of the existing public secondary school system or made into a separate public system under separate control. Those favoring a separate system, including most industrialists and manufacturers and only a few educators, argued that "efficiency in vocational education requires different methods of school administration, different courses of study, different qualifications of teachers, different equipment, different ways of meeting the needs of pupils, and a much greater flexibility in adapting means to ends than is possible of development under the ordinary routine of the public school system."[119] Those advocating an integrated system, including most parents, teachers, and educators, declared that it was easier and less costly to modify existing school systems to meet vocational needs than to create a new system of schools and administrators and also that greater harmony and unity would prevail if an integrated system were adopted.

Some states—New York, New Jersey, Ohio, and Maine—had already adopted the single system. Massachusetts had initially used the dual system but had abandoned it in favor of the integrated plan. Wisconsin had adopted the dual system; such an arrangement was being proposed to the Illinois legislature during the winter of 1912–13. Because other legislatures about to take up the issue were looking for leads, considerable attention was focused on the discussions and debates in the legislature and among interested observers in Illinois. "Vocational education, long a matter of national importance," wrote one observer, "is rapidly becoming one of popular interest. Witness the intense discussion that has been going on for six months in Illinois, where parents, educators, bankers, merchants and manufacturers have carried on a fight by press, pamphlet and report that has attracted the attention of interested persons throughout the country." [120]

Dewey aligned himself with those who favored a single, integrated system of education. He agreed that the dual system would involve costly duplication; that it would nullify much of what had been done in enriching and revitalizing traditional academic education by taking out of the traditional system those manual, industrial, and vocational activities just recently put in; and that it would tend to promote social cleavages among both children and adults.

This last consideration especially troubled Dewey, prompting him to write in behalf of the single system. "No question at present under discussion in education," he declared, "is so fraught with consequences for the future of democracy as the question of industrial education. Its right development will do more to make public education truly democratic than any other one agency now under consideration. Its wrong treatment will as surely accentuate all undemocratic tendencies in our present situation, by fostering and strengthening class divisions in school and out." Terming the plan to establish a dual system in Illinois "an undemocratic proposal," Dewey urged people and legislators to reject it, to adopt instead the integrated system already in use in some of the country's more progressive schools. "The old time general, academic education is beginning to be vitalized by the introduction of manual, industrial and social activities; it is beginning to recognize its responsibility to train all the youth for useful citizenship, including a calling in which each may render useful service to society and make an honest and decent living. Everywhere the existing school system is beginning to be alive to the need of supplementary agencies to help it fulfill this purpose, and is taking tentative but positive and continuous steps toward it." [121] The philosophy of education underlying the integrated system, Dewey pointed out, is "that industrial training shall be primarily not for the sake of industries, but for the sake of citizenship, and that it be conducted therefore on a purely educational basis and not in behalf of interested manufacturers." Dewey declared that "those who believe in the continued separate existence of what they are pleased to call the 'lower classes' or the 'laboring classes' would naturally rejoice to have schools in which these 'classes' would be segregated. And some employers of labor would doubtless rejoice to have schools supported by public taxation supply them with additional food for their mills." But all others, he urged, should unite and resist "every proposition, in whatever form advanced, to separate training of employees from training for citizenship, training of intelligence and character from training for narrow industrial efficiency." [122]

That Dewey felt strongly on the matter of industrial education is reflected in his efforts to circulate his views as widely as possible. His article "An Undemocratic Proposal" was reprinted with slight changes in the *Child Labor Bulletin* under the title "Some Dangers in the Present Movement for Industrial Education"; it appeared also as *Pamphlet No. 190* of the National Child Labor Committee and as Part II of an article in *Survey* entitled "Industrial Education and Democracy." [123] Other statements appeared in the recently founded liberal magazine, *New Republic*, with the titles "A Policy of Industrial Education," "Industrial Education—A Wrong Kind," and "Education vs. Trade-Training." [124] On 23 October 1913 Dewey addressed the National Society for the Promotion of Industrial Education at its seventh annual convention in Grand Rapids, Michigan, on the topic, "Should Michigan Have Vocational Education under 'Unit' or 'Dual' Control?" [125] Two years later, on 30 December 1915, he read a paper entitled "The Need of an Industrial Education in an Industrial Society" to educators attending the Second Pan-American Scientific Congress at George Washington University in Washington, D.C.[126]

Another proposal relating to the public schools in which Dewey had much interest was the introduction of religious instruction in the schools during the school day. Many parents, teachers, civic and religious leaders were troubled by the fact that most children attending public schools received little or no religious training. They were concerned that the lack of such training might have an adverse effect on the moral lives of the children and on society. Among plans suggested for bringing religious instruction into the schools, the one most generally favored was to release an amount of time from the regular school day for instruction in religion. At specified hours, children would be excused from their regular school work and turned over to teachers from their respective churches or denominations. Such a plan, its proponents argued, could be put into operation with a minimum of confusion and expense; it would also recognize and respect sectarian differences.

The proposal was vigorously opposed by various groups and individuals, primarily because of its disruptive influence on school life. Up to this time, opponents argued, the public schools of

America had been remarkably successful in assimilating children of different ethnic and cultural groups, making them feel as one. Under the "released time" plan, children would be segregated into denominational groups; religious differences, mostly unnoticed before in the children's school life, would be brought into sharp focus, undoing much of what the schools had done to establish unity.

Dewey agreed fully with these arguments, adding that it was scarcely an auspicious time to emphasize sectarian instruction in religion. For, as Dewey saw the situation in religion, large numbers of persons were finding the ideas and practices of the traditional faiths inadequate; they were searching for a religion that would more fully satisfy the moral, intellectual, and religious needs of the present. Because Dewey's conviction was that the faith of the future would center in the ideals of democracy and the methods and findings of science, he urged that the possibilities of such a faith for the public schools be explored. "Bearing the losses and inconveniences of our time as best we may," he wrote, "it is the part of men to labour persistently and patiently for the clarification and development of the positive creed of life implicit in democracy and in science, and to work for the transformation of all practical instrumentalities of education till they are in harmony with these ideas." [127] It is better for the schools to continue along the lines they had been following, Dewey believed, "than that they should, under the name of spiritual culture, form habits of mind which are at war with the habits of mind congruous with democracy and with science." [128]

Still another matter affecting the public schools, one in which Dewey was intensely interested, was the professional organization of teachers. This movement was prompted by the fact that the vast majority of American teachers worked under unhappy conditions and were unable to correct them. With few exceptions, the schools were autocratically administered by principals and superintendents subservient to school boards that represented powerful political and business interests; teachers' salaries were low, often on the level of the most poorly paid unskilled laborer; jobs were insecure and teachers could be dismissed without reason; no provisions were made for sickness and old age; the working day was long; classes were too large; school buildings all too frequently were overcrowded, poorly equipped, and unsanitary. The situation in the public schools of New York City fitted this general pattern.

Teachers in New York City and elsewhere had long complained about these conditions, repeatedly making recommendations for their correction. But seldom were those in authority moved to act. This perennial inaction convinced the more perceptive and aggressive teachers that little could be hoped for until teachers established an organization that could back up its demands with appropriate action. Teachers groups in Chicago, Atlanta, Washington, and St. Paul had organized around the turn of the century with such outstanding results that teachers in other cities began to follow their example. In 1912, under the leadership of Henry R. Linville, head of the biology department at Jamaica High School, a group of New York City teachers founded a magazine entitled the *American Teacher,* to acquaint teachers and the people of New York with conditions in the schools and to give voice to the teachers' grievances. The editors adopted as the magazine's slogan: "Democracy in Education: Education for Democracy"; they immediately began to urge the teachers of New York to form an organization that could implement the slogan with action.

On 17 October 1912, a group of teachers headed by Linville sponsored a meeting in the Horace Mann Auditorium to consider such an organization. Prior to the meeting some 15,000 handbills had been distributed to teachers throughout the city with the result that the meeting place was filled to overflowing.[129] Despite the opposition of two district superintendents who recommended that teachers confine their interests to the classroom, leaving administrative details to those responsible for them, the teachers in attendance voted overwhelmingly to establish a Teachers League of New York. A "call to organize" appeared in the *American Teacher*; on 28 February 1913 an organizational meeting was held in Milbank Chapel at Teachers College.[130] At this meeting, Linville was elected president, other officers were elected, a committee structure set up, and a set of principles adopted.

Dewey, invited to address the February meeting, chose as his topic "Professional Spirit among Teachers."[131] He defined this spirit as involving not merely "the continuous study of the questions of teaching within the school room" but also "a responsibility as leaders, as directors in the formation of public opinion" in matters relating to educational policy and to the "thousand and one problems relative to children that have come forward with the great congestion of population in cities in the last generation."[132] He found that compared to the spirit prevailing in the medical profession, professional spirit among teachers was practically nonexistent. And the chief reason for this, Dewey believed, was that, under the organizational arrangement that dominated the educational system, teachers were relieved of all responsibility outside the classroom; despite the wisdom they might have acquired in their dealings with children, they had "no authorized way of transmitting or of communicating it, and of seeing it was taken account of by others." Hence, there was no "adequate impetus" among teachers to develop a professional spirit—no reason for taking a more genuine intellectual interest in the larger aspects of their work or for making education count as a social force. Dewey emphasized that responsibility for the educational system should not be concentrated in the few, however wise and competent they might be. "To concentrate responsibility" among the few, he argued, "is to diffuse irresponsibility" among the many.[133] Dewey was convinced that "if we could achieve a thorough professional spirit, permeating the entire corps of teachers and educators, we should have done more to forward the cause of education than can be achieved in any other way."[134]

In the years following, Dewey continued his involvement in teacher organization. In 1916, three years after the founding of the Teachers League of New York, he supported bringing the organization into the American Federation of Labor. In the 1930s, when the Communist element among New York teachers threatened to gain control of the local organization, Dewey was among those who led the anti-Communist group of teachers out of the local union.

The interest Dewey had had in social settlement work in Chicago continued in New York. Of the city's many social centers, the Henry Street Settlement on the lower east side was the most prominent. Its leader was Lillian D. Wald whose work over the years placed her in the forefront of women noted for pioneering work among the poor and underprivileged.[135] The reputation of the Henry Street Settlement came to rival that of Hull House in Chicago; distinguished persons from all over the world came to visit it. Tagore; Madame Naidu, an associate of Gandhi; Madame Suradji; Prince Kropotkin; and Ramsay MacDonald were among the many from abroad who called at the settlement.[136] Among the visitors in 1910 were "two stalwart men in Russian blouses and high boots." As Miss Wald reports the occasion, "I was much moved to learn that they had been sent to us by Tolstoy. Tolstoy had died while the two friends were on their way to America. They said they came to this country in the interests of free education, meaning, as they defined it, freedom from uninteresting, rigid, traditional instruction. . . . I wanted to help them in their pilgrimage, and asked what I could do. Without hesitation they answered, 'We want to meet John Dewey.' That, happily, could be arranged."[137]

Soon after his arrival in New York, Dewey familiarized himself with the work of the settlement; he was particularly impressed by the concern of the staff about children leaving school and going to work. The settlement had maintained for some years a system of scholarships to help these children get an industrial education, making up for their benefit a list of schools in the New York area where such an education was available. In 1913 the settlement decided to publish a directory with a more complete and detailed account of such schools, to which Dewey was asked to write an introduction. In it, Dewey stressed the need for vocational education, the failure of the public to meet this need adequately, and the indebtedness of the public to the Henry Street Settlement for "the thoroughgoing pains taken in the preparation of this Directory, which places before those interested an exhibit of existing facilities for industrial and trade education in Greater New York." [138]

Dewey usually accepted invitations to address academic and professional groups in and around New York. Three weeks after he began his duties at Columbia he gave on the campus a series of public lectures on "Some Problems in the Psychology of Conduct." [139] On six successive Sundays in February and March of 1906, he gave a series of talks on "Contemporary Ethical Problems" at the Brooklyn Institute of Arts and Sciences.[140] Also in March 1906, he gave an address at Teachers College on "Self-Activity in Education" to which interested University members were invited but with the warning that "the doors will close promptly at the beginning of the lecture." [141] In the fall of 1906, he gave a course of six lectures on "Philosophy of Education" to the members of the Normal Department of Pratt Institute in Brooklyn.[142] When Columbia University sponsored a series of public lectures during the winter and spring of 1909 on "Charles Darwin and His Influence on Science," commemorating the fiftieth anniversary of the publication of the *Origin of Species*, Dewey's contribution was his now well known lecture, "Darwin's Influence upon Philosophy." [143] During the same spring, the university arranged a series of public lectures on "Science, Philosophy, and Art," in which Dewey spoke on "Ethics." [144] When the Department of Philosophy and Psychology sponsored a series of public lectures in 1909–10 on "Contemporary Philosophic Thought," Dewey talked on the philosophy of Maurice Maeterlinck.[145] Dewey had few invitations to address church groups, but on 17 December 1911 he spoke at the Mount Morris Baptist Church on "The Evolution of Morality." [146] During January and February of 1913, he gave six weekly lectures on modern philosophy to the Colony Club of New

York City.[147] In the spring of 1913 he addressed the Teachers College Alumnae on "The Training of Thinking in Children"; [148] a few weeks later he read a paper entitled "Social Education" to the Association of Women High School Teachers.[149] In the winter of 1914, Dewey gave a course of five weekly lectures under the auspices of the Federation for Child Study at their headquarters at 2 West 64th Street.[150]

Out-of-town speaking engagements for Dewey were mostly at other colleges and universities. During the fall semester of 1906 he went to Baltimore each week to give a course of lectures on Greek philosophy to graduate philosophy students at The Johns Hopkins University.[151] During the second week in December 1907, he gave a series of six lectures on "The Relation of Philosophy to Educational Theory" at the School of Education at the University of Illinois.[152] In April 1908, he gave two talks on "The Psychology of Teaching" at the annual Teachers Convention in Philadelphia.[153] In the spring of 1909, he was invited to address the Philosophical Club of Smith College, choosing as his topic "A Short Catechism concerning Truth." [154] During January and February of 1910, Dewey was again at the Johns Hopkins, this time giving a course of six weekly lectures on "The Pragmatic Movement in Contemporary Philosophy." [155] In March 1910, he gave a talk on "Present Educational Tendencies" to the students and faculty of Rhode Island State Normal School,[156] as well as two lectures in April 1910 at Wellesley College—one on "The Development of Pragmatism" and the other on "The Problem of Truth." [157] In December 1910, he was invited by the University of Pennsylvania to give a series of three talks on the George Leib Harrison Foundation. The general subject of these talks was "The Problem of Truth." Dewey divided his material under the topics: "Why Is Truth a Problem," "Truth and Consequences," and "Objective Truths." [158] In June 1912, Dewey gave the annual address at the class-day exercise of Teachers College of George Washington University in Washington, D.C., and also the commencement address at the Walnut Hill School in Cincinnati.[159] In the winter and spring of 1914, he delivered a series of eight weekly lectures at Union College under the auspices of the Ichabod Spencer Foundation on the general topic "The Psychology of Social Behavior." [160]

Though Dewey enjoyed addressing audiences on his favorite topics, at times he wearied of the many demands his speaking engagements made on his time and energy; he would have liked to forego some of them. But invitations to speak usually carried with them honoraria which he could not well afford to overlook. His five children were now approaching high-school and college age; the responsibility of providing for their needs and financing their education was a heavy one. The reduction in income the family suffered when Dewey and Mrs. Dewey surrendered their posts at the University of Chicago accentuated the problem. The matter of finding a suitable place for the family to reside at a price they could afford, for example, was a troublesome one; between 1905 and 1914, the Deweys moved nine times.[161]

Because of the family's straitened finances, Alice Dewey did most of the cooking, baking, cleaning, knitting, and sewing for the family, also seeing to it that the children met their appointments on time and that her husband did not forget to meet his scheduled class. Though Alice Dewey did not dislike these tasks, she found them not a sufficient challenge. She missed the laboratory school in Chicago that had served as such an excellent outlet for her unquestioned abilities and powers of leadership; she felt frustrated at not being able to undertake more challenging ventures in school or society. She did attempt to keep abreast of her husband's studies and research in education; her conversations with him were generally a stimulus and help. In the preface to *How We Think,* Dewey acknowledged that "my fundamental indebtedness is to my wife, by whom the ideas of this book were inspired, and through whose work in connection with the Laboratory School, existing in Chicago between 1896 and 1903, the ideas attained such concreteness as comes from embodiment and testing in practice." [162] Despite her responsibilities at home, Alice Dewey was always ready to help out in university social affairs; in 1906 she was one of the committee of women who arranged a university tea at which Mark Twain was the guest of honor.[163]

Her deep sense of political justice prompted Alice to take an active part in the woman suffrage movement agitating the nation at this time. Dewey, who shared his wife's interest in woman suffrage, did what he could to advance it. When the *International* ran a symposium on woman suffrage, Dewey was one of those invited to state their views. The questions put to the participants and Dewey's answers to them were: First, "What in your opinion is the most powerful argument (a) For, or (b) Against woman's suffrage?" Dewey's reply to this was that no society can claim to be genuinely democratic until its women have the same political rights as the men. Second, "Are you in favor (a) Of a property, or (b) Of an educational qualification?" Dewey's answer was that a property qualification would be "a most reactionary move" in that it would deprive the poor of the protection which comes from the ballot. And if by an educational qualification is meant "a certain degree of literacy," then, Dewey declared, "it is a piece of academic foolishness to suppose that that ability to read or write is an adequate test of social and political intelligence." Third, "Are you in favor of militant methods?" Dewey's response was that militant methods are not now needed in this country; not being needed, they should not be adopted. Finally, "Should a woman's moral standing affect her right to vote?" Dewey's reply to this was, "There is enough of a double standard of morality now. When a man's 'moral standing affects' his right to vote, it should also affect a woman's—not till then." [164]

On 8 August 1912 Dewey addressed the summer students at Columbia on woman suffrage; according to one press report, "so many people came to hear him that many could not get inside the doors." [165] As reported, Dewey declared in his speech that as long as women are deprived of the right to vote they are "shut out from the culmination and seal for full citizenship, the outward and visible sign of the inward and spiritual grace which is liberty." [166] A few months later, in December, Dewey gave a lecture entitled "Woman's Suffrage" to the Current Events Club of Englewood, New Jersey.[167]

Dewey occasionally took part in the parades designed to publicize and help the woman suffrage movement. According to an anecdote widely circulated at the time, just before the start of one parade Dewey had thrust into his hands without his reading it a banner proclaiming: "Men can vote! Why can't I?" and was considerably puzzled by the amused smiles which greeted him as he proceeded on the march down Fifth Avenue.

The Deweys were noted for their hospitality; to their home came many people. They were particularly solicitous of oriental students who had come to New York to study and had not yet found rooms. An invitation was usually extended them to stay with the family till suitable lodgings were found.

The hospitality of the Dewey family became a matter of public interest in the spring of 1906 when it was extended to Maxim Gorky, the noted Russian revolutionary and writer, and his woman companion. When the press announced that Gorky was on his way to the United States to get financial and moral support for the Russian revolutionary movement, reaction in many quarters was immediate and strong. Some opposed his admission to the United States because of his radical socialist teachings. Later, when it was learned on his arrival that the woman who accompanied him was not his wife but the Russian actress, Madame Andreeva, opposition to his presence in the country grew more and more pronounced. Civic and religious leaders joined in the cry against him, declaring that the presence of

Gorky and Madame Andreeva here was subversive of the nation's morals. The press publicized the affair, denouncing Gorky as an anarchist, socialist, and free lover. Officials in Boston where he was scheduled to speak declared he would not be welcome there; Theodore Roosevelt announced that the couple would not be invited to the White House. The hotels where the two successively sought lodgings—the Belleclaire, the Brevoort, and the Rhinelander—fearing adverse publicity, asked them to leave.[168]

Distressed by the public treatment of Gorky and Madame Andreeva, Dewey invited the two to stay with his family. According to Max Eastman, "Dewey in turn was violently attacked for this act of magnanimity, so violently that he seemed for a time in danger of losing his job." Throughout this ordeal, the account continues, "Mrs. Dewey stood behind him like a rock. 'I would rather starve and see my children starve,' she said between clenched teeth, 'than see John sacrifice his principles'." [169]

To get the children and themselves out of the city during the summer months, John and Alice continued up to 1910 to go to their camp at Hurricane, New York, in the Adirondacks, near the place where Thomas Davidson ran Glenmore, a summer school centering on the cultural sciences. In 1910, they bought a farm on Long Island not far from Huntington on what is now Greenlawn Road. From 1910 to 1923, when the Deweys sold the property, the family spent their summers there.[170]

Dewey found life on the farm relaxing; during the summer months he spent all the time he could there.[171] He spent a portion of each day, usually shortly after dawn, working in the gardens. He liked to work the soil with his hands, taking pride in the appearance of the asparagus bed and the vegetable gardens. The Deweys' fondness for herbs made the variety of these in their garden unmatched anywhere in the neighborhood. Dewey saw to it that the peach trees were kept well pruned; he supervised and helped in picking the crop, and, with his son Sabino, sold and delivered peaches to families and stores in the neighboring villages. Surplus eggs from the farm's sizeable number of hens were taken by the children and sold to neighboring townspeople.[172] After his work in the gardens, Dewey would retire to the canvas tent under the tree at the side of the house, where, with typewriter and paper at hand, he would write, oblivious to the activities around him.

During the summer of 1910 Dewey learned of the death of William James at his summer home in Chocorua, New Hampshire, on 26 August. Circumstances had prevented a close intimacy from growing up between James and Dewey, but the two had known each other on friendly terms for a considerable number of years. Though the thinking of the two men agreed in most essentials, there were places where their philosophies diverged. Neither attempted to overlook these differences, though James, more than Dewey, was inclined to minimize their importance.[173] But they did not allow disagreements to separate them; rather, as James's biographer observed, "they sought by sympathy and understanding to emphasize the truth which they held in common, rather than by disputation to aggravate their differences." [174]

Dewey was quick to pay tribute to James. "By the death of Prof. William James, at the age of sixty-eight," he wrote, "America loses its most distinguished figure in the field of philosophy and psychology." [175] Dewey noted James's "sense of reality," his "power of literary expression," his "generous personality," and his "religious belief in the possibilities of philosophy." [176] Dewey stressed this union of philosophy and life in the thought of James, declaring that "if the common people read him gladly, it was not alone for a clearness and a picturesqueness that will long be the despair of other philosophers, but because of their instinctive recognition that here at least was a philosopher who believed in life and who believed in philosophy because of his belief in life." [177] "Our greatest act of piety to him to whom we owe so much," Dewey wrote, "is to accept from him some rekindling of a human faith in the human significance of philosophy." [178]

Four years to the month after James died, World War I broke out in Europe; in the spring of 1917 the United States entered the conflict, remaining a participant till the cease-fire order on 11 November 1918. These events and their aftermath precipitated a number of crises in American thought and practice, and Dewey was a leader of the intellectuals who faced up to them. In confronting them, Dewey's life and thought took on added dimensions, so that he became recognized the world over not only as a philosopher and educator, but also as one of America's foremost thinkers on national and international problems, a staunch supporter of liberal causes.

9. Columbia University, 1914–1919

THE OUTBREAK of war in Europe in August 1914 was a severe setback to those who had believed that armed conflict among major nations was a thing of the past. Many facts had led to this belief. There had been no widespread European war since the defeat of Napoleon in 1815. The strong peace movements flourishing in Europe and the United States had created in many influential quarters a climate of opinion opposed to war. Peaceful international cooperation had been under way in many areas where it was useful and in the common interest, resulting in such organizations as the Universal Postal Union, International Telegraph Union, Radio and Communication Union, and the Union for the Protection of Industrial Property. Tsar Nicholas II of Russia in 1899 and President Theodore Roosevelt in 1907 had summoned peace conferences at the Hague, where progress had seemingly been made on plans to reduce armaments, codify international law, and set up machinery for arbitrating disputes between nations. Then, too, expanding commercial and financial ties among the leading countries of Europe and America had made them economically so interdependent as to make war among them seem unthinkable.

Long convinced that peace among nations depended primarily on removing the barriers that separate peoples and in setting up international mechanisms to promote common interests and reduce international tensions and rivalries, Dewey had been cautiously hopeful that moves in these directions would continue, eventually rendering war outmoded. Consequently he shared in the general shock and disappointment when war was declared.

Though students of the European situation knew that the causes of the conflict were many and complex, attention centered initially on Germany as the main offender. Her nationalist and economic ambitions during the preceding half-century along with the rising tide of militarism and imperialism among her leaders had caused deep concern in neighboring countries. When in 1914 the German government declared war, ordering its armies to march into Belgium in violation of her neutrality, this concern was recognized as having been well grounded. When, in addition, Germany adopted a policy of unrestricted submarine warfare that included the sinking of the British liner "Lusitania" on 7 May 1915 with the loss of some 1,200 passengers, people wondered what underlying philosophy motivated the German government to resort to tactics as ruthless as these.

The wonder was even greater because of Germany's long adherence to philosophical idealism. As expressed in the philosophies of men like Fichte, Schelling, and Hegel, this tradition gave primacy to spiritual and cultural values; after the defeat of Napoleon, it had inspired and given direction to Germany's national life. The explanation generally given for Germany's war policy was that under the influence of the teachings of such men as Feuerbach, Bismarck, Treitschke, and Nietzsche, the nation had abandoned its earlier idealism, embracing in its place materialism, industrialism, practicalism, and militarism. This philosophy, it was argued, that had dominated the life of Germany in recent years, now supplied the ideological basis of its international policies.[1]

As a student of German thought and culture, Dewey also sought an explanation for German military policy. He could not accept the explanation generally advanced because it failed to account for the spiritual unity of the German people and their overriding conviction that the actions of their leaders were morally justified. This moral confidence and self-assurance, Dewey believed, could be explained only in terms of an idealism as pervasive and influential as the practicalism and militarism on which so much attention was being focused. An invitation to give a series of lectures on the John Calvin McNair Foundation at the University of North Carolina in February 1915 provided Dewey an occasion to develop his views, which he did under the general title, "German Philosophy and Politics."[2]

To understand the mind of Germany, Dewey argued, it is necessary to go back to Kant's well-known doctrine of a world of phenomena set over against a world of noumena. The world of phenomena is made up of that which is outer, physical, and subject to law, reflected in man's science, technology, industrialism, and the forms of organization in political, economic, and military affairs. The world of noumena relates to man's free, inner, spiritual life, outwardly manifested in man's pursuit of moral, spiritual, and cultural ends. Though both realms are integral parts of human existence, Kant gives priority to the world of spiritual values and ideals. Kant, however, failed to give these any concrete content, leaving them formal and empty. To correct this weakness, his successors like Fichte and Hegel, proceeding on purely *a priori* grounds, filled the void in Kant's doctrine with, as Dewey said, "the substantial figures of the State and its Historical Evolution and Mission." [3] Because German idealism taught that ideals are absolute and that pure reason alone, without considerations of utility, can determine what these ideals are and what means are to be employed in realizing them, it easily adjusted to the argument that industrialism, practicalism, and militarism are necessary means to achieve German cultural and spiritual goals. The result has been, said Dewey, that "combination of self-conscious idealism with unsurpassed technical efficiency and organization in the varied fields of action" that has characterized German national life for the last half century and that undergirded its war effort.[4]

The belief that war was a thing of the past, that the future held only peace, was just one aspect of the general optimism with which the twentieth century had opened. Faith in the inevitability of human progress that had so strongly characterized the thought of the latter half of the nineteenth century had continued into the twentieth. Democracy was advancing on most fronts in Europe and the United States, bringing civil rights, education, and opportunity for betterment to more and more people. Science and technology were opening up prospects of an era in which hunger, disease, and poverty would be largely overcome. Improved means of travel and communication gave promise of breaking down the barriers that separate nations, bringing more and more peoples into closer and friendlier relations. To most observers these developments seemed to indicate that progress was inevitable, that nothing could long impede the forward march of events.

The war forced people to rethink the nature of progress and to consider anew the possibility of realizing it. Dewey condemned the earlier optimism because it had rested on false grounds. "We confused rapidity of change with advance, and we took certain gains in our own comfort and ease as signs that cosmic forces were working inevitably to improve the whole state of human affairs." [5] What was overlooked, said Dewey, was that the changes that brought improvements in the lives of some all too frequently created new rivalries, tensions, and trouble spots. Before genuine progress can be claimed in any area, the problems created by change must themselves be solved and social mechanisms devised to prevent their reoccurrence. Change, Dewey pointed out, "affords an *opportunity* for progress, but is not itself progress." [6] Progress is not automatic and inevitable, something to be left to "nature, or Providence, or evolution, or manifest destiny." [7] It comes only to the extent that men apply intelligent and cooperative effort to solving problems caused by change. Dewey strongly condemned the theory that progress is automatic, doubting "if the whole history of mankind shows any more vicious and demoralizing ethic than the recent widespread belief that each of us, as individuals and as classes, might safely and complacently devote ourselves to increasing our own possessions, material, intellectual, and artistic, because progress is inevitable anyhow." [8] Terrible as the war is, he declared, "we may welcome whatever revelations of our stupidity and carelessness it brings with it; and set about the institution of a more manly and more responsible faith in progress than that in which we have indulged in the past." [9]

Almost immediately after the war in Europe started, antimilitarist groups in this country began a movement to keep the United States out of it. The United States, they believed, should direct its efforts to stopping the war and to planning for peace. Prominent men and women from all walks of life were in the movement, helping establish such organizations as the National Peace Federation, World Peace Foundation, League to Enforce Peace, American League for the Limitation of Armament, and Women's Peace Party. President Wilson also, shortly after the outbreak of the war, proclaimed the neutrality of the United States and set about seeking ways to stop the war and establish the foundations for an enduring peace. Apparently Dewey did not belong to any of these organizations, but he sympathized with their efforts, doing what he could to support them.

Because the possibility always existed that the United States might be drawn into the war against its will, some urged the United States to prepare itself militarily. "Preparedness" groups pressed for legislation to enlarge greatly the regular army and navy, provide funds for an increase in armaments, and expand the range of military training. The preparedness movement at first met determined opposition from the antimilitarist groups, but as the war progressed, conviction grew that the survival of the democratic way of life might demand our entry into the war; antimilitarism in most quarters gave way to a sentiment favoring preparedness.

Dewey was among those endorsing preparedness. One proposal, however, stirred him to protest: the recommendation that military training should be universal and compulsory because of its educational value in creating a feeling of responsibility and loyalty to the country. The argument in support of this plan was stated by General Wood in a Philadelphia speech. As reported by the press, General Wood said: "It is a pretty dangerous situation to turn loose in this country all kinds of humanity seen on the docks at Ellis Island, to turn them loose with no sense of responsibility to their new land. They come in racial groups, drift through our schools in racial groups and are controlled by a dialect press. We are doing absolutely nothing to make these people understand that they are Americans, at least in the making. . . . There is nothing like compulsory military service to accomplish this." [10]

Dewey opposed such a program because, first, it assumes that Americanization consists in reducing all immigrant peoples to a homogeneous group patterned after the country's Anglo-Saxon settlers, whereas the real problem is "to see to it that all get from one another the best that each strain has to offer from its own tradition and culture." [11] Second, it appeals to the dangers of foreign aggression to win support from immigrants; to Dewey, "to stir up fear and dislike of home countries as a means of securing love of an adopted country does not seem a promising procedure." [12] In the third place, it leaves untouched the two factors really responsible for the divided loyalties of immigrant Americans. These are the localism of our public school systems and the disadvantages that immigrants must contend with in the industrial order. To overcome the "spiritual localism" in our educational systems we need more interest and action on the federal level in vocational education for immigrants and in programs for continuing education among newly arrived groups. "We might at least try the experiment of making our Federal Bureau of Education at Washington something more than a book-keeping and essay-writing department before we conclude that military service is the only way of effecting a common mind." [13] In the world of industry, national legislation is needed to correct abuses in the economic order, providing more equal opportunity and security for newly arrived workers. Such legislation will show immigrant groups that their newly adopted homeland is intent on protecting the individual worker's integrity; this in turn will elicit the widespread loyalty and support so frequently lacking. Until we start nationalizing our education and eliminating the evils in our economic life, said Dewey, "it is premature to appeal to the army, to marching and to sleeping in barrack cots as the best way to remedy the evils of a lack of national mindedness." [14]

As the war went on, the United States wavered about becoming a participant. Some Allies sympathizers declared that our national uncertainty was due to the provincialism of our outlook, a provincialism that blinded us to the global implications of a German victory; that a sentimental attachment to peace prevented us from seeing our larger duty; that sordid self-interest kept us from risking life and money in a foreign war. In the 1916 presidential campaign that pitted Charles Evans Hughes against Woodrow Wilson, Theodore Roosevelt denounced the Wilson administration, declaring that Wilson was a president who appealed always to national self-interest and to safety-first and never once to "the stern enthusiasm of strong men for the right."[15]

Dewey believed that the nation's uncertainty—an uncertainty he undoubtedly shared—had a deeper origin than those stated. Our nation, he argued, is vaguely groping to find itself. It has severed the strings that tied its thinking to democratic Europe; it is in process of making up its own mind as to its long-range purpose. Though it recognizes its kinship with the democratic peoples of Europe, our nation is at the same time convinced that the democracy and civilization prevailing in Europe and being defended by the armies fighting in France are not the democracy and civilization it wants to see prevail in this country. Our nation desires to create within its borders a new society, one that will embody as fully as possible the dream of its founders. But the United States is not sure precisely what this new democratic society is to be. All it knows is that it will be different from the democracies of England and France. In its uncertainty, America hesitates to enter the war on the side of the Allies. It feels that "the gallant fight for democracy and civilization fought on the soil of France is not our fight."[16] And even if eventually we entered the war against Germany, our doubt and uncertainty would probably still be with us. "We shall have decided a small thing, what to do, but the great thing, the thing so great as to cause and perpetuate our hesitation, may remain."[17]

By the spring of 1917, President Wilson and the majority of the American people had become convinced that American attempts to stop the war were futile, that if democracy was to be saved the United States would have to enter the war. Accordingly, President Wilson asked Congress to declare war on Germany and the Central Powers; this it did in early April 1917. Much as he disliked war, Dewey approved this act. For the basic fact is, he wrote, "that in a world organized for war there are as yet no political mechanisms which enable a nation with warm sympathies to make them effective, save through military participation."[18]

In explaining the country's stand, President Wilson declared that America's fight was not with the German people but with their military overlords who brought on the war and who must be overthrown if the world is to be made safe for its inhabitants. "This is a peoples' war," Wilson emphasized in his Flag Day address on 14 June 1917, "a war for freedom and justice and self-government amongst all the nations of the world, a war to make the world safe for the peoples who live upon it . . . the German people themselves included." [19]

Dewey agreed wholeheartedly with this statement of aims. Addressing a group of teachers on 15 December 1917, he said: "Ever since President Wilson asked for a breaking of relations with Germany and afterwards for war against that country, more and more as he has stated why we are in this war, I have been a thoro and complete sympathizer with the part played in this country by this war and I have wished to see the resources of this country used for its successful prosecution. As has been said over and over again, this is not merely a war of armies, this is a war of peoples." [20]

With the declaration of war, the government took immediate steps to gear the life of the nation to its war needs, calling upon the people to unite in prosecuting the war. The response was widespread; leaders in business, industry, labor, and agriculture along with journalists, publicists, and intellectuals pledged their support. Institutions of higher learning considered ways to help the government; among the ventures undertaken by Columbia University was a series of "war papers" issued by the university's Division of Intelligence and Publicity. These pamphlets were designed to acquaint the public with "the problems and duties of American citizens in meeting the national needs in the present world conflict." Among the topics discussed were "German Subjects Within Our Gates," "Our Headline Policy," "How to Finance the War," "Food and Preparedness."

Dewey led off the series with a pamphlet entitled "Enlistment for the Farm," [21] in which he called attention to the serious food problem facing the Allied world. He explained that one factor in this was the shortage of labor on the farms caused by the shift of rural workers from the farms to the armed forces and munitions factories; he suggested that school children and their teachers could reduce the shortage by enlisting for farm work. Such work, Dewey declared, provides the child with an opportunity for "Constructive Patriotism." [22] At the same time it links the school with life, thus giving the child "a sense of reality which means so much to children." [23]

Some Americans could not accept Wilson's thesis that the war in Europe was different from all preceding ones in that it aimed at ending all future wars. Many radical socialist and intellectual groups viewed it as just another imperialist war used by the ruling classes to advance their own interests. A sizeable number of hyphenated Americans opposed America's role in the war either because of pro-German sympathies or anti-British feelings. Pacifists strongly condemned the war and our participation in it; those among them eligible for the draft frequently refused to bear arms against the enemy.

Because it was important that the nation present a united front to the enemy and guard against subversion from within, these dissenting groups were viewed with suspicion, at times even with open hostility. As tensions mounted, the emotionalism approached hysteria. Socialists and radicals often saw their organizations crushed and their leaders imprisoned. Books, magazines, and newspapers containing material opposing the war or criticizing government policy were confiscated or denied use of the mails. Teachers in schools, colleges, and universities, and clergy were closely watched to be sure they taught no subversive doctrines. Pacifists and conscientious objectors were regarded as unpatriotic or hopelessly idealistic; they were held up to scorn and ridicule by much of the press.

Along with other liberals, Dewey was deeply distressed by this treatment of dissenting groups. "I do not think that to defeat Prussianism abroad," he wrote, "it is necessary to establish Prussianism at home." [24] He opposed using threats and force to stop dissenting views because history has shown it to be futile, with long-lasting, evil effects. Force merely drives unpopular views underground where they breed and foster additional ones. Also, to prevent discussion is to stifle thinking, rendering people unprepared to meet the problems of war and peace. Such intellectual unpreparedness, Dewey thought, presents a danger much greater than any that might conceivably arise from free discussion of controversial issues. In Dewey's words, "There is not a tithe of the danger to our effective participation in the war from those who think wildly and erratically than there is from those who do not think enough." [25]

However, Dewey saw no permanent threat in these wartime invasions of civil rights or in the hostile attitudes toward those with unpopular views. They all represented a "lapse" in our otherwise deep national concern with democratic rights, growing out of our inexperience in carrying on the activities of a nation at war. They were "merely a part of our haste to get into the war effectively, a part of the rush of mobilization, which, thank heaven, had to be improvised because of our historic and established unmilitarism." [26] Dewey, therefore, was inclined to be rather lenient in judging those responsible for the frequently harsh treatment of dissenting groups. "It is not to our discredit," he declared, "that we were unfamiliar with the ways and usages of war, and that we were incapable of displaying, for example, the ordered decency of the French who have lived for decades in the sobering presence of a national danger." [27]

The invasion of civil rights came home to Dewey when Columbia University became involved in cases of its own. Columbia had long been regarded as a center of academic freedom where faculty and students could air their views without fear of recrimination. America's entry into the war changed this. Aware that many considered the university a haven for pacifists, socialists, and radicals of various sorts, President Butler and the trustees were anxious to change the university's image and to portray it as a citadel of loyalty, patriotism, and genuine Americanism. The board of trustees, therefore, with the strong endorsement of President Butler—himself held suspect in many conservative quarters because of his long and close association with prewar peace movements—let it be known that faculty members who expressed views or engaged in activities judged detrimental to the war effort would be dismissed. They announced the formation of a special committee of the trustees to keep watch over faculty instruction and activity and to bring cases of suspected disloyalty to the attention of the board. To give this plan a democratic flavor, the trustees authorized the appointment of a Committee of Nine, drawn from the University Council, to cooperate in the investigations.[28] Dewey was made a member of this committee. The committee of trustees immediately went to work, announcing in a few weeks, on 1 October 1917, the dismissal of two faculty members, James McKeen Cattell, professor of psychology at Columbia since 1891 and Henry Wadsworth Longfellow Dana, an instructor in English. The dismissal of Cattell grew out of a letter he had sent on 23 August to members of Congress urging them to support a measure then before Congress to prohibit sending conscripts to fight in Europe against their will. Cattell defended his act on the ground that any citizen had the constitutional right to petition his government. But because the letter had aroused the anger of several who had received it, the trustees voted to dismiss Cattell on the ground that his act was injurious to the war effort and showed a lack of patriotism. The firing of Dana stemmed from his activities as a member of the People's Council, an organization regarded in conservative circles as a radical group working, under the guise of promoting peace, to undermine the prosecution of the war. Butler had warned Dana not to participate in the council's activities but Dana had insisted on his right to do this and was subsequently dismissed.

When considering Cattell's case, the trustees had taken into account but rejected the recommendations of the Committee of Nine. When reviewing the case of Dana, the trustees had acted without consulting the committee. This ignoring of the faculty committee led Dewey to resign from it, writing to E. R. A. Seligman, the committee chairman: "In view of the fact that the President has asked for the resignation of Professor Dana under penalty of dismissal without securing an inquiry by or hearing before any representative body of the Faculties, there seems no reason for the continued existence of the Committee of Nine, and I herewith present my resignation. . . . Conspicuous ignoring of the Committee on an occasion when it would have been conspicuously appropriate to clothe it with authority . . . seems to me, [to render] the continued activity of the Committee inconsistent with professional self-respect." [29] Dewey felt so strongly about the highhandedness of the trustees that he devoted an entire class period to condemning the methods used in the dismissals.[30]

An issue engaging a large portion of Dewey's attention during the war years was that raised by pacifists and conscientious objectors; he believed their claims were of critical importance in a time of war. Also a large number of Dewey's friends among social workers, professional people, and writers, including his longtime friend Jane Addams, were strong pacifists; Dewey felt more than an ordinary obligation to state the reasons for his own antipacifist stand.

Dewey distinguished pacifists such as Jane Addams from those whom he called "professional pacifists." [31] Jane Addams and others like her, though opposed to all war, at least assumed a positive role and bent their efforts to building an international order that would reduce the possibilities of war. He acknowledged, "The best statement which I have seen made of the pacifist position since we entered the war is that of Miss Addams." [32] Professional pacifists, on the other hand, are so convinced that anything is better than war that they take on the purely negative role of opposing all war, neglecting whatever interest they might have in general international reorganization. "The pacifist literature of the months preceding our entrance into war," said Dewey, "was opportunistic—breathlessly, frantically so. . . . Hence the continuous recourse to concessions and schemes, devised *ad hoc* over night, to meet each changing aspect of the diplomatic situation so as to ward off war." [33]

The pacifists' argument was that not only the war in Europe but all forms of war are inherently evil and have no rightful place in the economy of human life and progress. They found it inconsistent that men should kill and destroy now in order to stop killing and destroying in the future. They declared that law should be substituted for force, that arbitration should take the place of armed might in settling disputes between nations. They asserted that war grows out of man's evil impulses, which must be changed through education, example, and an appeal to man's higher sentiments; only then will wars cease.

Dewey refused to admit that war per se is always evil. War, he declared, is a form of force; the real question is, "What is force and what are we going to do with it?" [34] This, he believed, is "the acute question of social philosophy in a world like that of today." [35] Dewey pointed out that force is involved in everything we do, that "not to depend upon and utilize force is simply to be without a foothold in the real world." [36] Therefore, those pacifists who scornfully refer to "the 'philosophy of force' " are in somewhat the same position as an engineer who "should speak deprecatingly of the science of energy." [37] The important thing, said Dewey, is to distinguish good and bad uses of force. This he did by differentiating force as power and force as violence. Force as power is force that is ordered, organized, under control, and capable of realizing the ends sought. The use of this type of force is justified because it represents the rational, most efficient way of getting desired results. Force as violence is force without direction and control, running amuck. Use of this kind of force is not justified; it embodies the irrational, the destructive, the wasteful in seeking ends. Thus, moral justification for using force must be determined in each particular case in terms of its effectiveness in gaining desired results. It is intolerable, said Dewey, that "men should condemn or eulogize force at large, irrespective of its use as a means of getting results." [38]

When pacifists argue that law must be substituted for force, said Dewey, they betray their confusion of language. For law can never be a substitute for force; it is merely a statement of "a method for employing force economically, efficiently, so as to get results with the least waste." [39] Therefore, "literally to substitute law for force would be as intelligent as to try to run an engine on the mathematical formula which states its most efficient running." What pacifists undoubtedly mean by the phrase "substitution of law for force" is that some method must be devised to regulate the expenditure of force in ways that will avoid the wastes and evils attending present methods. But their "emotional animosity to the very idea of force" prevents them from saying this; their "badly mixed" language all too frequently results in "a harmful mixture in ideas" that in turn leads to ill-advised acts.[40]

The pacifists' claim that war springs from the evil impulses of human nature is only a half-truth. "The avarice of munition-makers, the love of some newspapers for exciting news, and the depravity of the anonymous human heart," said Dewey, "doubtless play a part in the generation of war." But these evil inclinations are able to cause war only because "there are specific defects in the organization of the energies of men in society which give them occasion and stimulation."[41] If social and international arrangements existed to meet the needs of competing groups and nations, the power of men's wicked desires to bring on war would be largely nullified.

Because they neglect this aspect of the problem of peace, said Dewey, "pacifists have had little recourse save to decry evil emotions and evil-minded men as the causes of war," reducing the peace movement to "the futile plane of hortatory preaching." Using as an analogy the heavy traffic on a busy highway, Dewey said that "the ordinary pacifist's method is like trying to avoid conflict in the use of the road by telling men to love one another, instead of by instituting a rule of the road."[42]

These considerations, according to Dewey, suggest what pacifists must do if they are to be a factor in shaping the future. They must cease their essentially negative role of opposing war at every turn, putting their faith instead in constructive, collective intelligence. They must cooperate with others to create international arrangements and agencies that will reduce the need for war. "Until pacifism puts its faith in constructive, inventive intelligence instead of in appeal to emotions and in exhortation, the disparate unorganized forces of the world will continue to develop outbreaks of violence."[43]

Dewey was particularly interested in the plight of conscientious objectors to war who refused to bear arms against the enemy. He sensed the inner struggle of these youths as they attempted to reconcile the demands of loyalty, service, and unity on the one hand with the dictates of conscience on the other; he believed that "such young people deserve something better than accusations, varying from pro-Germanism and the crime of Socialism to traitorous disloyalty, which the newspapers so readily 'hurl' at them—to borrow their own language."[44] A good practical solution to the problem, Dewey judged, was the Selective Service

Act provision that conscientious objectors when drafted should be given tasks that put least strain on their consciences. "The country ought to be great enough in spirit as it is great enough in men and in the variety of tasks to be performed to make this a matter of course." [45]

But Dewey went on to inquire why so many young men are morally opposed to war. As he saw it, conscientious objectors are the "victims of a moral innocency and an inexpertness which have been engendered by the moral training which they have undergone." This training, Dewey explained, is dominated by the evangelical Protestant tradition which "emphasizes the emotions rather than intelligence, ideals rather than specific purposes, the nurture of personal motives rather than the creation of social agencies and environments." [46] Putting war under the commandment against murder, it teaches that by abstaining from war themselves, by urging others to abstain, and by exhorting peoples and nations to forsake their evil ways and to love one another, people are fulfilling their duties in regard to eliminating war from human existence.

What such an education overlooks, said Dewey, is that war is as much the outgrowth of inadequate international and social mechanisms as it is the product of men's selfish impulses; to abolish war it is as necessary to establish appropriate international agencies as to change men's attitudes. Had pacifist education recognized this truth, it would have instructed youth not simply to oppose and denounce a war already engulfing them but rather to use the war as an occasion for establishing international mechanisms to ward off future wars. "If at a critical juncture," said Dewey, "the moving force of events is always too much for conscience, the remedy is not to deplore the wickedness of those who manipulate events. . . . The remedy is to connect conscience with the forces that are moving in another direction. Then will conscience itself have compulsive power instead of being forever the martyred and the coerced." [47]

Intellectuals who considered Dewey their leader applauded his vigorous defense of those who were denied the exercise of their civil rights. But some of his followers were deeply shocked and disappointed at other stands he took on the war. Perhaps the most articulate of these was Randolph S. Bourne, a brilliant young student of Dewey's at Columbia just a few years before and one of his most devoted followers. Bourne liked particularly Dewey's concern with the needs and well-being of the masses of people and his stress on intelligence, cooperation, and experiment in solving social problems. Instrumentalism more than any other philosophy, Bourne believed, offered the best hope for realizing the American dream.[48] But Bourne was not able to reconcile Dewey's wartime stands with his peacetime philosophy. Dewey's wholehearted approval of America's entry into the war, his readiness to explain if not to condone the various invasions of civil rights, his attacks on the pacifists, and his cavalier treatment of the plight of conscientious objectors seemed to Bourne a betrayal of Dewey's humane instrumentalist philosophy that put him outside the circle of young intellectuals for whom Bourne spoke. "A philosopher who senses so little the sinister forces of war, who is so much more concerned over the excesses of the pacifists than over the excesses of military policy, who can feel only amusement at the idea that any one should try to conscript thought, who assumes that the war-technique can be used without trailing along with it the mob-fanaticisms, the injustices and hatreds that are organically bound up with it, is speaking to another element of the younger intelligentsia than that to which I belong." [49]

Bourne's criticisms seemed to have no immediate effect on Dewey's thinking about the war; but when the war ended and Wilson's war aims were defeated at Versailles, exposing the war as just another imperialist one, Dewey admitted that "the consistent pacifist has much to urge now in his own justification; he is entitled to his flourish of private triumphings." [50] Nevertheless he reaffirmed his earlier position that ideals must be backed by intelligence and force if they are to have any real standing in the world of affairs, declaring that the collapse of Wilson's war aims was really the result of America's failure to use enough force intelligently, especially in the months and weeks preceding our entrance into the war. We foolishly gave the Allies vast amounts of military, financial, and material aid without first requiring that they declare their war aims, publicly and in detail, so that we could determine whether these aims coincided with ours. Our sentimentalism, our naïve faith in the good will of the Allies, our inveterate belief that ideals somehow can and will work themselves out, Dewey declared, had blinded us to the hard realities of nationalist ambitions and international rivalries, to the need of backing our ideals with all our forces. "The ideals of the United States have been defeated in the settlement," Dewey observed, "because we took into the war our sentimentalism, our attachment to moral sentiments as efficacious powers, our pious optimism as to the inevitable victory of the 'right,' our childish belief that physical energy can do the work that only intelligence can do, our evangelical hypocrisy that morals and 'ideals' have a self-propelling and self-executing capacity." He believed it unfair to regard as "a failure of idealism what ought rather to be charged against our own lack of common sense." [51]

A matter that for some years had been troubling Dewey and the teaching profession generally, one that became more urgent under the stresses of war, was the way many schools, colleges, and universities in this country were being administered. Most institutions had no definite, settled rules of procedure concerning the hiring of teachers, their rates of pay, promotion, tenure, and dismissal. Trustees and the school officials representing them ran their institutions as they judged best, without allowing the teachers a decisive voice in the proceedings. This system produced instances of administration that outraged the teaching profession, stirring some of its more articulate members to protest and to agitate for change in the government of educational institutions. Cases often occurred when reactionary or overly conservative trustees wanted to rid their institutions of instructors with ideas and activities distasteful to them. Dewey was in the forefront of those protesting current modes of school and college government; he expressed his opposition on a number of occasions.

One was the case of Scott Nearing at the University of Pennsylvania. On 14 June 1915 the board of trustees of the university refused to reappoint Nearing as assistant professor of economics for the academic year 1915–16. Nearing had been active in behalf of labor unions, antitrust laws, and laws prohibiting child labor. These activities displeased Joseph R. Grundy, an industrialist and powerful political boss. Grundy threatened to use his considerable influence to pressure the Pennsylvania legislature to withhold funds from the university's Wharton School of Business unless the board fired Nearing. Despite the outcry of faculty and public-spirited citizens, the board capitulated to Grundy, denying reappointment to Nearing.[52]

The conservative press applauded this act; the *New York Times,* in an editorial entitled "The Philadelphia Martyr," declared that the trustees, as the legally appointed guardians of the university, had the unquestioned right to fire members of the teaching staff who they believed were injuring the university's good name and that they need give no other reasons for their act.[53]

Dewey, in a letter to the editor, strongly objected to the position taken by the *Times.* The editorial, he wrote, proceeds on the assumption "that a modern university is a personally conducted institution like a factory, and that if for any reason the utterances of any teacher, within or without the university walls, are objectionable to the Trustees, there is nothing more to be said." Such a view, he declared, makes the university a private undertaking and leaves the trustees responsible only to themselves. A more careful reading of the facts reveals something quite different. Modern universities, committed as they are to the pursuit and transmission of truth, are really and essentially public institutions with responsibilities to the public. Those who teach in them are responsible primarily not to their legally established employers but to their "moral employer," which is society as a whole. College and university faculties resent more and more the "arbitrary exercise of a legal right based upon the conception of the relation of a factory employer to his employe." University professors, Dewey emphasized, are not asking for special privileges in speech and discussion under the guise of academic freedom. "They will be content," he said, "for their own protection, with any system which protects the relation of the modern university to the public as a whole." [54]

The dismissal of Cattell and Dana from Columbia gave Dewey another occasion to press the case against prevailing methods of university rule.[55] In an article entitled "The Case of the Professor and the Public Interest," [56] he emphasized that what disturbs the university professor in such instances as those of Nearing, Cattell, and Dana is not the alleged curtailment of their academic freedom, but the procedures used in handling their cases. Referring to the Nearing case, Dewey pointed out that "the condemnation of the Pennsylvania authorities was based essentially upon prosaic details of failure to define grounds, failure to allow a hearing, upon details of time and method of dismissal, with presentment of collateral evidence that these irregularities of procedure were due to unacknowledged objections to the tenor of his economic doctrines. This case affords a reasonably fair symbol of the usual situation." [57] Dewey quoted with approval a statement of President Schurman of Cornell that "the university is an intellectual organization and the American professor wants the government of the university to conform to that essential fact. His indictment of the existing form of government is that it sets up and maintains an alien ideal, the ideal of a business corporation engaging professors as employees and controlling them by means of an absolute and irresponsible authority." [58] If this statement is correct, if university professors are striving to safeguard the university as an intellectual organization and resisting the intrusion of alien and sinister influence into its life, they are working in the public interest and merit the support of the public. "In the end," wrote Dewey, "it is the public, not the teachers nor their legal employers and regulators, whether in the university or in other schools, which will determine the settlement of the issue. It is not too much to say that the final issue is how much the American people cares about the integrity and responsibility of the intellectual life of the nation."[59]

The unsatisfactory situation in colleges and universities had its counterpart in most of the country's public schools. Dewey had occasion to point out that this was certainly true of the public schools of New York City when he spoke in defense of three teachers dismissed from their jobs at the De Witt Clinton High School for "holding views subversive of good discipline and of undermining good citizenship in the schools." Addressing a meeting held to protest this action, Dewey attacked both the charges and the dismissal procedures. The charges, he argued, were so vague and general that they would never stand up in court, and the questioning which preceded the firing was more akin to that of an inquisition than of a fair trial. Anyone studying the case, Dewey said, cannot escape the conclusion that "it is not the teachers who are under indictment; it is the method of administering the public school system of New York City in relation to the teachers."[60]

Dewey also made concrete, practical efforts to win for the members of the teaching profession a more responsible and decisive role in the government of their institutions. In 1913 he had helped the teachers of New York City found the Teachers League of New York. Three years later, in 1916, when members of the league were debating whether to dissolve the league and organize a union, Dewey helped win the case for a New York Teachers Union. A few months later, when the members of the union were divided as to the advisability of joining the American Federation of Teachers, an affiliate of the American Federation of Labor, Dewey urged that the New York union become a part of the general labor movement.

In a talk entitled "Professional Organization of Teachers"[61] at a mass meeting called by the American Federation of Teachers during the National Education Association convention in New York City on 6 July 1916, Dewey pointed out the advantages of membership in a union affiliated with the general labor movement. Such membership, he argued, would raise the general morale of teachers, make them more conscious of their calling, more aware of their responsibilities to each other and to the community, and more confident of their power to get needed things done. Aware that many teachers disliked the thought of becoming identified with the rank and file of labor unions, Dewey deplored the snobbish overtones of this attitude, pointing out to his listeners "that these labor unions are engaged in useful service; that they also are servants of the public" and that no shame attaches to affiliating with them. He reminded his audience that in any past emergency when teachers needed help and support, they had always turned as though instinctively "not to manufacturers' associations and bankers' associations and lawyers' associations, and the so-called respectable elements of the community" but to bodies of organized labor. Dewey also told the teachers that in joining organized labor they would not only integrate the labor movement by bringing brainworkers and handworkers together in the same organization, but they could also provide the insights and intelligence needed to formulate an effective philosophy of the laboring classes. It may be, he said, "that if the more enlightened, more instructed—that is to say, the more lettered portions of the community like the teachers—put themselves fairly and squarely on a level with these other bodies of people who are doing needed and useful service, that they will hasten the time when all of these unions will look at all of their work and labor, not merely from the standpoint of their personal interests and the protection of these personal interests, important as that is; but also from the standpoint of service to the general public." [62]

When the New York Teachers Union joined the American Federation of Labor through its affiliate the American Federation of Teachers, becoming identified as Local No. 5, Dewey became a charter member of the local; for three years he served as its first vice-president.

About the time he was working to organize teachers in the New York City public schools, Dewey was also helping to get under way an organization of university professors. In the spring of 1913, a group of professors at The Johns Hopkins University wrote to selected members of nine other universities inviting them to a meeting to consider forming such an organization.[63] Dewey was one of those invited; at the meeting held in Baltimore on 17 November 1913, he was appointed chairman of a committee to draw up plans of organization. His committee worked at this during most of 1914 and by November was ready with its report. A meeting was then called for 1 and 2 January 1915 at the Chemists' Club in New York City; some two hundred and fifty professors from colleges and universities throughout the country attended.

As chairman of the committee on organization, Dewey called the meeting to order and gave a short introductory address concerning the purposes and possibilities of an association of university professors. The chief point he stressed was that such an association could become the voice of the American university teaching profession just as the American Bar and American Medical Associations were the authentic voices of the legal and medical professions. It could educate the public on the needs and problems of higher education; it could foster public support of faculty attempts to gain a more responsible role in college and university government. Dewey discounted the fear frequently expressed by professors that a national organization of university professors would tend to create a spirit of trade unionism, leading its members to center their efforts on improving the profession's economic and material lot while neglecting the educational side. He declared that such a fear had no solid basis; while the organization would certainly concern itself with the economic well-being of its members, it would work equally to improve higher education and to protect the university from hostile outside influences. Equally unfounded, said Dewey, was the fear that trustees and administrators would not take kindly to such an organization and would penalize faculty members who belonged to it. Dewey believed that authorities, instead of opposing such an organization, would welcome it as providing a way to discuss matters of higher education with a truly representative group of university professors. "I can not believe," Dewey told his colleagues, "that we are fallen so low that association for the purpose of careful investigation and discussion of common educational interests can be interpreted by any right-minded person as a rebellious and mercenary organization." [64] The upshot of the meeting was the establishment of an American Association of University Professors with Dewey as its first president.

His year as president of the association was a busy one for Dewey and for the Committee of Inquiry set up to investigate cases of alleged unfair treatment of faculty members. In addition to the investigations at the University of Pennsylvania in the Scott Nearing case and at Columbia in the dismissal of Cattell and Dana, inquiries were made into cases at the Universities of Utah, Montana, Colorado, and at Wesleyan. At the end of his term of office on 31 December 1915, Dewey addressed the association's first annual meeting in Washington, D.C., summing up the activities of the year. He expressed regret that the Committee of Inquiry had had to spend so much time and energy on cases of alleged unfair treatment of faculty members. But these cases, he declared, had been literally thrust upon the association; its officers had no alternative but to face up to them. "To have failed to meet the demands would have been cowardly; it would have tended to destroy all confidence in the Association as anything more than a talking body." [65]

Dewey continued to be active in the association's affairs, giving his power and prestige to support it throughout subsequent years. Because of this, the association bestowed on him a rarely given honor—honorary life membership.

The attacks on academic freedom and the high-handed manner in which trustees and administration frequently treated faculty members with unpopular views prompted a group of distinguished scholars, mostly at Columbia, to consider founding a center of learning where pressing political, economic, and social problems could be discussed by adult men and women in an atmosphere of genuine freedom, without fear of recrimination. Dewey took a lead in this venture as did Charles Beard, Thorstein Veblen, James Harvey Robinson, Wesley Clair Mitchell, and Alvin Johnson. Herbert Croly, editor of the *New Republic,* was also deeply interested in the idea, and the group frequently met at the *New Republic* offices for their discussions. As plans began to crystallize, the interest and support of some influential civic leaders including Mrs. Thomas W. Lamont, Mrs. George W. Bacon, and Mrs. Learned Hand were enlisted.

As a result of these efforts, the New School for Social Research was founded in 1919 as a small informal center where vital social problems and ways of solving them could be discussed by mature men and women under expert leadership. The school began operation in the spring semester of 1919, providing its first students with an imposing list of lecturers from among its founders and others. The institution was first headed by Robinson and Beard, then, in 1921, by Alvin Johnson. During his term of office for the next quarter of a century, Johnson helped make the school an outstanding center of adult higher education. Dewey gave an occasional course of lectures at the New School during its early years. As one of its founders, he maintained a continuing interest in its growth and development.[66]

Another organization started at this time to which Dewey lent his support was the American Civil Liberties Union. This organization grew out of the National Civil Liberties Bureau, itself the outgrowth of the American Union against Militarism founded in 1916 to keep the United States out of the war in Europe. Leaders of the National Civil Liberties Bureau were deeply concerned about the frequent and widespread violations of the civil rights of those who held unpopular views about the war and social issues; they believed the situation called for an organization whose sole purpose would be the defense of anyone whose civil rights were threatened. They enlisted the aid of about fifty prominent Americans of different political, economic, and social views, including Dewey, Jane Addams, Felix Frankfurter, Clarence Darrow, Roger N. Baldwin, Helen Keller, and Norman Thomas. Together, in 1920, they helped found the American Civil Liberties Union, a nonpartisan, national organization dedicated to defending the rights guaranteed by the Constitution whenever and wherever these rights were violated.[67]

Dewey was a loyal supporter of the union throughout the 1920s; for many of these years he was a member of its National Committee. During the 1930s, however, when Communists infiltrated the organization and disrupted its proceedings, Dewey with a few others resigned from the organization. By a vote of the board in 1940, communists and fellow-travelers with antidemocratic views were denied membership in the union, but Dewey, then in his eighties, did not resume any of his former responsibilities. He did, however, continue to endorse and to support morally the union's main efforts till his death.[68]

Despite his many involvements in nonacademic matters, Dewey kept up his studies in philosophy and education, making notable contributions to each.[69] Of his philosophical writings at this time, two essays reflect particularly interesting developments of Dewey's thought. One is "The Subject-Matter of Metaphysical Inquiry"; [70] the other is the lengthy "Introduction" to the *Essays in Experimental Logic,*[71] a collection of previously published articles.

In his earlier essay entitled "The Postulate of Immediate Empiricism," [72] Dewey had declared that this postulate suggests primarily a methodology. It bids us go to experience to see how the item referred to by a term functions in experience in order to get at the meaning of the term. The postulate is indifferent to metaphysics or ontology; it can offer no "offhand demonstrations of God, freedom, immortality, nor of the exclusive reality of matter, or ideas, or consciousness, etc." [73] Indeed, it is self-contradictory, Dewey had written in another article, for an empirical, functional, instrumentalist philosophy "to set up claims to supplying a metaphysics or ontology." [74] Further deliberations, however, prompted partly by discussions with his colleague F. J. E. Woodbridge, led Dewey to see that strict adherence to empiricism and instrumentalism does not necessarily rule out a metaphysics. It can provide a metaphysics that is itself empirical and analytic and at the same time different from science. In his "The Subject-Matter of Metaphysical Inquiry," he stated the general outlines of such a metaphysics.

Dewey began by pointing out that science deals with the specific traits of the universe. It studies individual causes and effects to discover the particular laws or regularities manifested in the behavior of individual things. But the question can be asked whether the existences studied by science have traits universally and always present irrespective of the particular time and place of their occurrence. That is, would studies of the subject matter of the several sciences reveal certain ultimate traits of existence? If so, could these be appropriate objects of study for a special kind of discipline? Dewey replied to both questions in the affirmative: "In all such investigations as those referred to above we find at least such traits as the following: specifically diverse existences, interaction, change. Such traits are found in any material which is the subject-matter of inquiry in the natural science. They are found equally and indifferently whether a subject-matter in question be dated 1915 or ten million years B.C. Accordingly, they would seem to deserve the name of ultimate, or irreducible, traits. As such they may be made the object of a kind of inquiry differing from that [of science] which deals with the genesis of a particular group of existences, a kind of inquiry to which the name metaphysical may be given."[75] The use of the term "metaphysics" to denote such an inquiry would not be unusual, said Dewey, since it "at least has the sanction of the historical designation given to Aristotle's consideration of existence as existence."[76]

Such a metaphysics, Dewey declared, differs in important ways from traditional metaphysics. First, it abandons as futile and meaningless the search for "ultimate origins and laws of causation with which the 'universe' is supposed to have been endowed at the outset."[77] The only origins and laws it recognizes as meaningful are those with which science concerns itself. It rejects the notion that there was some "absolute original,"[78] radically different from what now exists, declaring that however far back in time we might go, we would always find "the same situation that we have at present: diversity, specificality, change."[79] Thus, while an empirical metaphysics deals with "ultimates," it "frees these traits from confusion with ultimate origins and ultimate ends—that is, from questions of creation and eschatology."[80]

Moreover, a metaphysics dealing with ultimate and irreducible traits repudiates the idea of potentiality as a causal principle.

It rejects the notion of an " 'undifferentiated universe' which, by some immanent potential force, determined everything which has happened since." [81] It rejects potentiality as denoting certain mysterious, inherent powers, replacing it with the notion of potentiality as "a certain limitation of present powers, due to the limited number of conditions with which they are in interaction plus the fact of the manifestation of new powers under different conditions." [82] Taking as an example a decaying apple, Dewey pointed out that "to say that an apple has the potentiality of decay does not mean that it has latent or implicit within it a causal principle which will some time inevitably display itself in producing decay, but that its existing changes (in interaction with its surroundings) will take the form of decay, *if* they are exposed or subjected to certain conditions not now operating upon them." [83]

Also, the metaphysics Dewey was suggesting resists attempts to reduce the universe to one or another kind of being, such as a cosmic mechanism, an absolute life, mind, or consciousness. It accepts the physico-chemical entities of science, declaring that, with certain interactions and changes in arrangement among them, they take on organizations that behave mechanically, vitally, consciously, or intelligently. It admits, therefore, that the universe contains mechanisms and organisms including those with consciousness or mind, but denies that this warrants anyone to claim that the universe as a whole or in some prior, original state was mechanical or vital or sentient or intelligent.[84]

As for evolution, Dewey asserted that it also is one of the irreducible traits of the world because it tells us something ultimate, that is, it is a world in which changes and interactions "in the direction of vital and intelligent organization" can and do take place.[85] This holds true of any matter irrespective of its date. For, Dewey argued, "it is not the matter of 1915, as caused by matter that has now ceased to be, which lives. The matter which was active ten million years ago now lives: this is a feature of the matter of ten million years ago." [86] But, again, this does not justify anyone to conclude that the matter from which life and intelligence emerged was itself "biocentric or vitalistic or psychic." [87]

The "Introduction" to the *Essays in Experimental Logic* gives an account of experience that goes beyond any Dewey had previously given. In his earlier writings he had been especially concerned with refuting the notion that experience is something subjective, psychical, going on exclusively in the mind. In contrast he had argued that for anyone taking seriously the findings of evolutionary biology, experience is "a matter of functions and habits, of active adjustments and re-adjustments, of co-ordinations and activities, rather than of states of consciousness."[88] It is itself a "mode of *existence*," "an act-of-a-certain-specific quality" and "objective."[89] This analysis of experience made the presence of an organism essential to its occurrence; it also made experience a factor within and continuous with nature.

In his "Introduction," however, Dewey gave an interpretation in which experience and nature tend to merge. So intent was he on making experience objective that he ended with a conception of experience that seemed to his critics to make it identical with nature. For Dewey now argued that the factors making up an environment on the one hand and the desires and interests that attach to an organism on the other, can be extended indefinitely till both organism and environment are lost in what he called "experience." To illustrate, he described a person using a typewriter:

> The word which I have just written is momentarily focal; around it there shade off into vagueness my typewriter, the desk, the room, the building, the campus, the town, and so on. *In* the experience, and in it in such a way as to *qualify* even what is shiningly apparent, are all the physical features of the environment extending out into space no one can say how far, and all the habits and interests extending backward and forward in time, of the organism which uses the typewriter and which notes the written form of the word only as temporary focus in a vast and changing scene.[90]

In this scene, Dewey also said experience as conscious "is only a very small and shifting portion of experience."[91]

This account of experience seemed to many of Dewey's readers clearly to identify it with nature. For here the term "experience" is applicable to virtually everything to which terms such as "nature," "world," "universe," "existence" have traditionally been applied. This being the case, the question arises as to why the term "experience" should enter into one's discourse at all. Dewey's reply was that the term "experience" suggests something indispensable, something the other terms do not express, namely, "an actual focusing of the world at one point in a focus of immediate shining apparency."[92] The term "experience" indicates that something here and now attracts, repels, interests, frightens, satisfies, etc.

Explaining how and why the term "experience" came into use, Dewey declared that it was a way "to refer peremptorily to what is indicated in only a roundabout and divided way by such terms as 'organism' and 'environment,' 'subject' and 'object,' 'persons' and 'things,' 'mind' and 'nature,' and so on."[93] But if this is so, said his critics, experience is the more inclusive term, and, instead of experience being a factor or "mode of existence" in nature, "nature," "world," "environment," are factors within experience.

Dewey's writings on education included articles on such subjects as industrial education, the teaching of science, educational ideals in wartime, American education and culture, education for democracy, as well as a revised edition of *The School and Society*.[94] But, in addition, two books on education are worthy of special note. One, written in collaboration with his daughter Evelyn, was entitled *Schools of To-morrow*.[95] The other was *Democracy and Education*,[96] one of Dewey's best known and most highly regarded books.

Schools of To-morrow combines an exposition of the principles underlying an education based on the child's natural growth with a description of some schools where these principles are put into practice. The exposition of principles, written by Dewey, uses the doctrines of such persons as Rousseau, Pestalozzi, Froebel, and Montessori as foils in the development of his own views. The description of schools, written mostly by Miss Dewey, details the different methods used by several schools to make education fit the growing child's needs and interests. Programs of more than a dozen schools in different parts of the country are described, including such outstanding ones as the Fairhope School in Fairhope, Alabama,[97] the public schools of Gary, Indiana, and the kindergarten at Teachers College at Columbia.

Schools of To-morrow won wide praise from progressive educators, one reviewer declaring that "a better or more convincing presentation of the new spirit in education could not well be made. I regard the appearance of this book as the most significant educational event of the year.[98]

Dewey undertook in *Democracy and Education* to state the kind of education required by a twentieth-century democratic society, as suggested by the findings of the biological and psychological sciences. The discussion brings to a focus the several aspects of Dewey's philosophy so that, as he remarked some years later, the book was "for many years that in which my philosophy, such as it is, was most fully expounded." [99] This accounts for the familiar ring of much of the book as well as for one reviewer's hailing it as a book with not only insights for the progressive educator but also with "that wisdom which democracies need, the common wisdom which must lie beneath the diverse activities of all the professions." [100]

Dewey began his discussion by pointing out that education is the means by which new meanings are discovered and old ones renewed and transmitted through communication—communication being a process of "sharing experience till it becomes a common possession." [101] Education, therefore, can be defined as growth—growth toward more and better shared experience, with "no end beyond itself." [102] Put in technical terms, education is "that reconstruction or reorganization of experience which adds to the meaning of experience, and which increases ability to direct the course of subsequent experience." [103] Because a democratic society allows the individual to develop and entertain a wide diversity of interests and helps him to communicate his experience by removing barriers separating individuals and groups, it is the form of society in which education can best flourish, the one in which the individual is most likely to attain his highest and fullest stature as a human being.

In working out the details of the education best suited for a democratic society and most in keeping with the results of modern science, Dewey made generous use of ideas previously developed. Among the more important of these are: education in the school must be continuous with the child's experience outside of the school; subject matter should center on the current interests of the child, not on the adult he will eventually be; as the child's interests grow and expand under the guidance of the teacher, subject matter must widen and deepen; since learning and doing, theory and practice develop together, opportunity should be provided in the classroom for projects and activities in which the child's ideas can be tested; vocational subjects have potential cultural meanings that should be brought out; the significance of the natural sciences for human life should be made clear to the child; the school or classroom should be organized as a cooperative community so that the child can develop the attitudes and dispositions necessary for a responsible member of a democratic society; interest in subject matter and in the success of the class project should bring about the effort and discipline characteristic of a well-ordered, effective classroom.

The assumption underlying this theory of education, said Dewey, is that of continuity—an assumption that rejects dualisms such as man and nature, mind and body, theory and practice, the individual and society, leisure and work, etc., accepting instead their continuity, interdependence, and organic relationships. These dualisms developed at a time when society was divided into classes like rich and poor, noble and baseborn, ruler and ruled, people of leisure and people who worked. These divisions and antitheses were carried over into the educational system where they left their mark, a "setting up of different types of life-experience, each with isolated subject matter, aim, and standard of values" so that "the scheme of education, taken as a whole, is a deposit of various purposes and procedures." [104] Continuity, in contrast, gets its cue both from modern science, which sees things as continuous and organically related, and from the democratic movement, which views individuals as organically related, affecting each other.

Dewey attacked all dualisms in education but especially that of culture and utility. From the perspective of a democratic society, this dualism is "probably the most fundamental." For where it prevails, the danger always exists that children of the cultured, leisured, upper classes will have a liberal education and those belonging to the laboring masses a vocational education. Such an arrangement establishes and fixes class distinctions, thus striking at the heart of a democratic society. "The problem of education in a democratic society," said Dewey, "is to do away with the dualism and to construct a course of studies which makes thought a guide of free practice for all and which makes leisure a reward of accepting responsibility for service, rather than a state of exemption from it." [105]

Dewey's purpose in chapter 24 of *Democracy and Education* was "to extract and make explicit the idea of philosophy implicit in these considerations"; [106] he reached the conclusion, startling to his philosophical colleagues, that philosophy is essentially "the general theory of education." [107] He arrived at this conclusion by arguing that all philosophy is at bottom social philosophy and all social philosophy is at bottom philosophy of education.

Dewey's contention was that philosophy, like all other forms of reflective thinking, has its origin in situations that are uncertain and problematic. What distinguishes philosophical thinking is that "the uncertainties with which it deals are found in widespread social conditions and aims, consisting in a conflict of organized interests and institutional claims." [108] Philosophy seeks to determine the basic issues underlying surface conflicts and to suggest ways of overcoming the conflicts. Its inquiries into nature and human nature, into metaphysics, epistemology, and theory of value are undertaken, at least originally, with the hope of getting insights to help solve social problems. Plato's *Republic,* as Dewey pointed out elsewhere, is perhaps the most illustrious example of this fact.[109] Therefore, "if we are willing to conceive education as the process of forming fundamental dispositions, intellectual and emotional, toward nature and fellow men, philosophy may even be defined *as the general theory of education.*" [110]

Democracy and Education almost immediately became a best

seller among professional educators. Before long it was widely regarded as a classic in the literature of philosophy of education. One reviewer judged it to be on a par with Plato's *Republic* and Rousseau's *Emile,* the three representing "epochal stages" in the history of philosophy of education.[111] As the book's reputation spread, it was translated into many languages, among these being Arabic, Chinese, German, Italian, Japanese, Persian, Portuguese, Spanish, Swedish, and Turkish.

Dewey's frequent and continuous contributions to the *New Republic*[112] led many readers to believe he had some official connection with the magazine; some of his friends began to send him manuscripts of articles to be considered for inclusion in the *New Republic.* But, as Dewey explained to a friend who queried him on this: "I have no editorial relationship to the New Republic, and have to be rather careful about acting as a medium of transmission."[113] A business arrangement, however, did exist. According to Bruce Bliven who joined the *New Republic* in 1923 and became its leading editor in 1930, "Instead of paying him for each article, as is usual, we put him on the regular payroll for some modest sum like $50 a week, and he wrote an article for us at irregular intervals whenever he felt he had something to say." Bliven went on to remark: "I remember him as a model contributor. As you know, he had a difficult style, involved and tortuous, and he needed very heavy editing, and sometimes complete rewriting, to meet the standards of magazine journalism. Never once, so far as I remember, did he complain of a single change, or make any alterations on proof. This was in marked contrast to some other contributors I could name, who also wrote badly, but would not permit a word to be changed."[114]

Despite his busy schedule of teaching, study, writing, and sundry other activities, Dewey found time to address organizations requesting his presence—usually in New York, but occasionally at a considerable distance from the city. As already noted, in February 1915 he gave three lectures at the University of North Carolina on German philosophy and politics. On 30 December of the same year, he read the paper discussed earlier (143), "The Need of an Industrial Education in an Industrial Society," at George Washington University in Washington, D.C.[115] Seven months later, on 7 July 1916, he addressed the National Education Association at its fifty-fourth annual meeting in Madison Square Garden, New York, selecting as his topic, "Nationalizing Education."[116] On 28 December 1916, when the American Psychological Association celebrated in New York the twenty-fifth anniversary of its founding, Dewey read a paper on "The

Need for Social Psychology." [117] At the annual meeting of the Public Education Association in the Biltmore Hotel in New York on 20 February 1917, he spoke again on vocational education, this time on the topic: "Learning to Earn: The Place of Vocational Education in a Comprehensive Scheme of Public Education." [118] The following month he spoke to the Conference on Child Labor at its Thirteenth Annual Conference in Baltimore, choosing as his subject "Federal Aid to Elementary Education." [119] That vocational education was a matter in which Dewey continued to be deeply interested is attested by still another talk on this topic, delivered on 25 January 1918 in Chicago to the Vocational Education Association of the Middle West, with the title "Vocational Education in the Light of the World War." [120] One week later, on 3 February 1918, he addressed the Detroit Open Forum on "Education for Democracy." Some three weeks later, on Washington's birthday, he delivered an address at Smith College on "America in the World." [121]

Dewey was in his late fifties during the years of World War I; his active and strenuous life began to take its toll in the form of physical and nervous tensions. Long hours at his desk produced stiffness and soreness in the muscles and ligaments of his neck and upper shoulders, also affecting his eyes. From friends he learned of Dr. F. Matthias Alexander from Australia, who had an unusual and interesting theory as to the cause of most of contemporary man's ailments and a technique for treating them. Alexander contended that most of civilized man's ills came when the development of man's body failed to keep pace with that of his brain and nervous system. Man's brain and nervous system developed rapidly in exceedingly complex ways under the stresses of expanding and intricate physical, social, and cultural environments. His body, on the other hand, remained very much as it had been when it served a much less developed and less complicated brain and nervous system. Consequently, civilized man's brain and nervous system have had to get along with a body not adequately designed to serve them. The result has been nervous breakdowns, emotional instabilities, and physical and mental exhaustions. To correct this state of affairs, Alexander declared, man must consciously undertake to change or modify his bodily activities, including his postural habits and muscular controls, to better serve the needs and requirements of a brain and nervous system coping with a highly complex civilized culture.

Despite the low esteem in which the theories of Alexander were held by members of the medical and related professions, Dewey was sufficiently intrigued by the doctrines to become

Alexander's patient. His relations with Alexander were friendly, cordial, and helpful. When Alexander set forth his views in a book entitled *Man's Supreme Inheritance: Conscious Guidance and Control in Relation to Human Evolution in Civilization,*[122] he asked Dewey to write an introduction to it, which Dewey did, declaring that as regards Alexander's technique for treating his patients, he could testify to "the efficacy of its working in concrete cases."[123] Dewey acknowledged elsewhere that contact with Alexander influenced "my theories of mind-body, of the coördination of the active elements of the self and of the place of ideas in inhibition and control of overt action."[124]

Throughout the war years, Dewey maintained a strong interest in the peace that would follow the end of the war in Europe. As early as September 1917 he had cautioned against a peace treaty designed exclusively to punish Germany and to exact "justice" from her. In an article entitled "Fiat Justitia, Ruat Cœlum," he had written, "How often is it argued that 'justice' demands this or that, while the terms of an enduring peace are under consideration, when the context makes it clear that justice means taking it out on Germany as the chief offender, irrespective of the influence upon the future of the punishment inflicted. . . . It is not sentimental pity for Germany but a wise self-interest which dictates that a pragmatic regard for the future and not a passion for abstract justice shall control discussion of the aims of war and the terms of peace."[125]

When President Wilson announced his famous Fourteen Points to a joint session of Congress on 8 January 1918, Dewey's thinking became more definitely focused. Among the points mentioned by Wilson were open diplomacy, freedom of the seas, the elimination of trade barriers, the reduction of armaments, the adjustment of international boundaries according to the principle of self-determination of the peoples affected, and an "association of nations" designed to provide "mutual guarantees of political independence and territorial integrity to great and small nations alike."[126]

Dewey was in complete accord with Wilson's stand, especially in regard to a league of nations. He was convinced that the fourteen conditions of peace set forth by Wilson "cannot be effectually realized in detail without the continuing support of an international organization which shall be administrative in character, and not merely judicial."[127] In a series of four articles in the *Dial,* Dewey undertook to explain the nature of such a league and its implications for future international relations.[128]

Dewey argued that the kind of league implied in Wilson's

Fourteen Points is one that focuses on the modern world of industry and commerce, that asks how this world can be organized to serve best the urgent economic needs and wants of the peoples of the world. This sort of league, he declared, is in marked contrast to the traditional conception of a league that centers attention primarily on political and military arrangements and seeks "to enforce peace by an extension of legal mechanisms of controversy and litigation." [129] Such a league, said Dewey, might endure during periods of recuperation and quiescence, but would surely collapse when challenged by a powerful nation or group of nations intent on expansion or on a redistribution of the centers of power. "But an organization of nations which grew out of common everyday necessities, and which operated to meet the commonplace needs of everyday life with respect to food, labor, securing raw materials for the reparation of a devastated world, and so on—an organization which grew out of wants and met them would, once formed, speedily become so indispensable no one could imagine the world getting on without it." [130] And, once in operation, such an organization of nations would generate the legal and political mechanisms needed to handle controversies and conflicts of interests. Dewey was convinced that "the hopeful approach to a concert of nations is along the economic road which aims to further common interests, rather than by the negative and legal road which contents itself with litigation and the adjudication of disputes." [131]

Dewey declared that a league of nations taking the economic approach to international problems requires a new type of diplomacy to function effectively. This new diplomacy would transfer management of international affairs from career diplomats interested and trained primarily in political and military matters, drawn mostly from the aristocratic and ruling classes, to international administrative commissions with members trained and skilled in the areas of production and distribution of goods, international trade and finance, commerce, industry, etc. Whereas the old diplomacy gave priority to the "ethics of honor and dignity, the idealization of their assertion and defense . . . in all that concerns the relationships of states to one another," the new diplomacy would emphasize the "ethics of industry and of reciprocal contractual service" and would aim at providing the economic base for the material and spiritual well-being of the peoples of the world.[132]

Dewey admitted that the problems confronting such a new diplomacy would be complex and difficult. But he insisted that they were not insurmountable. The successful prosecution of the war, he said, showed what can be done when men skilled in different fields cooperate in a cause in which they have faith and to which they are sincerely devoted. The successful prosecution of peace after the war would be similar. "The resources and abilities are at hand, if we choose to use them. The question is as to the depth and endurance of our desire." [133]

By late summer of 1918 it was obvious that Germany was losing the war; in August General Ludendorff so informed Emperor William II. In October Germany announced willingness to accept Wilson's peace terms, and on 11 November 1918 an armistice halted the fighting. On 18 January 1919 the Peace Conference officially opened at Versailles; on 28 June 1919 the Treaty of Versailles was signed. In the peace negotiations, Wilson succeeded in getting a covenant for a League of Nations included in the settlement. However, he was not able to prevent the Allied Powers from imposing on Germany unusually harsh terms, boding ill for future world peace. The German nation was deprived of its overseas possessions; it was forced to pay crushing reparations; and it lost large areas of its national territory in Europe in the readjustment of national boundaries on that continent.

When the terms of the treaty became known in this country, general disillusionment set in. The feeling spread that the war the American people had been led to believe was good had been just another imperialist war, that the terms of the peace treaty followed the traditional pattern of awarding the spoils to the victors.

Dewey shared the general disillusionment; he joined other intellectuals in denouncing the treaty as too vindictive, as not taking sufficiently into account the bearings of its terms on future peace. He referred to the "iniquities" in the treaty, declaring that "when the war aims were gained, the peace aims were lost." [134] He believed that "quite probably it is fortunate for us that nationalistic ambitions and imperialistic aggressions were so undisguisedly powerful in the peace negotiations. We owe monuments to Clemenceau, Sonnino and Balfour. Probably in our excited idealism nothing less flagrant than the exhibition they gave could have averted our becoming innocent and ignorant accomplices in the old world game of diplomacy. As it was, the contrast between prior professions and actual deeds was so obvious as to evoke revulsion." [135]

The United States refused to be a party to the treaty. During the next few years Congress debated the terms of separate peace treaties with the several enemy countries. It also debated whether the United States should join the League of Nations as set up in the Treaty of Versailles, a debate joined by others. Among intellectuals many argued that the United States should become a member of the league because it seemed to be the only hope for an eventually peaceful world. Other intellectuals opposed America's participation in the league because it seemed nothing more than a device to perpetuate the old imperialist order. When President Wilson toured the country in September 1919 to win support for the league, these liberals, along with formerly favorable magazines such as the *New Republic* and the *Nation,* opposed him.

Dewey was opposed to America's entry into the league, but as he was in the Far East from 1919 to 1921, not until his return to this country did he publicly express his views.

10. The Far East, 1919–1921

ON SABBATICAL leave from Columbia University during the academic year 1918–19, Dewey spent the first half of the winter lecturing at the University of California. As his duties there neared an end, he and Mrs. Dewey made arrangements for a trip to Japan. He explained in a letter to a friend, "Mrs. Dewey and I have decided that we may never again get as near Japan as we are now and that as the years are passing, it is now or never with us. Consequently we have sent for passports and tentatively engaged berths for Jan. 22nd."[1]

When word reached Japan that Dewey was about to visit that country, plans were immediately made for him to lecture at the Imperial University in Tokyo. The leader in this planning was Dr. Ono Eijiro who some years before had received a Ph.D. degree in political science at the University of Michigan where he had met Dewey. After teaching a few years at one of the universities in Japan, Ono had left the academic world in 1896 for banking, where he was highly successful. At the time of Dewey's visit he was vice-governor of the Industrial Bank of Japan.

Ono, desiring help in financing a lectureship for Dewey, turned to Baron Shibusawa Eiichi, one of the most prominent men in Japanese financial and philanthropic circles. The Baron had made trips to the United States in 1902, 1910, and in 1915 to study American business and banking techniques, many of which he had then introduced into the Japanese economy. Shibusawa, eighty-three at the time of Dewey's visit, had retired from business but had kept up his philanthropic and humanitarian activities; he readily agreed to help underwrite the Dewey venture. Thus, with the hearty endorsement of authorities at Imperial University, Ono cabled Dewey in San Francisco inviting him to lecture at Imperial University in Tokyo. Dewey accepted the invitation with pleasure both because of the financial arrangements involved and because, as he wrote, it "ought to be helpful in getting us into closer relations with things than might otherwise be the case." [2]

The Deweys sailed from San Francisco as planned on 22 January 1919 on the Japanese liner *Shunyu Maru.* During the voyage of two and one-half weeks, Dewey had ample time to converse with the Japanese passengers, particularly with a group of returning Japanese school principals who had just finished a tour of elementary schools in the United States. On 9 February at 11:00 A.M., the *Shunyu Maru* reached Yokohama Harbor, where it docked only after some hours delay because of heavy snows. Photographers, newsmen, and selected individuals came aboard to meet the more prominent and publicized passengers. Dr. Ono, Professor Anezaki Masaharu, who was to be Dewey's official host at Imperial University, and Professor Tomoeda Takahiko, professor of ethics at the university, boarded the ship to welcome the Deweys to Japan.

The Deweys were at once approached by reporters requesting pictures and statements. Dewey posed in turn with Mrs. Dewey, with Professors Anezaki and Tomoeda, and with the group of returning school principals. Asked for a statement, Dewey replied that he and Mrs. Dewey were pleased to be in Japan, that a sizeable number of his former Japanese students were now in Japan, and that he and Mrs. Dewey planned to be in Japan about five months. He said that he had had some very worthwhile talks with the school principals and that he himself hoped to give special attention to Japanese elementary and secondary schools. He stated further that he wanted very much to talk with Japanese leaders on matters of domestic and international importance and to report his findings in the *New Republic* and *Dial.* In reply to a question about the general topic of his lectures at Imperial University, Dewey said he had not definitely decided on this, but had left the matter open till he had conferred with the people at the university. After finishing with the newsmen, the Deweys left for their hotel in Tokyo.[3]

The Deweys were at the Imperial Hotel about a week when they were invited to use a suite of rooms in the home of their long-time friends, Dr. and Mrs. Nitobe Inazo. Mrs. Nitobe was a native American who had been brought up in the Quaker tradition. Her husband, some four years younger than Dewey, had studied in both Germany and the United States; it was while he and Mrs. Nitobe were in New York that they came to know the Deweys. Dr. Nitobe, who had attained prominence both as an author and educator, was at this time president of the Japanese Christian College.

That the Deweys were pleased with their new quarters is evident in Mrs. Dewey's letter to their children: "Here we are, one week after landing, on a hill in a beautiful garden of trees on which the buds are already swelling. The plums will soon be in bloom, and in March the camellias, which grow to fairly large trees. In the distance we see the wonderful Fuji, nearby the other hills of this district, and the further plains of the city. Just at the foot of our hill is a canal, along which is an alley of cherry trees formerly famous, but largely destroyed by a storm a few years ago." Referring to the rooms, Mrs. Dewey said: "We have a wonderful apartment to ourselves, mostly all windows, which in this house are glass. A very large bedroom, a small dressing room, and a study where I now sit with the sun coming in the windows which are all its sides. . . . We are surrounded by all the books on Japan that modern learning has produced, so we have never a waiting moment." [4]

After conferring with the members of the Department of Philosophy at Imperial University, Dewey chose as the overall subject of his talks "The Position of Philosophy at the Present: —Problems of Philosophic Reconstruction." The plan was for a series of eight public lectures at 3:30 on Tuesday and Friday afternoons, beginning Tuesday, 25 February and ending Friday, 21 March 1919. As eventually worked out, the program was:

Tuesday, 25 February: Conflicting Ideas as to the Meaning of Philosophy.

Friday, 28 February: Knowledge as Contemplative and Active.

Tuesday, 4 March: Social Causes of Philosophic Reconstruction.

Friday, 7 March: Modern Science and Philosophic Reconstruction.

Tuesday, 11 March: The Changed Conception of Experience and Reason.

Friday, 14 March: The Reconstruction as Affecting Logic.

Tuesday, 18 March: The Reconstruction as Affecting Ethics and Education.

Friday, 21 March: Reconstruction as Affecting Social Philosophy.

Dewey prepared a syllabus for each lecture with a short list of readings for listeners who desired to delve further into the subject matter of the lectures.[5]

The lectures were given in a large room in the Law Building

of the university. Dewey's fame and the publicity given the lectures drew an audience for the first lecture of around one thousand—mostly professors and students of the several normal schools, colleges, and universities in and around Tokyo, with a sizeable sprinkling of non-Japanese men and women. The press reported that the talk was very well received and that the series of lectures was off to an auspicious start.[6]

The audiences continued to be of respectable size during the first part of the series; on 5 March Dewey wrote home: "I have now given three lectures. They are a patient race; there is still a good-sized audience, probably five hundred."[7] But as the lectures continued, the attendance dwindled until toward the end only thirty to forty people were present to hear him.[8]

Dewey said that his purpose in the lectures was "to set forth the forces which make intellectual reconstruction inevitable and to prefigure some of the lines upon which it must proceed."[9] In keeping with this aim, he first pointed out that traditional philosophy has always been concerned with justifying certain fixed moral, social, and religious values, relying primarily on reason and proof to do this; it has argued in favor of some absolute or transcendent reality to guarantee perpetuation of these values. The emergence of modern science, technology, and industrialization, and the political and social trends toward democracy have led men to think along new lines. They are now concerned with what is specific, concrete, and undergoing change rather than with the universal, changeless, and eternal; they rely less on the pronouncements of traditional authorities for truth and more on the power of individual minds trained and disciplined in the methods of science; they entertain the idea of progress and stress the future rather than some allegedly golden age of the past; they believe that knowledge of nature brings control over her and that this is the path by which progress is to be achieved.

Dewey went on to say that philosophy needs to be reconstructed and oriented to these new trends in contemporary life. As a first step, he examined the traditional philosophical antithesis of experience and reason, concluding that the antithesis is false because reason and experience come together and cooperate in intelligent inquiry. He examined next the traditional opposition between the real and the ideal, declaring that instead of their being opposed or inhabiting different realms, the ideal is simply the real developed and elevated to its higher or ideal dimensions under the guidance of creative intelligence. In spelling out the needed reconstruction in logic, Dewey gave an account of the logic of experimental inquiry. In detailing the reconstruction needed in moral and social thinking, he emphasized that concern with specific, concrete moral and social problems and their practical solution through collective thinking must replace interest in abstract moral and social concepts and their rational systematization.

Though Dewey rarely used the term "pragmatism" or "instrumentalism," trying to avoid "a partisan plea in behalf of any one specific solution of these problems,"[10] his talks reflected his philosophical bias. Thus, when the lectures appeared in book form in the United States under the title *Reconstruction in Philosophy,* reviewers hailed it as an excellent summation of Dewey's own philosophy.

Dewey's lectures had little lasting appeal for most of the professional philosophers of Japan,[11] particularly the older men. Conditioned by German philosophy, these thinkers preferred the rationalistic, absolutistic, and systematic philosophies to the more empirical, concrete, and practical doctrines of Dewey and the pragmatists.[12]

But Dewey was not without followers in Japan. Some were men who had taken courses under him in America. Others had been won over to his philosophy through a study of his works. Waseda University in Tokyo was a center of Deweyan learning. Included in the "Waseda Group" were Tanaka Odo, Hoashi Riichiro, and Tasei Saju. Tanaka, following Dewey, urged that philosophy forsake its academic ways and become involved in the affairs of men. Hoashi's *Reconstruction in Education,* published in 1929, showed strong traces of Dewey's influence. Tasei's translations of Dewey's *Democracy and Education* in 1918, *Schools of To-morrow* in 1920, and *School and Society* in 1923 reflect his interest in Dewey's philosophy of education.[13]

Japanese philosophy students took advantage of Dewey's presence in their country to interview him. Nagano Yoshio was one of these. Then a student at Imperial University, Nagano eventually became one of the most productive and influential of Japanese Deweyan scholars and one of the founders in 1957 of the John Dewey Society of Japan.[14] Okabe Yataro, whose uncle had known Dewey at the University of Chicago, also had an interview. During this conversation, Dewey pointed out the great need in Japan for more work in educational psychology. Impressed by Dewey's remarks, Okabe turned to educational psychology and became an outstanding Japanese authority in the field. Okabe later declared that this meeting had marked the turning point in his life.[15]

Thus there were in Japan a number of devoted adherents to

Dewey's philosophy, especially his philosophy of education. After World War II, when the occupational forces under General MacArthur took over control of Japan, these men played an important role in putting the educational system of Japan on a modern, democratic basis along lines suggested by Dewey's philosophy.

Outside the academic world, the aspect of Japanese life that immediately caught Dewey's attention was the widespread affirmation of political and social liberalism. "Liberalism is in the air," he wrote,[16] "and everyone is talking 'De-mo-kras-ie'."[17] The defeat of Germany, Dewey learned, was mainly responsible for this. Long regarded by the ruling classes as the model state, Germany's defeat had thoroughly discredited the militarist and bureaucratic party. With the collapse of Germany, "it became possible, almost popular, to say out loud what liberals had been saying quietly and steadily in the class room, or in the public press in language sufficiently veiled to pass the eye of the police."[18]

The home of liberalism Dewey found to be the universities. Even Imperial University, long regarded as the citadel of conservatism and reactionism, was now harboring liberal thinkers; one report declared that the majority of the members of the Faculty of Political Science were active liberals[19] and another that many members of the university's faculty were "the most active members of a society called The Dawn, which is openly carrying on propaganda by public lectures for democratic ideas." Similarly, students throughout Japan were becoming "infected with radical ideas." At Imperial University a group of them were publishing a liberal journal called *Democracy.* In fact, Dewey learned that "magazines with titles like *Reconstruction, The New Society,* are born almost every month."[20]

Political liberalism in Japan had to be satisfied with limited objectives; it was difficult, Dewey found, to imagine "a coherent and unswerving working policy for a truly liberal political party in that country."[21] Political opportunism was the only workable policy for liberals. Business and military interests were so powerfully entrenched in government that these two groups could be said to constitute the state. Bolstering this power was the myth, taught in all the schools, that the Emperor as "Son of Heaven" was the supreme ruler to whom the people owed unquestioning obedience. Since as a matter of fact the Emperor was mostly a figurehead, "this permeating religious sanction accrues to the benefit of the bureaucracy that actually runs things."[22] Thus, unless liberals wanted to risk religious and social upheaval, they had to be content with the form of government as it was, while working for increased representation of the people within that government. "The extension of the suffrage," the Deweys found, "is the great question under discussion at present."[23]

The "fusion in the popular mind of political with religious and theocratic ideas"[24] was a severe handicap to liberals working on the international front, for it was used by the bureaucracy to support its claim that Japan had a divine mission in Asia, especially in China, and that those who opposed Japan's aggressive and military policies in Asia were opposing God as well as country. Thus, though liberals in general were critical of Japanese militarism and imperialism, they could do little without arousing a hostile public opinion.

One matter of foreign policy on which liberals and reactionaries agreed was the elimination of race discrimination among the nations of the West. Long incensed over America's oriental exclusion acts, Japanese liberals and conservatives alike urged their annulment, pleading for a clause in the Covenant of the League of Nations to prohibit the practice. Dewey favored such a clause, pointing out that when the Peace Conference at Versailles failed to include such a clause, liberalism in Japan suffered a severe setback. Reactionaries could now argue that Wilson's idealistic and liberal war aims were "merely disguises behind which materialistic America was hiding her commercial and territorial ambitions in China, Siberia, and other parts of the world" and that the League of Nations was simply a "scheme of Anglo-American capitalism to dominate the world without the trouble and expense of maintaining an army."[25]

Economic liberalism in Japan was stimulated by the enormous industrial expansion caused by the war. This industrialization, Dewey found, sharpened the division of economic classes. "The Marxian division into the proletariat and the millionaire," he wrote, "is rapidly going on";[26] in intellectual circles the question currently debated was "whether Japan must in its economic development pass through the stage of antagonism of capital and labor characteristic of Western development."[27] One school of thought, taking as its point of departure the "principle of 'kindness'," maintained that such an antagonism is neither inevitable nor necessary. Members of this school, representing the old Confucianist oligarchy, held that the feudal principle of master and man, of protection and dependence, could be carried over into the modern relation of employer and employee. Such industrial paternalism would include not only decent treatment of employees but also health and unemployment insurance, suitable housing and recreation facilities. Another group rejected this doctrine as essentially a relic of the past, bound to fail because it placed too great a dependence on the good will of the employer. Appealing to the "principle of 'rights'," these intellectuals declared that workers have rights as human beings and must organize to win for themselves the rights to which they are morally entitled.

Though liberalism in Japan had made "a mighty forward leap—so mighty as to be almost unbelievable," [28] Dewey believed its immediate outcome was still in doubt, "that however, a party still entrenched in education, the army, and the civil service should be so completely discredited as to surrender without a struggle does not seem probable." [29] Also, every move away from democratic ideals in other countries, such as the refusal to abolish racial discrimination and the continued exploitation of backward peoples by imperialist countries, set back the liberal movement in Japan as elsewhere. "But unless the world overtly and on a large scale goes back on democracy," said Dewey, "Japan will move steadily towards democracy." [30]

Dewey wanted while he was in Japan to study its primary and secondary schools. What he found was not reassuring for the liberal cause. He saw much in the way of learning by doing, but he also found heavy stress on the emperor-cult and its values. The younger children, he learned, accepted the myths about the Emperor as literally true; the older ones accepted them—if not intellectually then at least emotionally and practically till they became "a part of the sub-conscious mental apparatus of all the pupils." [31] As for the teachers, Dewey found that "it would be worth any teacher's position for him to question any of their patriotic legends in print." [32] Teachers in the public schools, he was told, were perhaps the most fanatical patriots in the country. "More than one has been burned or allowed the children to be burned while he rescued the portrait of the Emperor when there was a fire." [33]

Though Dewey was usually the center of attention, Mrs. Dewey was by no means overlooked. The publicity given Dewey in the press often included statements about her and her contributions to elementary education in the United States.[34] Women intellectuals, eager to learn her views on public matters relating to women, arranged in March a question-and-answer meeting with her in Tokyo.

One question put to Mrs. Dewey concerned woman suffrage, an issue agitating women in liberal Japanese intellectual circles. Mrs. Dewey, who had been active in the woman suffrage movement in New York, argued that since women were as intelligent and emotionally stable as men, they could be depended upon to do at least as well as men in voting. Another question related to the education of girls. In her reply, Mrs. Dewey pointed out that inasmuch as girls have the same native intelligence as boys, any society that refuses to give its girls the educational opportunities it gives boys is depriving itself of the contributions that one-half the population could make to the economic, social, and cultural life of the people. Asked her opinion on licensed prostitution in Japan, Mrs. Dewey declared that it was more to the point to educate young girls, preparing them for some socially approved and worthwhile work, than futilely to deplore the existing evil state of affairs.[35]

Despite his busy schedule of preparing and delivering his lectures, Dewey and Mrs. Dewey managed to crowd a wide variety of experiences into their three-months stay in Japan. Their letters home refer to the theaters, museums, temples, shrines, and schools they visited. They mention the several festivals, the Geisha and garden parties to which their friends took them, and the Japanese style meals in the homes of their Japanese friends as well as in the restaurants. And Mrs. Dewey wrote about the shops and department stores where they stopped to make purchases.

The Deweys liked to mix with the crowds on the streets; Dewey noted especially the children in their bright kimonos and the almost complete absence of bullying and quarreling among them.[36] Both were impressed by the universal courtesy and politeness they encountered. "Whatever else you think about the Japanese," wrote Dewey, "they are about the most highly civilized people on earth, perhaps overcultivated." [37]

Upon completing the lectures at Imperial University, the Deweys left Tokyo for Kyoto and Osaka. In each of these cities Dewey gave talks to teachers and university groups; after the lectures they were elaborately entertained at dinners by city and university officials.[38]

The Japanese government publicly recognized Dewey's visit when the Emperor announced he intended to confer on Dewey the "Order of the Rising Sun." This was being done, according to the announcement, both to honor Dewey as a scholar and to promote friendly relations between the United States and Japan.[39] Dewey, however, declined to accept the honor because for him it carried certain undemocratic connotations he disliked.[40]

The Deweys' stay in the Far East was unexpectedly extended when Dewey, while still in Japan, received an invitation to lecture at the National University in Peking during the academic year 1919–20, his duties to begin in June 1919 and end in March 1920. The invitation was the result of the efforts of some former Chinese students of Dewey who believed that he could make a significant contribution to the liberal movements then taking root in China. Enlisting the aid of five Chinese progressive educational organizations, they had succeeded in raising money to finance the project.[41]

The Deweys left Japan for China on 28 April on the steamer *Kumano Maru,* arriving in Shanghai on 30 April. They spent most of May sightseeing in Shanghai, Hangchow, Nanking, and Peking. With the help of guides and interpreters provided by their friends, they visited mills, factories, schools, temples; in Peking went to the "Forbidden City" with its old palaces, shrines, museums, and audience halls. As they jostled with the crowds on the streets, the Deweys found the people easygoing, good natured, tolerant, noisy, and extremely courteous. This way of life, Dewey believed, had developed not despite the dense crowds but because of them. "Live and let live is the response to crowded conditions. If things are fairly well off, then let well enough alone. If they are evil, endure them rather than run the risk of making them worse by interference." [42] The Deweys were shocked at the extreme poverty they saw in some quarters, a situation Dewey said he had "no idea of before coming here." [43] They were also distressed to find that so many of the children, having to work and take on responsibilities at an early age, "are grown up so soon. . . . The children on the street are always just looking and watching, wise, human looking, and reasonably cheerful, but old and serious beyond bearing." And Dewey wrote that he would like to donate "a few millions for playgrounds and toys and play leaders." [44]

One of the highlights of these first days in China was Dewey's dinner meeting with Sun Yat-sen in Shanghai on 12 May. The year before, in May 1918, Dr. Sun had surrendered his posts as Generalissimo and as one of the seven Directors-General in Canton because militarists of the old type had taken over control in that area, leaving Sun with no official duties. Consequently, he went to live in Shanghai, where, at the time of Dewey's visit, he was putting the finishing touches on a book of plans for reconstruction of the several areas of Chinese life. Sun was particularly interested in the relation of thought and action; during their time together the two men discussed this problem, especially in relation to the Chinese people. Dewey later referred to the "evening pleasantly spent with ex-President Sun Yat-sen" [45] and to the fact that Sun had philosophical as well as revolutionary interests.[46]

Dewey's lectures at National University in Peking included sixteen on "Social and Political Philosophy," sixteen on "Philosophy of Education," fifteen on "Ethics," eight on "Types of Thinking," and three lectures each on "Three Philosophers of the Modern Period—William James, Henri Bergson, and Bertrand Russell," "Modern Trends in Education," and "Democratic Developments in America." The lectures were delivered in English, interpreted in Chinese as they were being given, and written down by recorders for use by the daily press and learned periodicals. Dewey always typed in advance a brief summary of each lecture, which he gave to the interpreter as a help and guide in the translation.[47]

Fifty-eight of the lectures were published in book form, in Chinese, under the title *Dewey's Five Major Series of Lectures in Peking*, edited by Hu Shih.[48] Many others, either in whole or in summary form, appeared in numerous Chinese philosophical and educational journals. Since Dewey did not save the original English versions of the lectures, their content has remained relatively unknown to the non-Chinese scholarly world until the recent publication of English translations in *John Dewey: Lectures in China, 1919–1920*.[49]

Dewey gave his lectures at a time when the intellectual climate in Chinese philosophical circles was highly invigorating. The reason for this was the influx of Western philosophical ideas and thought systems, notably American and British neo-realism, especially that of Bertrand Russell, the several Neo-Kantian and Neo-Hegelian idealisms, Marxism, and pragmatism. As these philosophies met each other and such strongly entrenched oriental systems as Neo-Confucianism and Neo-Buddhism, there resulted, as one historian of recent Chinese philosophy noted, "an intense philosophical boiling and bubbling." [50] Dewey's presence at National University added to the intellectual ferment; his lectures were eagerly awaited and his ideas vigorously debated.

While in Peking, Dewey lectured regularly at Tsing-Hua College, the school established by American Boxer Indemnity funds. The college was actually a high school with two years of college work added, whose graduates were usually sent to American colleges to complete their undergraduate training. Dewey went once a week to lecture at this school, located about ten miles outside of Peking. His experience at the school convinced him that because the average Chinese student at the end of his sophomore year was not mature enough to be sent to America, "Tsing Hua should become a four year college and send to America a smaller number, but more mature and advanced, for specialized graduate work." [51]

As Dewey's duties at National University neared an end, the family, including Lucy, who had joined her parents in July 1919, prepared to leave Peking for Nanking, where Dewey was scheduled to lecture at the National Teachers College. His lectures included ten on the "Philosophy of Education," ten on the "History of Philosophy," and three on "Experimental Logic." [52] Commenting on his work at the college, Dewey wrote: "I'm lecturing here on philosophy of edu., rather popular, history of Greek philosophy and logic, 8 hours altogether, but the interpretation has to come out of the time, so it is rather a lesson in selection, condensation and illustration." [53]

The Deweys' residence in the Far East continued for still another year when Dewey was urged to stay on as visiting professor of philosophy at the National University in Peking for the academic year 1920–21. As Dewey explained to John Jacob Coss, "Suh Hu and a few others are very anxious to modernize the university, and to do [this] means not only getting teachers but material in shape. He is anxious to have me give a course in the interpretation of the history of western philosophy, which can become for a while a kind of standard basis for that subject." [54] Coss expressed the sentiments of the department at Columbia about Dewey's prolonged absence when he wrote: "We all feel that it is very hard to get through another year without you, but we are glad you are going to stay long enough to get inside the Eastern shell." [55]

While the plan was for Dewey to devote his major efforts to National University, it also provided that he would give lectures at National Teachers College in Peking and at National Teachers College in Nanking. But the lectures this time were to be "of a more intensive character" than those of the previous year; they were to be given without the aid of an interpreter; and they were to be open only to advanced and graduate students.[56]

One of Dewey's pleasant experiences at the start of his second year in Peking was receiving an honorary Ph.D. degree from the National University. The degree was conferred before a large audience of men and women students and Chinese and American educators. In his citation, Dr. Fai Yuan-pei, acting rector of the university, referred to Dewey as the "Second Confucius"; those in attendance expressed their approval with prolonged applause.[57]

His second year in Peking afforded Dewey an opportunity to

become more personally acquainted with another famous philosopher, Bertrand Russell. Russell, with his secretary, Dora Winifred Black (daughter of Sir Frederick Black), had been touring eastern Russia and China during the summer and fall of 1920 prior to delivering a series of lectures at National University in Peking during the winter and spring of 1921. The Deweys, Russell, and Miss Black had met previously in the fall of 1920 when their travels brought them at the same time to Chang-sha in Hunan Province. The governor of the province, upon learning of the presence of such distinguished persons in the city, had arranged a dinner party for the travelers. Russell later referred to that meeting with the Deweys: "The first time I met Professor and Mrs. Dewey was at a banquet in Chang-sha, given by the *tuchun*. When the time came for after-dinner speeches, Mrs. Dewey told the *tuchun* that his province must adopt co-education. He made a statesmanlike reply, saying that the matter should receive his best consideration, but he feared the time was not ripe in Hunan." [58]

After Russell arrived in Peking, he and Dewey frequently got together for informal philosophical discussions, sometimes joined by others in philosophy at the university. Their differing points of view and the skill with which each man defended his position added excitement to the general interest in philosophy already prevailing at National University.

In March, Russell became seriously ill with pneumonia and for a while was not expected to live. The British press, anticipating the worst, announced his death on 28 March in Peking; the *Manchester Guardian* published a lengthy obituary. Dewey attended Russell during the critical stage of his illness, and, according to the *Japan Advertiser*, took down his will.[59] Another account states that, "during Dewey's visit to a dying Russell in Peking in 1921, Russell outlined plans for ending national disputes, discussed avidly the situation in China and his debates with the leader of the Chinese Communist Party, Chen Tu-hsu, debates which had gripped China's intellectuals and which influenced the young Mao Tse-tung and Chu Teh. Dewey broke down before the passion, sense of fun and restless intelligence radiating from Russell on his presumed death-bed." [60]

Because Dora Black was not yet married to Russell, she was not accepted in American and British social circles although Russell himself was. This struck Mrs. Dewey as very unfair, her argument being that if Russell was socially acceptable, Dora Black should be also. Consequently, her invitations to the Dewey home included both Miss Black and Russell despite the disapproval of many of her friends.[61]

During his two years in China, Dewey's schedule of classes at the colleges and universities was arranged so that he could make trips out into the provinces to address nonacademic as well as academic groups there. Indeed, it was planned by the organizations sponsoring his visit that Dewey should lecture to as many groups as possible to give his ideas wide circulation. While living in Peking, he visited such northern provinces as Manchuria, Shansi, Shantung, and Shensi. After his lectures in Nanking in May 1920, he went "on circuit round and about the Yangtse provinces,"[62] and visited Chekiang, Kiangsu, Kiangsi, Hunan, and Hopei provinces. During the spring of 1921 he went to the southern provinces of Fukien and Kwangtung. Altogether Dewey visited thirteen of the twenty-two provinces of China, speaking in the capitals of most of these.[63]

Mrs. Dewey and Lucy usually went along on these trips; invariably they were seated on the platform with Dewey so that the audience could have a clear view of all of them. Lucy has recalled that "the lectures in the provincial cities were in the biggest hall available and all schoolchildren from kindergarten to university level were there. . . . The little ones behaved beautifully all thru the two hours of lecture and interpretation. Once in a while a toddler would quietly leave his seat, come to the center aisle, study us intently for a couple of minutes and quietly return to his seat."[64]

The lectures Dewey delivered in the provinces covered a variety of topics. In Fukien Province, for example, his four lectures to the Foochow elementary and secondary school teachers, were: "Spontaneity in Learning," "Habit and Thinking," "The Relationship between Natural and Social Environment and Human Life," and "Industry and Education." He gave one lecture on "Self-motivation and Political Democracy" to a group of junior college instructors, another on "Teachers Are Leaders of Society" to the students of Provincial Normal School. At a meeting of the Provincial Education Association, he spoke on "The Influence of American Educational Organizations on American Society." He addressed the students and faculty of the Private School of Law and Administration on "The Essentials of Democratic Politics." He talked to the members of the Nai Tai Young Men's Association on "The Relation between Education and the Nation" and to the members of the Fukien Shang-iou Club on "The Meaning of a Democratic Government."

Mrs. Dewey was also called upon to give talks, usually to women's groups. In Fukien Province she spoke to the students and faculty of the First Provincial Normal School on "The Necessity of Education of Chinese Women." At the Private School of Law and Administration she talked on "The History of the American Woman's Struggle for Voting Rights." She gave two talks to a group of students at the Hwa Nan Girls School, one on "The Education of Girls in America," the other on "The Parallels between the Struggle of American and Chinese Girls for Coeducation." She spoke to a joint meeting of students and faculty of the Girls Normal School and the Girls Vocational School on "Putting What You Learn to Work." She addressed a meeting of the Young Women's Association on "How We Women Should Help Society." [65]

Wherever the Deweys went they were met by a committee and given a big welcoming party attended by government dignitaries and representatives of civic, professional, and educational organizations. On their departure, there would be a farewell party at which speakers expressed appreciation of the Deweys' lectures and the pleasure of the people in having them as their guests. Organizations addressed by the Deweys would then give them gifts—vases, lacquered boxes, silk shawls and scarves—as mementos of their visit.

Such cordial and generous treatment left a lasting impression on the Deweys. Nearly forty-six years after her stay in China, Lucy wrote: "The Chinese are a wonderful people, their consideration and generosity were boundless. Those two years are among the richest and most pleasant of my life and both my parents felt the same way." [66]

Though the personal circumstances for Dewey's lectures were pleasant and friendly, the background of political and social upheaval far exceeded anything he had experienced in Japan. On the international front China was futilely attempting to get rid of the foreign powers that were exerting a stranglehold on her economy and political life and taking over portions of her territory. In Peking, a weak and corrupt government gave Japan, in exchange for a series of loans, additional rights and controls that made China virtually a Japanese vassal. This act sparked expression of a long-suppressed anger and disgust at the government. Young intellectuals, especially, felt action was necessary; on 4 May 1919, just a month before Dewey began to lecture there, students at the National University in Peking staged a demonstration against the pro-Japan government, demanding a purge of government officials and a halt to cooperation with Japan. They urged a boycott of Japanese goods along with a general strike of merchants and shopkeepers till the government gave in to their demands. These demonstrations spread among students at universities, colleges, and secondary schools throughout China, winning the support of patriotic groups everywhere. When merchants in Shanghai, Tientsin, and Nanking went on strike and those in Peking and other large cities prepared to do so, the government yielded and promised reforms.

This "May the Fourth Movement," as it became known in history, was accompanied by the great literary and cultural development generally referred to as the "New Culture Movement." Participants in this movement attacked many traditional institutions and customs of China that they believed tied her to an outmoded past, preventing her from joining the family of modern nations. They declared China must learn from Western culture, must modernize herself, must adjust to the opportunities and demands of the twentieth century. They urged the creation of a popular literature written in the language of ordinary people; they wanted school texts and reference books written in this language rather than, as in the past, in classical Chinese. Leaders in the movement started periodicals in the vernacular dealing with problems of current importance throughout China.

Thus when Dewey arrived in China, widespread movements for the rejuvenation of Chinese life were occurring. These caught his attention at once; he became an interested observer and interpreter of the events around him. "Simply as an intellectual spectacle, a scene for study and surmise, for investigation and speculation," he wrote, "there is nothing in the world to-day—not even Europe in the throes of reconstruction—that equals China." [67] And, busy as he was with classroom duties and outside speaking engagements, Dewey took time to write articles, primarily for the *New Republic* and *Asia,* on the situation in China.[68]

Coming just four days after Dewey's arrival in China, the student revolt was the first event he wrote about. In "The Student Revolt in China," [69] he gave a detailed account of the students' actions and the government's response. To Dewey the revolt signified a shift by China from a state of passive acceptance to one of positive and aggressive action, demonstrating "the possibilities of organization independent of government, but capable in the end of controlling government." [70] He was particularly impressed that young people, many of them mere children, had done this. He wrote to his family, "To think of kids in our country from fourteen on, taking the lead in starting a big cleanup reform politics movement and shaming merchants and professional men into joining them. This is sure some country." [71]

Other articles such as "Chinese National Sentiment," [72] "The New Leaven in Chinese Politics," [73] "A Political Upheaval in China," [74] "Industrial China," [75] "Is China a Nation?" [76] explored the political and economic problems of China, stating her need for a stable, centralized, democratic government, a unified and nationwide currency, a unified and comprehensive transportation and communication system, and a national consciousness to supplement local loyalties with strong nationalist feelings and sentiments.

Still other writings considered the social and cultural reform movements. Among these are "Transforming the Mind of China," [77] "What Holds China Back?" [78] and "New Culture in China." [79] What Dewey stressed is that China, in making changes, should avoid dualism in her national life. He pointed out that Chinese acceptance of Western science and technology would of necessity cause changes in attitudes, practices, and institutions, but he believed these changes should be guided to fit in with China's past and to take into account her peculiar present and future needs. What is required, he wrote, is "a new culture, in which what is best in western thought is to be freely adopted —but adapted to Chinese conditions, employed as an instrumentality in building up a rejuvenated Chinese culture." [80]

Dewey commented frequently on the policies of foreign powers in China. In such articles as "On Two Sides of the Eastern Sea," [81] "Shantung, as Seen from Within," [82] "The Far Eastern Deadlock," [83] "China's Nightmare," [84] "The American Opportunity in China," [85] "The Consortium in China," [86] and "Shantung Again," [87] he discussed the problems created by the presence of foreign countries in China. He singled out Japan for special comment because of her aggressive and belligerent policy and because of her claim that she was "the defender of the integrity and sovereignty of China against European aggression." [88] The truth, Dewey found, was that Japan's actions, especially her twenty-one demands of 7 May 1915, a day which the Chinese have since commemorated as their "Day of National Humiliation," had so embittered the Chinese that they were hostile to almost everything Japanese. "As a matter of fact," Dewey wrote to his family, "I doubt if history knows of any such complete case of national dislike and distrust; it sometimes seems as if there hadn't been a single thing that the Japanese might have done to alienate the Chinese that they haven't tried." [89]

In his "The International Duel in China,"[90] Dewey saw the conflict in China as basically one of political ideologies. "The duel concerns the ideas and ideals which are to control China's internal political development. Is it to become a genuine democracy or is it to continue in the traditions of autocratic government?—whether under the name of a republic or an empire being a secondary consideration."[91]

Dewey was convinced that the Chinese people were inherently democratic rather than autocratic in feeling and disposition, that they desired a government modeled after the democracies of the Western world, especially that of the United States. "Although this democracy is articulately held only by a comparative handful who have been educated," he wrote, "yet these few *know* and the dumb masses *feel* that it alone accords with the historic spirit of the Chinese race." And, he said, "No one can understand the present idealization of the United States by China who does not see in it the projection of China's democratic hopes for herself."[92]

Dewey saw no threat to China from communism at this time. A few faculty and students were adherents of Marxism, which was studied at the universities. But there was no strong Communist movement with support from Russia, herself still in the throes of her revolutionary period and in no position to engage actively in revolutionary movements in other countries. The new culture movement, Dewey found, was distinctly democratic, with no trace of direct Russian influence. But he did not write communism completely off as a threat to China. With prophetic insight he declared that "it is conceivable that military misrule, oppression and corruption will, if they continue till they directly touch the peasants, produce a chaos of rebellion that adherents of the existing order will certainly label Bolshevism."[93]

As a result of his two-year stay there, Dewey's impact on China was varied.[94] His influence on Chinese philosophical circles was only temporary; his lectures on technical philosophical subjects did not result in establishing a strong school of pragmatic thought. Hu Shih, a former student of Dewey's who had been converted to instrumentalism while at Columbia, had upon his return home introduced it in China, succeeding in winning some youthful, minor figures to it. But Hu Shih's early shift of interest from technical philosophy to the cultural reform movement of which he became an outstanding leader, had left pragmatism without a strong, vigorous advocate. Dewey's lectures focused attention on pragmatism, giving it renewed life as large numbers of professional philosophers heard him speak or read the texts of his talks in the press and learned journals. But this interest waned a year or two after Dewey left; eventually pragmatism became one of the least influential of philosophical schools in China.[95] Chinese philosophers, like those of Japan, generally preferred the more abstract, rationalistic, comprehensive systems of western Europe or their own oriental traditions over the empirical, concrete, relativistic, practical philosophy of pragmatism.

Dewey's influence on Chinese educational thought and practice was much more marked and enduring. His presence and his lectures on education without doubt strengthened the efforts of those who for some years prior to his arrival had been spreading his ideas and applying them in the schools of China. After his visit, these efforts were expanded to the point that Dewey's philosophy of education was a dominant one in China. When Chinese Communists gained control of the country, establishing the People's Republic of China on 1 October 1949, Dewey's philosophy of education immediately became a main target of attack by those who wanted to reconstruct Chinese education along lines suggested by Communist ideology. "If we want to criticize the old theories of education," declared a Communist educator, "we must begin with Dewey. The educational ideas of Dewey have dominated and controlled Chinese education for thirty years, and his social philosophy and his general philosophy have also influenced a part of the Chinese people." [96]

The virulence of the attack on Dewey is illustrated by the forced recantation of Ch'en Ho-ch'in, who had been one of Dewey's ablest and most devoted followers: "How was Dewey's poisonous Pragmatic educational philosophy spread over China? It was spread primarily through his lectures in China preaching his Pragmatic philosophy and his reactionary educational ideas, and through that center of Dewey's reactionary thinking, namely, Columbia University, from which thousands of Chinese students, for over thirty years, have brought back all the reactionary, subjective-idealistic, Pragmatic educational ideas of Dewey. . . . As one who has been most deeply poisoned by his reactionary educational ideas, as one who has worked hardest and longest to help spread his educational ideas, I now publicly accuse that great fraud and deceiver in the modern history of education, John Dewey!" [97]

The effect of Dewey's lectures on the cultural reform movement also strengthened the hand of those already at work bringing the ideas of democratic liberalism to the people. Dewey's appraisal of his efforts in this connection was: "Whether I am accomplishing anything as well as getting a great deal is another matter. China remains a massive blank and impenetrable wall, when it comes to judgment. My guess is that what is accomplished is mostly by way of 'giving face' to the younger liberal element. It's a sort of outside reinforcement in spite of its vagueness. Other times I think Chinese civilization is so thick and self centred that no foreign influence presented via a foreigner even scratches the surface." [98]

As for China's effect on Dewey, the record is clear. His stay in that country, he wrote, was the "most interesting and intellectually the most profitable thing I've ever done." [99] "It has been a worth while experience," he explained, "not so much for things specifically learned as for the entirely new perspective and horizon in general. Nothing western looks quite the same any more, and this is as near to a renewal of youth as can be hoped for in this world." [100] In an essay on her father, Jane Dewey summed up the experience: "Whatever the influence of Dewey upon China, his stay there had a deep and enduring influence upon him. He left feeling affection and admiration not only for the scholars with whom he had been intimately associated but for the Chinese people as a whole. China remains the country nearest his heart after his own. The change from the United States to an environment of the oldest culture in the world struggling to adjust itself to new conditions was so great as to act as a rebirth of intellectual enthusiasm. It provided a living proof of the value of social education as a means of progress." [101]

11. Columbia University, 1921–1925

UPON HIS RETURN to this country, Dewey immediately took up his duties at Columbia. He was especially pleased to resume his philosophical studies and writings because, as he had written to Coss, he felt he was "getting rather stale" and needed "a fresh start."[1] His university lectures in Japan and China, his talks in the Chinese provinces, his articles for the *New Republic* and *Asia,* and the numerous social occasions into which he was of necessity drawn had left him little time for study and reading. Now, back at Columbia, he could settle down again to his studies and undertake new ventures in his philosophical thinking.

At the same time, however, Dewey had to prepare for publication the series of lectures he had delivered at Leland Stanford Junior University upon the West Memorial Foundation in the spring of 1918. According to the agreement with the foundation, they were to have been ready by 1920, but the directors of the foundation had given him an extension of time because of his absence from the country. The lectures, with an introduction and conclusion added, appeared in 1922 in book form with the title *Human Nature and Conduct.*[2]

Dewey's purpose in these lectures was to give a strictly empirical and naturalistic account of morals. Much of what he wrote in the book had already appeared in the chapters he had contributed to the *Ethics,*[3] but his treatment in *Human Nature and Conduct* is more detailed than in the earlier work, throwing considerable new light on his views.

The main argument of the book centers on the ideas of impulse, habit, and intelligence, and the role of each in conduct. Dewey pointed out that original human nature is a complex of impulses and tendencies that, left to themselves, manifest themselves in blind, chaotic activity. But since each individual is born within a group with already established ways of acting, this impulsive activity is immediately guided into channels set by the group's demands and customs. Such channeling results in habits of conduct and of disposition in the individual, helping to make him the kind of person he is. Habits, however, are constantly challenged, as when one habit comes into conflict with another or with a desire, or is confronted with a problematic or novel situation in which it proves unworkable. In such cases habit is blocked; blind impulse or desire is ready to take over. To avoid this, intelligence intervenes to mediate impulse and habit. Thus the moral life may be said to be a process in which impulse, habit, and intelligence play a role in modifying or reinforcing each other to bring about an ever widening and deepening harmony among themselves, with a corresponding integration of conduct. In this interplay, habit reflects the thinking of the social group while impulse and intelligence reflect the mental activity of the individual.

In the course of his discussion Dewey showed how such moral concepts as "good" and "bad," "right" and "wrong," "duty" and "conscience" emerge naturally out of human life situations, needing no transcendental source to give them meaning or to make the demands of the moral life more binding.

That the individual's habits reflect social thinking and conduct, Dewey emphasized again and again. Throughout his discussion he stressed that habits are "social functions," that there is no hard and fixed dualism of individual and society. "Honesty, chastity, malice, peevishness, courage, triviality, industry, irresponsibility," he declared, "are not private possessions of a person. They are working adaptations of personal capacities with environing forces."[4] Thus the habits acquired by an individual give as much insight into the social whole he adjusts to as into the character of the individual himself. This consideration explains Dewey's statement that "an understanding of habit and of different types of habit is the key to social psychology."[5] It explains also why he used as the book's sub-title "An Introduction to Social Psychology."

Human Nature and Conduct had a very favorable reception among intellectuals. Reviewers generally believed that Dewey had shown conclusively that the moral life can be explained on a strictly naturalistic and empirical basis without recourse to some nonempirical, transcendental realm. The book's radical empiricism, declared one writer, "dethrones all the idols of the moralists and reinstals them in the living pertinence in which they had their origin, in the specific functions, services, attributes and operations of the drab immediacies of the daily life. The moralists themselves, their high priests, it turns into the outer darkness. It points out that, if they seek initiation into efficacy and relevance in the life of man, they must replace fancies with observations, speculations with statistics, dialectic with scientific method."[6]

Human Nature and Conduct was reprinted in 1930 with a new introduction as a Modern Library volume. In 1944, during World War II, it was again reprinted, this time in a paperback edition for use by the armed forces in educational programs. Since then, it has continued to be one of Dewey's most widely read and popular books.

An opportunity to organize and state some new ideas he had been entertaining came to Dewey when he was asked in 1922 to deliver the Carus Lectures on the newly established Paul Carus Foundation. Paul Carus, born in Germany in 1852, had been educated at the Universities of Strassburg and Tübingen. While still a young man he came to this country, becoming editor of the *Open Court* magazine in 1888. Somewhat later he founded the *Monist*, which eventually became one of America's outstanding philosophical journals. When the Open Court Publishing Company was established, Carus served as director of its editorial policies. Carus's own thinking centered on the philosophy of science and comparative religion, fields in which he authored a number of articles and books. After his death in 1919, his family founded in his memory the Carus Lectures, designed to encourage and perpetuate philosophical studies of a high order and to bring these to bear on human problems. Commenting on Dewey's being chosen the first lecturer on the foundation, the chairman of the selection committee wrote: "It is more than happy that the first series of the Paul Carus Lectures should have been delivered by John Dewey, for there is no living American philosopher of whom it can more truly be said that his influence is of the type which represents Dr. Carus's ideal."[7]

Dewey delivered the lectures before a joint meeting of the Eastern and Western Divisions of the American Philosophical Association, held at Union Theological Seminary in New York City on 27, 28, and 29 December 1922. The titles of the three lectures were: "Existence as Stable and Precarious," "Existence, Ends, and Appreciation," and "Existence, Means, and Knowledge."[8] During the next three years, as time and energy permitted, Dewey expanded these lectures, adding considerable material; in 1925 the results of these endeavors were published with the title *Experience and Nature*.[9]

Part of this volume repeats what Dewey had written earlier. It reaffirms, for example, that experience and nature are continuous; that reality can be had and known only to the extent it enters into experience; that denotation is the method most appropriate for a philosophy of experience; and that ideas are instrumental and not revelatory in function. But new strains are also prominent in the book and, since the older ideas are put and discussed in new contexts, *Experience and Nature* was a fresh statement of Dewey's experimental naturalism.

Three of the new strains in Dewey's thinking at this time should be mentioned. One is his emphasis on the social and cultural dimensions of experience. He repeated that experience is interaction between organism and environment, but whereas in earlier writings he had tended to stress the biological and psychological factors of this interaction, he now added to these the anthropological elements involved, finding in anthropology "material more pertinent to the task of philosophizing than that of psychology isolated from a theory of culture." [10] The customs, traditions, and social organizations that anthropologists study became for Dewey authentic philosophical documents because they indicate the kind of world that men throughout the ages have encountered and adjusted to. This biological-psychological-anthropological approach marked a new departure in Dewey's thinking, attesting the influence of his colleagues in cultural anthropology.

Another novel feature is Dewey's constant reference to ancient Greek philosophy, especially that of Aristotle, and his use of Greek philosophy in formulating some of his own theories. He found in Greek philosophy insights and approaches that enabled him to escape the assumptions and methods of modern science and philosophy, to approach reality with a fresh outlook. This feature of Dewey's thinking suggests the influence of his colleague, F. J. E. Woodbridge. Woodbridge for some years had found inspiration in the philosophy of the ancient Greeks, using it in establishing some of his own views; this he had communicated to Dewey in numerous conversations with telling effect.[11]

Dewey's inclusion of a philosophy of art in his general philosophy was also new. Prior to *Experience and Nature,* Dewey's views on art were fragmentary and scattered, but here they are more carefully thought out and organized, exercising a pervasive influence on his philosophy. More than in any previous work, Dewey stressed the "consummatory" object as found in aesthetic experience; in so doing he undermined the claim of critics who declared that his instrumentalism has a place for instrumental values only. This emphasis attests the influence of his associates in the Barnes Foundation, especially Albert C. Barnes, well-known art critic and owner of a fabulous collection of modern French painting.

Though *Experience and Nature,* ranging over a wide variety of topics, constitutes the most systematic and comprehensive statement of Dewey's experimental naturalism up to this time, its main thrust is metaphysical. For what Dewey attempted to do in the book was "to set forth the implications of experience for philosophy," and more particularly for "a theory of nature, of the world, of the universe." [12]

Dewey defined metaphysics as "cognizance of the generic traits of existence"; he believed this definition was akin to that of Aristotle when he defined metaphysics as the study of Being *qua* Being.[13] Though Dewey's definition seems to imply that his metaphysics will take into account the generic traits of *all* of existence, actually in *Experience and Nature* the discussion centers on those generic traits that relate to man and are of help in formulating a theory of human life and happiness.

Viewed from the perspective of human experience, existence is immediately seen to be a mixture of the precarious and stable. As the studies of cultural anthropologists show, early men, recognizing the perilous character of existence, devised religions with their magic, rites, and ceremonies to help ward off the forces that threatened their survival. Modern man, who faces the same kind of world, has devised his own means of understanding and controlling the unpredictable, precarious elements in nature. "Our magical safeguard against the uncertain character of the world," wrote Dewey, "is to deny the existence of chance, to mumble universal and necessary law, the ubiquity of cause and effect, the uniformity of nature, universal progress, and the inherent rationality of the universe." If civilized modern man's science and technology are superior to the incantations and rites of primitive man, it is because the former fasten upon verifiable stabilities and regularities of nature whereas the latter are tied to imaginary and fanciful ones. "But when all is said and done," declared Dewey, "the fundamentally hazardous character of the world is not seriously modified, much less eliminated." [14]

The changes continually taking place everywhere in nature suggest that movement or process is another general and pervasive trait of existence. Dewey spoke of the "stable" in nature, but, as he pointed out, this is a relative term. For even the most stable and enduring things are subject to outside conditions that force them to change. But, because the rate of change in some things is so slow and rhythmic compared to the rapid, irregular changes of other things, the former are called structure and the latter process. Actually, everything is process, or, as Dewey put it, "every existence is an event." [15] Dewey rejected the metaphysics of enduring and changeless substances that somehow underlie and cause the changes that are observed, substituting for it a metaphysics of events.

This consideration applies to such things as matter, life, and mind, which are not special kinds of metaphysical substances or entities but rather qualities of events, qualities that appear when events take on certain intricate and complex forms of organization. These terms are adjectival, not substantive, in character and function; they refer to qualities of events, not to something underlying events. "The idea that matter, life, and mind represent separate kinds of Being," wrote Dewey, "is a doctrine that springs, as so many philosophic errors have sprung, from a substantiation of eventual functions. The fallacy converts consequences of interaction of events into causes of the occurrence of these consequences." [16] Dewey called this "*the* philosophic fallacy." [17]

Dewey's theory of nature, thus, includes a version of the doctrine of emergent evolution, according to which each new organization of events results in the emergence of new qualities and capacities that could not have been predicted on the basis of what had occurred previously. And, like most adherents to the theory, Dewey distinguished three main levels or "plateaus" of existence—matter, life, and mind.[18]

Since every existence is a process or event, nature itself is a vast complex of "histories," characterized by beginnings, developments, and endings. Aristotle recognized this when he declared that nature contains ends, terminals, finishings. But Aristotle went beyond empirical evidence, falling into error when he maintained that the ends in nature reflect purposes on the part of nature. He confused simple endings or terminals in nature with ends-in-view, "things viewed after deliberation as worthy of attainment and as evocative of effort." [19] Simple endings in nature can and constantly do become ends-in-view but only when a sentient organism wants and deliberately strives to get them. "Classic metaphysics," Dewey declared, "is a confused union of these two senses of ends, the primarily natural and the secondarily natural, or practical, moral. Each meaning is intelligible, grounded, legitimate in itself. But their mixture is one of the Great Bads of philosophy." [20]

Besides the simple endings or terminations of processes in

nature, Dewey also included as ends or finalities in nature the qualities given in immediate experience. "Empirically," he wrote, "things are poignant, tragic, beautiful, humorous, settled, disturbed, comfortable, annoying, barren, harsh, consoling, splendid, fearful; are such immediately and in their own right and behalf. . . . These traits stand in themselves on precisely the same level as colors, sounds, qualities of contact, taste and smell. . . . *Any* quality as such is final; it is at once initial and terminal; just what it is as it exists. It may be referred to other things, it may be treated as an effect or as a sign. But this involves an extraneous extension and use." [21] These considerations led Dewey to declare that "qualitative individuality" is another of the pervasive generic traits of existence.[22]

Dewey emphasized that qualities belong to nature; they are not mere subjective states of mind or consciousness as modern philosophy has often taught. Qualities, he said, have a "natural existential status" [23] and are "qualities *of* cosmic events." [24] They are "qualities of inclusive situations" [25] created when sentient organism and environment interact; they are located where immediate experience finds them to be located.

Because the qualities that characterize events are the aspects of things that are enjoyed or suffered, they therefore determine the worth or value of life itself. As Dewey remarked, "The realm of immediate qualities contains everything of worth and significance." [26] The things in this realm are what Dewey called "consummatory" objects; they are the things men seek to attain or avoid.[27] Consequently, men are interested in the control of the processes that produce qualities in order to control the qualities themselves.

Science is the instrument by which modern man attempts to control events, histories, endings. It concerns itself with "those connections of things with one another that determine outcomes and hence can be used as means." [28] The ideas and concepts of science, Dewey argued, are not revelations of the inner nature of things, nor are they descriptions of a world separate from or underlying the world of qualitative experience. Rather they are tools or instruments that enable men to get and perpetuate the qualities they want and to avoid those they do not desire. "Physical science," Dewey wrote, "does not set up another and rival realm of antithetical existence; it reveals the state or order upon which the occurrence of immediate and final qualities depends. It adds to casual having of ends an ability to regulate the date, place and manner of their emergence." [29]

Man is an integral part of nature, and in him nature attains consciousness of meanings. Meanings arise in experience; they acquire public and general status through the give and take of community life. As individual mind is a function of social life, the first meanings it acquires have their origin in tradition and custom. "From his birth," wrote Dewey, "an individual sees persons about him treat things in certain ways, subject them to certain uses, assign to them certain potencies. The things are thereby invested for him with certain properties, and the investiture appears intrinsic and indissoluble." [30]

With the coming of language and communication, the world of meanings is tremendously enlarged. Words, which are signs or symbols of objects and events, can be substituted for them in daily discourse, so that objects can be discussed, interpreted, experimented with, and their meanings multiplied even though they are not physically present. "Ability to respond to meanings and to employ them, instead of reacting merely to physical contacts," said Dewey, "makes the difference between man and other animals; it is the agency for elevating man into the realm of what is usually called the ideal and spiritual." [31] "Mind" is defined by Dewey as "the whole system of meanings as they are embodied in the workings of organic life." [32]

Dewey singled out creative art as the experience that best exemplifies the nature of man's encounter with existence and the successful culmination of this encounter. Art is "a continuation, by means of intelligent selection and arrangement, of natural tendencies of natural events"; [33] it aims at "consummatory fulfillment." [34] In successful artistic production means and ends, the instrumental and the consummatory, process and product, the contingent and the necessary, the irregular and the settled, the precarious and the stable, the subjective and the objective no longer work at cross purposes but mingle in harmony till consummation is achieved.[35] Artistic production, Dewey believed, "sums up in itself all the issues which have been previously considered"; [36] a correct understanding of artistic production and of the factors involved in it "solves more problems which have troubled philosophers and resolves more hard and fast dualisms than any other theme of thought." [37]

Reference to the consummatory fulfillments toward which art strives led Dewey in the last chapter of *Experience and Nature* to a further discussion of value and of philosophy's role in the selection of values. Values, as Dewey maintained, are the "intrinsic qualities of events in their consummatory reference"; [38] in their immediacy nothing more can be said of them than that they are what they are. But experience teaches that "some things sweet in the having are bitter in after-taste and in what they lead to." [39] The question therefore arises as to the "real" as contrasted with the immediate value of an object. When this question is raised, the appeal is to criticism and to value judgments; "the court of appeal decides by the law of conditions and consequences." [40]

Since judgments of value are of crucial importance in man's quest for security and happiness in a perilous world, his great need is for wisdom, wisdom of the sort traditionally associated with philosophy. Philosophy as wisdom is in essence criticism, concerned with the evaluation of existing goods and values so as to render them "more coherent, more secure and more significant in appreciation." [41]

Metaphysics as cognizance of the generic traits of existence is a prerequisite to philosophy as wisdom. By discovering, analyzing, and defining the general and pervasive traits of existence, metaphysics provides "a ground-map of the province of criticism, establishing base lines to be employed in more intricate triangulations." [42] "Barely to note and register that contingency is a trait of natural events has nothing to do with wisdom. To note, however, contingency in connection with a concrete situation of life is that fear of the Lord which is at least the beginning of wisdom." [43]

Experience and Nature was immediately proclaimed one of the most important philosophical works of the first quarter of the twentieth century. More than thirty critical reviews appeared in the period just after its publication and it has since prompted numerous articles supporting or attacking its views.

Critics were unanimous in recognizing the book's rich store of insights and wisdom. "Occasionally," declared one writer, "a book breaks in upon us like a new sun—shedding life-giving light and warmth over the very human world—on rich and poor, alike, on the just and on the unjust. John Dewey's most recent book, Experience and Nature, is such a sun." [44] The remark of Justice Oliver Wendell Holmes is well known: "But although Dewey's book is incredibly ill written, it seemed to me after several rereadings to have a feeling of intimacy with the inside of the cosmos that I found unequaled. So methought God would have spoken had He been inarticulate but keenly desirous to tell you how it was." [45] One of the most highly respected students of the history of philosophy, writing twenty-seven years after the first appearance of the book, declared that "*Experience and Nature* is the greatest new addition to metaphysical knowledge since

Spinoza."[46] In philosophical circles generally the book has been considered Dewey's *magnum opus.*

Some critics complained, however, that Dewey's theory of the relation between experience and nature was too elusive. Dewey denied that the two are coextensive, declaring that experience takes place within a larger nature and therefore is not to be equated with all nature or all existence. "There is no evidence," he wrote, "that experience occurs everywhere and everywhen."[47] But throughout his discussion Dewey used the terms "nature" and "existence" as though they were interchangeable with the term "experience." Consequently his intended view is hard to pin down. "It darts about weasel-like. . . . It peeps out at us for a moment, to disappear immediately and almost before we are aware of it, behind expositions and criticisms and comparisons of general standpoints."[48]

Other readers said the book told more about experience than about the nature in which experience takes place. "We hoped," wrote one critic, "that the experience which men have and have had would be surveyed, analyzed, and interpreted so as to throw light upon—not the experiences which are 'had'—but upon the nature of that world or worlds which comprise the environment of human life and experience."[49] *Experience and Nature,* it was said, focuses upon human experience and upon nature as involving human experience but never on nature as it exists in its own right and apart from human perspectives. Consequently, the book is primarily "an inquiry into the nature of human goods and meanings and the possibility of their intelligent liberation and control, an inquiry and interpretation which proceeds throughout upon the assumptions of a type of metaphysical naturalism."[50]

Santayana in a famous review emphasized this point. Dewey, he said, concerned himself with the "foreground" of nature, that is, with nature as experienced, neglecting the larger and deeper dimensions of nature, nature as it is apart from experience. This *"dominance of the foreground"*[51] in Dewey's philosophy and his failure to inquire into the background of nature leave his naturalism "half-hearted and short-winded." Moreover, because Dewey always approached nature by way of human experience, his account of it was "relative to human discourse,"[52] to human perspectives. Consequently, Dewey's naturalism is anthropocentric, giving an account not of the world as it actually is but only of the world as it affects man. Nature, viewed objectively and independently of human experience, said Santayana, is found to possess "no foreground or background, no here, no now, no moral cathedra, no centre so really central as to reduce all other things to mere margins and mere perspectives." [53]

In a rejoinder Dewey argued that Santayana's case against him grew out of his separating experience and nature. Santayana, said Dewey, was willing to include in nature man as a physically extended body but not man as "institutions, culture, 'experience'." [54] For Santayana, "the former is real, substantial; the latter specious, deceptive, since it has centers and perspectives." Santayana's naturalism puts a break in nature which is not there. Human affairs, Dewey insisted, are "projections, continuations, complications of the nature which exists in the physical and pre-human world." "To me, then," wrote Dewey, "Santayana's naturalism appears as broken-backed as mine to him seems short-winded." [55]

Dewey also questioned Santayana's charge that his concern with the foreground of nature led him to neglect its background. The foreground, he argued, must of necessity come first because inquiry must begin with clues given in the foreground, proceeding from these to a discovery of the background. When preparing the second edition of *Experience and Nature,* Dewey elaborated this point. "A geologist living in 1928," he wrote, "tells us about events that happened not only before he was born but millions of years before any human being came into existence on this earth. He does so by starting from things that are now the material of experience. Lyell revolutionized geology by perceiving that the sort of thing that can be experienced now in the operations of fire, water, pressure, is the sort of thing by which the earth took on its present structural forms." [56] Considerations such as these, said Dewey, show that "experience, if scientific inquiry is justified, is no infinitesimally thin layer or foreground of nature, but that it penetrates into it, reaching down into its depths, and in such a way that its grasp is capable of expansion; it tunnels in all directions and in so doing brings to the surface things at first hidden—as miners pile high on the surface of the earth treasures brought from below." [57] Experience tells us not only what nature is here and now but also what it was before men arrived.

Dewey emphasized that experience properly used and interpreted is a means of discovering the realities of nature—not a barrier cutting man off from nature. "Nature and experience," he declared, "are not enemies or alien. Experience is not a veil that shuts man off from nature; it is a means of penetrating continually further into the heart of nature." [58] When man is experiencing, "it is not experience which is experienced, but nature—stones, plants, animals, diseases, health, temperature, electricity, and so on."[59]

Dewey wrote only a few essays on technical philosophical and educational topics between 1921 and 1925; most of his articles were devoted to public issues, especially those which arose as the aftermath of World War I. He shared the general disillusionment that took hold in this country when the terms of the Treaty of Versailles became known in June 1919. He joined with those who condemned the treaty as too vindictive and as laying the ground for future war; he approved the decision of the United States not to become a signatory but to work out separate peace treaties with the enemy countries.

Two issues in particular caught Dewey's attention during the years immediately following his return from the Far East. One of these was America's proposed entry into the League of Nations; the other was outlawing war. Though Dewey had been a staunch supporter of the idea of a League of Nations when President Wilson first proposed it in 1918, he strongly opposed America's entry into the league as set up in the Treaty of Versailles. In an article entitled "Shall We Join the League?"[60] Dewey gave his reasons for opposing America's entry. Among the points he made were: the league as provided in the Treaty of Versailles could do little more than give support to the terms of the treaty; Russia and Germany were excluded from membership and so the league was not strictly international; the organization was not honestly named: it was not a league of nations representing the several peoples of the world but a league of governments representing the same ruling classes that had brought on the war; the "international cooperation" in which the United States was invited to participate was so ill-defined that the nation did not know with whom to cooperate or for what end.

Dewey emphasized that until the international cooperation in which the United States was asked to take part was spelled out in detail to our satisfaction and backed by guarantees that the agreed upon cooperative program would be put into operation, it was premature for America to join the league. To join it without such terms, said Dewey, would be to repeat the mistake this country made when it entered the war without first coming to an agreement concerning specific war aims and guarantees that promises would be kept. The truth is, said Dewey, "Europe does not want and will not tolerate our cooperation except on its own terms. . . . The notion that we have only to offer ourselves as universal arbiter—and paymaster—and all will be well is childish in the extreme."[61] The ruling statesmen of Europe want us to join the league "for the same reason that they wanted us during the war—to add power to *their* policies."[62]

Dewey's stand on the league did not mean he favored a return to prewar isolationism. "The war itself," he had declared in an earlier article,[63] "is sufficient demonstration that aloofness and neutrality have gone by the board; their day is over."[64] Nevertheless, he did advise that in international matters the people of the United States should "certainly tread warily," confining themselves "to the irreducible minimum, and that most specifically stated." The reason for such caution, Dewey argued, is that international foreign policy, even that of such democratic countries as England and France, is too little influenced by the principles of democracy. "Diplomacy," Dewey declared, "is still the home of the exclusiveness, the privacy, the unchecked love of power and prestige, and one may say the stupidity, characteristic of every oligarchy." By becoming a steady and willing participant in such diplomacy, he argued, we retard rather than advance international democracy. Only when the management of international matters rests in the hands of persons more representative of the masses of the world and more responsive to their needs and desires will diplomacy be the sort we can heartily participate in. "We are not holier than other nations," said Dewey, "but there is an obligation upon us not to engage too much or too readily with them until there is assurance that we shall not make themselves and ourselves worse, rather than better, by what is called sharing the common burdens of the world, whether it be through the means of a League of Nations or some special alliance."[65]

Dewey's interest in the outlawry of war movement grew out of his friendship with Salmon O. Levinson, who first conceived the idea of outlawing war and worked out a plan to implement the idea.[66] Levinson was a corporation lawyer in Chicago with a deep interest in public and philanthropic affairs. He had married Nellie B. Haire, a student of Dewey's at the University of Michigan who was also, during her college years, a classmate and close friend of Alice Chipman, the future Mrs. Dewey. When the two families settled in Chicago, they renewed old contacts, establishing a friendship that lasted long after the Deweys moved to New York.[67]

As World War I continued, its evils became increasingly apparent. Levinson was struck by the fact that because war as an institution had legal standing in international law, it was recognized as a final and legitimate way to settle disputes between nations. Levinson believed that the conscience of the civilized world was ready to outlaw war, that the time was ripe for nations to draw up a code making war illegal. This code, he believed, should brand those responsible for starting a war as criminals, provide an international tribunal before which these criminals could be tried, and establish a supernational organization to execute, by force if necessary, the decisions of the tribunal. Levinson elaborated these ideas in an article entitled "The Legal Status of War."[68]

In support of Levinson's ideas, Dewey wrote an essay entitled "Morals and the Conduct of States,"[69] arguing that individuals have to be moral because they live under conditions that permit them to be moral—an organized society that confers on them certain rights and responsibilities. States, on the other hand, cannot be moral under present international circumstances because there is no inclusive society of nations that specifies for them their rights and responsibilities as members. Hence nations have no alternative but to define for themselves their duties and rights. Those who believe nations ought to be subject to moral laws just as individuals are, Dewey declared, should welcome Levinson's proposals, which would make it possible for nations to be moral and to be held responsible for their acts.

When the terms of the Treaty of Versailles were announced, it was learned that the Covenant of the League of Nations had made no provisions for outlawing war. Levinson and his supporters thereupon denounced the league, redoubling their efforts in behalf of the plan to outlaw war. The American Committee for the Outlawry of War was organized, headquartered in Chicago, with Levinson as chairman; a similar committee was established in New York City with Dewey as its moving spirit.[70] In December 1921 the Chicago Committee issued a pamphlet by Levinson entitled *Outlawry of War,* and distributed over two hundred and fifty thousand copies of it during the next few months. In this essay, Levinson urged that international law include provisions abolishing the legal status of war, making it a crime against humanity; that existing international law be revised where necessary to make its several parts consistent with the new provision outlawing war; that an international court of justice be established with jurisdiction over all purely international disputes; and that international law give each state, rather than an international court, the responsibility for trying and punishing its own war criminals.

The outlawry of war movement received powerful support on 14 February 1923 when Senator William Borah, after numerous discussions and much correspondence with Levinson, introduced in the Senate a resolution to put that body on record favoring the outlawry of war principle and basing American foreign policy on a plan practically identical with that suggested by Levinson.

With the issue thus before Congress and the people, the American Committee for the Outlawry of War and its supporters undertook a widespread educational campaign to win popular approval of the plan. Dewey helped in this endeavor, writing a number of articles designed to clarify the plan and to meet the principal objections to it. Among his articles were: "Ethics and International Relations"; "Political Combination or Legal Cooperation"; "If War Were Outlawed"; "What Outlawry of War Is Not"; "Shall the United States Join the World Court?" and "War and a Code of Law."[71] The Chicago Committee for the Outlawry of War judged the two articles, "What Outlawry of War Is Not" and "War and a Code of Law," such an excellent exposition and defense of the outlawry plan that it brought them together in pamphlet form as *Outlawry of War: What It Is and Is Not*,[72] and distributed twenty thousand copies.[73]

Levinson admired and deeply appreciated Dewey's contribution to the cause; he wrote to Dewey: "I don't know how to write you without making it appear like fulsome flattery. You are certainly doing the most heroic work for Outlawry of anybody. You have delivered smashing blows in all directions."[74]

The outlawry of war movement achieved its major political objective some years later when the Pact of Paris, also called the Kellogg-Briand Pact, was signed on 27 October 1928 by fifteen nations including France, the United States, Great Britain, Germany, and Japan. The pact condemned war as an instrument of national policy, binding the signatories to employ only peaceful means for settling international disputes. The United States ratified the treaty on 15 January 1929; by the summer of that year practically every other principal power had promised adherence.

Dewey judged the Pact of Paris to be one of the most significant international developments of modern times. "If it is considered," he wrote, "that for many centuries war has been the recognized means of settling disputes between nations, that it is one of the oldest of all historic institutions and that the minds of statesmen and diplomats as well as of the military have become adjusted to war as the ultimate juridical method of settlement, the change that has been effected in the legal status of war in a short period of ten years is striking."[75]

Because Levinson was the person most responsible for the outlawry of war idea and for the movement to achieve it, Dewey believed that Levinson merited the Nobel Peace Prize for 1930.

Accordingly, he enlisted the support of a number of prominent Americans in nominating Levinson for the honor.[76] The move failed, but in 1934 the French Government elected Levinson a chevalier of the French Legion of Honor for his contributions to international peace.[77]

On the domestic front at the end of the war, the people of the United States were eager to return to the ordinary routines of life. Having had enough of war's dislocations, they wanted to get back to "normalcy." During the early twenties the progressive movement of prewar years had all but disappeared, because during the war years the progressives had split, first on the issue of America's participation in the war, later upon the country's becoming a member of the League of Nations. With progressives thus divided, conservatives were able to take control; during the administrations of Harding and Coolidge, they enjoyed a degree of power unmatched since the days of McKinley. Tariffs were raised, income and corporation taxes were reduced, trusts were allowed to go their own way, and fiscal policy, with Andrew W. Mellon as Secretary of the Treasury, was designed to favor business and industry.

Dewey noted the conservative take-over, writing: "The Bourbons are always Bourbons, even when victorious, and the greater the reactionary victory now, the greater the democratic reaction later—tho I wish the latter policy could be established without the confusion and conflict this wasteful method entails. I didn't set out to play the role of a prophet, but the situation is so clear that it is hard to realize the stupidity that makes the present reactionaries unable to see it." [78]

A temporary resurgence of the progressive movement occurred in 1924 when progressives backed Robert M. La Follette as a third-party candidate for the presidency. Dewey joined this movement, actively supporting La Follette in the campaign of that year. On one occasion he appeared as the principal speaker at a La Follette rally of college men and women in New York City.[79]

A friendship with important bearings on Dewey's life and thought grew up during this time with Albert C. Barnes. In the academic year 1917–18 Barnes enrolled as a special student in one of Dewey's seminars at Columbia; [80] from this initial contact developed a close friendship lasting till Barnes's death in 1951. Though many found Barnes an exceedingly difficult person to get along with,[81] Dewey found him friendly and cooperative, almost unmatched for "sheer brain power" among the scholars Dewey knew.[82]

In the years immediately after he received the M.D. degree from the University of Pennsylvania in 1892, Barnes had been more interested in experimental chemistry than in the practice of medicine. This interest led to his developing Argyrol, a silver nitrate solution with strong antiseptic powers but without the burning qualities ordinarily associated with silver. The manufacture and sale of Argyrol brought Barnes a huge fortune that enabled him to indulge another of his interests—art and, more particularly, painting. As profits from his business mounted, Barnes began buying, usually at bargain prices, the works of modern French painters such as Cézanne, Renoir, Picasso, Matisse, Monet, and Degas. Eventually he owned one of the world's most valuable collections of modern French painting.

Barnes wanted his collection to serve educational purposes; this interest in education prompted him at the age of forty-five to enroll in Dewey's seminar. To further his aim, Barnes established the Barnes Foundation in 1922, endowing it with ten million dollars. Dewey was appointed to the staff of the foundation as educational adviser and consultant. Located in Merion, Pennsylvania, the foundation was formally dedicated in May 1925 with Dewey as one of the main speakers.[83]

Dewey's considerable influence on the thought and practice of the foundation is attested by Barnes himself. He dedicated *The Art in Painting* to Dewey "whose conceptions of experience, of method, of education, inspired the work of which this book is a part." [84] The director of education at the foundation, Violette de Mazia, in 1945 characterized the institution as "a dream of John Dewey's—fifty years ago." [85]

Dewey in turn owed much to Barnes and the foundation staff, which he acknowledged in the preface to his *Art as Experience*.[86] Referring to Barnes he wrote: "I have had the benefit of conversations with him through a period of years, many of which occurred in the presence of the unrivaled collection of pictures he has assembled. The influence of these conversations, together with that of his books, has been a chief factor in shaping my own thinking about the philosophy of esthetics. Whatever is sound in this volume is due more than I can say to the great educational work carried on in the Barnes Foundation. . . . I should be glad to think of this volume as one phase of the widespread influence the Foundation is exercising." [87]

Barnes made a practice of taking his more promising students to the museums of Europe where they could view the works of masters and listen to Barnes's discussions of them. In the summer of 1926 Dewey went with such a group to visit the museums of Madrid, Paris, and Vienna.[88]

Prior to his death in 1951, Barnes provided for the financial support of his oldest and most loyal employees upon their retirement; he also established for Dewey a stipend of five thousand dollars a year for life.[89]

An organization Dewey joined at this time, and of which he remained a devoted member throughout his life, was the League for Industrial Democracy. Predecessor to this organization was the Intercollegiate Socialist Society founded in 1905 under the leadership of Upton Sinclair to acquaint students with the inherent evils in the American economic and social system under laissez-faire and to urge the establishment of a socialist order. Chapters of the society were organized during the next several years on a number of college and university campuses; speakers noted for their liberal views were invited to address the student groups. Encouraged by the response to its efforts, the society in 1921 reorganized itself into the League for Industrial Democracy, opening its active membership to anyone interested in its work. One of the league's statements described this work as follows: "The League for Industrial Democracy is a membership society engaged in education toward a social order based on production for use and not for profit. To this end the League conducts research, lecture and information services, suggests practical plans for increasing social control, organizes city and college chapters, publishes a monthly bulletin and books and pamphlets on problems of industrial democracy, and sponsors conferences, forums, luncheon discussions, and radio talks in leading cities where it has chapters." [90]

Because the aims of the league and the means used to attain them coincided so completely with ideas he had been advancing over the years, Dewey became an early and loyal supporter of the organization. He was for a number of years a member of its national board; in the late twenties he was elected a vice-president; in 1939, he was elected president of the league for a two-year period. As president, he presided at the monthly meetings of the board of directors, participated in policy making, and helped prepare appeals for financial support and statements to the press. Also while president, he presided over the large annual dinner of the organization; on 28 November 1940 he delivered an address of welcome at the league's thirty-fifth anniversary dinner at the Hotel Edison in New York City. In recognition of his long service, Dewey was elected Honorary President of the league in 1941; he continued to be consulted on matters relating to the organization till his death.[91]

A memorable experience for Dewey during the first half of the 1920s was his visit to Turkey in the summer of 1924, in response to an invitation by the Turkish government to survey the country's educational system and to recommend ways for its improvement. Turkey, under the presidency of Mustapha Kemal later called Ataturk, was at this time undergoing a series of reforms that touched almost every aspect of its national life. State and society, long under the dominance of Islamic rules and regulations, were secularized; many traditional Moslem practices were discouraged if not actually forbidden. Special privileges were abolished and all citizens were given equal rights under the law. Nationalism was stressed to instill in the people a pride in their Turkish heritage. To free Turkish economic and industrial life from dependence on foreign interests, the State took over many important industries.

Education was among the areas singled out for reform. The high illiteracy rate in the country prompted the government to declare a policy of universal and compulsory education for children between the ages of seven and twelve, a policy that required an enlarged and improved educational system. For guidance and advice the government turned to Dewey, whose philosophy of education fitted the democratic aims of the Turkish educational reform movement.

Dewey left New York with Mrs. Dewey during the first week in June, arriving in Constantinople some two weeks later. They made Ankara their headquarters, but Dewey spent the major portion of his time traveling through the provinces. Since the schools were not in session during the weeks Dewey was in Turkey, his efforts were confined to viewing school structures and facilities and, with the aid of interpreters, talking with parents, teachers, officers of teachers organizations, and with members of the Ministry of Public Education in Ankara.

Dewey's report, entitled "Report and Recommendation upon Turkish Education,"[92] covered topics relating to administration, teachers, curricula, and school buildings on all levels of the Turkish educational system. It urged that schools, especially in rural areas, become "centers of community life" where adults could gather after school hours for instruction, recreation, and especially for training in matters relating to health and hygiene. The report stressed that the organization of the classroom should be patterned after a democratic society so that the pupils would acquire the attitudes and habits necessary for the successful operation of the emerging democratic social order in the new Turkey.

The *Report and Recommendation upon Turkish Education* received careful study by Turkish authorities; many of the progressive steps in Turkish education in the years following Dewey's visit either grew out of or were given added momentum by his recommendations. His report continued to be read for many years. A Turkish printed edition of it appeared in 1939 with the title *Turkiye Maarifi Hakkinda Rapor*; another edition or printing was issued at Istanbul as late as 1952.

Though his time in Turkey was taken up mostly with educational matters, Dewey had periods of leisure when he could observe and discuss with informed Turks the changes taking place in Turkish life. He stated his reactions in a series of articles in the *New Republic*: "Secularizing a Theocracy: Young Turkey and the Caliphate"; "Angora, the New"; "The Turkish Tragedy"; "Foreign Schools in Turkey"; and "The Problems of Turkey."[93] The articles manifest Dewey's sympathy with the Turkish government's attempts both to break the shackles binding the country to an outmoded past and to organize Turkish national life after the pattern of a western democracy.

12. Columbia University, 1926–1930

DURING the late twenties and the thirties Dewey became increasingly interested in problems attending the changing character of American democracy. In an attempt to analyze broad trends in American society and their bearing on the future of democracy in this country, he wrote *The Public and Its Problems*, published in 1927, then *Individualism, Old and New*, *Liberalism and Social Action*, and *Freedom and Culture*, all published in the 1930s.

The Public and Its Problems[1] examines the status of the public *as public* in the changing society of America. Walter Lippmann had just written a thought-provoking volume entitled *The Phantom Public*,[2] pointing out the great difference between the public as it appears in democratic theory and the public as it functions in actual experience. The "public" of democratic theory is a "phantom" public that does not really exist; Lippmann argued that as long as democratic theory clings to this conception it cannot supply the insights needed to guide democratic society in present-day America. Dewey wrote a favorable review of the book in the *New Republic*,[3] commenting that it suggested "the need of further analysis."[4] *The Public and Its Problems*, delivered first as a series of lectures at Kenyon College in Ohio during January 1926, was this follow-up to the Lippmann volume.

Adopting a strictly empirical approach, Dewey noted that man is essentially an associative creature, made so by his biological and psychological needs. He further observed that man's social activities have two kinds of consequences. Some, which are confined to the people directly responsible for them, are called private. Others indirectly affect other people and are consequently called public. When these indirect consequences are perceived and those affected desire to regulate them for the sake of

Dewey's birthplace at 186 South Willard Street in Burlington, Vermont.

Home of Dewey's maternal grandparents in Richville, Vermont, where he spent many summers in the 1860s.

John Rich, a cousin; John, Davis, and Charles Dewey. About 1865, when Dewey's mother went to join his father in Virginia.

Lake View Seminary, Charlotte, Vermont, where Dewey taught during the winter term, 1881–82.

Archibald S. and Lucina R. Dewey, parents of John, in Ann Arbor in the late 1880s.

Dewey (center front) and the editorial staff of the University of Michigan student monthly, *The Inlander,* about 1890.

Portrait placed in Newberry Hall at the University of Michigan a few days before Dewey left for Chicago.

Glenmore Camp, Keene Valley, New York, probably 1893. Standing: John Dewey, Rabbi Max Margolis, William Torrey Harris, A. J. Leon (Ibn Abi Sulaiman): Sitting: Josiah Royce, J. Clark Murray (not clear), Thomas Davidson

Dewey, early in his career at Columbia University.

John and Alice Dewey, Nanking, May 10, 1920.

John, Lucy, Alice, and Evelyn Dewey at Pei-ta-ho Station, August 11, 1920.

Dewey, flanked by Lucy and Alice, center front row, Foochow, April 18, 1921.

Dewey with Chinese child, Foochow, probably 1921.

John Dewey and John Dewey II, son of Frederick and Elizabeth, 1921.

Looking through mementos of China trip.

Doctor honoris causa,
University of Paris, 1930.

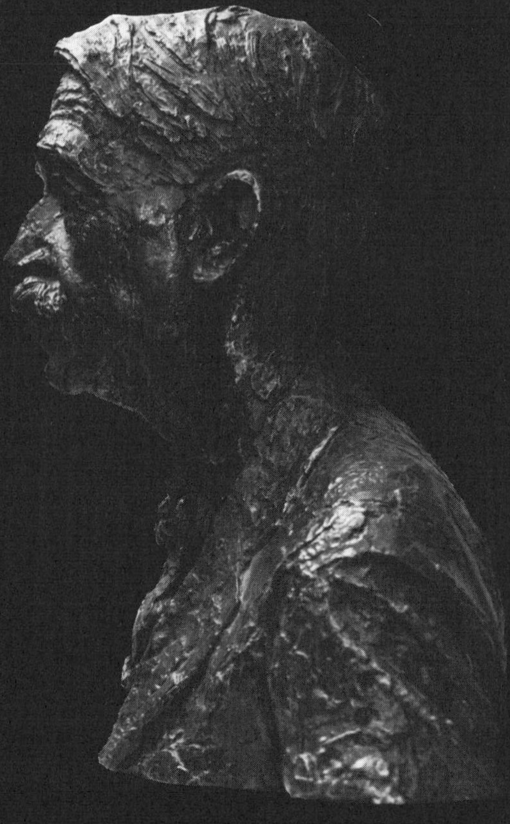

Heroic size bust by
Sir Jacob Epstein.

Surrounded by former Columbia students, at conference of New Education Fellowship, Capetown, South Africa, 1934.

With Albert C. Barnes, early 1940s.

Watercolor portrait by Joseph Margulies.

Dewey characteristically occupied at Hubbards, Nova Scotia.

Opposite page:
With Robert M. La Follette and Sumner Welles before radio broadcast in 1944.

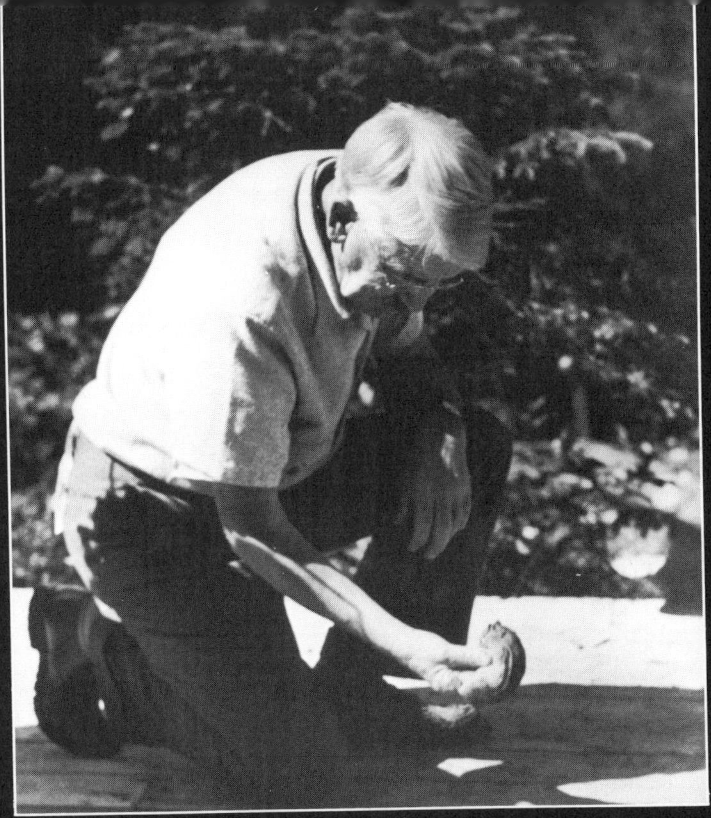

Relaxing and working at Hubbards, Nova Scotia, mid-1940s.

Top: John and Roberta Grant Dewey, late 1940s.

Bottom: With Pandit Nehru at ninetieth birthday observance.

Nearing ninety, looking ahead.

John and Roberta cutting the ninetieth birthday cake at the Commodore Hotel.

Ninetieth birthday homecoming at the University of Vermont: George Dykhuizen, John Dewey, President Elias Lyman.

Memorial monument at the University of Vermont where interment services were held in October 1972.

preferred ends, a public comes into being. A "public," according to Dewey, is made up of "all those who are affected by the indirect consequences of transactions to such an extent that it is deemed necessary to have those consequences systematically cared for." [5]

The proper overall regulation of these indirect consequences calls into being a special group of agents or officials who act in behalf of the public's interest. A state then comes into existence, for a public organized and functioning through its officials is the state. Government also emerges since the body of officials charged with safeguarding the interests of the public is the government. The criterion for determining the effective functioning of a particular state is "the degree of organization of the public which is attained, and the degree in which its officers are so constituted as to perform their function of caring for public interests." [6]

Social developments over the last one hundred years have caused an eclipse of the public or publics. "The machine age," wrote Dewey, "has so enormously expanded, multiplied, intensified and complicated the scope of the indirect consequences, has formed such immense and consolidated unions in action, on an impersonal rather than a community basis, that the resultant public cannot identify and distinguish itself." [7] Governments—officials, legislators, judges, etc.—are still very much in evidence. "But where," asked Dewey, "is the public which these officials are supposed to represent? How much more is it than geographical names and official titles?" [8]

The reestablishment of a democratically organized public, which Dewey believed to be one of the urgent needs of present-day democratic society, can be effected in the ways he suggested: there must be complete freedom of scientific inquiry into social problems; the resulting knowledge must be disseminated among the people; full publicity must be given to plans and policies currently in operation or about to be put into operation; the indirect effects of these on people not directly involved must be publicized; freedom of thought and expression, of discussion and debate, must be expanded so as to include the great masses of people. Because these conditions, Dewey recognized, are difficult to attain, the task of reestablishing an effective public is a formidable one. He believed, however, that the machine age can perfect the social and political mechanisms needed.

The Public and Its Problems was well received by critics. Particularly impressed by Dewey's empirical approach to the problems of the origin of the state and government, they found his views fresh and enlightening. That Dewey's account also pointed to the future was an added attraction. "Forgetting insights and excellencies that alone would be enough to distinguish lesser works," wrote one reviewer, "this book has one high and rare virtue: it analyzes and defines and criticizes political philosophy in such a way as to leave disclosed important next steps for practice." [9]

Dewey was also sensitive to some outstanding social evils accompanying the business boom of the Coolidge administration and the first years of the Hoover administration. Despite optimism engendered by business prosperity, months before the stock market crash of 29 October 1929, he and other serious observers were concerned about chronic unemployment in the bituminous coal and cotton textile industries, the economic plight of the farmers, the uneven distribution of the national income, and the deplorable standard of living and lack of opportunity among low income groups.

In the presidential campaign of 1928, which pitted Herbert Hoover against Al Smith and in which Norman Thomas ran as a candidate for the Socialist party, Dewey's sympathies were with Thomas and the Socialist party. "If I had any special confidence in what can be accomplished by any party, with reference to our specifically political needs," he wrote, "I should vote for Norman Thomas, because I think those needs are connected with a much more fundamental facing of the issues of economic reconstruction than we shall obtain from the Democratic party under any conceivable circumstances." [10] But because he believed that as a matter of practical politics the real choice was between Hoover and Smith, Dewey supported the latter. Among his reasons was the "humane and sympathetic spirit" with which Smith approached social problems as contrasted with Hoover's "hard 'efficiency'," an efficiency that "works out to strengthen the position of just those economic interests that most need weakening instead of strengthening." [11]

Despite his respect for the Socialist party and for many of the measures it advocated, Dewey never became a confirmed socialist embracing socialist dogma. His pragmatic approach to social problems precluded his commitment to socialism or any other "ism." "The person who holds the doctrine of 'individualism' or 'collectivism'," he declared, "has his program determined for him in advance. It is not with him a matter of finding out the particular thing which needs to be done and the best way, under the circumstances, of doing it. It is an affair of applying a hard and fast doctrine which follows logically from his preconception of the nature of ultimate causes." [12]

Among responsibilities Dewey assumed at this time was the presidency of the People's Lobby, an organization that was the outgrowth of two previous ones: the first was the People's Reconstruction League, formed shortly after the First World War to lobby in behalf of labor unions; later, when the unions withdrew their financial support, the league changed its name to the Anti-Monopoly League, extending its lobbying activities to matters of general public interest. When the president of the league died in 1929, the board voted at the suggestion of Benjamin C. Marsh, its executive secretary, to invite Dewey to become the new president. Taking the matter up with Dewey, Marsh explained that the Anti-Monopoly League was really a people's lobby in that it operated in behalf of all the people, not in the interest of a particular group. Though Dewey at first protested that he was a philosopher, not a lobbyist, he eventually agreed to accept the presidency if the organization called itself what it tried to be—a People's Lobby. When the board agreed to the change of name, Dewey became the new president, serving from 1929 to 1936.[13]

Though Marsh was the actual lobbyist in Washington as well as editor-in-chief of the lobby's monthly organ, the *People's Lobby Bulletin,* Dewey also kept active in behalf of the lobby. He contributed a number of articles to the *Bulletin* during his presidency; more significantly, he used his office as a platform to make public statements to the press, especially during the months following the stock market collapse in October 1929. He urged Congress to legislate a more equitable distribution of the national income by taxing incomes over ten thousand dollars; [14] he supported the pending Wheeler-La Guardia bill to create a Federal Child Relief Board and to appropriate twenty-five million dollars for its immediate use; [15] he urged President Hoover to ask Congress for two hundred and fifty million dollars as an initial aid to the three to five million men and women left without work by the depression; [16] and he strongly recommended that Hoover call a special session of Congress to take steps toward a system of unemployment insurance.[17] When Hoover failed to do this, Dewey urged in a statement to the *New York Times* that Hoover ask the next Congress for five hundred million dollars of the two billion needed for unemployment relief, the rest to be raised by state, municipal, and other local governments. Pointing out the gravity of the situation, Dewey wrote: "The solemn question to be answered, probably within a decade, is whether we can change our present policies of governmental fostering of the concentration of wealth, while over a tenth of the population suffer; or whether the adoption of human policies by government shall be forced upon us by other countries which have freed themselves from the conception of government as the private property of predatory and stupidly selfish interests."[18]

The continuing failure of the two major political parties to offer programs getting at basic causes of social evils convinced liberals generally that it was futile to expect any lasting improvement while both parties were under the control of conservative forces. Both parties, Dewey said in a radio broadcast, have "surrendered abjectly to domination by big business interests and become their errand boys."[19] What the situation urgently called for, these liberals declared, was a new political alignment to include a party representing the interests of the great mass of working people.

As a first step toward forming a new political party, a group of liberals met on 8 September 1929 to organize the League for Independent Political Action, with Dewey as its first president.[20] The initial aims of the league as stated by Dewey were "to discover and to co-operate with liberal groups and individuals throughout the country; to bring them into conscious contact with one another and to promote that sense of solidarity among them which is the condition of further effective political action. In being a clearing house for liberal sentiment and ideas, it will also carry on the work of research and of education in order to build up that body of positive and constructive political policies which can alone give unity and endurance to a progressive party movement."[21]

But after the stock market crash of October with its resultant emergencies, officers of the league recognized that this program was not enough. Concrete political action was called for; this required the immediate formation of a third political party. Accordingly, in the early 1930s a movement got under way to organize such a party, an endeavor in which, as noted later, Dewey played a leading role.

Dewey continued to watch developments in the field of education carefully, and, as in the past, he was frequently called upon to address groups on matters relating to education and the teaching profession. When the Teachers Union of New York City held a meeting in November 1927 to spark a membership drive, Dewey was one of three speakers invited to address the gathering on the subject, "Why I Am a Member of the Teachers Union." Among the reasons he cited were: a union can protect the teaching profession's economic interests; it can resist efforts of those who would exploit the schools for private ends; by joining the American Federation of Labor teachers would become part of an organization that has done much to advance the cause of public education; and by joining the labor movement teachers can contribute ideas, gaining in return increased awareness of the harsh realities confronting working men and women in their everyday lives. Dewey had little patience with teachers who were reluctant to join a union because of its alleged overemphasis on teachers' salaries. "I never had that contempt for the economic aspect of teaching, especially not on the first of the month when I get my salary check. I find that teachers have to pay their grocery and meat bills and house rent just the same as everybody else."[22] Dewey also chided those teachers who held back from joining a union because they did not want to become identified in the public mind with manual workers. Such "academic snobbery," Dewey declared, ill becomes a profession that has had such gallant and loyal support from labor. He urged teachers to recognize that they belonged to the great mass of working men and women and to cooperate with them in advancing their own and the public interests.[23]

When Dewey was the principal speaker at the National Consumers' League banquet 28 November 1927 in New York City, he used the occasion to attack strongly the proposal of the National Manufacturers' Association that children between the ages of fourteen and sixteen who are unable to profit any further from conventional forms of education be allowed to drop out of school and seek employment in industry. Dewey urged instead that special schools be set up with programs designed for these children. Boys and girls of this age, he argued, should be put under the care of educators, not in charge of industrialists interested primarily in exploiting them.[24]

Dewey also addressed one of the meetings of the eighth annual conference of the Progressive Education Association in New York 8 March 1928 at the Commodore Hotel, reminding his listeners that "the negative phase of the movement was over and that it was time to contribute something more constructive to the science of education."[25]

At a meeting called by the New York Teachers Union on 9 November 1928 in New York City, Dewey discussed with others the recommendation of the Executive Council of the American Federation of Labor that labor unions withdraw their support of the Brookwood Labor College because of its liberalism and alleged Communist sympathies. So concerned was Dewey about the implications of the matter for the future of adult education within the labor movement that he wrote a lengthy article in the *New Republic* detailing the situation. He pointed out that the action was taken without any investigation of the school, without submitting charges to the faculty and students, and without giving the school an opportunity to reply. He called attention to the ultraconservative affiliations and biases of Matthew Woll, the vice-president of the Federation who had led the move against the college; he declared that labor politics rather than genuine concern for workers' education prompted the action against Brookwood. Dewey warned that the action against Brookwood was no isolated event but the first step in a policy "to eliminate from the labor movement the schools and influences that endeavor to develop independent leaders of organized labor who are interested in a less passive and a more social policy than that now carried on by the American Federation of Labor in its close alliance with the National Civic Federation." [26]

Dewey spent the summer of 1926 at the University of Mexico where he had been invited to lecture during the summer session. Although no record has been found of what he taught at the university, his articles indicate reactions to the changes that were taking place in Mexico's national life. President Elías Plutarco Calles, who had succeeded to the presidency two years before Dewey's arrival, was vigorously putting into effect the revolutionary programs voted during the regimes of his immediate predecessors. Despite the opposition of conservative forces, Calles was breaking up the large landed estates, advancing the rights of labor, expanding and reforming education, restricting the rights of foreign commercial and industrial interests, and severely limiting the powers and activities of the Catholic clergy in Mexico. Dewey's careful observations of what was going on appeared in a series of four articles in the *New Republic* sketching the situation in Mexico and expressing his general sympathy with the revolutionary movement.[27] As had his earlier trip to Turkey, Dewey's stay in Mexico "confirmed his belief in the power and necessity of education to secure revolutionary changes to the benefit of the individual, so that they cannot become mere alterations in the external form of a nation's culture." [28]

Dewey experienced great personal loss in the death of his wife in July 1927. Alice had accompanied her husband to Mexico City but had not been there long when an unexpected heart condition made her return home. During the fall and winter of 1926 her heart continued to weaken, causing a general deterioration of her health. Her poor condition became so marked that Dewey took a leave of absence from Columbia during the spring semester of 1927 in order to be with her.[29] Early in July she had a series of small strokes, leading to her death on 14 July.[30]

Alice's death was a blow to Dewey. Married almost forty-one years, the two had been unusually close. Alice shared her husband's intellectual interests, especially in the fields of education and social affairs, and Dewey was quick to acknowledge his wife's influence on his thinking in these areas. Whenever Dewey joined a movement directed toward social or educational reform, he was always assured of his wife's understanding and strong moral support.

Alice and John had derived much pleasure from their home life. They both loved children and the loss of two young sons during the early years of their marriage was a shattering experience. They enjoyed young people; both were noted for their kindness and helpfulness to young people in need, especially foreign students during their first months at Columbia. Together they had entertained famous people from this country and from abroad, extending to them all an unpretentious and genuine hospitality. The family's domestic life had surrounded Dewey with the warmth, stability, and rich human relationships his temperament required; in this Alice had played an important role. Referring on one occasion to the personal conditions of happiness, Dewey declared that the "deepest source of happiness in life comes to one, I suppose, from one's own family relations; and there too, though I have experienced great sorrows, I can truly say that in my life companion, in my children, and in my grandchildren, I have been blessed by the circumstances and fortunes of life." [31]

Feeling the need of rest after the months of caring for his wife, Dewey left shortly after the funeral for Nova Scotia to join his son Frederick, who had gone there with his family for a vacation.[32] Because Dewey was quite taken with the area, during one of his subsequent vacations there he purchased a cottage on Lake Sawlor, a small freshwater lake about one-half mile from a bay of the ocean at Hubbards, some thirty-five miles southwest of Halifax. This remained Dewey's favorite summer vacation spot where he continued going till his death in 1952. On the open veranda of this cottage, overlooking the lake, Dewey did some of his most important work, including *The Quest for Certainty* and *Logic: The Theory of Inquiry.*

After their mother's death, as circumstances allowed, one or another of Dewey's children moved in with him so as not to leave him alone. During these years they lived in a number of places. After moving from 2880 Broadway, where the Dewey family had lived while the children were still at home and where Mrs. Dewey had died, Dewey lived at 125 East 62nd Street, 320 West 72nd

Street, 1 West 89th Street, and in 1945 moved to 1158 Fifth Avenue. Here, in a handsome apartment overlooking Central Park, Dewey lived the rest of his life, first with his daughter Jane, and later upon his remarriage in 1946, with his second wife, Roberta Grant Dewey.

An event that deeply disturbed Dewey at this time and outraged his sense of justice was the execution of Nicola Sacco and Bartolomeo Vanzetti in the summer of 1927. On 15 April 1920, the paymaster and guard of a shoe factory had been robbed of $16,000 and murdered in South Braintree, Massachusetts. Sacco and Vanzetti, two Italian workers at the factory, professed anarchists, were accused of the crime and brought to trial on 31 May 1921. Though no money was traced to them and no evidence introduced that they ever owned the automobile in which the murderers had escaped, a jury found them guilty on 14 July 1921 of first degree murder. Protests arose in several quarters, many persons feeling these men had been convicted not because of evidence adduced against them, but because of their radical views. Dewey, who was in the Far East when the murder occurred, arrived home shortly after the trial began and followed it closely. His studies convinced him that the two men were innocent, that the conduct of the trial had been unfair, and he joined with others in demanding a new trial. In the meantime, in 1925, a condemned criminal confessed he had been a member of the gang that had committed the crime. As demands for a retrial were revived all over the world, the case became an American *cause célèbre*. This increasing criticism led Governor Allan T. Fuller to appoint an advisory committee to study the conduct of the trial. Dewey was hopeful that the committee would find for the defendants; he was shocked when it reported it could find nothing unfair about the way the trial had been conducted. Fuller thereupon allowed the death sentence to stand and the two men, protesting their innocence, were executed on 23 August 1927.

Dewey regarded the Sacco-Vanzetti case as very significant in the history of America because it revealed the ways prevailing fears, tensions, and prejudices could affect methods of insuring justice for persons of heterodox political, social, and religious beliefs. He believed that the report of the Fuller advisory committee illustrated some of these ways; he analyzed the report in an article in the *New Republic* entitled "Psychology and Justice," showing how antecedent attitudes on the part of the committee rather than strict adherence to the impartial laws of inquiry determined their conclusions.[33] Dewey believed that history would confirm his judgment that the generation which killed

Sacco and Vanzetti was itself on trial in the case. He believed that Americans generally should feel profoundly humiliated at this revelation of the national mood, that they should experience a sense of guilt "as if for a share in permitting such a state of mind as is exhibited in the record to develop in a country that professes respect for justice and devotion to equality and fraternity."[34]

Close friends and associates of Dewey, long desirous of giving him some token of their affection and esteem, found an opportunity in 1927 when Jacob Epstein, famous for his portraits and abstract sculpture, visited this country. They arranged with Epstein to make a bust of Dewey. A national advisory committee was set up, with James Harvey Robinson as chairman and Joseph Ratner as executive secretary-treasurer,[35] to raise the necessary money and see the project through. Upon its completion, the bust was presented to Dewey at a ceremony in the Henry Street Settlement Building on 16 May 1928. At Dewey's request, the bust was later transferred to the library room of Teachers College. Here it was formally unveiled on 9 November 1928 before an audience of students and faculty of the college. Dewey was present for the occasion when William Heard Kilpatrick gave the main address extolling Dewey's contributions to philosophy and education.[36]

During the winter of 1928 the Soviet Commissar of Education notified the American Society for Cultural Relations with Russia that his country would welcome a group of American educators to visit schools in the Leningrad and Moscow areas. The society thereupon arranged for a delegation of twenty-five persons, including Dewey, to go to Russia and observe the schools.[37] The trip was to be entirely unofficial with members of the delegation paying their own expenses. The group left New York on 23 June 1928 for Gothenburg, Sweden, from where they proceeded by rail to Leningrad.[38]

Because he wanted to visit some of the more famous art galleries in London and Europe, Dewey, accompanied by his daughter-in-law Elizabeth (Mrs. Frederick Dewey), left New York a month before the delegation, sailing from this country on 19 May on the *George Washington*, arriving in Plymouth, England, on 27 May.[39] Dewey and Elizabeth spent about three weeks in western Europe, mostly in London, Paris, and Berlin, and then went by plane to Leningrad, arriving 2 July. Here Dewey's daughter Evelyn joined them.

Because the other members of the delegation were not due to arrive for a few days, Dewey took advantage of this free time to visit the museums in Leningrad. He was especially drawn to the famous collections in the Hermitage, which he visited repeatedly. Dewey was not like the ordinary, casual visitor to an art gallery. Elizabeth Dewey has recalled that in the museums he visited, he would frequently stay for a long time before a painting that interested him and study it intently. On one occasion, at the Hermitage, after they had been there for some time, she and Evelyn "finally dragged Dad away at three having been there since 11—no lunch." [40]

The works of art were not the only things that impressed Dewey in the Hermitage. His attention was also caught by the number and kinds of people who came to the museum, "groups of peasants, working men, grown men and women much more than youth, who came in bands of from thirty to fifty, each with a leader eager and alert. Every day we met these bands, twenty or thirty different ones." [41] This experience was repeated in every other museum—artistic, scientific, historical—that the Deweys visited. Such widespread interest by the masses of people in cultural things led Dewey to wonder whether there was not an aspect of the Revolution generally overlooked—the attempt "to use an economic change as the means of developing a popular cultivation, especially an esthetic one, such as the world has never known." [42]

When the other members of the delegation arrived in Leningrad on 7 July, the Deweys immediately joined them. During the five days the Americans had in Leningrad, they visited several schools in the city, making short trips outside Leningrad to view certain other institutions. Among these were an Academy of Science, a Nature Study School, and a Children's Colony located on the estate of a former Grand Duke. In Leningrad some Russian friends took Dewey on a nonofficial visit to the "House of Popular Culture," supported and run by workers in the factory section of the city. It had been established to encourage interest in the various arts and to provide facilities for recreation. Dewey was told that some five thousand persons made daily use of the center. "The contrast with the comparative inactivity of our own working men and with the quasi-philanthropic quality of similar enterprises in my own country," wrote Dewey, "left a painful impression." [43]

The group stayed in Moscow much longer than in Leningrad, arriving there 13 July and remaining till late July. The program arranged for the delegation was similar to that in Leningrad: visits to several of Moscow's public schools, teacher training institutes, research centers, and the University of Moscow. Outside Moscow, members visited a Children's Summer Kindergarten, a

"School in the Forest" where children threatened with tuberculosis were cared for, an Institute for Homeless Children, a Rehabilitation Center where persons convicted of minor offenses underwent rehabilitation, and a Sanitarium, formerly a palace, where ailing scientists and intellectuals could go for a nominal fee to recuperate.

The group was also provided entertainment. The members were taken on numerous sight-seeing tours including visits to Moscow's museums and art galleries and to the Kremlin. They also attended some trotting races and a soccer game between teams of Russian and Austrian workers. When Dewey was struck by the large attendance at these sporting events, he learned that the government was encouraging and fostering sports and athletics among the people.

An outstanding event of the Moscow stay was a banquet in honor of the American visitors. Hostess for the occasion was Mme. Kamenoff, president of the Soviet Society for Cultural Relations with Foreign Countries and Trotsky's sister. Among Russians who attended were some of the country's most prominent officials and educators; several gave short talks expressing appreciation again and again for the spirit of unbiased, practical criticism that had characterized the comments of the American educators. One American newsman covering the event reported that the party was unusual in that "it was the first time in a fairly extensive experience of such affairs that there was a striking absence of 'hokum' propaganda." [44]

Upon his return to this country Dewey wrote a series of six articles for the *New Republic* summarizing his impressions of what he had found in Russia. The titles of the articles were: "Leningrad Gives the Clue," "A Country in a State of Flux," "A New World in the Making," "What Are the Russian Schools Doing?" "New Schools for a New Era," and "The Great Experiment and the Future." [45] These articles together with those he had written earlier on Mexico, China, and Turkey were brought together in the book *Impressions of Soviet Russia and the Revolutionary World: Mexico—China—Turkey.*

What most attracted Dewey's attention about the Russian schools was that they were made to serve the needs and interests of a Communist society. The curriculum, he found, stressed the central role of work in human life, relating it on the one hand to materials and natural resources and on the other to social and political history and institutions. Classroom methods and procedures were designed to develop habits and dispositions that would lead people to "act coöperatively and collectively as readily as now in capitalistic countries they act 'individualistically'."[46] Rules governing the school activities of the children were not regulations externally imposed upon the children by teachers and authorities so much as natural outgrowths of "the carrying on of some line of work needed in the school itself, or in the neighborhood."[47]

Dewey learned that though all the schools had a common social aim, they were not all alike in regard to specific programs. "Soviet education," he said, "has not made the mistake of confusing unity of education with uniformity: on the contrary, centralization is limited to the matter of ultimate aim and spirit, while in detail diversification is permitted, or rather encouraged."[48] Schools started with local needs and conditions in setting up their specific programs but fitted these into the larger life of the nation. Thus the numerous minority populations in Russia were able to preserve a high degree of cultural and local autonomy while at the same time remaining loyal to Soviet political and economic ideals.

Dewey found an immense amount of indoctrination and propaganda in the schools, much of it distasteful. But he believed that the broad general effort to make the schools serve social ends was justified and could not be cavalierly dismissed as mere propaganda without "relegating to that category all endeavor at deliberate social control."[49]

Firsthand observation of Soviet society led Dewey to change drastically the ideas he originally had of Russian national life under the Revolution. Upon arriving in Leningrad he had expected to find a people subdued and resigned to a way of life not of their own choosing. Instead he found a people full of "movement, vitality, energy,"[50] with an interest in life and its possibilities probably unsurpassed in any other country. Though Dewey was quite aware that behind the façade of Russian life there lurked secret police, that arrests, inquisitions, imprisonments, deportations, and executions were common occurrences, he found that these touched mostly those in high public places who posed threats to the Bolshevik regime. "Life for the masses," he declared, "goes on with regularity, safety and decorum."[51]

From all his observations and conversations, Dewey became convinced that the really significant Soviet revolution was not that which had occurred in the political and economic areas of Russian life but that which had taken place in the attitudes of the masses of people. The primary revolution, he declared, was "a revolution of heart and mind, this liberation of a people to consciousness of themselves as a determining power in the shaping of their ultimate fate." [52] Though Marxist theories and expectations "operated to pull the trigger that released suppressed energies," [53] Dewey believed that these energies themselves, coping with domestic and international realities, rather than Marxist doctrine, would be the decisive factor in fashioning the future of Russian national life.

Summing up his impressions, Dewey suggested that the most instructive way to view events in Russia was as a great national experiment whose outcome was still in doubt. Like all experiments, the Soviet one involved continuous adjustments, risks, inconveniences, and uncertainties; because of this Dewey was frank to admit that "for selfish reasons I prefer seeing it tried in Russia rather than in my own country." [54]

Dewey believed strongly that the United States should change its stand in regard to Russia and extend political recognition to the Soviet Union. Such recognition, he declared, would provide contacts between the peoples of the two countries and create a better understanding between them. To insist upon maintaining the barriers that separate the Soviet and American peoples and prevent mutual understanding and knowledge is "close to a crime against humanity." [55]

The generally favorable account of the Soviet schools and of Russian life as a whole that Dewey gave was so unlike the opinions commonly set forth in the United States that many people were led to believe that, having been won over to communism, he was trying to sow its seeds in this country. The more conservative newspapers called him "Bolshevik," "red," or "Communist"; at its November 1928 convention in New Orleans, the American Federation of Labor expunged its tribute to Dewey after its conservative vice-president, Matthew Woll, denounced Dewey as "a propagandist for Communist interests." [56] This suspicion continued for a long time in various conservative quarters despite Dewey's later persistent attacks on communism. As late as 1961 an administrator at the University of Vermont received a letter from Texas asking whether it was true that Dewey's ashes had been sent to Moscow as a rumor in that state claimed.[57]

Early in March 1928, Dewey received a letter from Sir Alfred Ewing, principal of Edinburgh University, inviting him to give the Gifford Lectures there some time during the academic year 1928–29. Although this lectureship was one of the most highly regarded in philosophical and theological circles, up to this time only two American philosophers, William James and Josiah Royce, had been appointed to it. "The duties of the lecturer," wrote Ewing, "are to give a course (usually of ten lectures) at any time convenient to the lecturer within the academic year, that is to say, from October 1928 to June 1929. . . . The lecturer's remuneration, which comes from an endowment, is about £1140." [58]

Dewey, accepting the appointment with pleasure, delivered the lectures at the university on Wednesday and Friday afternoons at five o'clock, beginning Wednesday, 17 April and ending Friday, 17 May 1929. The large and interested audiences drawn by the talks generally received them well. Dewey's attack on traditional philosophy and religion, however, stirred considerable comment in Scottish academic and religious circles.

Upon his return home Dewey prepared the lectures for publication in book form later in the year with the title *The Quest For Certainty: A Study of the Relation of Knowledge and Action.*[59] The volume restates Dewey's general philosophy in a fresh and instructive way. He began by explaining how philosophy took on its traditional form, pointing out that early man lived in a hazardous world and sought above all else to escape its perils and achieve absolute security. Finding this impossible, early man invented religion, which pictured for him a supernatural realm where he could find the complete certainty and security denied him here, if only he employed the appropriate religious means of attaining them. Thus there was established in men's minds an awareness of two realms: a higher and transcendent one of absolute certainty and security and the lower one of ordinary experience in which man had to rely on his own factual insights and skills to win whatever limited and temporary certainty and security he could.

Philosophy, Dewey contended, inherited this notion of two realms, "reflected upon it and gave it a rational formulation and justification." [60] It transformed the mythical, picturesque, and imaginative world of religion into a more perfectly ordered and rational realm of eternal, changeless, and ultimate objects and values. It discarded "the story told in imaginative and emotional style" and adopted instead "rational discourse observing the canons of logic." [61] But despite this difference in outward form, the content of both remained essentially the same. Traditional philosophy differed from traditional religion only in that "for deliverance by means of rites and cults, it substituted deliverance through reason." [62]

Philosophy's acceptance of the notion of two realms, Dewey declared, determined its main tasks and shaped its future. In theory of knowledge its aim was to make known by means of reason the antecedently real, "the Real in itself, of Being in and of itself." In theory of value its work was to identify and clarify by means of reason the eternal, changeless, and antecedently real values inhering in ultimate Being and "to superimpose upon acts ends said to flow from the nature of reason." [63]

The emergence of sixteenth and seventeenth century science should have alerted philosophy to a new view of the knowing process, a view that sees thought and action cooperating to fashion ideas to cope with the specific, concrete problems encountered in ordinary experience; the triumphs of science and technology should have aroused philosophy to a new awareness of the ideal possibilities of ordinary experience. But philosophy's deep-seated desire (often unconscious) for absolute certainty caused it to continue its futile "search for the immutable" [64] by means of reason and to refuse to put its faith exclusively in scientific ways of knowing and doing.

To sustain this charge Dewey cited and epitomized the philosophies of thinkers such as Spinoza, Locke, Newton, Kant, Fichte, Hegel, Spencer, and present-day idealists and realists. He pointed out how in each case thought is separated from action and regarded as capable in itself of revealing ultimate reality and value. "Quest for complete certainty can be fulfilled in pure knowing alone. Such is the verdict of our most enduring philosophic tradition." [65]

A considerable portion of *The Quest For Certainty* is devoted to restating the instrumentalist theory of knowledge in terms of the idea of "operationalism" as it had been developing in the thought of physicists such as P. W. Bridgman, A. S. Eddington, Albert Einstein, and Werner Heisenberg. Dewey quoted with approval Bridgman's definition of meaning that "we mean by any concept nothing more than a set of operations; *the concept is synonymous with the corresponding set of operations.*" [66] He referred also to Eddington's statement that Einstein's theory should be interpreted to mean that "each physical quantity should be defined as the result of certain operations of measurement and calculation." [67] Combining the operational theory of meaning with the instrumentalist emphasis on consequences and ends, Dewey restated his position as follows: "Our conceptions and ideas are designations of operations to be performed or already performed. Consequently their value is determined by the outcome of these operations. They are sound if the operations they direct give us the results which are required. . . . The business of thought is not to conform to or reproduce the characters already possessed by objects but to judge them as potentialities of what they become through an indicated operation. . . . To think of the world in terms of mathematical formulae of space, time and motion is not to have a picture of the independent and fixed essence of the universe. It is to describe experienceable objects as material upon which certain operations are performed." [68]

Operational thinking, Dewey declared, applies also to the realm of value. He held that values, as distinguished from goods that are immediately had and enjoyed, are objects that remain good after critical examination and testing. "Without the intervention of thought, enjoyments are not values but problematic goods, becoming values when they re-issue in a changed form from intelligent behavior." [69] Thus, value-objects are not antecedently given as traditional theories of value have maintained, but are, like the objects of scientific inquiry, outgrowths of operational thinking. And value judgments, like judgments of matters of fact in science, derive their validity not from their correspondence to something antecedent but from their success in bringing about anticipated value consequences when the designated operations have been performed.

The operational theory of ideas, Dewey believed, is "one of three or four outstanding feats of intellectual history," [70] amounting to a "Copernican revolution" in philosophy.[71] It frees thinking from the alleged need of always referring back to what is antecedently real and finding its validity there, and enables it to focus on the possibilities of the future and to find its justification in them. Operational thinking calls forth "an idealism of action," an idealism "that is devoted to creation of a future, instead of staking itself upon propositions about the past." Dewey emphasized that reference to something antecedently real is irrelevant to an idealism of action. "The claims of the beautiful to be admired and cherished do not depend upon ability to demonstrate statements about the past history of art. The demand of righteousness for reverence does not depend upon ability to prove the existence of an antecedent Being who is righteous." [72]

The Quest For Certainty was generally considered an outstanding contribution to contemporary thought. Though it did not measure up to *Experience and Nature* as a statement of a comprehensive, systematic philosophy, the volume nevertheless was "so rich in statements of a positive character that a considerable book might easily be made of them." [73] The work was praised for its "penetrative criticism, its ardent idealization of the era in which we live, its ethical and social vision, and the virility of its challenge to present-day philosophy." [74] Admiration was expressed for "the sustained and unrelenting vigour with which its argument is driven home." [75]

Reviewers noted particularly Dewey's attack on traditional religion and philosophy. "Classical philosophy and institutional religion receive here a bolt that has been a-forging for them many a year," declared one writer. "If they survive this, they survive Dewey." [76] Traditional theories of knowledge, observed one reviewer, are subjected to "such incisive and persistent criticism on page after page that the cumulative impression is one of stupendous destruction," and "one scarcely knows whether to admire most the daring of the attempt, the knowledge and experience brought to bear, the strategy employed, or the relentless energy of the attack." [77]

One major objection to the book was to Dewey's insistence that the only effective and worthwhile kind of knowing is that exemplified in science. "In his eagerness to have philosophy take an active part in the attempt to make this a better world, has not Dewey been unduly impatient with its interest in the problem of knowledge, where knowledge is other than scientific?" [78]

Closely related to this criticism was the charge that Dewey's argument unjustifiably limits the sphere of philosophical inquiry and also directs such inquiry to fields that are not strictly philosophical. "If thinking is only a function of action, then all speculative thinking is futile, idle, and vain, and philosophers should seek to determine not the nature of reality as a whole but which hypotheses to try next in social experimentation. But will man cease theorizing? And should philosophers become practical sociologists? Who then would procure for us, God, Freedom, and Immortality? Shall we not rather recognize that man's intelligence has a speculative and transcendent function as well as a practical and immediate function? And even that the theoretical function faces reality as a whole while the practical function deals with a part of the world? On this basis the practical life of man is completed by the theoretical and the temporal by the eternal." [79]

As Dewey neared his seventieth birthday on 20 October 1929, friends and colleagues made plans to commemorate the occasion. A "National Committee for the Celebration of the Seventieth Birthday of John Dewey" was organized, with members drawn from various walks of life and all parts of the country. From this an Executive Committee was set up with William H. Kilpatrick of Teachers College, Columbia, as chairman and Henry R. Linville, president of the Teachers Union of New York City, as secretary.

The plan eventually worked out by the Executive Committee was for a two-day celebration with three separate sessions on

18 and 19 October. The first was to be devoted to a discussion of the general topic "John Dewey in Education"; the second was to focus on "The Philosophy of John Dewey"; and the third, combined with a luncheon meeting, was to center on "John Dewey and Social Progress."

The first session, on Friday evening 18 October in the auditorium of the Horace Mann School at Broadway and 120th Street, was presided over by Frank P. Graves, Commissioner of Education for New York State. Ernest C. Moore, Director of the University of California at Los Angeles, spoke on "John Dewey's Contribution to Educational Theory"; Jesse H. Newlon, Director of Lincoln School in New York, addressed the meeting on "John Dewey's Influence in the Schools"; and I. L. Kandel of Teachers College, Columbia, gave a paper on "John Dewey's Influence on Education in Foreign Lands." Several hundred persons attended this meeting and the one the following morning.

This second session, also in the Horace Mann School auditorium, was chaired by Ralph Barton Perry, Professor of Philosophy at Harvard University. The speakers were George Herbert Mead of the University of Chicago, who talked on "The Philosophies of Royce, James and Dewey in Their American Setting" and Herbert W. Schneider, Professor of Philosophy at Columbia University, who delivered a paper entitled "The Prospect for Empirical Philosophy." At this meeting, Dewey received as a tribute a decoratively bound volume of essays written by colleagues, former associates, and former students, entitled *Essays in Honor of John Dewey on the Occasion of His Seventieth Birthday October 20, 1929.*[80]

The luncheon gathering in the Hotel Astor climaxed the celebration. Almost 2,500 persons—including leaders in government, civic affairs, education, labor, and social welfare as well as friends, colleagues, students, and former students—met to honor the man they all admired. James Roland Angell, President of Yale University and one of Dewey's first graduate students, presided at the formal part of the meeting. Addressing the guests, Angell declared: "I can recall in the history of American life no parallel for this distinguished gathering which is here today, for what it expresses of grateful appreciation of a great personality and a great contribution to our national life, unless one should go back to the days of Benjamin Franklin and to the occasion of his triumphal return from the Continent and particularly from Paris, where he had left the impress of his powerful mind upon all the contemporary thinking of his day."[81] Noting the many telegrams and cablegrams that had arrived from places as far away as China, Japan, Turkey, and Russia, Angell was moved to remark that the "great mass of messages coming from literally all over the world" bore eloquent testimony to how deeply people throughout the world felt about Dewey's contribution to the world of thought and to how much they desired to be identified with those now paying honor to him.[82]

Invited to give formal papers at the luncheon meeting were Jane Addams, who spoke on "John Dewey and Social Welfare," and James Harvey Robinson, who read an essay entitled "John Dewey and Liberal Thought."

Dewey was greeted with prolonged applause when he rose to acknowledge the honors accorded him. He expressed his gratitude to all those who had helped make the celebration a success; he said the whole affair had been enjoyable to him although there had been many times he felt that estimates of the significance of his work had been exaggerated.

Dewey called attention to what he considered one of the basic problems in American social life: the changing character of individuality and the need to safeguard its integrity. He declared that the "externalism" which characterized much of American life, the attempt to find happiness in external things, resulted from the fact that "we do not really possess our own souls."[83] What America urgently needs, he continued, is a "revival of faith in individuality and what belongs to the internal springs and sources of individuality." Only through such a revival, he declared, can America attain "calm, repose, and a sense of beauty in the multitude of distractions of our modern life and action."[84]

Through arrangements made previously for book publication, the addresses delivered at the three sessions of the celebration appeared the following year with the title *John Dewey, the Man and His Philosophy: Addresses Delivered in New York in Celebration of His Seventieth Birthday.*[85]

The New York press noted the anniversary; tributes to Dewey appeared in the editorial columns of the *New York Times,*[86] the *New York Herald Tribune,*[87] and the *New York World.*[88] Feature articles on him appeared in leading periodicals: Irwin Edman wrote an essay for the *New York Times Magazine* entitled "Our Foremost Philosopher at Seventy";[89] Herbert W. Schneider had an article in the *New York Herald Tribune* Magazine Section on "He Modernized Our Schools";[90] Scott Buchanan wrote an essay in the *Nation* entitled "John Dewey";[91] and Robert Morss Lovett contributed an article to the *New Republic* entitled "John Dewey at Seventy."[92]

Dewey's interest in the problem of the individual in a changing society, briefly indicated in his remarks at the anniversary luncheon, found fuller expression in the volume *Individualism, Old and New*.[93] This book repeats some material from *The Public and Its Problems* about changes science and technology have brought about in American society. But whereas the earlier work traced the effects of these on the public *as public*, *Individualism, Old and New* examines their effects on individuality, endeavoring to show the urgent need to rethink traditional ideas concerning individualism.

The old individualism, Dewey pointed out, was shaped by the pioneer conditions of early American life. The individual during this period had to contend mainly with the forces of physical nature; to do this successfully he needed freedom, initiative, resourcefulness, self-reliance, and persistence. The results of his labor were there for him to see, appreciate, and enjoy. His associations with his fellows were direct and personal, on a neighborly basis. Thus his way of life developed attitudes, habits, loyalties, and allegiances that gave his existence meaning and substance.

The conditions of pioneer days no longer exist. Group action has largely replaced individual action; the work the individual participates in is most often a minor part of a larger whole of activities remote from and of little direct concern to him; his relations with his fellows and with the organizations for which he works have become increasingly impersonal. The individual has difficulty finding in such a situation something with which he can or cares to identify, something that captures his emotions and enlists his loyalties. "The tragedy of the 'lost individual'," said Dewey, "is due to the fact that while individuals are now caught up into a vast complex of associations, there is no harmonious and coherent reflection of the import of these connections into the imaginative and emotional outlook on life."[94]

The individual can recover himself, Dewey argued, only to the extent he takes into account the realities of the present, making them the means for realizing individually chosen ends. "True integration," he said, "is to be found in relevancy to the present, in active response to conditions as they present themselves, in the effort to make them over according to some consciously chosen possibility."[95] The old individualism was meaningful and effective precisely because it grew out of conditions that prevailed then. The new individualism, if it is to be similarly relevant and effective, must develop out of present realities and opportunities. The old individualism took form in response to the pressures of a physical frontier. The new individualism must take its shape mainly in response to the demands of a largely "unsubdued social frontier." [96] The construction of a new individuality, Dewey believed, is "the deepest problem of our time," [97] involving nothing less than the formation of a "new psychological and moral type." [98]

Dewey was not prepared to say what the new individualism will be. "I am not anxious," he declared, "to depict the form which this emergent individualism will assume. Indeed, I do not see how it can be described until more progress has been made in its production." [99] He believed that the initiative lies inescapably with the individual, because individuality is "a manner of distinctive sensitivity, selection, choice, response and utilization of conditions"; in these matters no one can substitute for the individual.[100] "If, in the long run, an individual remains lost, it is because he has chosen irresponsibility; and if he remains wholly depressed, it is because he has chosen the course of easy parasitism." [101]

Individualism, Old and New was on the whole well received; reviewers agreed with Dewey's general thesis that a revitalized individuality requires that the individual face up to the realities of the machine age and make them serve the needs and demands of a new individuality. They valued Dewey's factual approach to the problem. "It is a pleasure, after dalliance with a number of panaceas for the plight of industrial civilization," wrote one critic, "to come back to John Dewey. For he, more than any one else, keeps his eyes on actualities—and the possibilities he envisions have this merit: at least they are possibilities in terms of trends that we all may observe." But the same reviewer went on to criticize Dewey for not indicating some of the first steps an individual should take in forging a new individuality. "We should like to know, in brief," he wrote, "what the Deweyan individual is to do in the transitional period between present realities and the industrial Utopia which 'Individualism Old and New' beckons us toward." Dewey may not be able to tell his readers the final form which the new individualism will eventually assume, but he should be able to tell them some of the concrete things that could be done now. Not to do this is to deprive his followers of a starting point from which to proceed to a new and better individuality. "It is the lack of an initial leverage in Dewey that lends such force to the attacks of Randolph Bourne, Waldo Frank and Lewis Mumford, all of whom have accused Dewey, at one time or another, of 'prostrate' pragmatism." [102]

Shortly after the beginning of the academic year 1929–30,

Dewey wrote President Butler asking to be relieved of his teaching duties at Columbia at the end of the school year and placed on retirement. Though he was in excellent physical and mental condition, Dewey felt this step was necessary if he was to do the writing he still wanted to do and to devote himself more fully to some of the causes in which he was deeply involved. Besides, his teaching career had spanned a period of approximately forty-five years, which he undoubtedly felt was long enough. President Butler agreed to bring the matter to the attention of the board of trustees, but expressed the hope that Dewey would not sever all connections with Columbia. "It will be of the greatest advantage to the University," he wrote Dewey, "if you will keep your stated office on Morningside Heights, offer occasional lectures, meet graduate students for conferences and direction, and do all the other things which are appropriate and interesting in themselves to a life-long university scholar." [103]

At their meeting on 3 March 1930, the trustees accepted Dewey's resignation; at the same time, on the recommendation of President Butler, they appointed him Professor Emeritus of Philosophy in Residence, the appointment to take effect upon his retirement from active service on 30 June 1930. In notifying Dewey of the action of the trustees, Butler wrote, "You understand, I know, that as Professor Emeritus of Philosophy in Residence your compensation will continue undiminished in order that you may be called upon for counsel and advice to advanced students and research workers without conducting any course that leads to a degree." [104]

Dewey found this arrangement agreeable. During his nine years as professor emeritus, he maintained his office in Philosophy Hall on the Morningside Heights campus and made himself available to graduate students in philosophy and education.

Dewey's career at Columbia had been a brilliant one; his affiliation with the institution had added greatly to its prestige. "Forever Columbia will be honored as the academic home of John Dewey," wrote one historian of the university,[105] a statement the years have tended to confirm. The university itself was aware of its debt to Dewey. Commenting on Dewey's retirement, the Dean of the Faculties of Political Science, Philosophy, and Pure Science, declared: "The University is grateful to have been the precinct from which John Dewey fired so many of his luminous bolts. Fortunately he is not wholly lost to us; he becomes Emeritus Professor of Philosophy in Residence. While breath survives his quiet voice of wisdom and of guidance will be heard among us." [106]

Despite the fact that the Department of Philosophy had always been administered by others, it had become known in philosophical and academic circles as Dewey's department. The impact of his thought on other members of the department and on advanced students left little doubt that Dewey's influence was the dominant one or that the department regarded him as its intellectual leader.[107]

The same was true of Dewey's relation to Teachers College. Though the college had been a center of educational reform before he arrived, with new ideas circulating among faculty and students for quite some time, Dewey's thinking served to give these ideas more definite form, coherence, and direction so that "they left an indelible and inestimable impression upon the institution." [108]

As a classroom lecturer, Dewey seemed to lack all the essentials of a good teacher.[109] Entering the classroom with a pile of books and some notes on a few crumpled yellow sheets, he would seat himself at his desk and remain there throughout the hour. In looks, Sidney Hook has reported, he resembled "a cross between a philosophical anarchist and Robert Louis Stevenson"; [110] in manner he was mild and unaffected. Unless Mrs. Dewey had checked his appearance before he left for class, his tie was likely to be askew and his hair disheveled.

Beginning his lecture, he spoke slowly, with no attempt at rhetorical persuasiveness. He directed his gaze for the most part out of the window, seemingly little aware of the presence of the class. His facial expression was serious and grave, although he was quick to smile and chuckle when he recalled some homely anecdote to press home a point. Developing his theme, Dewey would approach it from various angles, struggling to put his ideas into intelligible language. As the lecture continued most of his listeners despaired of following his trains of thought and let their minds wander.

To most of the thousands, both on and off campus, who over the years came to his classes, Dewey's lectures were a boring experience; the wonder was how one who so stressed the role of interest in the educative process could himself fail so abysmally to create it in his own classes. But to those who tried seriously and faithfully to follow his thinking, who conscientiously took notes and studied them afterwards, Dewey's lectures eventually became an exciting educational experience. As Irwin Edman explained, in his own case, "it was then a remarkable discovery to make on looking over my notes to find that what had seemed so casual, so rambling, so unexciting, was of an extraordinary coherence, texture, and brilliance. I had been listening not to the semi-theatrical repetition of a discourse many times made—a fairly accurate description of many academic lectures—I had been listening to a man actually *thinking* in the presence of a class. . . . To attend a lecture of John Dewey was to participate in the actual business of thought. Those pauses were delays in creative thinking, when the next step was really being considered, and for the glib dramatics of the teacher-actor was substituted the enterprise, careful and candid, of the genuine thinker. Those hours came to seem the most arresting educational experiences, almost, I have ever had. One had to be scrupulously attentive and one learned to be so. Not every day or in every teacher does one overhear the palpable processes of thought." [111]

Advanced students of Dewey's agreed that he was at his best in a small seminar group, where the atmosphere was that of a group of thinkers cooperatively engaged in inquiry. Members of the class prepared papers on the seminar's general theme, shared in the discussions, and evaluated each other's ideas. Dewey joined in this, being careful not to take more than his share of the time. What particularly impressed his students about Dewey was his "gift for pointing to the exact difficulty or the exact limitations of a man or a paper; his capacity for sympathetically seeing what a student was driving at, even when he did not quite succeed in saying it, and Dewey's candid expression of his own position or his own prejudices." [112]

The influence Dewey had on his students, especially those who did considerable work with him and so came to know him better, was more than academic. The man himself, his personality, elicited a warm response and left a lasting impression on them. "For those who were his students, and for many who were his colleagues throughout the University," wrote J. H. Randall, "Dewey became a part of their very lives and selves. . . . It was not alone what he did and thought, it was what he was, that drew men to him—simple, sturdy, unpretentious, quizzical, shrewd, devoted, fearless, genuine—a true Yankee saint. For Woodbridge, students and colleagues developed admiration; for Adler, respect; for Montague, affection. For Dewey it was unashamed love." [113]

13. Emeritus, Columbia University, 1930–1935

THE LEAGUE for Independent Political Action had been organized with the plan of devoting its first few years to education, acquainting liberal groups throughout the country with each other, and formulating a set of principles around which liberals and progressives everywhere could rally. With the ground thus properly prepared, steps would then be taken to organize a third political party to compete with the two major ones. But as the depression following the stock market crash of 29 October 1929 deepened, as bread lines lengthened and the ranks of the unemployed grew, as legislation came to a virtual standstill because leaders in Congress could not agree on what ought to be done, those in charge of the league became convinced that the establishment of a third party could not be postponed. "The officers of the League were never more certain than they are now," declared a 1930 statement of the league, "that the American people must have a party that will represent their interests. With growing insecurity for the many caused by unemployment, low wages, the scrapping of men at forty-five and fifty years of age, the old parties just play with the problem. The injustice heaped upon the farmer by the tariff scandal is notorious. The control of public utility commissions by the utility companies is a disgrace. The European situation is serious and may easily lead to war within five years. America is not exerting the influence for peace that might be exercised. Every interest of the people demands a new political alignment with a party that will throw the searchlight upon these problems and bring results." [1]

Casting about for someone to lead a new party, the league chose Senator George W. Norris of Nebraska. Norris was an insurgent Republican with a long record of supporting liberal causes; league officers were hopeful that he could be persuaded to leave his party to head the new movement. Consequently, Dewey wrote to Norris on 23 December 1930 pointing out the need of a new party and urging him to accept leadership of it. "Millions of progressives over the United States," wrote Dewey, "are disgusted with the old parties and are longing for a new political alignment. At this Christmas season will you not renounce both of these old parties and help give birth to a new party based upon the principle of planning and control for the purpose of building happier lives, a more just society and that peaceful world which was the dream of Him whose birthday we celebrate this Christmas Day?"[2] Dewey went on to say that though the new party could not expect to win the presidential elections of 1932 and 1936, it could conceivably win in 1940. By so doing, he wrote, "we could drive the conservatives in desperation into one of the old parties and we should then have a real conflict of ideas and a vital party of opposition which would make for rapid political progress and give desperate workers and farmers a constructive vehicle of political expression."[3]

Though agreeing that liberal legislation and changes were very much needed, Norris did not believe that these required the formation of a third party. He believed, rather, that a constitutional amendment abolishing the electoral college, allowing the people to vote directly for a presidential candidate apart from traditional party allegiances, was a more realistic and promising way of getting needed reforms. Accordingly, in his reply to Dewey, Norris wrote, "If we would all unite in a demand for a constitutional amendment such as I have indicated, I have no doubt but that success would crown our efforts within a reasonable time."[4] Norris therefore declined the leadership of a new party; in an interview with the press afterward he declared himself a "good Republican" and expressed his determination to "purify" the party from within.[5]

Dewey was disappointed with Norris's refusal and disillusioned with liberal congressmen in general. In a speech before the New History Society on 30 December 1930 heard by some two thousand persons, he attacked Norris, Borah, and other insurgents in the Senate. He accused them of lacking "the courage to break away from the safe and comfortable moorings of the Republican party" and to affiliate openly with a party aggressively committed to a reorganization of the economy in order to secure the ends they seemingly professed. He declared that they were content to be merely "snipers" taking as their target now this and now that social evil, but refusing to face up to the real need, namely, a socially controlled and planned economy.[6]

The exchange of letters between Dewey and Norris dramatically projected Dewey and the league into the political limelight. Leading newspapers throughout the country published the league's call for a new party and debated its wisdom. Opinion was almost entirely against the idea. "If Professor Dewey has been reading editorial comments on a third party, brought forth by his suggestion," declared the *New York Times,* "he knows that his idea fared no better with the press than with the Insurgents at Washington. . . . When the press was not politely skeptical it was frankly scornful." [7] The same paper editorialized that Dewey's proposal "seems to 'smell of the lamp' rather than to have been composed by a man in close touch with the hard realities of political life." [8]

Despite the cool reception accorded the proposal in the Senate and in the press, the league continued its efforts in behalf of a new party. Dewey wrote and spoke extensively on the issue, best summarizing his position in a series of four articles in the *New Republic.* Using as his general theme, "The Need for a New Party," he wrote on "The Present Crisis," "The Breakdown of the Old Order," "Who Might Make a New Party," and "Policies for a New Party." [9] In these articles Dewey stressed that a new people's party was urgently needed because the old parties no longer represented the interests of the people; that the old parties' leadership was blind to the fact that laissez-faire capitalism had collapsed and could no longer function effectively; that the membership of the new party would include laborers, farmers, white collar workers, owners of small businesses, professional people, and intellectuals; and that its policies would include a socially controlled and planned economy to give hitherto neglected and underprivileged minorities a more just share of the nation's goods.

The election of Franklin D. Roosevelt and the coming of the New Deal did not change Dewey's conviction that a new party was needed.[10] He admired Roosevelt's humaneness and recognized that many New Deal measures were identical with those advocated by the league.[11] But he feared that once the emergency was over, pressure from big business would cause the traditional parties to revoke much of what was most worthwhile in New Deal legislation, especially since Roosevelt and his advisers had declared that the more radical policies were of an emergency and temporary nature only. *"The only way to preserve as well as to extend whatever is good in the Rooseveltian measures,"* Dewey declared, *"is the formation of a strong united radical new party."* [12]

Dewey's chief objection to the New Deal was that it did not go far enough. It was a "half-way house" in the nation's endeavor to build a more just and democratic social order.[13] Its primary aim was to repair and bolster the old capitalist system, to cushion the blows that system might inflict on those unable to cope with it. For Dewey this was too little. Further steps were needed to establish a socially controlled and planned economy like that advocated by the more radical parties in England and on the continent. Dewey's conviction was that "we cannot achieve a decent standard of living for more than a fraction of the American people, by any other method than that to which the British Labor Party and the Social Democratic Parties of Europe are committed—the socialization of all natural resources and natural monopolies, of ground rent, and of basic industries. Classification as Democrat or Republican means nothing in America today—the only vital distinction is on such socialization." [14]

Dewey's hope and that of the league for a strong new radical party turned out to be futile. Despite its shortcomings, labor unions, farmers' organizations, small business men, white collar workers, many liberal members of professional and intellectual groups, the needy, and the underprivileged rallied around the New Deal to help Roosevelt win spectacular victories in the elections of 1936 and 1940. Sensing the hopelessness of its cause under these circumstances, the league ceased operations in the late thirties.

Dewey continually called attention to the plight of those suffering from the depression. Using mostly the *People's Lobby Bulletin* as his channel, he cited instances of groups requiring help; he urged governments on the different levels to act immediately in their behalf. His ideas were expressed in such articles as: "Full Warehouses and Empty Stomachs," "Challenge to Progressive Senators to Act for Relief," "You Must Act to Get Congress to Act," "Voters Must Demand Congress Tax Wealth Instead of Want," "Get Mayor and Governor to Demand Relief," "Relief Is Vital," "The Drive against Hunger," and "President's Policies Help Property Owners Chiefly." [15]

The correspondence between Dewey and his close friend Salmon O. Levinson contains at this time numerous references to the economic crisis. Levinson, legal consultant to banks and corporations, was more conservative than Dewey in his approach to the problems created by the crisis. In one of his letters, written while Hoover was still in office, Levinson remarked that it was "a terrible mistake" for Dewey's radical group to oppose the proposed increase in railroad freight rates. This increase, Levinson argued, would ease the financial crisis of the railroads, undergird investments in railroad stocks and bonds, and indirectly help railroad employees and workers in industries supplying material to the railroads.[16]

Dewey replied:

> I'm not enough of an economist to balance the stimulus given to the railway business and those who furnish them supplies etc., with the effect on depressed industries and shippers of a rise in rates. But I am sure there is something completely topsy turvy when Hoover refuses to do anything for the actually starving, when Mellon's idea is a sales tax on the consumer and higher taxes for the low brackets and the now exempt; and it is proposed to subsidize the holders of investments in stocks and bonds. It's a good illustration of the present system.
>
> Our "leaders" political and economic seem to me as mad as the nobility in France before the revolution. That doesn't apply to Hoover —it takes brains, I've always understood, to go insane and he is just socially and politically dumm [*sic*].
>
> Don't they know what the actual condition of the country is?[17]

In the spring of 1932 Levinson wrote: "The economic world seems to be cracking completely and does not stop. The past few years we have heard much about stabilizing this, that and the other thing, but nobody seems to try to stabilize the crisis, especially market securities, at any level. Here after 2½ years of panic, the situation grows daily almost hopelessly worse."[18]

Some months later, toward the end of the presidential campaign, Dewey declared in a letter: "I should think you would feel in need of sympathy in seeing or hearing Hoover's last speeches—they sound like the snarlings of a defeated man; I always thought there was a strong petulant streak [in] him but he is worse now than I anticipated. My own chief regret is that he is making persons who had decided to vote for Thomas switch to Roosevelt to make sure of beating H."[19]

After Roosevelt's election in 1932, just before the inaugural address, Levinson sent Dewey a letter in which he wrote:

> Economically and financially I am greatly baffled. Of course Roosevelt will make a big play, which he has a grand opportunity to do, at his inaugural. Whether the patient has got beyond the point of recovery or not, I don't know, but perhaps a transfusion of presidential serum may pull us up.
>
> Don't be too hard on the capitalistic system because I don't want to wade through the period of broken down systems and demolished business through the rest of my journey this side of the moon.[20]

In his reply Dewey assured Levinson that: "If the 'capitalistic system' survives its own blunders and crimes, it certainly can endure any blows that I may direct against it!" [21]

The public schools were among the first victims of the economic crisis. Communities, hard hit by the depression and looking for ways to economize, made the schools one of their first targets. The Division of Research of the National Education Association made a brief state-by-state survey in November 1931 of conditions in the schools. It found that two-thirds of the city school systems were forced to operate on reduced budgets despite increased enrollments; that in many rural areas schools had had to close completely and in others to operate on a shortened school year; that certain educational services such as kindergartens, school health work, special classes for handicapped children had been discontinued or curtailed; that in many schools the so-called "frill" courses—manual training, domestic arts, music, physical education, art work—had been abolished or were about to be abolished; that teachers' salaries had been drastically cut in many communities and in others experienced and competent teachers had been replaced by inexperienced ones at lower salaries; that teaching load and class size had increased to a point that threatened the efficiency of instruction; and that long overdue building programs had been suspended, leaving classrooms more crowded than ever.[22]

Dewey was acutely aware of the situation in the schools and frequently called attention to it. In a talk before the Department of Supervisors and Directors of Instruction of the National Education Association in Minneapolis on 1 March 1933, he warned that if not corrected the condition would "wipe out the gains in security of teachers and in enrichment of instruction which are the outstanding gains of the last forty years." [23] He urged teachers "to assert themselves more directly about educational affairs and about the organization and conduct of the schools," [24] not to leave matters to those who would sacrifice the welfare of the schools "under cover of the depression and to the cry of economy." [25] All thoughtful citizens recognize that in a time of national emergency certain retrenchments and economies are necessary; but the form these should take, he continued, should be determined by those working in and for the schools, not by those who have the least connection with them.

Among other talks and papers given by Dewey on educational problems arising from the depression were: "Teachers as Citizens," delivered before Local 195 of the American Federation of Teachers at Cambridge, Massachusetts, on 9 April 1931; "The

Economic Situation: A Challenge to Education," read before the Department of Supervisors and Teachers of Home Economics of the National Education Association at Washington on 22 February 1932; "The Crisis in Education," given before Yale Local 204, American Federation of Teachers and the New Haven Teachers Association at New Haven, Connecticut, on 22 January 1933; "Shall We Abolish 'Frills'? No"; "The Teacher and the Public," delivered over WEVD University of the Air on 16 January 1935; and "Can Education Share in Social Reconstruction?" [26]

While communism never gained a wide mass following in the United States, it succeeded during the early depression years in winning a sizeable number of adherents in literary, artistic, and intellectual circles.[27] These persons saw in communism a way out of the depression and the promise of a more just and worthwhile social order. Its goal of bettering the lot of the underprivileged masses and its steps toward a "planned economy" had greater appeal to many intellectuals than the confused, wavering goals and programs of capitalist America. "To join the Communist party became a confession of past error and an act of faith in a better future. Developments in the Soviet Union scarcely supported such a faith, but during the early 1930s Stalin's ruthlessness received less publicity than Russia's progress toward clearly formulated economic goals. America's drifting economy stood in glaring contrast to Soviet planning." [28]

In keeping with traditional Communist practice, American Communists infiltrated various areas of the nation's life and culture through the familiar tactic of "boring from within," seeking to win control of labor unions, civic organizations, professional associations, literary magazines, liberal publishing houses, the theater, and the movies.

Teachers' unions, especially in big cities, became objects of attack; among these was Local No. 5 in New York City, the union Dewey helped organize and of which he was a charter member. Employing the well-known Communist methods of delay, obstruction, misrepresentation, and name-calling, a militant Communist minority within the union was able to bring the affairs of the union to a virtual standstill, preventing action on policies supported by the majority. Dewey served as chairman of a "grievance committee" to straighten matters out; when these efforts failed,[29] the officers of the union petitioned the American Federation of Teachers to revoke the original charter and to draw up a new one that would enable the union to protect itself against obstructionists. This petition was denied at the Cleveland convention of the federation in 1935.

Unable to get help from the parent organization and with Communist members becoming increasingly dominant, officers of Local No. 5 withdrew from the organization taking with them six to seven hundred members including Dewey. This group shortly afterwards founded the independent New York Teachers Guild,[30] leaving Local No. 5 under the control of its Communist members.

Affiliated so long and so closely, first with Local No. 5 and later also with the American Federation of Teachers, Dewey found the decision to resign from the local a painful one. But he felt that he had no alternative. He could not in good conscience remain a member of a teachers union when "that union was used for promoting a particular political opinion rather than for educational purposes." [31]

Though deeply involved in political, economic, and educational matters, Dewey did considerable writing. He contributed a steady stream of articles and reviews to professional journals; he wrote a revised version of his portion of the Dewey and Tufts *Ethics* [32] and a new edition of *How We Think*.[33] In addition, he published a number of important books, one of which was *Art as Experience*.[34]

Art as Experience was the outgrowth of a series of ten lectures that Dewey delivered at Harvard during the winter and spring of 1931. The talks were under the sponsorship of the newly founded William James Lectureship to which Dewey was the first appointee. The volume brings together and greatly enlarges upon many ideas on the philosophy of art that Dewey had been developing ever since his affiliation with the Barnes Foundation, ideas he had stated or touched upon in various articles and scattered passages in books. *Art as Experience* was dedicated to Albert C. Barnes.

Dewey viewed the aesthetic as a form of experience. First he singled out the factor that makes an experience an aesthetic one; this distinguishing feature, he said, is identical with that which separates *an* experience from the ordinary run of experiences. Experience, Dewey reminded the reader, is always the interaction of the live creature and its environment. Furthermore, because of conflicts and tensions within the self, resistances and obstacles encountered in the environment, experience is all too frequently one of starts and stops, attempts and frustrations. "We put our hands to the plow and turn back; we start and then we stop, not because the experience has reached the end for the sake of which it was initiated but because of extraneous interruptions or of inner lethargy." But occasionally an experience occurs that has a beginning, a continuous development, a fulfillment, and a satisfying emotional quality because of the experience's inner and consistent movement toward the intended fulfillment. "A piece of work is finished in a way that is satisfactory; a problem receives its solution; a game is played through; a situation, whether that of eating a meal, playing a game of chess, carrying on a conversation, writing a book, or taking part in a political campaign, is so rounded out that its close is a consummation and not a cessation. Such an experience is a whole and carries with it its own individualizing quality and self-sufficiency. It is *an* experience." [35]

Aesthetic experience belongs to this latter type of experience. It is "the clarified and intensified development of traits that belong to every normally complete experience." [36] The artist takes a thing enjoyed in everyday experience and gives it special treatment, a treatment designed to bring out the object's fuller, richer meaning and value so as to make possible a new and aesthetic experience. "Through art," said Dewey, "meanings of objects that are otherwise dumb, inchoate, restricted, and resisted are clarified and concentrated, and not by thought working laboriously upon them, nor by escape into a world of mere sense, but by creation of a new experience." [37]

A substantial portion of Dewey's discussion centers in the artist's creation of a work of art. On the one hand is the artist with his background of experience, summed up in his skills and interests, likes and dislikes, biases and prejudices, some operating consciously and others unconsciously while he works. Also in the artist is the vague and dimly imagined goal to which he aspires in his creative endeavor. On the other hand, there is the material or medium with which the artist works. This constitutes his environment and includes obstacles and difficulties to as well as opportunities for the realization of his goal.

In the struggle to mold the material according to his purpose, the artist finds that difficulties presented by the material compel him constantly to modify his plan, while the material itself continually undergoes change as it submits to the artist's purpose. Thus the creation of a work of art is like all experience "a prolonged interaction of something issuing from the self with objective conditions, a process in which both of them acquire a form and order they did not at first possess." [38]

The enjoyment of the finished work of art, if this enjoyment is to be genuinely aesthetic, requires that the beholder go through the same sort of experience as did the artist in the making of the object. In imagination he must experience the same type of struggles, successes, frustrations, adjustments leading to final fulfillment as did the artist. "We lay hold of the full import of a work of art," said Dewey, "only as we go through in our own vital processes the processes the artist went through in producing the work." [39] And he added: "The one who is too lazy, idle, or indurated in convention to perform this work, will not see or hear. His 'appreciation' will be a mixture of scraps of learning with conformity to norms of conventional admiration and with a confused, even if genuine, emotional excitation." [40]

Because works of art grow out of the experiences of a people, they tell us much about the culture in which they had their origin. Objects of art, embodying as they do the consummatory experiences of a people, are "a record and celebration of the life of a civilization." [41] Dewey saw art as "the most universal and freest form of communication"; [42] he believed that more than any other single factor it breaks down the barriers which separate peoples. Viewing works of art from primitive times to the present, people become aware of the continuity of human hopes and aspirations and conscious of "their union with one another in origin and destiny" [43]—a sense of oneness which may take on "a definitely religious quality." [44]

In *Art as Experience,* Dewey elaborated a point already suggested in *Experience and Nature*: [45] that aesthetic experience, being a fully realized experience, provides all the insights needed for a philosophy of experience. Aesthetic experience is "experience in its integrity"; [46] it is therefore the kind of experience to which the philosopher can go in order to discover what experience is. Philosophers have traditionally viewed aesthetic experience as a separate and special kind of activity, as supplying insights applicable only to itself. Dewey's position is that aesthetic experience, like all experience, is the prolonged and continuous interaction of a self and environmental material and that the consummatory fulfillment in aesthetic experience is potential in all experience.

Art as Experience was acclaimed as "the most important contribution to æsthetics that America has yet produced." [47] Dewey's empirical approach to the problems of aesthetics was widely welcomed. His success in handling aesthetic subject matter led one reviewer to assert that "empiricism in æsthetics need no longer be on the defensive; the burden of proof has been decisively shifted." [48]

Dewey's volume was also welcomed as putting his instrumentalism in its larger context. Critics had long attacked Dewey's philosophy because of its emphasis on means, its exaltation of the practical, and its preoccupation with science and technology. In *Art as Experience* Dewey stressed that consummation and fulfillment as found in aesthetic experience are what make life worthwhile and give it meaning. Means and instruments are of importance and deep concern, but only because they determine the success or failure of mankind's endeavors to reach desired ends.

Dewey's next book, *A Common Faith*,[49] followed quickly after *Art as Experience*. It, too, was the outgrowth of a series of lectures, the three talks given on the Dwight Harrington Terry Foundation at Yale University in January 1934. Dewey's aim in these lectures was to restore religion to its proper place in human experience by putting it in its naturalistic and humanistic setting.

His account begins with a distinction between "religion" and "religious." "Religion" is a collective term referring to the sum total of religions, each with its own particular set of beliefs and observances, and unique institutional organization.[50] "Religious" signifies a "quality of experience" applicable to two kinds of experience: that which relates the individual to the universe of things and persons in such a way as "to effect an adjustment in life, an orientation, that brings with it a sense of security and peace,"[51] and that which is "any activity pursued in behalf of an ideal end against obstacles and in spite of threats of personal loss because of conviction of its general and enduring value."[52]

The great historic religions also accept these two kinds of experience as genuinely religious, but they have tied them in with ideas of the supernatural and the transcendent, centering attention on these. They have made faith in a supernatural Being and the observances growing out of that faith of central importance, tending to obscure or push into the background the role of man and nature in bringing about a more ideal existence. In doing this, religion has alienated large numbers of people who, primarily for intellectual reasons, cannot accept faith in the supernatural or participate in the practices required by such a faith. The results have been a widespread indifference to religion in many quarters and a general lessening of its influence in human affairs.

If religion is to recapture its place in human life and play the effective role in human culture that it formerly did, it must abandon the ideas and practices inherited from a prescientific and pretechnological age and substitute ideas of man and nature in keeping with modern science and with present-day moral and social idealism. Religion must free itself from the "weight of historic encumbrances," [53] allowing the natural religious quality of experience to come to consciousness and find appropriate expression. Religion must recognize that the only meaningful, ideally satisfying life is that which relates to existence here and now, which can be attained only through human powers cooperating with the appropriate forces in nature. "Were the naturalistic foundations and bearings of religion grasped," wrote Dewey, "the religious element in life would emerge from the throes of the crisis in religion. Religion would then be found to have its natural place in every aspect of human experience that is concerned with estimate of possibilities, with emotional stir by possibilities as yet unrealized, and with all action in behalf of their realization." [54]

The process by which the actual is transformed into the ideal Dewey called "God" or the "divine." He believed he was justified in this because the "working union of the ideal and actual" is "identical with the force that has in fact been attached to the conception of God in all the religions that have a spiritual content." [55] He knew that using the word "God" laid his doctrine open to misinterpretation because of the term's long association with the supernatural. Despite this, he believed he ought to employ the term because it draws attention in a striking way to the notion of an operating union of the actual and the ideal, and "in a distracted age the need for such an idea is urgent." [56]

Dewey emphasized that the realization of ideals depends as much on the cooperating forces of nature as on man's endeavors. Without the materials nature supplies and without the help nature gives, man's efforts would be groundless. Consequently Dewey criticized both atheism and religious humanism insofar as these view mankind as living in an alien and hostile world, depending solely on itself for the realization of a good life. He charged them with a "lack of natural piety." [57] A genuinely religious attitude, he argued, requires "the sense of a connection of man, in the way of both dependence and support, with the enveloping world that the imagination feels is a universe." [58]

Institutional religions, Dewey believed, have little to lose and much to gain from abandoning belief in the supernatural and the practices associated with it, focusing attention upon ideal possibilities here and now. "The transfer of idealizing imagination, thought and emotion to natural human relations," he declared, "would not signify the destruction of churches that now exist. It would rather offer the means for a recovery of vitality. The fund of human values that are prized and that need to be cherished, values that are satisfied and rectified by *all* human concerns and arrangements, could be celebrated and reinforced, in different ways and with differing symbols, by the churches. In that way the churches would indeed become catholic." [59]

The book's concluding paragraph eloquently sums up Dewey's ideas of the faith that can and should inspire the efforts of mankind:

The ideal ends to which we attach our faith are not shadowy and wavering. They assume concrete form in our understanding of our relations to one another and the values contained in these relations. We who now live are parts of a humanity that extends into the remote past, a humanity that has interacted with nature. The things in civilization we most prize are not of ourselves. They exist by grace of the doings and sufferings of the continuous human community in which we are a link. Ours is the responsibility of conserving, transmitting, rectifying and expanding the heritage of values we have received that those who come after us may receive it more solid and secure, more widely accessible and more generously shared than we have received it. Here are all the elements for a religious faith that shall not be confined to sect, class, or race. Such a faith has always been implicitly the common faith of mankind. It remains to make it explicit and militant.[60]

A Common Faith was eagerly read in scholarly circles, causing considerable excitement, especially because of Dewey's use of the word "God." Those who had followed the development of his philosophy had long desired a book comprehensively stating and defending his religious views. *The Quest for Certainty* had disappointed many readers because it had failed to deal specifically with the religious problem, leaving Dewey's position in some respects open to question. Reviewers were agreed that *A Common Faith,* though quite brief, helped to round out Dewey's position by adding insights that greatly enriched the reader's understanding of Dewey's religious humanism.[61]

Some believed that Dewey had too lightly dismissed the experiences within institutionalized religion. He judged these to be based on outmoded beliefs, therefore not meriting too much attention from philosophy of religion. His treatment of religion in this respect contrasts sharply with that he accorded to art. As one reviewer, otherwise sympathetic to Dewey's general philosophy, put it:

In art, Dewey is quite aware that criticism not intimately acquainted with a variety of traditions is limited, one-sided, and distorted. For him art is the gateway to appreciating alien cultures, and his perception is both catholic and discriminating. But religion must reject the past for the best in the present; and here his sympathies are both protestant and unimaginative. Art is to be enjoyed wherever it is found excellent; religion is not to be enjoyed, but to be emancipated from historic encumbrances the better to foster an intelligent humanism. Whatever one's agreement with the specific criticism and program, the fact remains that while Dewey has clarified the meaning of the whole artistic side of man's experience, he has merely stated the case for American liberal humanism today.[62]

The summer of 1934 found Dewey, accompanied by his daughter Jane, participating in the South African Education Conference. This conference was sponsored by the New Education Fellowship, a loosely organized international body founded in 1915 to draw together teachers, parents, social workers, and others to promote education more suited to changing needs. The conference was financed and otherwise supported by numerous government agencies, educational institutions, churches, and civic organizations throughout South Africa.[63]

The first session of the conference was held in Capetown from 2 July to 13 July; the second in Johannesburg from 16 July to 27 July. Over four thousand persons attended the two sessions, and over three hundred formal addresses were delivered by one hundred and forty-five speakers.[64] Dewey, one of twenty-five specially invited overseas speakers, had his travel expenses and those of his daughter paid by the Carnegie Corporation of New York.[65]

The general theme of the conference was the adaptation of education to meet the rapidly changing needs of society, with special application to South Africa. Three main issues were discussed: the ultimate aim of education, the problem of method, and the problem of the curriculum. Dewey spoke at each session, choosing as his subjects: "The Need for a Philosophy of Education," "What Is Learning?" and "Growth in Activity."[66] In these talks Dewey expressed ideas familiar to readers of his earlier works on education: that without a guiding philosophy education merely drifts or improvises; that learning is organically one with doing; and that education has no aim beyond that of individual growth.

Apart from the meetings devoted to discussions of educational problems, there was much in South Africa to interest members of the conference. Perhaps more than any other place at the time, South Africa was a unique laboratory in racial and cultural relations. A small white population of less than two million, occupying the tip of a continent with a black population of one hundred and forty million, sought to keep its European way of life intact while at the same time establishing suitable working relations with the country's nonwhites. In addition, within the white population tensions were built up by those of English and Dutch descent as each group clung tenaciously to its unique cultural traditions.

The conference provided several tours so that members could observe at firsthand the patterns of life prevailing in the country as well as programs aimed at improving the lot of the masses. Dewey and Jane, who took advantage of many of the tours, also went on unscheduled trips. According to Jane, "There was a good deal of time for travel and we saw the country. I think these trips were not at all part of the agenda. We saw a good many missions, medical and religious, to see what was going on in the education of the natives and to improve their conditions. . . . I remember that the agents for the native reservations took us on very interesting trips, probably very much to the detriment of their regular work. I mean just one day tours but we saw a great deal more than we could have on our own." [67] Unfortunately, Dewey did not record his impressions of South Africa as he had those of his trips to Japan, China, Turkey, Mexico, and Russia.

Still another volume by Dewey, *Liberalism and Social Action,* was published in 1935.[68] This work is an elaboration of the series of three lectures that Dewey delivered at the University of Virginia upon the Page-Barbour Foundation and is dedicated to the memory of Jane Addams. The book reflects Dewey's concern with the rising tide of antiliberalism during the troubled years of the 1930s when various brands of conservatism, radicalism, and liberalism were competing for supremacy. The spate of articles, pamphlets, and books on political and social issues at this time is a measure of the general interest and general concern with these topics. The main argument of Dewey's book is that liberalism needs to be restated in terms relevant to twentieth century realities, that it must be linked to radicalism in action if it is to survive and serve as a guide in the solution of today's pressing social problems.

Tracing briefly the history of liberalism, Dewey noted that it arose in the seventeenth and eighteenth centuries as a protest against the innumerable restrictions imposed on individual activities by organized society. Governmental restraints were particularly resented because they were considered unnecessary in most cases, especially in economics. A laissez-faire economy was regarded as most in keeping with individual freedoms in that it allowed a maximum of individual liberties and a minimum of government restraint in the conduct of business. During this early stage liberalism was emphatically individualistic in the sense in which individualism is opposed to organized social action.

As the industrial revolution developed and great masses of workers and their dependents became its victims, this early liberalism was found to be inadequate. A laissez-faire economy could not be trusted to bring the good life automatically to all. The conviction among liberals then was that government must intervene through legislation to protect and help the laboring and underprivileged groups who were otherwise at the mercy of the captains of industry and of the economic process. By the end of the nineteenth and into the twentieth century, the spirit and meaning of liberalism had changed. As Dewey put it, "It came surely, if gradually, to be disassociated from the laissez faire creed and to be associated with the use of governmental action for aid to those at economic disadvantage and for alleviation of their conditions." [69]

But this type of liberalism, Dewey argued, has in turn become outmoded, as the depression made abundantly clear. Occasional reforms and isolated public services have proved inadequate; as improvisations designed to meet special emergencies, they fail to get at such underlying causes of social evils as private ownership of natural resources and public utilities, the unequal and unjust distribution of national income, and the absence of overall social planning. Only a radical reorganization of the economic order will get at fundamental causes and bring into existence a more just society; present-day liberalism must strive in behalf of such reorganization if it is to continue.

As to the precise form the new economy should take, Dewey repeated what he had said on previous occasions: "The only form of enduring social organization that is now possible is one in which the new forces of productivity are coöperatively controlled and used in the interest of the effective liberty and the cultural development of the individuals that constitute society." [70] And if radicalism is defined as awareness of the need for drastic changes in the organization of the economic order, then "any liberalism which is not also radicalism is irrelevant and doomed." To play an effective and significant role in the life of today, liberalism must be radical, radical in the sense of seeing "the necessity of thorough-going changes in the set-up of institutions and corresponding activity to bring the changes to pass." [71]

A cooperatively controlled and used economy requires a high degree of difficult, complex planning, which in turn calls for "a new conception and logic of freed intelligence as a social force."[72] Liberalism, as Dewey pointed out, has always been committed to the use of freed intelligence as a means of directing social change. Early liberalism emphasized the use of reason by the individual, championing freedom of thought, expression, and debate. But valuable as these freedoms are, they are not enough to originate and develop the intricate, comprehensive planning required in a socially controlled and directed economy. This demands the type of intelligence characteristic of a community of scientists—intelligence that is socially organized, cooperative, experimental, always concerned with the solution of concrete problems. The value of such an intelligence is attested by its remarkable triumphs in areas where it has been allowed to function, most notably in the natural sciences. Dewey was convinced that if this type of intelligence were applied to the solution of human problems, equally remarkable results would follow. "Great as have been the social changes of the last century," he had written a few years earlier, "they are not to be compared with those which will emerge when our faith in scientific method is made manifest in social works."[73] The depression, he believed, is a small price to pay if it induces men to think more scientifically in their search for its causes and of ways to control them.

For organized, cooperative, experimental intelligence to come into existence and function effectively, changes are needed in our basic ideas, attitudes, and habits of thought and conduct. Up to now these have been determined mostly by an individualistic philosophy and way of life, whereas now the need is for patterns of thought, feeling, and action geared to a cooperative, intelligent, experimental society. Dewey called upon all the educational forces in society to bring about this change, declaring that educational work is "the primary, though not by any means the ultimate, responsibility of a liberalism that intends to be a vital force."[74]

In contrast with communism, Dewey opposed violence as a way of effecting social change, emphasizing that it has no place in the liberalism he espoused. Violence is to be rejected because the means it employs destroys the ends it strives for. Force, he argued, breeds counterforces, so that in the society which eventually emerges, the values originally aimed at are sacrificed to the interests of one or another of the conflicting parties. "I know of no greater fallacy," he wrote, "than the claim of those who hold to the dogma of the necessity of brute force that this use will be the method of calling genuine democracy into existence—of which they profess themselves the simon-pure adherents. It requires an unusually credulous faith in the Hegelian dialectic of opposites to think that all of a sudden the use of force by a class will be transmuted into a democratic classless society." [75]

Most liberals applauded *Liberalism and Social Action*, finding that while it remained faithful to the fundamental values of traditional liberalism, it suggested ways these could be secured and extended in the realities of current existence. "Dewey's 'Liberalism and Social Action'," declared one reviewer, "restates in the language and under the conditions of his times what Jefferson's Declaration of Independence affirmed in the language and under the conditions of his." [76] Sidney Hook, referring to the work a few years later, declared that it could "very well be to the twentieth century what Marx and Engels' *Communist Manifesto* was to the nineteenth." [77]

Some, however, believed that Dewey's liberalism rested on a too naïve faith in the goodness and perfectibility of human nature and in the ability of freed intelligence to direct social change. These critics declared that Dewey failed to appreciate adequately the decisive role that competing selfish interests play in determining these changes. Reinhold Niebuhr's remarks are typical of this line of criticism: "[Dewey's liberalism] does not perceive the perennial and inevitable character of the subordination of reason to interest in the social struggle. Its ideal of a 'freed intelligence' expects a degree of rational freedom from the particular interests and perspectives of those who think about social problems which is incompatible with the very constitution of human nature." [78]

Though deeply concerned with problems at home, the people of the United States were not unmindful of developments on international fronts during the early 1930s. Mussolini and his Fascist party, having come into power in Italy, were making plans to invade Ethiopia; Hitler and the Nazis, having gained control in Germany, were demanding the restoration of territories in Europe taken from Germany by the Versailles Treaty; there was political unrest in Spain; Japanese militarists, upon becoming the dominant force in their country, had taken steps to expand Japan's control over Manchuria. Thoughtful observers recognized that unless these developments were halted and peaceful arrangements worked out, war on a wide scale was inevitable.

Opinion in the United States in both liberal and conservative quarters was that the nation should stay out of such a conflict should it occur. The feeling was that America's entry into

World War I had been a mistake; that the people of the United States had been taken in by British propaganda, by a militarist press at home, and by the undercover activities of bankers and munitions manufacturers; that the government's insistence on certain neutrality rights had been unwise. The prevailing attitude was that the United States should not repeat the mistakes attending the outbreak of the First World War but should remain strictly neutral in case of war.

Dewey shared this general mood. He expressed his stand in his answers to the questions put to him and to some other prominent persons in a June 1935 symposium sponsored by the *Modern Monthly*. Replying to the first question, "What will you do when America goes to war?" Dewey wrote: "Do my best first to keep the country out and then if it happens to keep myself out." To the second question, "Will your decision be altered if Soviet Russia is an ally of the United States in a war with Japan?" Dewey answered, "No." The last question was, "Would a prospective victory by Hitler over most of Europe move you to urge U.S. participation in opposition to Germany in order to prevent such a catastrophe?" Dewey's reply was: "No, as at present informed." [79]

The anti-Jewish and antiliberal stand of the Nazi government in Germany and the persecution of distinguished scholars in other countries under totalitarian rule greatly disturbed scholars in this country. Letters describing the plight of foreign scholars and protesting the treatment accorded them were circulated among the faculties and staffs of universities; suggestions were solicited as to what might be done to help the victims of this persecution, but nothing of consequence resulted from this action. At this point Alvin Johnson, then president of the New School for Social Research, proposed a plan for his institution. He conceived the idea of establishing, as an integral part of the New School, a University-in-Exile where refugee scholars could pursue their studies without interference from government, where they could conduct their classes on the graduate level along the lines of instruction characteristic of European universities. The Board of Directors of the New School agreed to the proposal and authorized raising funds to finance the project. When these became available, a number of scholars, mostly from Germany, were invited to the New School; in 1933, they became the first faculty of the University-in-Exile.[80] Inspired by the example of the New School, other institutions of higher learning added refugee scholars to their faculties so that by the end of World War II a sizeable number of Europe's foremost scholars and educators were contributing significantly to the enrichment of American higher education.

Dewey became involved from the beginning in the venture at the New School when, along with other prominent Americans, he was appointed a member of the advisory committee of the University-in-Exile.[81] He closely followed the activities of the new organization and was aware of the contributions many of its members were making to the cultural life of the nation. But he also recognized the shortcomings of some of them. In a letter to Arthur F. Bentley, he remarked that "so many of the Germans in the New School were so bound up with their 'idealisms' as to be more or less out of step with American life."[82] Two years later, in 1942 in another letter to Bentley, he expressed the hope that "in the long run the influx of German refugees will contribute something, but meantime a lot of them are committed to advertising the goods they brought over with them . . . and those who have 'phenomenology'—whatever this is—to sell seem the worst."[83]

Dewey's interest in civic affairs continued to be strong. Charges of widespread corruption in the government of the City of New York in the early thirties led to an investigation of conditions in the courts and other departments of the city's government. Samuel Seabury, a prominent lawyer and citizen of New York who was appointed chief investigator, made an exhaustive study of conditions. His findings shocked civic leaders and other thoughtful citizens who believed that the disclosures ought to be called to the attention of the people at large. To this end, a committee of civic workers and prominent educators was formed, with Dewey as chairman. This committee in 1933 prepared a pamphlet that summarized the findings of the Seabury investigation, explaining what such corruption meant to the citizens of New York.[84]

The death in April 1931 of George Herbert Mead, Dewey's former colleague at the University of Michigan and at the University of Chicago, ended a friendship of some forty years. At the family's request, Dewey gave the principal address at the services in Bond Chapel on the University of Chicago campus. In his remarks Dewey referred to Mead's kind and generous nature, his wide range of knowledge, and his varied interests, including the work of the University of Chicago Settlement House. He paid tribute to Mead as an original and profound thinker, declaring that Mead's studies in the social nature of the self and his philosophy of the complete act were scholarly contributions of the first order that had inspired much study and research by others. "His mind was germinative and seminal," said Dewey; "one would have to go far to find a teacher of our own day who started in others so many fruitful lines of thought." As to Mead's influence on his own thought, Dewey declared, "I dislike to think what my own thinking might have been were it not for the seminal ideas which I derived from him." [85]

Honors continued to come to Dewey after his retirement. In November 1930, the University of Paris granted him the degree of Docteur de l'université *honoris causa.* Dewey was one of a number of persons of international prominence, including King Albert of Belgium, who were given degrees at this time.[86] Dewey's daughter Lucy and her husband Wolf came from their home in Vienna to attend the ceremonies, and Lucy has recalled the large, friendly, vivacious, and altogether enjoyable dinner that preceded the meeting at which the degrees were given.[87] In reading the citation for Dewey, the Dean of the Faculty of Letters referred to him as "the most profound, most complete expression of American genius." [88] After the ceremonies, Dewey left with the Brandauers for a few weeks of rest and relaxation in Vienna.

Another honorary degree came to Dewey when Harvard University conferred the LL.D. degree on him at its commencement exercises on 23 June 1932. In making the citation President Lowell declared: "John Dewey: Doctor of Laws—Most renowned of living American philosophers, we rejoice to add our sprig of laurel to his crown." [89]

The National Education Association, in response to a resolution introduced by the New York delegation, at its meeting in Atlantic City, 25 June to 1 July 1932, elected Dewey one of two honorary presidents of the association.[90]

Tragedy struck the Dewey family when the infant daughter of Lucy and Wolf Brandauer died in the summer of 1931. In a letter to Mrs. Levinson, Dewey wrote, "We had a cable from Lucy that they have lost their little girl, and I feel that I must go over and be with her for a few weeks. . . . I expect to sail from N.Y. about Aug. 20." [91] Levinson replied, "Your letter to Ruth contains the sad news of which you have had all too many in your family. To me there is something abnormally sad in the loss of a budding infant that has already made its deep impression on the lives around it, although not having reached the point of thought and expression. We extend our deepest and most affectionate sympathy to you and to Lucy." [92]

Another death in the family occurred when John, the thirteen-year-old son of Fred and Elizabeth, died in the Flushing, New York, hospital on 29 December 1934, from a skull fracture suffered when he had run into an automobile the day before. A student in a school in Colorado Springs, Colorado, he had been home for the Christmas holidays [93] when the accident occurred. Levinson, ever thoughtful, wrote: "It was with bleeding heart that we read yesterday (Sunday) of the terrible accident to your namesake grandson. All our love and sympathy to you, Fred, and to the boy's mother." [94]

14. Emeritus, Columbia University, 1935–1939

THE 1930s witnessed an unprecedented interest in American education. The depression had raised the question of costs and the need for retrenchment in various areas of school life, but discussion soon went beyond the economics of education to focus on topics of a social and professional nature. Among issues that became subjects of debate were: the wisdom of discussing controversial political, economic, and social matters in the classroom, indoctrination, academic freedom, loyalty oaths for teachers, religious instruction in the public schools, and the perennial question of the relative merits of traditional and progressive education. Not only professional educators but leading figures in government, business, religious organizations, and the professions joined in the debates, raising public interest in education to an unusually high pitch.

Aware of the importance to American education of the issues being debated, Dewey devoted a large portion of his time to considering them. Many of his articles on education and related themes appeared in the *Social Frontier,* a newly established progressive journal dedicated to educational criticism and reconstruction.[1] "The Teacher and His World" urged teachers, parents, and others responsible for the direction of public education to keep informed of current social movements and lend support to those promising a better and happier future.[2] "Youth in a Confused World" and "The Need for Orientation" argued that subject matter in the school should include controversial political, economic, and social topics, for only by acquainting students with current conditions while they are in school will they understand the kind of world they are about to enter, the direction it is moving, and their role in it.[3]

Unlike many liberal educators, Dewey opposed indoctrination in the classroom if it means the conscious inculcation of a fixed set of social beliefs. Indoctrination, he believed, is the antithesis of education. Indoctrination demands that the teacher give a biased account of a controversial issue and attempt to win the pupil to a particular point of view. Education requires that the teacher present all sides of an issue as objectively as he can, encouraging the student to think these through critically and make his own choice from among social alternatives. In "The Crucial Role of Intelligence," Dewey declared that the main safeguard against the massive attempts of press and radio to indoctrinate the public is a critical intelligence informed of all sides of an issue. "War propaganda and the situation in Hitlerized Germany," he wrote, "prove that unless the schools create a popular intelligence that is critically discriminating, there is no limit to the prejudices and inflamed emotion that will result."[4] Dewey's faith was that intelligence, if allowed to function freely and to examine all sides of a controversial issue confronting the nation, will support a reconstructed and more effective democratic order.

Academic freedom became a pressing concern when conservative groups, alarmed at the liberal and radical ideas circulating in many academic quarters, took measures to stop the discussion of such views in schools and colleges. Powerful forces, frequently organized on a nationwide scale, moved to make the schools safe for conservatism. Chambers of Commerce, the conservative press—especially that of William Randolph Hearst—the American Legion, the D.A.R., the American Liberty League, and other "patriotic" organizations denounced the radicalism of educators, demanding the dismissal of teachers found guilty of harboring "un-American" views. Twenty-two states and the District of Columbia, under pressure of conservative groups, passed laws sharply restricting the right of teachers to discuss unpopular and radical views.[5]

The conservative attack stirred strong, vigorous counterattacks by members of the teaching profession and by liberals in government, the press, religious organizations, business, and the professions. In books, articles, and public addresses, champions of academic freedom condemned the attack upon freedom, warning that if this attack succeeded, the schools and colleges of this country would be reduced to the same condition as schools in totalitarian countries.

Because Dewey had many times over the years come to the defense of academic freedom, his stand on the issue was well known. However, his 1936 article, "The Social Significance of Academic Freedom," develops an idea not previously elaborated: the bearing of academic freedom on methods of social reconstruction. He argued that if social changes are to be brought about in a peaceful, intelligent way, people must be trained in the art of free and enlightened discussion as exemplified in schools where academic freedom prevails. Without such training, wrote Dewey, "without freedom of inquiry and freedom on the part of teachers and students to explore the forces at work in society and the means by which they may be directed, the habits of intelligent action that are necessary to the orderly development of society cannot be created."[6] As events in totalitarian countries have shown, he wrote, the usual alternative in such a situation is violent and directive force.

A practice that evoked vigorous dissent from the teaching profession was the requirement that teachers take loyalty oaths. Teachers in New York were particularly concerned because the Ives Law, passed in 1934, required that all teachers take a special oath of loyalty to the Constitution of the United States and of the State of New York. Conservatives were solidly behind the law; they felt it did no injustice to loyal teachers while at the same time serving as a useful device for identifying Communists and other teachers with un-American views. Liberal and radical teacher leaders saw in the oath a threat to academic freedom and to teacher organizations. They feared that in a period of public hysteria, the law could be used to oust from the school system teachers who were critical of the current political and economic system as well as teachers who were most forthright in their demands for teachers' rights.

Dewey had no objection to requiring citizens to take oaths of allegiance to the Constitution. He did object, however, to singling out members of the teaching profession, requiring only them to do this. He opposed this practice because it was so obviously designed to be "one phase of the general movement calculated to prevent freedom of education in all matters that relate to economic and political conditions and policies."[7]

Disturbed at the increase in juvenile delinquency and crime, the decline in church and Sunday School attendance, and the growing indifference of young people to religion, prominent representatives of religious organizations took the lead in a movement to introduce religious instruction in the public schools. It was charged that the public schools in becoming secularized had neglected education in moral and religious values and that this neglect was the chief cause of prevailing evils. The remedy, it was argued, was to bring religious instruction back into the schools to train children in the ways of morality and religion.

Such instruction, it was suggested, could take the form of Bible readings, prayer, and the observance in the classroom of special religious occasions, such as Christmas and Easter; it could take the form also of courses focusing on the religious heritage of the several religions or denominations, a child taking only that course dealing with the religion to which his parents belonged; or it could be provided under a plan whereby school authorities would "release" a portion of the school day when children could attend classes in religion conducted by teachers supplied by the religious organizations involved, either within a school classroom or in quarters supplied by the religious organization. Children whose parents were opposed to instruction in any one religion would take a prescribed course in ethics.

These proposals stirred up heated controversy. Opponents pointed out the practical difficulties of carrying out some of the suggestions without offense to one or another of the several religious groups in a community; they declared that the proposals violated the time-honored American principle of the separation of church and state; they maintained that pupils in public schools were receiving moral, as distinguished from religious, training and that character building was a prime objective of the schools; they insisted that the public schools remain public rather than become instruments of vested religious interests.[8]

Dewey had expressed very similar opposition views in an article entitled "Religion and Our Schools" when agitation for religious instruction in the schools was just beginning in 1908. He particularly deplored the plan of "parcelling out pupils among religious teachers drawn from their respective churches and denominations" for religious instruction during the school day. Such an arrangement, he argued, made the pupils conscious of their differences, created divisions, and weakened the schools' efforts to inculcate the sense of social unity that is so important for the effective working of democracy.[9] When the Board of Education of New York City held an open hearing on 13 November 1940 on a bill providing released time for religious instruction during the school day, Dewey was one of those who appeared to urge defeat of the measure. His argument then, as in 1908, was that a released-time program would cause divisions in the children's school life and undermine the feeling of community the schools were attempting to foster. "I certainly hope," the press reported his saying, "that the Board of Education will think very,

very seriously before it introduces this division and antagonism in our public schools." [10]

Although long-standing, the question of the relative merits of traditional and progressive education was still debated spiritedly during the 1930s. Often Dewey was among the critics of progressive education, not because he had abandoned the principles upon which this sort of education rested but because he was disturbed by the interpretation and application of these principles in many progressive schools. In "How Much Freedom in New Schools?" he pointed out that in their zeal to avoid the formalism and regimentation of the traditional schools, many progressive educators had gone to opposite extremes, establishing programs that reflected their "enthusiasm much more than their understanding." [11] Believing that adult interests and aims should not be imposed on the child, many educators had gone so far as to allow the child to decide what he should study. Such educators forget that the immature and passing interests of the child are not adequate guides for his continuing, integrated growth and development. Also, rejecting the notion of the teacher as a taskmaster imposing his will on the children, many educators had reduced the teacher's role to that of chaperone or custodian. These persons fail to see that the mature, informed, skilled teacher is more fruitfully employed when he shares in the activities of the classroom, guiding them into channels that lead to genuine growth and education. Again, judging external authority and regimentation to be encroachments on the child's liberty, some educators, especially those farthest to the left, had abolished virtually all restrictions in the classroom; they had carried "the thing they call freedom nearly to the point of anarchy," allowing the pupils "unrestrained freedom of action and speech, of manners and lack of manners." Such educators overlook the fact that the attitudes, dispositions, and habits of conduct growing out of that kind of freedom ill prepare the child for life in organized and civilized society. There is much evidence indicating, Dewey declared, that "in some progressive schools the fear of adult imposition has become a veritable phobia." [12]

Dewey maintained that the weaknesses of many progressive schools stemmed from a lack of understanding of the laws of growth and learning and their detailed application to the work of the school. He urged progressive educators to acquire the needed information and to use it to correct existing evils. He warned that if progressive schools neglect this responsibility, if they become "complacent with existing accomplishments, unaware of the slight foundation of knowledge upon [which] they rest, and careless regarding the amount of study of the laws of growth that remains to be done, a reaction against them is sure to take place."[13]

Experience and Education,[14] Dewey's most important work in education during the 1930s, suggests the direction educational inquiry must take. Educators must go to experience to determine "the potentialities of education when it is treated as intelligently directed development of the possibilities inherent in ordinary experience."[15] Consequently the major portion of the book is concerned with analyzing experience and with applying the results of the analysis to educational theory and practice. *Experience and Education* can quite appropriately be regarded as an invitation to educators to construct "a philosophy of education based upon a philosophy of experience."[16]

Experience, Dewey found, involves the two principles of continuity and interaction. The principle of continuity holds that present experience grows out of past experience and leads into future ones. The principle of interaction states that experience is the interaction of individual, subjective, internal factors and external environmental ones—physical, social, and cultural. Dewey demonstrated in considerable detail that these principles serve as helpful guides in determining educational theory and practice.

The principle of continuity, for example, points to growth as the end or goal of education. It suggests that subject matter be organized to meet the interests and needs of the child at each stage of development. It implies that the methods of instruction and school organization be attuned to the child's continuously increasing maturity and responsibility.

The principle of interaction requires that both the child's present abilities, interests, likes and dislikes, and the present and future demands of the child's external world be taken into account when selecting subject matter, organizing the school, and adopting methods of discipline and control.

Whether a present activity is a genuinely educative experience depends upon its effect on the child's future growth. Many activities carried on in the classroom arrest, distort, or misdirect future growth and so are not truly educative. "Hence the central problem of an education based upon experience," Dewey wrote, "is to select the kind of present experiences that live fruitfully and creatively in subsequent experiences."[17]

Dewey's argument throughout is addressed to all educators in behalf of *Education* itself, not in support of any particular kind of education, either traditional or progressive;[18] he was as ready to criticize progressive education as to condemn traditional education whenever he believed it engaged in practices not genuinely educative.

Experience and Education received no extended reviews at the time it appeared. But the frequency of references to it in the decades following its publication attests its importance. What readers have found particularly helpful is that Dewey restated and clarified many of his ideas against the background of the criticisms, distortions, and misunderstandings they had evoked over the years. The book also demonstrates that he was not to be identified with everything that goes on in the name of progressive education.

The general and widespread interest in educational problems extended also to the nation's colleges and universities. Both professional educators and the informed public, disturbed for some years by the confused and patchwork nature of education on the higher levels, had been casting about for ways to correct the situation. Discussion came to a head in 1936 with the appearance of *The Higher Learning in America*[19] by Robert M. Hutchins, president of the University of Chicago, which examined the nature and causes of the chaos in American higher education and urged a return to reason in education. For Hutchins this meant essentially a return to traditional concepts and practices on all levels of education. On the college and university level it meant that studies should be limited to those with "intellectual content," that is, those exclusively concerned with broad, general, abstract principles and theories that challenge man's reason with no reference to any practical or vocational use. It meant making metaphysics the unifying discipline in the curriculum because, as the study of first principles, it supplies the intellectual framework within which each of the other studies finds its proper place and ultimate meaning. Though Hutchins mentioned no particular metaphysics for his plan, his frequent references to Aristotle and Saint Thomas as well as his close association with Mortimer Adler, a professed Neo-Thomist, led his readers to believe that some version of Neo-Thomism underlay his thinking.

Hutchins's proposals created a lively stir among educators, with traditionalists rallying to their defense and liberals wondering how "a young man connected with the University of Chicago" could suggest a theory that "rejects the essence of every intellectual advance of the last 300 years."[20] Though agreeing with Hutchins that American higher education was confused about its aims and subject matter, Dewey differed with him as to the remedy. He rejected particularly Hutchins's idea that subject matter with a vocational or practical bearing should be excluded from university curricula and only courses dealing with abstract, theoretical material allowed. Such an arrangement, he declared, means "the greatest possible aloofness of higher learning from contemporary social life" and manifests the old dualism of theory and practice.[21] If higher education is to be vital and relevant to existing needs, Dewey argued, it must concern itself with present-day social problems and help supply the insights needed for their solution.

Equally strong was Dewey's criticism of Hutchins's proposal that metaphysics should occupy the central place in a university curriculum. His objection was that this arrangement requires some individual or group to determine what particular metaphysics should prevail and the place each discipline should have in the hierarchy of studies. The authoritarianism implied in such a plan, he declared, does violence to the tradition of freedom in American education. It is "akin to the distrust of freedom and the consequent appeal to *some* fixed authority that is now overrunning the world."[22]

Dewey's conviction was that rationality and order will come to higher education to the extent it dedicates itself to the common good and accepts critical inquiry, the findings of science and technology, as the surest means of attaining this good. Within such a framework, he declared, the several disciplines would have a single unified goal and direction; they would cooperate and reinforce each other in achieving that goal. In such a situation the confusion, the dualisms, and conflict of aims harassing higher education would tend to disappear.

A notable honor came to Dewey in 1935 when a group of professional educators mostly from the New York City area founded an organization dedicated to the study of education and culture named The John Dewey Society.[23] After a modest start, the society expanded its membership till eventually it included persons from throughout the nation as well as some foreign countries.[24] One of the society's earliest accomplishments was publication of a series of yearbooks, some of which earned a secure place in the history of educational literature. In the late 1950s the society began a series of publications entitled The John Dewey Lecture Series; in the 1960s it started another called The John Dewey Society Studies in Educational Theory. More recently it has sponsored a number of annual awards for distinguished service to education in the spirit of John Dewey.

The Moscow Trials of August 1936 and January 1937, in which almost all the "Old Bolsheviks" who had helped engineer the 1917 revolution were tried, convicted, and ruthlessly shot, deeply shocked the civilized world. Men who had been regarded for years as belonging to the innermost circles of Soviet leaders were condemned as enemies of the Soviet Union, in league with its Fascist enemies. Especially mystifying were the "confessions" that supplied a major portion of the evidence against those brought to trial.

Among the accused, Leon Trotsky was the most important figure. The principal charges against him and his son Sedov were that they had directed terrorist attempts on the life of Stalin and other Soviet officials, organized acts of industrial sabotage to weaken the economy of the nation and undermine its military strength, and entered into secret agreements with Germany and Japan to wage war against the Soviet Union, to cede certain territory to these countries after the defeat of Russia, and to restore capitalism in Russia.

Trotsky, however, was beyond the immediate reach of Stalin's police and escaped execution. Throughout the course of the trials he was in exile, first in Norway, then in Mexico. Bitterly condemning the procedure of the trials, he requested a hearing for himself and his son before an impartial tribunal. To help Trotsky get this, a group of American liberals and radicals joined with American Trotskyites to establish the American Committee for the Defense of Leon Trotsky,[25] of which Dewey was elected honorary chairman.

After arriving in Mexico, Trotsky urged that a commission be set up at once to hear his case. In response to his plea, the American Committee organized in March 1937 a Commission of Inquiry to hear and study the charges against Trotsky. Dewey agreed to serve as chairman of this commission and also as chairman of a subcommittee that would go to Mexico for the hearings. This subcommittee became known as the Preliminary Commission of Inquiry.

Communists in the United States raised loud objections to this effort to give Trotsky a chance to be heard. They claimed the plan's main purpose was to discredit the Soviet Union and help its Fascist, capitalist enemies. Members of the committee were subjected to annoyances, verbal abuse, false charges, and physical threats. Some, including Dewey, were offered free trips to Russia to see for themselves the economic and social advances being made there. To offset the effect on public opinion that the Committee for the Defense of Leon Trotsky was having, Communist leaders drew up a statement condemning the committee's efforts, which they succeeded in having signed by scores of prominent American liberals, socialists, and radicals.[26]

Dewey became a particular target of Communist attack. Prior to his joining the committee, he had been held in high regard in Communist circles. His glowing report on Soviet education following his trip to Russia in 1928 and his sympathetic understanding of what Communist leaders were attempting to do for the Russian masses pleased American Communists, who considered him one of the most progressive and enlightened of liberals. His membership in the commission and his willingness to serve as chairman of the Preliminary Commission of Inquiry brought an abrupt change in attitude. The Communist press now charged him with being a "Fascist," "a Charlie McCarthy for the Trotskyites" and "a tool of reaction."[27] The *Daily Worker* declared that "liberals like Dr. Dewey, who in the face of the overwhelming evidence of Trotsky's guilt persist in stooging for this enemy of everything liberal and progressive, not only cover themselves with shame, but injure the cause of genuine liberalism and democracy."[28] An editorial writer of the *New Masses* asserted that the little group going to Mexico were all Trotskyites who were using Dewey as a "shield" in their attempt to whitewash Trotsky. The fact that Dewey was unaware of being so used showed that "even a famous philosopher may be extremely naïve in matters of this kind."[29]

Dewey's family was strongly opposed to his going to Mexico. Because he was seventy-eight years old, they believed that the changes in food and the inconveniences encountered in travel might affect his health. They believed, too, that he ran considerable physical danger in that Stalinist agents in Mexico would not hesitate to use violence if this best served their purpose. Dewey, however, was determined to go. He believed that the truth about the trials was of such historic importance that it needed to be brought out into the open. If, as many believed, the trials had been rigged and the accused falsely charged, this fact should be made known, especially to those in the United States who regarded Russia as a model for economic and social change.

The Preliminary Commission of Inquiry left New York for Mexico City on 2 April 1937, opening the hearings eight days later. The meetings were held in the villa of Diego Rivera in Coyoacán, a suburb of Mexico City. Barricades had been erected around the house; a contingent of police guarded the estate closely. Spectators, including representatives of the Mexican and foreign press, were carefully screened before being allowed to enter the meeting room.

Thirteen hearings were held from 10 April to 17 April. The sessions, usually two a day, generally lasted three hours except the last one which continued for five hours. This made for long and exhausting days that taxed the strength and energies of persons much younger than Dewey. The meetings themselves were of absorbing interest; those in attendance listened intently as Trotsky gave his testimony and as members of the commission and each side's counsel cross-examined him.

Dewey presided at each of the sessions, participating also in the questioning of Trotsky. His manner of conducting the hearings and his verbal encounters with Trotsky have been strikingly described by an eye-witness:

> Dewey's attention was unflagging. In a most unobtrusive way, he guided the proceedings when guidance was necessary. He was alert to see to it that all that was needed was put into the record. He would intervene when any point required clarification. When he cross-questioned Trotsky, his questions were apt, and they were part of a logical structure of questions which led to some clear and significant point or idea. He addressed Mr. Trotsky politely, and usually in the casual tone which marks so much of his conversation. Once or twice, in instances where Trotsky's own statements ran clearly counter to Dewey's own democratic ideas, there was a scarcely noticeable change of tone. In these rare instances, Dewey's own independence of mind, in the face of Trotsky's brilliance, was apparent. At the same time, there was here no violation of his role, no tactlessness. At these points, there was a revelation of temperament in intellectual exchange. . . . Dewey was more relaxed, more even-tempered than Trotsky, but then, their circumstances were so different that this specific contrast is not too significant. . . . Dewey's relaxation here is a sign of an unsuspected strain of worldliness in his personality. He was as much at home in the world as Trotsky.[30]

Trotsky was quite satisfied with the way the hearings were conducted. In his closing remarks at the last session thanking the commission, he paid special tribute to Dewey. "Allow me," he said, "to express to all of you my warm gratitude, which in this case does not bear a personal character. And allow me, in conclusion, to express my profound respect to the educator, philosopher and personification of genuine American idealism, the scholar who heads the work of your Commission."[31]

Upon its return to the United States, the Preliminary Commission drew up a report to present to the Commission of Inquiry. The report, almost six hundred pages in length, appeared in published form under the title *The Case of Leon Trotsky*.[32] In addition to a verbatim account of the proceedings in Coyoacán, it included a statement that the testimony and evidence submitted at the hearings warranted a thorough investigation as to Trotsky's guilt or innocence.

The Commission of Inquiry with Dewey as chairman thereupon took up the task of examining the evidence to determine the innocence or guilt of Trotsky and his son. After long hours of careful study the commission declared at its 21 September 1937 meeting that the Moscow Trials were frame-ups and that Trotsky and his son were innocent of the charges brought against them. The commission's argument, covering some four hundred pages, was published in book form with the title *Not Guilty: Report of the Commission of Inquiry into the Charges Made against Leon Trotsky in the Moscow Trials.*[33]

Dewey believed the Mexican hearings brought home a truth that needed to be emphasized, especially to those in this country sympathetically disposed toward Communist theory and practice. That truth was the organic oneness of means and ends. "The great lesson for all American radicals and for all sympathizers with the U. S. S. R.," he declared, "is that they must go back and reconsider the whole question of means of bringing about social changes and of truly democratic methods of approach to social progress. . . . The dictatorship of the proletariat has led and, I am convinced, always must lead to a dictatorship over the proletariat and over the party. I see no reason to believe that something similar would not happen in every country in which an attempt is made to establish a Communist government." [34]

The situation in Russia as revealed in the trials and in the Mexican hearings was "a bitter disillusionment" to Dewey personally. The revelations shattered his earlier optimism about the future of freedom in the Soviet Union, forcing him to revise the favorable impressions he had brought home from Russia in 1928. He reaffirmed his faith in the great capabilities of the Russian people, but confessed that "how a change can be brought about under the present conditions of suppression of individuality, falsification, and terrorism I have not the faintest conception." [35]

With his work on the commission completed, Dewey returned to the studies with which he had been preoccupied just prior to his trip to Mexico, studies in logical theory that culminated in his *Logic: The Theory of Inquiry.*[36] This volume synthesizes Dewey's previous contributions to logical theory, stated most notably first in his *Studies in Logical Theory*, then in popularized form in *How We Think*, and finally in a somewhat expanded version in *Essays in Experimental Logic*. These four books, covering a span of thirty-five years, testify to Dewey's continuing interest in logic and to his conviction that theory of knowledge is most basic to philosophy.

In his earlier writings Dewey had identified logical thinking with reflective thinking and problem solving. In his *Logic,* as the subtitle shows, he substituted the term "inquiry" for "reflective thinking," probably because he felt that inquiry connotes a more objective, impersonal, and operational process than does reflection. The *Logic,* therefore, is essentially an inquiry into inquiry; it sets forth the biological and cultural matrix of inquiry, the structure or pattern of inquiry, and the place or function of the several logical forms and distinctions within the process of inquiry. Dewey defined inquiry as "the directed or controlled transformation of an indeterminate situation into a determinately unified one,"[37] declaring that it represents the organism's attempt to pass from an uncertain, problematic situation to a condition of settled adjustment to an environment. Though the term "pragmatic" does not appear in the text, Dewey said his theory is "thoroughly pragmatic," if pragmatism is taken to mean that the function of consequences in inquiry is to serve as "necessary tests of the validity of propositions, *provided* these consequences are operationally instituted and are such as to resolve the specific problem evoking the operations."[38]

The portions of the book dealing with the matrix of inquiry and the structure of or steps in the process of inquiry repeat, but in considerably more detail, what he had previously written. The part of the volume showing that the several logical forms and distinctions ordinarily encountered in logical theory can best be understood when viewed as aspects or phases of inquiry contains much that was new and controversial, thus holding the greater interest for students of Dewey's logical theory.

Among the theories Dewey expounded and defended is that relating to the so-called "laws of thought." According to him, these are not to be regarded as *a priori* principles or "first truths" mysteriously implanted in the mind, intuitively known by a faculty called "pure reason." Rather they are to be viewed as general ways or habits of thinking that have originated in inquiry and continued throughout human existence because of their success in bringing inquiry to a satisfactory conclusion. They are "intrinsically postulates of and for inquiry";[39] they state the conditions inquiry must satisfy if it is to change the indeterminate situation to a determinate one. These principles are *a priori* only in the sense the law of contracts is *a priori* when it sets forth in advance the rules regulating the drawing up of certain kinds of business commitments.

Dewey went on to argue that to be a "datum" or a "given" in logical theory is "to have a special function in control of the subject-matter of inquiry";[40] that the different kinds of propositions—particular, general, hypothetical, disjunctive, etc.—"mark stages of progress in the conduct of inquiry"; [41] that judgment is the "settled outcome of inquiry"; [42] and that propositions derive their logical, coherent relationships with each other from the fact that they are "phases in the divisions of labor in the conduct of inquiry." [43] Dewey discussed these and the numerous other topics of logical theory in a highly technical way of interest primarily to professional logicians.

One of the more striking doctrines in the *Logic* is that propositions and judgments are not to be regarded as true or false. Propositions are simply some of the means by which inquiry is carried on, and, "since means as such are neither true nor false, truth-falsity is *not* a property of propositions." [44] Like other means they may be effective or ineffective, wasteful or economic, relevant or irrelevant, but not true or false.

Judgments are the conclusions reached by a process of inquiry aimed at removing doubt and replacing it with knowledge or belief. But the knowledge or belief that is the product of a particular inquiry is not to be taken as true in some fixed and final sense. Inquiry is a continuing process; a belief which held good at one time may not be acceptable at another. The most that inquiry can properly claim for any of its judgments or conclusions is that the evidence and reasoning employed in establishing it are of such a nature as to warrant its assertion. Dewey therefore would replace such phrases as "true conclusion" and "true judgment" with such terms as "warranted assertions," [45] "warranted assertibility," [46] "warranted conclusions," [47] "warrantably assertible conclusions" [48] and "*justified assertion.*" [49]

Dewey's general criticism of modern logicians is that they have been too faithful to the teachings of Aristotelian logic and too little concerned with the logical procedures of modern science. They have juxtaposed Aristotle's deductive logic and the inductive logic of such thinkers as Bacon and Mill without seriously attempting to bring the two together in a single coherent theory that would explain the logical procedures of science and of ordinary common sense. Believing that his instrumentalist logic was a step in this direction, he invited other logicians to follow his lead. "My best wishes as well as my hopes," he wrote, "are with those who engage in the profoundly important work of bringing logical theory into accord with scientific practice, no matter how much their conclusions may differ in detail from those presented in this book." [50]

In the last chapter of the *Logic*, entitled "The Logic of Inquiry and Philosophies of Knowledge," Dewey returned to the discussions that had occupied so much philosophical attention during the first quarter of the century: the relative merits of such epistemological theories as presentative and representative realism, perceptual and absolute idealism, pragmatism and instrumentalism. Taking his theory of inquiry as a point of departure, Dewey argued that whatever plausibility and strength each of these noninstrumentalist theories possesses derive from its borrowing certain conditions and factors from the actual pattern of inquiry, that its weaknesses stem from its isolating these factors from the inquiring process in which they function. Thus none of the theories is completely wrong but neither is any essentially correct. The theories are to be criticized, said Dewey, not "on the ground that they violate all conditions of inquiry as means of attaining knowledge, but on the ground that the selections are so one-sided as to ignore and thereby virtually deny other conditions which give those that are selected their cognitive force and which also prescribe the limits under which the selected elements validly apply." [51] The result of such extraction is that the material selected is viewed as "structural instead of functional, ontological instead of logical." [52]

Logic: The Theory of Inquiry was acclaimed as the most rigorous, comprehensive, and stimulating account of instrumentalist logic that had yet appeared. Reviewers agreed that this work of surpassing significance assured Dewey a place in the history of logical theory commensurate with that of Aristotle, Bacon, and Mill. Had Dewey written nothing else, one writer observed, his *Logic* "would have been sufficient to earn for him an illustrious place in the history of philosophy." [53]

But the *Logic* was not the rallying point around which all logicians could gather. Realists and idealists, of whatever variety, continued unconvinced of the validity of Dewey's basic teachings that knowledge is exclusively the outcome of inquiry and that truth is determined by the results of inquiry. Formal logicians were also critical of Dewey's work because it failed to do justice to mathematical logic, one of the most important factors in recent scientific procedures.[54]

Paralleling Dewey's long-standing concern with the problems of logic was his continuing interest in theory of value. His "Logical Conditions of a Scientific Treatment of Morality," "The Problem of Values," "The Objects of Valuation," and "Valuation and Experimental Knowledge" were among the essays attesting this interest.[55]

As the titles indicate, each of these articles dealt with a particular aspect of value theory, with no attempt at a rounded theory. But in the tenth chapter of *Experience and Nature* entitled "Existence, Value and Criticism," [56] and again in the tenth chapter of *The Quest for Certainty,* "The Construction of Good," [57] Dewey brought his ideas together in a brief but general theory of value. These chapters, both written in the 1920s, were the most complete statements of Dewey's philosophy of value till his *Theory of Valuation* [58] appeared in 1939. This essay, written at the invitation of the editors of the newly projected International Encyclopedia of Unified Science, was published as Monograph No. 4 of the second volume of the Foundations of the Unity of Science, the two-volume work that was the initial unit of the proposed encyclopedia.

Theory of Valuation covered much the same ground as the chapters mentioned, reaffirming Dewey's earlier positions, but was more polemical in that a considerable portion of the essay is a critical examination of rival theories. As before, he distinguished goods that are *desired* and those that are *desirable,* goods that are immediately enjoyed because they satisfy some impulse, habit, or desire as it first presents itself and those that are judged good after a consideration of the means used to produce them and of the consequences attending their realization.

Value judgments, Dewey argued, are not mere expressions of subjective, individual personal preferences as some other theories maintain. Nor do they refer to some transcendent, eternal realm of value to which human judgments must conform if they are to have validity, as claimed by absolutist and some idealist theories. Rather, said Dewey, value judgments are statements of man's moral, aesthetic, social, and religious ideals as these have emerged in the course of human experience. They are empirically determined; so far as their logical form is concerned, they are identical with the matters-of-fact judgments of the natural sciences. Like these, they are prompted by a problematic situation and they proceed by way of observation, hypothesis, and experiment to its solution. Values are as amenable to scientific treatment, broadly conceived, as are the matters-of-fact in scientific inquiry. Value judgments differ from judgments of matters-of-fact only in subject matter, just as judgments in geology differ only in content from those in astronomy.

Dewey's behavioral account of the value experience helped buttress this position. A value experience, he pointed out, is not confined to states of consciousness or feelings as mentalistic psychologists have taught but is to be identified with the behavior that aims at the attainment of value objects and relationships. "In empirical fact," he wrote, "the measure of the value a person attaches to a given end is not what he *says* about its preciousness but the care he devotes to obtaining and using the *means* without which it cannot be attained." [59] This puts value phenomena out in the open where they can be observed; theories about them can be formulated and tested in experience.

Theory of value was regarded by Dewey as an "outline of a program." [60] Value judgments are essentially practical in nature, having to do with "things *to be* brought into existence." [61] They focus on ends-in-view, the means necessary to acquire them, and the consequences that result from their attainment. When aided by the insights that an adequate psychology, biology, and cultural anthropology can supply, judgments of value can become intelligent and decisive factors in determining the "direction of human affairs." [62] This statement reflects the general thrust of Dewey's argument in *Theory of Valuation.*

As he followed discussions of theory of value during the next few years, Dewey came increasingly to feel that "little headway is being made in determining the questions or issues fundamentally involved." [63] As a step in correcting this situation, Dewey wrote an article entitled "Some Questions about Value" [64] listing four questions that he believed any adequate theory of value must take into account. Briefly, they were: 1. What connection is there, if any, between prizing or holding dear and desiring, liking, enjoying, etc.? 2. What connection is there, if any, between valuing and valuation in the sense of evaluating? 3. Are judgments of value *as judgments* inherently different from judgments of matters-of-fact? 4. Is the scientific method of inquiry applicable to evaluation, or judgments of value? To make the significance of the questions stand out more clearly, he then stated some possible answers to each of the questions. Because of his particular interest, he added as a sort of postscript a fifth question: "Are values and valuations such that they can be treated on a psychological basis of an allegedly 'individual' kind? Or are they so definitely and completely socio-cultural that they can be effectively dealt with only in that context?" [65]

Dewey hoped that his article would prompt other writers to state their views as to what questions and issues were fundamental to value theory. When this hope did not materialize, some interested persons explored the possibility of a symposium on value with Dewey's article as the point of departure. A number of outstanding scholars consented to take part in the endeavor; the result was the volume entitled *Value: A Cooperative Inquiry.*[66] The first part of this work contained the essays in which each of the fourteen contributors stated his views; the second part was made up of the criticisms and rejoinders directed by the writers toward each other. Dewey's contribution was an essay entitled "The Field of 'Value'," [67] in which he attempted to defend the thesis that "the field in which value-facts belong is *behavioral,* so that the facts must be treated in and by methods appropriate to behavioral subject-matter." [68]

The volume as a whole could scarcely have satisfied Dewey; as its editor acknowledged in the preface, "the present cooperative study has not produced unanimity among the various participants—even with regard to proper methods of approach or the most elementary and basic concepts." [69] One reviewer's comment was: "Supposedly centering their papers on four questions raised by Dewey, many of the authors pay only a polite bow to his queries and develop special theses of their own. Individually a number of the essays are of high quality—they make important distinctions and advance cogent arguments—but collectively the effect is too scattering to be very significant." [70]

During the late thirties it became increasingly clear that Europe was drifting toward another war. Mussolini invaded Ethiopia in 1935; the United States and the members of the League of Nations did nothing to prevent it. In 1936 Mussolini and Hitler helped General Franco establish his dictatorship in Spain. Later that year Germany and Japan formed the Berlin-Tokyo Axis to which they admitted Italy in 1937. During the summer of 1937 Japan renewed her invasions of China begun in 1931. Early in 1938 Hitler seized Austria and later that year took possession of most of Czechoslovakia. In the spring of 1939 he took the rest.

Throughout this time most Americans, whether liberal or conservative, were convinced that the United States should not become involved in European affairs and that if war came this country should stay out. Not wishing to be drawn a second time into a world war, they hoped that the Neutrality Act of May 1937 would safeguard the nation against this eventuality.

Dewey believed there were strong reasons the United States should not become engaged in a general European war; he expressed these in his contribution to a symposium entitled "If War Comes, Shall We Participate or Be Neutral?" [71] For one thing, he believed that mobilizing the nation's economic and social resources for war purposes would postpone indefinitely the social advances the United States was attempting to make. He pointed out that this had happened to the progressive movement under way just prior to World War I and that in all probability it would also happen to the liberal movement then taking place. He feared that the political, economic, and military organizations needed to prosecute a war successfully would have to be carried over following the war, to the impairment of our democratic way of life. "It is quite conceivable," he wrote, "that after the next war we should have in this country a semi-military, semi-financial autocracy, which would fasten class divisions on this country for untold years. In any case we should have the suppression of all the democratic values for the sake of which we professedly went to war." He argued finally that by staying out of the war the nation could save its resources and use them later to help "a stricken Europe after the end of its attempt at suicide." [72]

Dewey insisted that it was not inevitable that the nation would be drawn into the war when it came. Whether it did or not was up to the people. "If we but make up our minds that it is not inevitable, and if we now set ourselves deliberately to seeing that no matter what happens we stay out, we shall save this country from the greatest social catastrophe that could overtake us, the destruction of all the foundations upon which to erect a socialized democracy." [73]

Dewey's attitude, along with that of Americans generally, changed after war broke out in September 1939 and German armies overran Poland, Denmark, Norway, Holland, Belgium, and France in quick succession. Nazi totalitarianism, he recognized, was a grave threat to the survival of democratic institutions in Europe and had to be destroyed. Hitler, he now argued, must not be allowed to make good his boast that he would annihilate the "decadent" democracies of the West, extend his superstate to all Europe, and establish a reich that would last a thousand years. Dewey therefore supported Roosevelt when he urged Congress in March 1940 to pass the Lend-Lease Bill and to make the United States the "arsenal of democracy." After the attack on Pearl Harbor on 7 December 1941, he approved America's entry into the war, hoping for the defeat of totalitarian forces.

The gradual erosion of freedom and the rise of totalitarian regimes in several European countries and in Japan led Dewey to wonder whether a similar course of events could occur in the remaining free countries of the world, including our own. His *Freedom and Culture* [74] explored the problem of freedom in its larger cultural context, suggesting the general direction a free society must take if it is to preserve and expand its democratic freedoms and institutions.

Dewey pointed out that freedom in general breaks down into many individual and group concrete freedoms. Each of these, he explained, is a function of the interaction of an individual or group with particular aspects of the prevailing culture. The number and kinds of freedoms existing in a given culture at a given time will be determined by a culture's politics and economics, science and technology, system of education, art, morality, religion, and family life—all interacting with each other and with factors in human nature. No single factor, either in human nature or in culture, can be isolated and judged so dominant that it is the cause of all that occurs in the life of a people. "For example," said Dewey, "if our American culture is largely a pecuniary culture, it is not because the original or innate structure of human nature tends of itself to obtaining pecuniary profit. It is rather that a certain complex culture stimulates, promotes and consolidates native tendencies so as to produce a certain pattern of desires and purposes." [75] To single out one factor, whether in human nature or in the environment, making it the decisive one, is to oversimplify a situation and prevent clear understanding and intelligent action.

However, since various social theories in the past, including communism, have done exactly this, Dewey devoted a considerable portion of the book to a critical examination of these theories. But he concentrated mainly on Communist theory "both because of its present vogue, and because it claims to represent the only strictly scientific theory of social change and thereby the method by which to effect change in the future." [76]

Communism, as Dewey pointed out, selects the economic factor as the determining one, maintaining that "the state of the forces of economic productivity at a given time ultimately determines all forms of social activities and relations, political, legal, scientific, artistic, religious, moral." [77] To this idea it adds the notion of class conflict. Conflict of economic classes is declared to be the law of history, in operation at all times and in all places. Marx admitted he derived this law not from an observation of historical and sociological data but from Hegelian metaphysics. He transformed Hegel's dialectic idealism into his own dialectic materialism that pitted an oppressor class against an oppressed class till in the course of history the classless society of communism would emerge. Thus, as Dewey remarked, "the law of history became the law for revolutionary action;—and all was accomplished that can possibly be accomplished in behalf of a clear vision of a goal and the concentration of emotion and energy in its behalf." [78]

Dewey recognized, of course, that the economic factor plays an important role in any culture; he admitted that it could well have been the dominant influence in the complex of factors making up the culture Marx examined. But he declared it an error to generalize this situation and to insist, as communism does, that the economic element is always and everywhere the decisive one; the importance of this factor must be determined by a study of prevailing cultural conditions. Communist theory rules out such observation and inquiry. Like any dogmatic and absolutistic theology, it claims it already has "the Truth," making further study of the causes of social events superfluous and unnecessary. It supposes, wrote Dewey, that "a generalization that was made at a particular date and place (and made even then only by bringing observed facts under a premise drawn from a metaphysical source) can obviate the need for continued resort to observation, and to continual revision of generalizations in their office of working hypotheses." [79] "It is ironical," Dewey added, "that the theory which has made the most display and the greatest pretense of having a scientific foundation should be the one which has violated most systematically every principle of scientific method." [80]

Because the liberties enjoyed in any culture depend upon the ways various aspects of that culture interact with the components of human nature, it follows that the fight to preserve and extend them must be waged in the several areas of activities making up the culture. "The struggle for democracy," as Dewey remarked, "has to be maintained on as many fronts as culture has aspects: political, economic, international, educational, scientific and artistic, religious." [81] A democratic society committed to moral and humanist ends requires that its members be alert and morally sensitive to what is going on in the several areas of its life. "It says, Find out how all the constituents of our existing culture are operating and then see to it that whenever and wherever needed they be modified in order that their workings may release and fulfill the possibilities of human nature." [82] Dewey noted how easy it is for people to be sensitive to deprivation of freedom in one area while overlooking it in another. For example, "persons acutely aware of the dangers of regimentation when it is imposed by government remain oblivious of the millions of persons whose behavior is regimented by an economic system through whose intervention alone they obtain a livelihood." [83]

Because they subvert the democratic ends sought, Dewey repudiated violence, authoritarianism, and totalitarianism as methods to bring about desired social changes. He urged instead the adoption and application of such democratic means as cooperative, intelligent inquiry, discussion, and persuasion. He was aware that using such methods may at times be long, difficult, and frustrating and that people may be tempted to adopt nondemocratic means with their promise of attaining ideal ends more quickly and effectively. The first defense against such temptation, said Dewey, is to realize that "democracy can be served only by the slow day by day adoption and contagious diffusion in every phase of our common life of methods that are identical with the ends to be reached and that recourse to monistic, wholesale, absolutistic procedures is a betrayal of human freedom no matter in what guise it presents itself." [84]

Dewey was not prepared to say that under rapidly and radically changing conditions human nature can, in the long run, sustain a democratic culture. This issue, he believed, is still an open one. But he believed that faith in its potential is an important factor in creating the will to bring it to pass. "For in the long run," he wrote, "democracy will stand or fall with the possibility of maintaining the faith and justifying it by works." [85]

Freedom and Culture won high praise. Reviewers recognized the worth and timeliness of its message; one of them declared that "of all recent writing on the democratic ideal this is probably the most deeply thoughtful and suggestive." [86] To follow Dewey's account, wrote another reader, is "one of those great experiences which his readers have come to expect as they have awaited book after book from John Dewey's pen." [87]

What adverse criticism appeared concerned Dewey's neglect of the question as to what a democratic society should do when ruling interests, threatened by the use of free, critical inquiry, attempt by force to suppress it, as had happened in totalitarian countries. Shall the people, before it is too late, resort to force to defend their right to free discussion? If so, "is this defensive force antithetical to the method of intelligence or does it now become an instrument, an antecedent condition, for the operation of that method?" [88] Dewey, said his critics, did not come to grips with this problem, leaving his readers uncertain as to what he thought on this important matter.

During the spring of 1939 Dewey joined a small group of liberals to organize under the leadership of Sidney Hook the Committee for Cultural Freedom. A committee manifesto published in the *Nation* called attention to the suppression of freedom in the several areas of cultural activities in Germany, Italy, Russia, Japan, and Spain, warning that similar curtailments of freedom were beginning to appear in the United States. To help prevent the spread of such practices, the statement continued, the committee was undertaking "to expose repression of intellectual freedom under whatever pretext, to defend individuals and groups victimized by totalitarian practices anywhere, to propagate courageously the ideal of untrammeled intellectual activity." The manifesto called on others, irrespective of social philosophy, to join the committee in "defense of creative and intellectual freedom." [89] Dewey was one of the original signers; when the committee was formally organized, he became its first chairman.[90]

Because the manifesto included Russia among the countries suppressing freedom, American Communists and Communist sympathizers immediately attacked the committee, accusing it of wrongly equating fascism and communism. "In lumping together the Fascist powers with the USSR," declared an editorial in the *New Republic,* "the committee shows, we feel, a regrettable lack of historical perspective. It clearly implies that fascism and communism are both completely incompatible with freedom for the individual. But while this charge is true of fascism, it is certainly not true of the theory of a socialist commonwealth." [91]

In a counterattack Communist leaders circulated a letter, later published in the *Nation,* urging liberals, progressives, and radicals to repudiate "the fantastic falsehood that the U. S. S. R. and the totalitarian states are basically alike" and to cooperate with Communists in resisting world fascism. "Soviet aims and achievements make it clear," declared the letter, "that there exists a sound and permanent basis in mutual ideals for cooperation between the U. S. A. and the U. S. S. R. in behalf of world peace and the security and freedom of all nations." [92] The purpose of the Committee for Cultural Freedom in issuing the manifesto, the letter charged, was to "create dissension among the progressive forces whose united strength is a first necessity for the defeat of fascism." [93]

The Committee for Cultural Freedom immediately became active, and, as chairman, Dewey took a leading part in its work. When, for example, the Board of Education of New York City held public hearings on 13 November 1940 on the proposal providing released time for religious education in the public schools, Dewey appeared before the board as the committee's representative to argue against its adoption. Again, when Bertrand Russell was attacked upon his appointment to a chair of philosophy in the College of the City of New York in 1940, the Committee for Cultural Freedom was one of the first organizations to condemn this assault on educational and cultural freedom, with Dewey playing an active role.[94] Also, aware of the widespread influence of Communists in various political, economic, cultural, and civic organizations in the country and of their practice of suppressing the freedom of non-Communist members while supporting and encouraging that of Communist members, the committee issued reports containing lists of organizations under the complete or partial control of Communists for the guidance of those having relations with these bodies.[95]

In addition to his writing and other activities, Dewey spoke to numerous organizations, for, despite his advancing years, he was still in wide demand as a speaker, especially by professional educational groups. On 22 February 1935, for example, he spoke at the general session of the Department of Superintendence of the National Education Association at its meeting in New Orleans on the topic "Democracy and Educational Administration."[96] During April 1936 in Ann Arbor, Michigan, at the fiftieth anniversary meeting of the Michigan Schoolmasters' Club, which Dewey had helped found in 1886, he spoke on "The Integrity of Education."[97] In the fall of 1936, as one of the scholars invited to speak at the Harvard Tercentenary Celebration, he read a paper on 4 September entitled "Authority and Resistance to Social Change" to the Tercentenary Conference of Arts and Sciences.[98] A month later, in October, at Antioch College's Horace Mann Conference, he spoke on "Education, the Foundation for Social Organization."[99] On 13 November 1936, he spoke to more than 2,000 teachers at the Eastern States regional convention of the Progressive Education Association at the Hotel Pennsylvania in New York City[100] on "The Challenge of Democracy to Education."[101] Dewey addressed still another educational organization at the John Dewey Society meeting in New Orleans on 21 February 1937 on the topic "Education and Social Change."[102]

One of Dewey's speaking engagements was at the University of Vermont, his alma mater, where he was invited to give the annual Founder's Day Address on 1 May 1939. In his talk on "Education: 1800–1939," he discussed some of the important changes in education during this period—changes that had seen education supplementing the educational ideals of a professional, cultural, and leisure class with those more closely related to the vocational and practical demands of a democratic society oriented to a scientific and technological age.[103] At the same ceremonies a portrait of Dewey by Edwin B. Child was presented to the university in behalf of friends and members of the institution.[104]

Dewey had arrived a few days early in his native city, and, on the Sunday afternoon preceding the day of his address, Delta Psi, the fraternity to which Dewey had belonged as an undergraduate, held a reception in his honor. Over two hundred alumni of the fraternity, faculty members, and university officials attended the occasion. In the evening he met informally with the members of the John Dewey Club, an undergraduate organization founded in the winter of 1927 by faculty and students of the Department of Philosophy and Psychology. At the end of a question-and-answer period, Dewey wished the club well, saying he hoped that his name would not serve as a "blight" on the organization.[105]

During his years as professor emeritus, Dewey went regularly to his office in Philosophy Hall, continuing his personal contacts with members of the department. Woodbridge, Montague, Bush, Schneider, Randall, Edman, Friess, Gutmann, and Nagel, who had offices in the same building, saw him frequently. When spending the day on the campus, Dewey usually had luncheon at the Faculty Club where he met other close friends and associates in the university. He also maintained his long-time membership in the Philosophic Club whose members came from a variety of institutions and professions in the New York City area; whenever possible, he attended its monthly meeting.[106]

Sidney Hook and Joseph Ratner, both former students, maintained a close association with Dewey. Hook, a distinguished disciple and exponent of Dewey's philosophy, spent much time in conversation and discussion with him. During Dewey's later years, he regularly called upon Hook to read his manuscripts before publication to suggest improvements. Ratner, a devoted follower of Dewey and his philosophy, was also a frequent guest in Dewey's home. His interest in Dewey and his teachings led him to edit a collection of Dewey's articles on current affairs in the two-volume *Characters and Events*.[107] It also prompted him to bring together with a valuable interpretive essay a collection of passages from Dewey's philosophical works, systematically arranged according to topics, in a volume entitled *Intelligence in the Modern World*,[108] as well as to edit with a foreword a collection of passages from Dewey's educational writings in *Education Today*.[109]

A practice Dewey continued during these years was to attend outstanding ice skating events in Madison Square Garden with an old friend, Richard Ward Greene Welling.[110] The usual arrangement was for the two to meet at 7:30 P.M. at Childs Restaurant in Madison Square Garden, and after a leisurely meal, to attend the performances in the Garden.[111] Referring later to these occasions, Welling wrote: "As a member of the Skating Club at Madison Square Garden, and as an occasional donor of a cup for the youngsters in their competitions, my interest is kept up to date, although my grapevines and arabesques on two feet are wholly out of date. For a number of years John Dewey has joined me in attending the finals of the international skating championship in Madison Square Garden where spins, arabesques, curlicues, counters and chocktaws, are a delight to watch." [112]

Dewey customarily spent a portion of the summer and winter away from New York. During July and August he was usually at his cottage on Lake Sawlor in Hubbards, Nova Scotia, where he did much of his writing, including the *Logic,* on the veranda overlooking the lake. Part of the winter and early spring months were spent in Key West, Florida, where the sharp contrast of wealth and poverty impressed him deeply. In a letter to Welling he wrote: "If the old muckraking magazines days were back one of them could profitably investigate this town—it's a sample of what monopolistic economic control can do joined to administrative, especially tax control. A few people have the town by the throat, so that federal relief is necessary,—& then the men responsible can howl at gov. for failing to balance the budget." [113]

As the eightieth anniversary of Dewey's birth drew near, friends and admirers took steps to insure a proper celebration. A committee of fifteen, with Horace M. Kallen as chairman, Jerome Nathanson as secretary, and Frederick L. Redefer as treasurer, was set up to work out details for a celebration in New York. Nine local and national organizations agreed to sponsor the event; [114] leading figures in philosophy and education accepted invitations to read papers.[115] Disappointment prevailed when it was learned Dewey would not be present at the celebration. In reply to a letter from Nathanson telling about arrangements and inviting him to be present as guest of honor, Dewey wrote that he did not find himself "equal to going through with an elaborate celebration" and that he planned to spend the coming weeks with his daughter Evelyn's family on their ranch at Green Castle, Missouri. He wrote, though, that he wanted to cooperate with the committee and would send a short paper to be read at a meeting as suggested earlier by Kallen and Sidney Hook.[116]

The celebration, a two-day conference on 20 and 21 October, took place in the Hotel Pennsylvania. Invited speakers read papers analyzing and interpreting Dewey's philosophy and theory of education. The highlight of the conference was the dinner on the evening of 20 October, attended by some one thousand persons who heard Horace Kallen, presiding at the meeting, read the paper Dewey had sent for the occasion. In this essay, entitled "Creative Democracy—The Task Before Us," Dewey emphasized that a democratic society does not perpetuate itself automatically but requires for its survival "conscious and resolute effort" by its members.[117] This effort must be directed not only at preserving the form and organization of a political democracy but also at creating in the people the feelings, attitudes, and day-by-day relationships necessary for the successful operation of democracy as a way of life. We cannot very well denounce nazism for its intolerance, cruelty, and stimulation of hatred, he declared, if in our own lives we are moved by racial, religious, color, or other class prejudice. The society that must be created is one in which artificial barriers are broken down and experience is shared so that each individual can grow and develop according to his own special powers, abilities, and interests. Since this is an unending process, "the task of democracy is forever that of creation of a freer and more humane experience in which all share and to which all contribute." [118]

Dewey was honored in other ways at the time of this birthday. His colleagues in the American Philosophical Association at the December 1938 meeting adopted a resolution which declared: "To John Dewey on the approach of his eightieth birthday we tender hearty congratulations; and as a token of our admiration and affection we ask him to accept and to retain for the duration of his life the title of Honorary President of the American Philosophical Association." [119] The volume *The Philosopher of the Common Man: Essays in Honor of John Dewey to Celebrate His Eightieth Birthday* [120] was written especially for the occasion. Also, the publication of the first volume of The Library of Living Philosophers, *The Philosophy of John Dewey* [121] edited by Paul A. Schilpp, was timed to coincide with the year in which Dewey's eightieth birthday was celebrated, as was Sidney Hook's work, *John Dewey: An Intellectual Portrait.*[122]

The *New York Times* was among the many newspapers and periodicals that took special notice of the anniversary. In addition to an editorial paying tribute to Dewey as "a truly American philosopher," [123] its magazine section featured an interview with Dewey. "Professor Dewey," the interviewer declared, "opened the door of his apartment for me himself when I went to his house the other day. I had not seen him for several years, but he had changed very little—the same white, straight hair with a yellowish tinge, the same kindly smile and the same unaffected manner. His short-cropped mustache, like his eyebrows, remains dark. The wrinkles in his face were no deeper than when I met him first, almost a decade ago." [124] The high point in the interview came when Dewey was asked how he reacted to a world as unsettled and troubled as the present one. "I should say," he was quoted as saying, "that my philosophy of life is based essentially on the single word patience. Perhaps this is the result of having lived eighty years and of benefiting from a position which permits a long perspective. I have seen too many changes during my lifetime to allow myself to predict the future by what is uppermost now. . . . My philosophy teaches me to look beyond the present. It sustains me in such times as these. Because it is the rational application of criticism it is based upon reason rather than emotion, but it serves the same purpose that religion does for the devout believer." [125]

On 20 December 1939, at a reception in the Hampshire House in New York City for persons prominent in American and Chinese cultural life, Dr. Tsune-chi Yu, Chinese Consul General in New York, formally bestowed on Dewey and Nicholas Murray Butler of Columbia the decoration of the Order of the Jade. The presentations were in recognition of Columbia University's contributions to Chinese education. In his citation of Dewey, Yu described him as "one of the greatest philosophers in the history of philosophy, a master of human nature, enemy of no nation or men but of international injustice." According to the press, Dewey in response expressed the hope that Americans and Chinese would work together "to keep the flame of knowledge burning in China in spite of adverse winds." [126]

During the academic year 1938–39 Dewey asked the administration at Columbia to change his status at the university from professor emeritus of philosophy in residence to professor emeritus of philosophy as of June 1939. The change meant a reduction in income for Dewey because he would receive a university pension instead of a regular salary, but with his advancing years, he wanted to be relieved of the obligations connected with being in residence at the university; he welcomed an arrangement which would free him from further university responsibilities. The trustees acceded to Dewey's wishes, listing him from 1939 to his death in 1952 as professor emeritus of philosophy at the university.

15. Retirement Years, 1939–1952

THE CONTROVERSIES of the 1930s concerning education continued unabated during the 1940s. Two contending schools of thought, broadly defined as traditionalism and progressivism, continued to widen their efforts to win general support. Traditionalism was represented as before by such men as Robert M. Hutchins, Mortimer Adler, Mark Van Doren, Stringfellow Barr, Alexander Meiklejohn, Jacques Maritain, and members of the Education For Freedom, Inc., group whose doctrines were broadcast from coast to coast over the Mutual Broadcasting System.

Traditionalists argued that education should make central the traditions and wisdom of the past embodied in the great books. This wisdom has vast importance because it provides man with a body of established and eternal truths about human nature, human values, and human destiny—truths which can serve as guides and standards in society's attempt to solve its current problems and escape from the errors and confusion of the present. Traditionalists believed, of course, that science and scientific method should be given a place in the curriculum but that they should not be allowed to take over roles properly belonging to the humanities with their rationalistic methods of acquiring truth.

Progressivism was expounded and defended by such thinkers as Dewey, William H. Kilpatrick, George Counts, John Childs, Sidney Hook, George Axtelle, Horace M. Kallen, and Boyd Bode. These men emphasized that education should focus on present-day problems, studying the factors that shape modern culture: science and technology, the experimental method in the field of knowledge, and the democratic spirit in human relations. They believed the past should be consulted, its famous books read insofar as they are relevant to the solution of present problems, but they insisted that the insights provided by the past should be viewed as tentative and hypothetical in their bearing on the present, not as fixed and final truths standing in authority over present thinking. The principle of free, open, critical discussion that is the heart of political democracy must also be the principle pervading American education; any attempt to substitute authoritarian principles for it, whether the authority be that of the great books of the past or the theological dogma of traditional religion, must be resisted.[1]

During these controversies, Dewey became the target of a new line of attack. His opponents, while continuing their assaults on his educational theories, began a parallel attack on his general overall philosophy, claiming that his experimental, humanistic naturalism was making its way into the classroom and adversely affecting the lives of the students. In public addresses as well as in widely read magazines and journals, critics denounced his philosophy as "godless," "completely atheistical," "pagan," and "anti-Christian." They declared that the leading ideas of this philosophy were "infiltrating" the schools and colleges of the nation, "poisoning" the minds of the students, undermining their faith in God and the moral law, stirring them to acts of delinquency and crime. For more than three decades, declared one speaker, John Dewey and his followers at Teachers College had made that institution their center of operations in their "attempted destruction of Christian aims and ideals in American education." [2]

Moreover, because he taught that the dignity of man and human rights have emerged naturally and gradually in the course of man's moral, social, and cultural advance, persisting because of their beneficent results in personal and social relations, Dewey was accused of holding a social philosophy that endangered human rights. For, according to these critics, human worth and human rights can be respected and secure only when it is recognized that they are supernaturally derived. In denying the supernatural basis of human rights, his opponents charged, Dewey's philosophy of life "is identical with that which underlies the modern forms of dictatorship." [3] Fascism, communism, and German national socialism, it was alleged, also hold that man is nothing more than a highly developed animal with no worth or rights other than those conferred by government or society. This idea, too, they said, has made its way into the classroom where it is undermining faith in America's democratic tradition. "It is in the educational system of our country," declared one writer, *"that there lies the danger of totalitarianism in the clothing of democ-*

racy."[4] Addressing a session of the First Conference on Science, Philosophy, and Religion in Their Relation to the Democratic Way of Life in New York City in September 1940, a speaker attacked the entire professorial profession, declaring, "Democracy has much more to fear from the mentality of its teachers than from the nihilism of Hitler. It is the same nihilism in both cases, but Hitler's is more honest and consistent, less blurred by subtleties and queasy qualifications, and hence less dangerous."[5]

Opposition to progressive ideas in education took a more concrete form when certain social science textbooks used by many public school systems came under attack. These texts, departing from traditional treatments of American life, tried to present a realistic and rounded picture of conditions in the United States. Alongside accounts of the happier aspects of life in this country appeared portrayals of the poverty, hunger, illiteracy, joblessness, and general feeling of frustration afflicting millions of lives. To help correct these evils, the texts recommended more government planning and control in such areas as business and industry, health care, housing, rehabilitation, etc., frequently citing Russia and the Scandinavian countries as examples of nations where social planning was accepted as a proper function of government. The texts of Harold O. Rugg of Teachers College were particularly effective in acquainting their youthful readers with social realities and in pointing up the need for increased government planning. Highly regarded by teachers and administrators, they had been put into use in over four thousand school systems in the United States.

Conservative groups, seeing in these texts a threat to the American way of life, denounced them as un-American, subversive, and aimed at the "sovietizing" of American youth.[6] A nationwide organized attack on the texts was mounted with the support of the conservative press and such organizations as the National Association of Manufacturers, the Advertising Federation of America, the American Legion, the Daughters of the American Revolution, and the Daughters of Colonial Wars, bringing powerful pressure to bear on school boards and administrators throughout the country to ban the texts. Succumbing to this pressure, many local school boards stopped using the books.

The banning of the Rugg texts from the Binghamton, New York, public schools in April 1940 at the instigation of the president of the New York State Economic Council prompted Dewey to send a letter of protest to the *New York Times*. In his capacity as chairman of the Committee for Cultural Freedom, Dewey acknowledged the right of a democratic society to investigate its schools to learn what is taking place in them. But such an investigation, he wrote, must have a clear-cut objective; it must be conducted by persons competent to pursue such a study without bias or prejudice; and its aim must be to advance the educational process. The investigations of the social science textbooks were not of this nature. Their objective was to expose and abolish "subversive" textbooks, with the investigators reserving for themselves the right to determine what "subversive" means; they were conducted by special-interest pressure groups who lacked competence in the field of education. By prohibiting discussion of ideas which the investigators judged subversive, they prevented freedom of inquiry in the classroom and reduced American schools to "the condition of bondage which exists in Italy, Germany, and Soviet Russia." [7] "We welcome any investigation of American education," Dewey declared, "that has as its goal the development of thoughtful, intelligent, critical-minded students and citizens; we welcome evidence that agents of foreign governments are using the schools to undermine confidence in democracy. But we stand unalterably opposed to those who would pervert a free educational system by opening it to the exploitation of prejudice, bigotry and unenlightenment; and we shall vigorously resist any attempt by pressure groups to gain control of the public schools by seeking to dictate what shall and what shall not be taught in them." [8]

This issue took on additional interest when, on 26 February 1940, the Board of Higher Education of New York City appointed Bertrand Russell to a chair of philosophy at the College of the City of New York. When the appointment was announced in the press, William T. Manning, a bishop of the Protestant Episcopal Church, sent a letter to the *New York Times* denouncing the board's action on the ground that Russell was "a recognized propagandist against both religion and morality" and a person who "specifically defends adultery." [9]

Manning's letter triggered a flood of protests against the appointment. The more conservative religious, civic, and patriotic groups in the city voiced strong objections to the board's action, making vigorous efforts to have it annulled. A diocesan paper of the Roman Catholic Church in Brooklyn reported that on one Monday and Tuesday it had received copies of resolutions from eighty-four Catholic organizations objecting to the appointment and urging that it be rescinded.[10] A columnist writing in the same paper asked, "Why should such a man from foreign shores whose teachings are so infamous be foisted upon teachers, youths, parents and taxpayers of Greater New York?" [11]

As the opposition grew, individuals and groups representing more liberal points of view rallied to Russell's defense. College and university professors throughout the country, past and present officers of learned societies, student groups, and liberal clergy and civic leaders urged that the appointment be sustained and that Russell be allowed to teach the courses in mathematics and logic for which he was being hired. A statement of the Committee on Cultural Freedom declared that "whatever his views on marriage, divorce, and birth control, Mr. Russell has the same right to hold them as have his opponents theirs. His critics should meet him in the open and fair field of intellectual discussion and scientific analysis. They have no right to silence him by preventing him from teaching."[12] One widely read liberal journalist viewed Russell as "a twentieth-century Socrates, with the Bishop brandishing the cup of hemlock in his face."[13]

The matter reached the courts when a Brooklyn mother brought suit in the New York Supreme Court against the Board of Higher Education asking that the appointment be rescinded. The petition argued that: the board had made an illegal use of its power in appointing Russell because he was an alien and aliens are not eligible for civil service jobs; Russell did not undergo a competitive examination to test his competence as is required of civil service candidates; in his books Russell taught doctrines which imperiled public well-being and morality.[14]

The lawyer for the plaintiff declared Russell's books were "lecherous, salacious, libidinous, lustful, venerous, erotomaniac, aphrodisiac, atheistic, irreverent, narrow-minded, untruthful, and bereft of moral fiber" and that "all his alleged doctrines which he calls philosophy are just cheap, tawdry, worn out, patched up fetishes and propositions, devises [*sic*] for the purpose of misleading the people."[15]

The judge who heard the case declared in his decision of 30 March 1940 in favor of the plaintiff, going to considerable length to point out alleged evils of Russell's teachings. Quoting passages from Russell's writings on premarital and extramarital sex, trial marriages, nudity, masturbation, and homosexuality, he asserted that these were sufficient evidence to sustain the petitioner's contention that the appointment of Russell menaced "the public health, safety, and morals of the community" and therefore ought not to be allowed.[16] "The appointment of Dr. Russell," the court said, "is an insult to the people of the City of New York"; the Board of Higher Education in making it is "in effect establishing a chair of indecency" at the College of the City of New York.[17] The court's order annulling the appointment was appealed without success and Russell was prevented from teaching at the college.

Dewey, following the case closely, was among the first to support publicly the appointment of Russell. Shortly after opposition to it began, he joined Alfred North Whitehead, William P. Montague, and Curt John Ducasse, all past presidents of the American Philosophical Association, to issue a statement defending the appointment and praising Russell's high scholarly and moral qualifications.[18]

The court's ruling, though not unexpected, nevertheless greatly upset Dewey. In a letter to Richard Welling a few days after the decision was announced, he wrote: "If groups of the Ancient Order of Hiberians [*sic*] plus Bishop Manning are going to dictate who shall & shan't teach philosophy in American colleges, I'm glad I haven't much time left." [19]

An article in the *Nation* expressed Dewey's strong feelings on the conduct of the trial. In this he denounced the "disgusting and loathsome aura" with which the attorney for the plaintiff and the presiding judge had surrounded the case; [20] he condemned the way passages from Russell's books had been quoted out of context, ignoring the spirit in which they were written. The trial, he declared, misled many otherwise fair-minded people into thinking that Russell belonged to the class of writers who appeal to the prurient interests of their readers whereas in truth he was a serious, high-minded scholar concerned with theories to help people overcome problems in their sexual and marital experience.

Convinced that the issues involved in the Russell case were of transcendent social significance and should be made a matter of permanent public record, Dewey collaborated with Horace M. Kallen in editing *The Bertrand Russell Case*, a volume of essays dealing with the several aspects of the case and their social implications.[21]

Dewey's contribution to the volume was a chapter entitled "Social Realities *versus* Police Court Fictions." [22] Citing passages from Russell's works in context, explaining how the views put forward grew out of data supplied by anthropologists, historians, sociologists, psychologists, and other recognized authorities, Dewey made clear the scholarly content and intent of Russell's studies.

But outrageous as was the treatment of Russell during the trial, it was quite secondary, Dewey declared, to another and socially more significant matter. This was "whether the issues and problems of social morals, in fields where conventional taboos are very strong, are or are not to be publicly discussed by scientifically competent persons." [23] Dewey emphasized that to suppress such discussion and abuse those who engage in it is to close the door to a possibly wiser and more humane approach to the problems of sex and marriage, while more firmly entrenching traditional and authoritarian views however harmful and undesirable these may be.

Academic freedom also became a topic of controversy at Columbia when President Butler called a special meeting at the beginning of the school year in October 1940, a month after the Nazi all-out bombing of London, to address the several faculties on the matter. Convinced that the United States would in all probability become involved in the war in Europe, and mindful of what had happened at Columbia during the First World War when two members of the faculty had been dismissed for their wartime activities and Charles A. Beard had resigned in protest, Butler wanted to make clear his and the university's stand on academic freedom.

After declaring that academic freedom could not be an issue for students since they were at the university to learn, not to express their own views, he said that while faculty members had the right to discuss freely and openly issues relating to the war, engaging in whatever activities they thought proper, this right must not come in conflict with the university's right to play what it considered its appropriate role in respect to the war. "Indeed," said Butler, "before and above academic freedom of any kind or sort comes this university freedom." When faculty members take positions in conflict with that of the university, they "should, in ordinary self-respect, withdraw of their own accord from university membership in order that their conduct may be freed from the limitations which university membership naturally and necessarily puts upon it." As to the current conflict in Europe, Butler wanted there to be "no doubt where Columbia University stands in that war." That war, he declared, is essentially one "between beasts and human beings"; Columbia stood ready to cooperate with the United States government in supporting the Allied countries in their life-and-death struggle with the Axis powers.[24]

Butler's remarks aroused widespread comment. Although members of the university's administrative staff generally supported Butler's position, an overwhelming majority of faculty and students opposed it on the ground that it struck at the heart of academic freedom. The president of the New York City Board of Education, the chairman of the American Civil Liberties Union, the president of the Teachers Union Local No. 5, and the executive council of the New York College Teachers Union all voiced vigorous objection. In Washington, Senators Bennett Champ Clark of Missouri and Rush Holt of West Virginia denounced the speech on the floor of the Senate.[25]

The New York press made much of the affair, interviewing a number of prominent faculty members and student leaders to learn their reactions to Butler's talk. When Dewey was asked for comment, he expressed strong disagreement with Butler's position that students are not involved in academic freedom. Students, he said, are after all an essential factor in the educational process; without freedom of inquiry and critical discussion on their part this process is deeply impaired. Dewey could not accept Butler's distinction between the freedom of the faculty and the freedom of the university because "I do not know what a university is apart from students and its teaching staff." Moreover, Butler's statement that the freedom of the university is higher and therefore takes precedence over that of the faculty perplexed Dewey. "I can hardly believe," he said, "that President Butler intended to place the university in a realm so lofty that it is above the students and faculty and has the right to control their beliefs in the way in which churches set the creeds to which their members must conform. Such an idea seems to be identical, as far as it goes, with totalitarianism. Since President Butler is an opponent of the latter, I am forced to conclude that what he said does not convey his real meaning." [26]

After the German invasion of Russia in June 1941 brought her on the side of the Allies, a tendency emerged among persons in high places to speak well of Stalin and his regime, sympathetically explaining, if not always justifying, most things they did. Joseph E. Davies, ambassador to Russia from 1936 to 1938, seemed to do this. His book, *Mission to Moscow*,[27] argued among other things that the Russian government had established its case against the defendants in the Moscow trials; [28] that Stalin had been forced to side with Hitler in the nonaggression pact of 1939 because the governments of Britain and France had turned down his proposals for a "realistic alliance" to stop Hitler; [29] that if Stalin were again to join Hitler in a treaty it would be because he believed that the governments of the Allied countries were about to double-cross him; [30] and that though terrorism of the most horrifying sort did in fact exist in Russia and reached down into every town and hamlet, its leaders thought it justified to "save their cause," and that history in the long run would approve their acts.[31]

Davies's book and the many favorable reviews that greeted its appearance greatly disturbed Dewey because he believed they misled the American people as to the true nature and aims of Stalin and his regime, thereby playing into the hands of Communists and their sympathizers in this country. Consequently, he wrote to the *New York Times* criticizing Davies's seeming view that Stalin was always right, that anything he did contrary to the best interests of the Allies was forced on him by the heads of these countries. The truth was, Dewey wrote, that "Stalin's actions—and those of his agents and sympathizers here—will be governed by his own interest as he conceives it, regardless of the efforts of or the consequences to his present democratic allies." [32] But this did not mean the United States should withhold military and other aid to Russia. On the contrary, there was no question that America should give "every possible aid against the Nazi invasion, which the Russian people and armies have so heroically withstood." But there was equally no question that "it is not only unnecessary but dangerous for Mr. Davies or any other public man to present the totalitarian despotism of Stalin in any but its true light." [33] Dewey suggested that the United States take a leaf from Stalin's book and learn from him: Stalin recognized a common interest with this country, so he cooperated, accepted our aid, and would even help us if forced by necessity. But at the same time he distrusted us. He knew that totalitarianism and democracy were diametrically opposed and, despite present harmony, would like to see each other destroyed. "Our future would be much more secure than it now appears," Dewey concluded, "if we were to emulate his circumspection instead of indulging in the fatuous one-sided love feast now going on in this country, of which Mr. Davies's book is merely one manifestation among many." [34]

Dewey was equally disturbed when the movie based upon the book appeared two years later. In another lengthy letter to the *New York Times*, in collaboration with Suzanne La Follette, he denounced the film, also called *Mission to Moscow*, for falsifying history, for departing from the book whenever it presented facts that did not fit the film's general pattern, and for subtly trying to undermine confidence in democratic processes in government by representing them as slow, inept, controlled by vested interests, while depicting Soviet despotism as a form of "advanced democracy." [35] He declared that the film is "the first instance in our history of totalitarian propaganda for mass consumption" and that the producers had contributed more to the confusion of public opinion than to its enlightenment.[36]

His persistent efforts to alert the American people to the true nature of Russian totalitarianism and the danger it posed for Western democracy earned Dewey the bitter hostility of Communists and fellow-travelers and made him a favorite target of Soviet and pro-Soviet American writers. The charge most commonly made against him was that he was the "flunkey," the "faithful lackey," the "spokesman and apologist" for American capitalism and imperialism. His pragmatic logic with its doctrine that truth is that which works is essentially a "class logic," designed to safeguard "the vested interests of the capitalist preserves." [37] His moral and social philosophy with its stress on social democracy is merely an attempt to "corrupt the mind of the workers by the illusion of so-called meliorism—'the amelioration' of the capitalist order on the basis of the inviolability of the foundations of capitalism." [38] Dewey's theory of progressive education, like all bourgeois educational theories, "is geared to turn out faithful and obedient servants of the capitalist class." [39] To bring this about Dewey would limit the education of the children of the masses to vocational training. For, "since the overwhelming majority are workers who are not 'intellectually-minded,' Dewey maintains that there is no need to give them knowledge or culture. All they need are 'useful rules of action' and training for jobs." [40] To safeguard capitalist interests further, Dewey's theory stresses the need for "class collaboration" and the "spirit of service" if the larger and better society of the future is to be brought into existence. But, "Dewey's 'larger society' is, of course, monopoly capitalism, and the 'lovely harmony' he seeks is between the workers and the monopolists." [41] His critics further charged that "like Hegel, Nietzsche and the German fascists, Dewey declares that 'warlikeness,' as well as the desire for private property, is 'a component part of human nature'." [42] On the basis of this conception of human nature Dewey develops his "philosophy of war and fascism" [43] and provides "moral 'rationalization' for the world expansion of American imperialism"—thus revealing himself as "a vicious enemy of the Soviet Union." [44]

Despite being now in his eighties, Dewey continued to write extensively for publication. Three books, *German Philosophy and Politics*, *The Public and Its Problems*, and *Reconstruction in Philosophy* appeared in new editions during the 1940s, each with a new and extended introduction. He wrote numerous reviews for professional journals, as well as responding generously to requests from authors to write prefatory notes or introductions to their books. His articles on philosophy, touching upon many areas—logic, ethics, metaphysics, theory of value, social philosophy, and philosophy of education—attest his continuing lively, many-sided interest in philosophy.[45] Many articles written in the 1940s were combined with the more important ones of the 1930s in a collection published in book form under the title *Problems of Men*.[46]

Dewey's major philosophical efforts during these years, however, were devoted to a study of the terms used in logic and theory of knowledge in an attempt to clear up the linguistic confusion he found in these areas. He worked closely in these endeavors with Arthur F. Bentley, a research scholar in the behavioral sciences, a man eleven years younger than Dewey. Bentley's two books, *Linguistic Analysis of Mathematics* and *Behavior, Knowledge, Fact*,[47] were landmarks in language analysis which had earned him a secure place in the history of this discipline. Their cooperative venture resulted in a number of articles published first in the *Journal of Philosophy* from 1945 to 1948, then in the volume, *Knowing and the Known*.[48]

To show the "linguistic chaos" [49] characterizing logic and theory of knowledge and to emphasize the need for reform, Dewey and Bentley first examined the use of such words as "term," "proposition," "definition," "sign," "symbol," "fact," "object," "reality" in some recent prominent books and articles in these fields.[50] They found that the several authors—and even a single writer in a single work—used the words in such different ways that communication and cooperation among them were virtually impossible. The obvious need, Dewey and Bentley declared, is for "firm names," names based on observation, so clear and definite in meaning as to be understood and generally accepted by scholars working in logic and theory of knowledge.

In their quest for firm names, the authors stressed "specification" and "transaction" as undergirdings for their names. "Specification," giving individual, concrete, definite meanings to things, develops when "inquiry gets down to close hard work" and concentrates experimentally and operationally on its subject matter, as in the physical sciences.[51] "Transaction" is that stage or level of the organization and presentation of inquiry in which things are viewed as inseparable "aspects" or "phases" of a larger spatial-temporal situation in terms of which they are to be understood. In analyzing a transaction the problem involved is "always a question of emphasis, never of separation." [52] Specification and transaction mutually affect each other; together "they make possible at once full spatial-temporal localization, and reference within it to the concrete and specific instance." [53]

The "trial group of names" proposed by the authors for general use among scholars in logic and epistemology comprises approximately one hundred items. Because "knowledge" is viewed as "too wide and vague a *name* of anything in particular,"[54] the authors substituted for it specific "knowings" and "knowns" where "knowings" are regarded as the organic phases and "knowns" the environmental phases of "transactionally observed behaviors."[55] "Truth" is said to lack accuracy even in technical contexts; the writers therefore replaced it with the "warranted assertion" of Dewey's *Logic*.[56] "Object" as currently used is beset with ambiguities but is acceptable if defined, as in the *Logic*, as that which "emerges as a definite constituent of a resolved situation, and is confirmed in the continuity of inquiry."[57] Words like "reality," "substance," "essence," "being," when referring to "something which lies underneath and behind all knowing, and yet, as Reality, something incapable of being known in fact and as fact"[58] are omitted because what lies beyond knowing and the known has no place in an inquiry into knowings and knowns.[59] Words like "sign," "signal," "symbol," "term," "proposition," etc., are carefully considered and in each case specifically and transactionally interpreted. Language itself, whether in its spoken or written form, is taken to be not a third kind of realm lying between speaker and thing spoken of but transactionally regarded as "man-himself-in-action-dealing-with-things."[60]

Knowing and the Known was accorded a friendly reception. Reviewers were in sympathy with the writers' broad aim, favoring their attempt to bring clearness and firmness to the terms employed in logic and theory of knowledge. Though doubts were expressed concerning the adequacy of some of the proposals,[61] reviewers in general were ready to accept the judgment of one critic that "a rich feast awaits semanticists and those interested in the history of ideas," and that "how successful this program will be depends in part upon the sensitivity of the philosophic community to the issues raised and proposals made."[62]

At the time he was developing the idea of transaction, Dewey's attention was called to the work of Adelbert Ames, Jr., Research Professor of Physiological Optics at Dartmouth, who was engaged in some highly original experiments in the psychology of visual perception that seemed to indicate a thing observed was constructed not only out of past experience but also in reference to future behavior. It was found to be not a short-span visual image corresponding to something in the external world but a significant factor in an ongoing life process.

Ames's experiments seemed to Dewey to provide empirical evidence that the transactional approach is valid in requiring recognition of long-span, temporal-spatial conditions such as are involved in a transactional situation and rejecting short-span, isolated relations as inadequate. After Dewey wrote to Ames expressing his interest, they corresponded from December 1946 to November 1950, exchanging forty-eight letters.[63] In one of his last letters to Ames, Dewey remarked that "I think your work is by far the most important work done in the psychological-philosophical field during this century—I am tempted to say the *only* really important work."[64]

Dewey's personal life took a new turn when, on 11 December 1946, he married Roberta Lowitz Grant, widow of Robert Grant, a mining engineer. Roberta was the daughter of Mr. and Mrs. Joshua Lowitz of Pittsburgh, Pennsylvania, whom Dewey had known since the early 1900s when Joshua was teaching in normal school and Roberta was a young child in the grades. Contact with the family had then lapsed till 1939 when Roberta came to live in New York City after her husband's death. The friendship between the two was renewed, culminating seven years later in their marriage when Dewey was eighty-seven years of age and Roberta forty-two.

The wedding took place in Dewey's apartment at 1158 Fifth Avenue where he and his daughter Jane had moved the year before. Mrs. Sabino Dewey, wife of Dewey's adopted younger son, attended the bride and Frederick A. Dewey, Dewey's older son, was best man. Dewey's good friend, Dr. Jerome Nathanson, a leader of the Ethical Culture Society of New York City, performed the ceremony. Also in attendance were Dewey's daughter Jane, Mrs. Frederick A. Dewey, Sabino L. Dewey, and Dr. and Mrs. Albert C. Barnes of Merion, Pennsylvania.[65]

By his marriage Dewey forfeited his right to share in the estate of his first wife, Alice Chipman Dewey. On her death in 1927 she had left a gross estate of $129,732 and a net of $68,565, derived mostly from the sale of the Dewey farm on Long Island, which had greatly appreciated in value during the years the Deweys owned it. Alice's will provided her husband a life interest in the estate except that, in the event of his remarriage, the principal was to be divided equally among the surviving children.[66]

Roberta contributed much to Dewey's happiness and well-being during his last years. She had an outgoing personality with much common sense, a quiet but lively sense of humor that matched Dewey's. Intelligent and well-informed, she was an interesting conversationalist. Their friends were impressed by Roberta's wholehearted devotion to her husband and his obvious delight in her companionship. Despite the initial misgivings of members of both their families, their relationship was congenial and happy.

Distressed at reports of the plight of children in post-war Europe, Dewey and Roberta shortly after their marriage adopted two small Belgian children, brother and sister, made orphans by the war. First adopted was a boy, John; a year later, his older sister, Adrienne, was found and adopted.

Always fond of children, Dewey was pleased when Adrienne and John joined Roberta and him. The four adjusted to each other in only a short time, soon becoming a tightly knit and affectionate family group. When his travels took him away from the city, Dewey's usual practice was to telephone the children to hear their voices and to learn how they were.

Dewey's age prevented his traveling abroad although he and Roberta did go to Montego Bay, Jamaica, during the winter of 1949 and to Honolulu during January and February of 1951. For the rest, their travels were confined to this country. During the hot summer months they went either to Dewey's cottage in Hubbards, Nova Scotia, or to Roberta's farm in New Alexandria, Pennsylvania. With the coming of winter they went to Florida, usually to Key West, but sometimes to Miami Beach.

Dewey's ninetieth birthday on 20 October 1949 was widely celebrated. Press releases from Canada, England, France, Holland, Denmark, Sweden, Israel, Mexico, Turkey, Japan, and India announced special programs honoring Dewey. The president of Austria and the prime ministers of Britain, the Netherlands, Norway, and Italy, along with scores of well-known scholars and educators throughout the democratic world sent messages to Dewey. In this country over one hundred colleges, universities, and learned societies held meetings at which Dewey's philosophy and its influence on American life and thought were discussed. The press gave the occasion extensive coverage; editorials paying tribute to Dewey appeared in many of the country's leading papers. Special feature articles appeared in the *New York Times*[67] and the *New York Herald Tribune*.[68] *Time Magazine* and *Life Magazine*[69] gave popular accounts of Dewey's life and thought, and the *New Republic*,[70] the *Saturday Review of Literature*,[71] and the *New Leader*[72] each brought out a special John Dewey issue containing articles on his philosophy. Both the *New Yorker* and the *Saturday Evening Post* expressed interest in publishing an article on Dewey, but plans for these were never realized.[73]

The main celebration was in New York City where a national John Dewey 90th Birthday Committee was set up to make plans.

A three-day program was arranged, with a banquet at the Commodore Hotel on 20 October and meetings on the evenings of 21 and 22 October.[74]

Commanding most attention, the banquet at the Commodore[75] was attended by over fifteen hundred people, including nationally and internationally known figures. During the formal part of the meeting a congratulatory message from President Truman was read, followed by greetings from representatives of various countries and from civic, educational, and labor organizations. Jawaharlal Nehru, Prime Minister of India, left at the end of a meeting in his honor at the Waldorf-Astoria Hotel in order to bring personally to Dewey the greetings of his country. Hu Shih, former Chinese ambassador to the United States, conveyed the best wishes of Dewey's Chinese friends. Carlos Delabarra, Consul-General of Chile, bestowed on Dewey the Chilean Order of Merit.

William P. Montague, acting for the John Dewey 90th Birthday Committee, read a citation by the committee honoring Dewey and his work, extending to him its "best wishes for many more years of wise and gallant service in the cause of a free and more radiant humanity."[76]

A huge three-tiered cake decorated with forty-nine candles was then presented to Dewey. On it was inscribed "Happy Birthday—Dr. John Dewey." While cameras clicked and bulbs flashed, and with Adrienne, John, and five of their little friends surrounding him, Dewey cut the cake with Roberta's assistance.

Dewey's words of response were brief. Reviewing his career, he declared that despite the many fields in which his thought had ranged, he regarded himself as being "first, last, and all the time, engaged in the vocation of philosophy" with his interest in other areas "specifically an outgrowth and manifestation of my primary interest in philosophy."[77] As philosopher, he continued, he had attempted to get beneath the surface of things to obtain "a moderately clear and distinct idea of what the problems are that underlie the difficulties and evils which we experience *in fact*; that is to say, in *practical* life."[78] Looking ahead, he reaffirmed his faith in democracy, in "human good sense and human good will as it manifests itself in the long run when communication is progressively liberated from bondage to prejudice and ignorance."[79] He declared that he would like to think that "the significance of this celebration consists not in warming over of past years, even though they be four-score and ten, but in dedication to the work that lies ahead."[80]

Before the meeting adjourned, the birthday committee announced that as part of the celebration a John Dewey 90th Anniversary Fund, Inc., had been established with the goal of raising $90,000 for "presentation to Dr. Dewey during his 90th year for distribution to those causes which he wishes to support."[81] Also announced was a project with Sidney Hook in charge to publish a volume of essays as a public tribute to Dewey.[82]

The one out-of-town celebration in his honor that Dewey attended was a homecoming on 26 October at the University of Vermont. In contrast to the celebration in New York when notables and celebrities from at home and abroad had met in the magnificence of a New York hotel, the reception in Burlington was simple. Dewey was welcomed home by his native city, his alma mater, and by people who had known him as a boy and had always regarded him as one of their own.

Dewey and Roberta arrived on an early train the day of the homecoming celebration and left the same day on a sleeper for New York. During the day the Deweys were taken on a tour to places in Burlington with which Dewey had had close ties while he was growing up in the city. These included his birthplace at 186 Willard Street and the homes on George Street and South Prospect Street where he had lived as a youth; the site of the grade school he had attended at North and Murray streets; the high school on College Street from which he was graduated; the First Congregational Church on South Winooski Avenue whose services he dutifully attended, where he taught Sunday School and led the Young People's Society; the store on Church Street where his father ran a cigar and tobacco shop; Burlington harbor where as a teen-ager Dewey worked in the lumber yards that lined its shores; Battery Park overlooking Lake Champlain where Archibald Dewey frequently took his young sons and told them stories of the battles fought on the lake during the War of 1812; and Green Mountain Cemetery where his parents and two of his brothers are buried in graves only a few paces from that of Ethan Allen. Throughout the drive, Dewey entertained Roberta and the others by recalling his youthful experiences, pointing out the changes that had taken place in Burlington since the time he lived there.

A visit to the University of Vermont campus completed the tour. Here the Deweys were welcomed on the steps of the Waterman Building by Acting President Elias Lyman and a large number of students and faculty, with the university band and cheerleaders joining to make the reception enthusiastic and hearty. Led by sweatered cheerleaders, the crowd broke out again and again in cheers and applause for Dewey; an observer remarked that the welcome was more like that accorded a returning football hero than one normally given a world-renowned scholar. Dewey, however, clearly enjoyed the occasion, and, in response to a request for a few remarks, touched briefly upon the university of his day, expressing pleasure at the way the university had grown and prospered since his undergraduate years.

The dinner that evening was held in the faculty dining room on the campus. About one hundred persons attended, including members of the university administration and faculty, officers of student organizations, representatives of sister colleges in Vermont, and some townspeople who had known Dewey as a boy. President Lyman served as toastmaster, with his warmth, friendliness, and informality setting the tone for the evening. He welcomed the Deweys by their first names and expressed the university's pride in having as one of its alumni a person as illustrious as Dewey. On Roberta he conferred the title "Honorary Vermonter," welcoming her into the university family. Representatives of the several organizations then expressed their greetings and best wishes to Dewey.

Dewey was visibly moved when six townspeople who had known him as a boy arose and explained their former acquaintance with Dewey. Dewey, who had not seen some of these friends since childhood days, was touched by the unexpected meeting and acknowledged each old friend with a nod and smile.

The meeting ended with a few remarks by Dewey. He declared his pride in being a native Vermonter, telling what the independent and democratic spirit that had prevailed in the Vermont of his youth had meant to him. He closed by reading a passage from a recent article that he had come across and scribbled on a piece of paper, a passage in which the author describes the planet Earth as a wonderful and beautiful place to live, where man can fashion a happy and worthwhile life provided he treats the earth and its resources with care and reverence and its inhabitants with intelligence and good will.[83]

The dinner was followed by a public address in the chapel on Dewey's work and influence by Herbert W. Schneider of Columbia. A packed house awaited the speaker, but Dewey and Roberta did not attend. The day had been long and strenuous and Dewey had asked after the dinner to be taken to the station so he and Roberta could return to New York.

The local press and university publications made much of the Dewey visit, printing detailed accounts of the day's activities.[84] The *New York Times* had sent a reporter and a photographer to cover the affair; stories and photographs relating to it were assigned a prominent place in the next day's issue.[85]

Dewey's deep satisfaction from his visit to Burlington, destined to be his last, is attested by his letter to President Lyman. "I could not have imagined in advance nor can I in retrospect imagine anything more heart-warming & genuinely home coming," Dewey wrote, "than your conduct of the dinner last night. I wish I knew how to tell you how deeply I am touched. . . . Of course the dinner here on the 20th was a wonderful occasion but the homecoming last night had something that went deeper." [86]

Dewey remained intellectually active during the last few years of his life. He wrote an occasional article for professional journals and contributed two substantial essays to *Democracy in a World of Tension: A Symposium Prepared by UNESCO* [87] and *The Cleavage in Our Culture: Studies in Scientific Humanism in Honor of Max Otto.*[88] He continued his collaboration with Bentley in exploring the use of terms in logic and theory of knowledge; between 7 July 1949 and 6 December 1951, sixty-four letters passed between them. In this connection Dewey wrote for publication two essays, "Means and Consequences" and "Importance, Significance, and Meaning," which he sent to Bentley for comment. Dewey died before he could send them to a journal for publication but they appear as Parts VIII and IX of *John Dewey and Arthur F. Bentley: A Philosophical Correspondence, 1932–1951.*

During his ninety-first year Dewey undertook a new edition of his *Experience and Nature.* In a letter to Bentley from Honolulu dated 18 January 1951, he reported that he had just begun a revised edition of the book and had in mind changing the title to *Nature and Culture,* adjusting the content to the new title. Nature and culture, he wrote, was a more accurate antithesis than nature and experience, and "I was dumb not to have seen the need for such a shift when the old text was written." [89]

Always interested in public affairs, Dewey maintained this concern to the very last. In 1947 he was one of the signers of a letter in the *New York Times* warning against the use of public funds for parochial schools.[90] When the question of allowing Communists to teach in public schools was being hotly debated during the late 1940s and early 1950s, Dewey wrote a letter to the *New York Times* expressing serious doubts about the practicality of banning Communists from teaching; such action, he believed, would lead most Communists to deny their Communist connections or else force them underground to engage in subversive activity there.[91] Later, when Secretary of State Dean Acheson was being attacked because of his foreign policy in Korea and the State Department's alleged coddling of Communists, Dewey wrote a letter deploring the attacks as unwarranted and as damaging America's image abroad.[92]

In recognition of his interest in public affairs and his contribution to liberal causes, Dewey was elected an honorary vice-chairman of the State Committee of the Liberal Party of the State of New York at its meeting in New York City on 3 May 1952.[93]

One of Dewey's last public appearances was at Yale University's two hundred and fiftieth commencement on 11 June 1951. On this occasion he was one of twenty-five of the nation's most outstanding scholars, including four Nobel prize winners, who received honorary degrees. Throughout the exercises, held under threatening skies and 55-degree temperature, Dewey, who had just undergone a serious illness, sat with a woolen robe draped across his knees, following all the proceedings with interest. The audience of eight thousand persons applauded each of the recipients as he came forward to receive his degree, but, according to one press account, reserved its loudest applause for Dewey as he left his chair on the platform to receive the Doctor of Letters degree.[94]

Throughout most of his life, Dewey enjoyed remarkably good health. Rarely was he forced to interrupt his activities because of illness; when a minor ailment did occur, he was able to rebound quickly. Even in his late years he impressed his friends and acquaintances with his vigor and vitality. When representatives of the press interviewed him on his eightieth, eighty-fifth, and ninetieth birthdays, they were unanimous in declaring that he looked and acted much younger than his age.

The advancing years, however, were taking their toll. Dewey's strength was waning and his powers of resistance were weakening. During his early eighties he had been afflicted with prostatitis, requiring a number of stays in the hospital over a period of months before the condition was remedied by surgery in the fall of 1943.[95] Also, as he grew older, references in his later correspondence show that he became increasingly subject to attacks of colds, flu, virus infections, congested sore throat, and bronchitis; in some of his letters he explained his delay in replying to a correspondent as due to his being "rather below par physically"[96] and to his lack of "needed strength."[97] Despite this, Dewey was able for the most part to keep to his usual routine of studying, writing, and corresponding; even a rather serious attack of pneumonia in the spring of 1951 did not prevent his attending the commencement at Yale in June to receive in person the degree awarded him then.

Shortly after his ninety-second birthday in November 1951, Dewey suffered an injury that incapacitated him to the end. While playing with Adrienne and John in the apartment, he fell and broke his hip. A surgeon set the fracture, but failure of the bones to knit properly kept him in the hospital till after Christmas. Upon his return home, recovery continued to drag, confining him to the apartment throughout the winter and spring months of 1952. When weather permitted, he was taken by elevator in a wheelchair to the roof of the building where he could sun himself.

Despite his physical handicap, Dewey felt well enough to work at some of the projects previously begun, and the clicking of his typewriter attested his activity. For relaxation he depended mostly on acrostic and crossword puzzles. Roberta and the children were company for him; visits from family and friends helped to brighten the days.

Though recovery was slow, Roberta and the family hoped that the hip would eventually heal so that Dewey would again be able to walk without too much difficulty. This hope received a jolt when, early on Saturday, 31 May, Dewey was again stricken with pneumonia. His physician saw no immediate danger since Dewey was helped considerably by an oxygen mask. However, late the next afternoon, his condition suddenly grew worse. His breathing became more labored and his skin took on an unusual pallor. Alarmed by these symptoms, Roberta called the physician and sent the children to the home of a neighbor. Dewey slowly lost consciousness, and his death, at seven o'clock on 1 June 1952, was quiet and peaceful.[98]

Many of Dewey's close friends and associates believed his funeral should be in keeping with his prominence; Columbia University volunteered use of its facilities and services for this purpose. Roberta, however, decided on a simple service, believing this was what Dewey would have wanted. Though Dewey had long ago ceased to belong to any organized religious group, she arranged for services to be held in the Community Church at 40 East Thirty-fifth Street. Such an arrangement was not out of keeping with Dewey's feelings because he had always respected the work of this church, believing it was one of those that most nearly embodied the type of religion he had advocated in *A Common Faith*. The church's statement of purpose was one Dewey could have heartily endorsed: "The Community Church seeks a religion as intelligent as science, as appealing as art, as intimate as home, as vital as the day's work, as inspiring as love and as universal as mankind. The core of its faith and the purpose of its life are the realization on earth of *The Beloved Community*."

Some five hundred persons attended the ceremonies on Wednesday, 4 June, including members of the family, friends, representatives of universities, learned societies, and civic and labor organizations. Donald Harrington, minister of the church, read passages from Proverbs, Ecclesiastes, and First Corinthians and stanzas from Matthew Arnold's "Rugby Chapel," George Eliot's "The Choir Invisible," and Samuel Taylor Coleridge's "Ode on Dejection." He also read the well-known last paragraph of Dewey's *A Common Faith*. In his brief eulogy, Harrington referred to Dewey as "one of the intellectual and moral giants" of all time, declaring that "when the full impact of his revolutionary thought reaches the heart of our society, some generations hence, scarcely a single social institution will remain as it is today." [99] Max C. Otto, professor emeritus of philosophy at the University of Wisconsin and a longtime friend of Dewey, briefly reviewed Dewey's contribution to philosophy and education and spoke eloquently of his qualities as a friend and philosophical companion. His philosophy, said Otto, was like that of a mountain climber who climbs in order to see farther, and who, once he has climbed one mountain, presses on to a higher one simply to see farther yet. It was that continual quest for new vision and new vistas that marked the greatness of Dewey's mind. A soloist sang "Swing Low, Sweet Chariot" and "The Balm of Gilead," the latter said to have been Dewey's favorite hymn. The service ended with the audience singing John Addington Symonds's hymn that begins: "These things shall be, a loftier race than e'er the world hath known shall rise."

Accounts of Dewey's death and funeral appeared in leading newspapers throughout the world. Journals of philosophy, education, and psychology here and abroad contained notices of his death and tributes to his work. Memorial minutes were read and placed in the files of the numerous learned and professional organizations with which he had been associated. At a meeting of the Columbia University Faculty of Philosophy on 17 April 1953, John Herman Randall, Jr., read a memorial minute written by him and Ernest Nagel. "We in this Faculty," the minute declared, "can recall with pride, and with an abiding sense of satisfaction, that for twenty-six of his ninety-two years, from 1904 to 1930, John Dewey was one of us. For those who were his students, and for many who were his colleagues throughout the University, the relation grew more intimate and prolonged—he became, and will remain, a part of our very lives and selves." [100]

Dewey's body was cremated the day after his death. Roberta

and Donald Harrington accompanied the body to the crematory where Dr. Harrington read a brief poem and said a prayer before the cremation.[101] A bronze urn containing the ashes was deposited temporarily in a safe in the Community Church. Roberta wanted the urn permanently placed at the University of Vermont and notices to this effect appeared in the press; [102] but while plans were being made by the university to receive the urn, Roberta decided that she wished to keep it near her during her lifetime.[103]

After her death in Miami Beach on 6 May 1970, the executor of Roberta's estate, with the consent of the two adopted Dewey children and the officers of the John Dewey Foundation, gave the urn containing Dewey's ashes and that containing Roberta's to the university for interment. Here on a quiet, shaded spot adjacent to the university's Ira Allen Chapel, a Dewey memorial monument was installed and the ashes interred. A program commemorating the event was given in the chapel on the afternoon of 26 October 1972 before an audience of some two hundred. George Dykhuizen, professor emeritus of philosophy at the University of Vermont, gave a talk on "Dewey and Vermont"; Sidney Hook, professor emeritus of philosophy at New York University and president of the John Dewey Foundation, spoke on "The Relevance of John Dewey's Thought." Edward C. Andrews, Jr., president of the University of Vermont, who presided at the meeting, expressed the university's deep satisfaction at being selected as Dewey's final resting place.

Dewey's career had been illustrious, establishing for him a leading place in the history of thought. That his writings inspired and continue to inspire widespread interest can be seen in the hundreds of books, articles, pamphlets, monographs, and theses written about his work. A "Checklist of Writings about John Dewey, 1886–1972," in preparation, lists almost 2,700 such items, exclusive of reviews.[104] The worldwide nature of this interest shows clearly in the large number of translations of his writings; a study at the Dewey Center listed 327 separate translations into 35 languages made between 1900, when the first translation of a Dewey work appeared, and 1967.[105] Many more have appeared in the ensuing years.

All Dewey's writings, comprising some forty books and over seven hundred articles, are being brought together in a definitive edition by a group of scholars centering at Southern Illinois University. This project, sponsored primarily by Southern Illinois University, is carried on at the university's Center for Dewey Studies under the direction of Jo Ann Boydston, with notable assistance from an advisory board of editors. The magnitude of the undertaking is manifest in the fact that five substantial volumes of Dewey's early works, those written between 1882 and 1898, have been published, with forty additional volumes to follow covering the other periods in Dewey's long career.

The memory of Dewey is being perpetuated by many formal undertakings. John Dewey Professorships and John Dewey Lecture Series have been established at numerous institutions of higher learning such as Columbia University and Antioch and Bennington Colleges. University buildings and schools have been named after him both in this country and abroad, one of the latter being the John Dewey School of Education at Hebrew University in Jerusalem. The John Dewey Society continues its practice, begun in 1964, of granting awards to individuals and institutions that have distinguished themselves by advancing the cause of education in the spirit of John Dewey. The John Dewey Foundation, established in 1964 by Roberta Dewey, seeks "to promote and support activities and projects relating to the life and works of John Dewey" and "to promote appreciation for and understanding of the democratic ideals for which John Dewey was known." Roberta's will generously endowed the foundation, opening a promising future for it. In recognition of Dewey's contribution to American life, the United States Post Office on 21 October 1968 with appropriate ceremonies in Burlington issued a 30-cent stamp, printed in light purple, with Dewey's portrait, as one in the Prominent Americans series. More recently, on 1 May 1971, the government of Grenada issued a five-cent stamp with Dewey's portrait, honoring him as one of the world's great educators.

Throughout his life, Dewey's mind had ranged and probed among various special fields, refusing to be bound by the narrowness of any. His more technical philosophical endeavors regarding the nature and function of sensations, ideas, knowledge, truth, value, and experience earned for him an outstanding place in the history of American philosophy. With Peirce, James, and Mead, he is regarded as a chief exponent and apologist for American pragmatism, or instrumentalism. Indeed, historians of philosophy generally agree that Dewey, with his closely reasoned, factually grounded arguments and with his wide scope of interests, gave this philosophy its most logical, comprehensive, and persuasive formulation. His early efforts in the field of psychology around the turn of the century represented the beginnings of a new school of psychology, gaining for him a secure place in the history of this discipline. His essay entitled "The Reflex Arc Concept in Psychology," written in 1896, is generally regarded as marking the beginning of functionalism as a definite movement in psychology.

Dewey's philosophy of education, even though often controversial, placed him at the head of the progressive movement in educational thought in this country, assuring him a prominent rank in the history of philosophy of education. His writings on social philosophy constitute a valuable account of American liberal thought during the first half of the twentieth century. More than any other philosopher of modern times, Dewey insisted that philosophy be made relevant to the problems of men and provide insights regarding individual self-realization and the reconstruction of society. "So faithfully did Dewey live up to his own philosophical creed," wrote one historian, "that he became the guide, the mentor, and the conscience of the American people: it is scarcely an exaggeration to say that for a generation no major issue was clarified until Dewey had spoken.[106] As Morris Cohen has said, if "there could be such an office as that of national philosopher, no one else could be properly mentioned for it."[107]

Indeed, if there were such a position as that of philosopher of the new world of the twentieth century, Dewey would be among the first of those whose names would necessarily come to mind. For though he left no formal system of thought, he did leave to posterity a philosophy rich in insights and in the wisdom to which philosophy has traditionally aspired. Much of this wisdom and many of these insights have already been absorbed, consciously or unconsciously, into twentieth century man's thinking and acting, functioning as guides for the reorganization of society and the attainment of individual human happiness. And, as long as there are people willing to open their minds to the ideas of a modest man who was at the same time a philosophical genius, those who come after him will continue to benefit from his teachings.

Notes — Index

Illustrations Credits

Dewey's birthplace in Burlington, Vermont. L. L. McAllister.

Home of Dewey's maternal grandparents. Lake View Seminary, Charlotte, Vermont. H. B. Eldred, University of Vermont Audio-Visual Services.

Glenmore Camp group, reproduced in *Coranto: Journal of the Friends of The Libraries,* University of Southern California.

Doctor honoris causa, University of Paris, 1930. Pacific and Atlantic photo.

Heroic size bust by Sir Jacob Epstein. Courtesy the John Dewey Foundation.

Dewey with Albert Barnes. Photo by Pinto Brothers. Courtesy *Saturday Evening Post.*

Watercolor portrait by Joseph Margulies. Courtesy Joseph Margulies.

Group of three at Hubbards, N. S., mid-1940s. Robert Norwood.

Dewey with Pandit Nehru. Alexander Archer.

Photograph by Ralph Morse. *Life Magazine.* Copyright, © 1949–72, Time Inc.

Ninetieth birthday homecoming at the University of Vermont. *Burlington Free Press.*

Memorial monument. John Smith, University of Vermont.

All other illustrations are from The Dewey Papers, Special Collections, Morris Library, Southern Illinois University-Carbondale.

Notes

CHAPTER 1. BOYHOOD AND YOUTH IN VERMONT, 1859–1879

1. John Gunther, *Inside U. S. A.* (New York: Harper & Bros., 1947), p. 493.
2. Irwin Edman, "America's Philosopher Attains an Alert 90," *New York Times Magazine,* 16 October 1949, p. 17.
3. For an account of Dewey's maternal ancestry, see Abby Maria Hemenway, ed., *The Vermont Historical Gazetteer,* vol. 1 (Burlington: Miss A. M. Hemenway, 1867), pp. 100, 101.
4. The house in which Dewey was born is still standing at 186 South Willard Street; see *Vermont Vital Records, Burlington, Vt., 1857–1869,* p. 96, and Town Records of Burlington, vol. 29 (handwritten), pp. 113, 114. Irwin Edman mistakenly said in an article some years ago that Dewey was born "on a Vermont farm" (see Edman, "Our Foremost Philosopher at Seventy," *New York Times Magazine,* 13 October 1929, p. 3).
5. The Deweys, having sold their house on South Willard Street when Lucina left for Virginia, bought the house at 14 George Street. This house was demolished in the summer of 1957 to make room for the new Federal Building on Pearl Street. The Deweys lived on George Street from 1867 to the spring of 1876 when they moved to the house, also still standing, at 178 South Prospect Street, their last residence in Burlington.
6. See S. W. Thayer, "Report of City Health Officer," in *Annual Report of Officers and Committees of the City of Burlington for the Financial Year, ending Feb. 1, 1866* (Burlington: Free Press Job Printing Office, 1866), pp. 84, 93. Sidney Hook has written that Dewey was brought up in "a community in which no great disparities in wealth or standards of living were to be found" (see Hook, *John Dewey: An Intellectual Portrait* [New York: John Day Co., 1939], p. 5). The facts indicate that the opposite was the case.
7. Irwin Edman speaks of Burlington in Dewey's day as having a

"homogeneous pattern of culture" (see "America's Philosopher Attains an Alert 90," p. 17). This was not true.

8. The United States Census for 1870 reports a total population for Burlington of 14,387. Of these, 8,219 were native born; 6,168 were foreign born, almost equally divided between immigrants from Ireland and from Quebec. U.S. Census Office, *9th Census, 1870,* 3 vols.
9. Joseph Auld, *Picturesque Burlington: A Handbook of Burlington, Vermont and Lake Champlain,* 2d ed. (Burlington: Free Press Association, 1894), p. 92.
10. Matthew H. Buckham, "Burlington as a Place to Live In," in *Vermont Historical Gazetteer,* 1:724.
11. Dewey to Angell, 19 July 1884, James Burrill Angell Papers, Michigan Historical Collections, University of Michigan, Ann Arbor, Mich. I am indebted to Dr. Willinda Savage for telling me of the existence of this letter.
12. Hook, *John Dewey: An Intellectual Portrait,* pp. 5–6.
13. Dewey began his grade-school work in District School No. 3, later called North Grammar School, located at North and Murray streets in Burlington. The building has long since been demolished; its site is now the playground of the Lawrence Barnes School.
14. See Eldridge Mix, "Report of the Superintendent of Common Schools," in *Annual Reports of the City of Burlington, 1868,* pp. 101–5; Matthew H. Buckham, "Report of the Superintendent of Common Schools," ibid., pp. 15–17; L. G. Ware, "Report of the Superintendent of Common Schools," ibid., p. 57.
15. See *Vermont School Register, 1867–1868,* District No. 3 (Burlington: R. S. Styles Book & Job Printers, 1867), attendance and department records of students attending District School No. 3.
16. J. E. Goodrich, "Report of the Superintendent of Common Schools," in *Fourth Annual Report of the City Government of the City of Burlington, Vt. for the Municipal Year 1868–9* (Burlington: R. S. Styles, 1869), pp. 44–69.
17. Ware, "Report of the Superintendent of Common Schools," p. 59.
18. Goodrich, "Report of the Superintendent," p. 48.
19. Ware, "Report of the Superintendent," p. 59.
20. *Vermont School Register, 1867–1868,* et seq.
21. The writer is indebted to the following people who knew Dewey well when he was growing up in Burlington for their impressions of him: Miss Cornelia Underwood, Mrs. Violet Hoyt (sister of Cornelia), Mr. James Wood, Miss Jane Wood (James's sister), Miss Barbara Northrop, Mr. Edward Northrop (Barbara's brother), Mrs. Delia Christman Wood (Dewey's first cousin), Dr. Lyman Allen, and Mrs. Margaret Ramsay-Smith.
22. *The Charter and Ordinances and Annual Report of Officers of the City of Burlington for the Financial Year ending Feb. 1, 1866* (Bur-

lington: Free Press Steam Job Printing Office, 1866), sec. 17, p. 52.

23. Dewey to Dykhuizen, 15 October 1949, George Dykhuizen Papers and Correspondence, Special Collections, Guy W. Bailey Library, University of Vermont, Burlington, Vt.
24. For accounts of Dewey's mother, see M. F. P., "Mrs. Lucina A. Dewey, An Appreciative Tribute to Her Worth," *Burlington Daily Free Press,* 28 March 1899; Sarah P. Torrey, "Women's Work in the First Church," in *The Hundredth Anniversary of the Founding of the First Church, Burlington, Vt.* (Burlington: Published by the Church, 1905), pp. 62–63; Mary C. Torrey, "A Brief History of the Sunday School," ibid., p. 97.
25. In a previous reference to this note (see my article, "An Early Chapter in the Life of John Dewey," *Journal of the History of Ideas* 13 [1952]: 566), I mistakenly asserted that John Dewey himself had written it. Since then, samples of Lucina's handwriting have come to light (cf. Names of Visitors to the North Grammar School, *Vermont School Register, 1870–1871,* North Grammar School [Montpelier: Polands' Steam Printing Works, 1870]), and there is no doubt that the note was written by her, as was also a companion note written in behalf of Davis Rich Dewey who joined the church at the same time that John did. Both these notes are in the files of The First Congregational Church of Burlington. The writer is indebted to the Prudential Committee of The First Church for permission to use the note. Dewey joined the church on 2 July 1871 (see Register of Church Members of First Congregational Church of Burlington, 21 February 1805–12 April 1925); Max Eastman has incorrectly stated that Dewey joined the church "during his sophomore year" in college (see his "John Dewey," *Atlantic Monthly* 168 [1941]: 672).
26. Sidney Hook, "Some Memories of John Dewey, 1859–1952," *Commentary* 14 (1952): 246.
27. Dewey, "The Place of Religious Emotion," *Monthly Bulletin,* Students' Christian Association, University of Michigan, November 1886, p. 24 [*The Early Works of John Dewey, 1882–1898,* ed. Jo Ann Boydston, vol. 1 (Carbondale: Southern Illinois University Press, 1969), p. 91].
28. The press reported the accident as follows:

> Distressing Accident.—We learn, with pain, that our friend and townsman, A. S. Dewey, has lost his oldest child, by a most distressing casualty. The child, a fine little boy, between two and three years old, was fatally scalded last evening, by falling backward into a pail of hot water. The customary appliances of sweet oil and cotton batting was made, when, by some accident the cotton took fire, and burst into flames upon the person of the child. This last mishap added to the pain of the little sufferer, as well as to his parents' distress, and death resulted (from the scalding principally, as we understand,) about seven o'clock this morning. The afflicted parents have the sincere and tearful sympathy of the community, in their sudden and most painful bereavement (*Daily Free Press,* 18 January 1859).

29. See Elvirton Wright, *Freshman and Senior* (Boston: Congregational Sunday School & Publishing Society, 1899).
30. Lewis O. Brastow, *The Work of the Preacher: A Study of Homiletic Principles and Methods* (Boston: Pilgrim Press, 1914), p. 188.
31. Ibid., p. 187.
32. Ibid., pp. 24–25.
33. Brastow left Burlington in 1884 to become Professor of Homiletics at Yale, where he remained till his death in 1913. In a memorial address at Yale University, Frank C. Potter, a colleague of Brastow's said:

> His preaching was especially helpful to those whose religious faith was unsettled by intellectual difficulties. One who is now a prominent teacher and leader in the department of philosophy wrote that he heard Mr. Brastow preach at the critical point in his life which comes to young men, when the old foundations are broken up and there is nothing clear, when irrational ways of putting religion had inclined him to skepticism. From him he got rational, philosophical thought which appealed to his best thoughts as well as feelings. "It was," he wrote, "the conviction obtained through you as to the reality of the spiritual and ideal elements that saved me to a belief in a living God and the meaning of existence" (Frank C. Potter, "Lewis Orsmond Brastow, D.D.," *Yale Divinity Quarterly*, January 1913, pp. 77–78).

Efforts to locate this letter and identify its writer have so far been unsuccessful. There are good reasons to believe it might have been Dewey.

34. Dewey, "The Place of Religious Emotion," p. 25 [*Early Works of Dewey*, 1:92].
35. Dewey, "Soul and Body," *Bibliotheca Sacra* 43 (1886): 262 [*Early Works of Dewey*, 1:114].
36. Dewey, "The Place of Religious Emotion," p. 25 [*Early Works of Dewey*, 1:92].
37. Dewey, "The Obligation to Knowledge of God," *Monthly Bulletin*, November 1884, p. 24 [*Early Works of Dewey*, 1:62].
38. John H. Randall, Jr., "The Religion of Shared Experience," in *The Philosopher of the Common Man: Essays in Honor of John Dewey to Celebrate His Eightieth Birthday*, ed. Sidney Ratner (New York: G. P. Putnam's Sons, 1940), pp. 106–45.
39. See *Laws of the University of Vermont and State Agricultural College* (Burlington: Free Press, 1874), pp. 7–8; see also chaps. 3, 4, and 5.
40. Marjorie H. Nicolson, "James Marsh and the Vermont Transcendentalists," *Philosophical Review* 34 (1925): 35.
41. Remarks of George W. Alger, in *John Ellsworth Goodrich, Class of 1853: Address by Darwin P. Kingsley and Tributes by Members of Delta Psi, with a Record of the Dedication of the Delta Psi Goodrich Memorial, June 21st, 1924* (Burlington: University of Vermont Lane Press, 1925), p. 45.
42. *Vermont Cynic*, 1 May 1939, p. 7.

43. Charles's fun-loving propensities caught up with him in college when the faculty voted to drop him from college for a year. (See Minutes of 28 November 1877, "Minutes of Faculty.") Charles did not return to college to continue his studies.
44. Minutes of 3 March 1876 and of 21 November 1877, "Minutes of Faculty."
45. *Vermont Cynic*, 1 May 1939, p. 7.
46. For Dewey's college reading, see Lewis S. Feuer, "John Dewey's Reading at College," *Journal of the History of Ideas* 19 (1958): 415–21.
47. See "Record Volume 'A' 1852–1892" (University of Vermont), p. 109.
48. Dewey, *Democracy and Education* (New York: Macmillan Co., 1917), p. 88.
49. Dewey, "Rationality in Education," *Social Frontier*, December 1936, pp. 71–73; "President Hutchins' Proposals to Remake Higher Education," ibid., January 1937, pp. 103–4; " 'The Higher Learning in America,' " ibid., March 1937, pp. 167–69; and Robert M. Hutchins, "Grammar, Rhetoric, and Mr. Dewey," ibid., February 1937, pp. 137–39. See also Dewey, "Challenge to Liberal Thought," *Fortune Magazine*, August 1944, p. 155; response by Alexander Meiklejohn, ibid., January 1945, pp. 207–8, 210, 212, 214, 217, 219; rejoinder by Dewey, ibid., March 1945, pp. 10, 14; further reply by Meiklejohn, ibid., p. 14; and letter by Dewey, ibid., p. 14.
50. Dewey said of his senior-year course that "it fell in with my own inclinations, and I have always been grateful for that year of my schooling" (Dewey, "From Absolutism to Experimentalism," in *Contemporary American Philosophy*, ed. George P. Adams and William P. Montague, vol. 2 [New York: Macmillan Co., 1930], p. 13).
51. "Record Volume 'A' 1852–1892," p. 109.
52. *Catalogue of the Officers and Students of the University of Vermont and State Agricultural College, Burlington, Vt., with a Statement of the Several Courses of Instruction, 1878–1879* (Burlington: Free Press, 1878), p. 18.
53. See Dewey, "From Absolutism to Experimentalism," p. 20.
54. John W. Buckham, "Ideals and Aims," in *The Very Elect: Baccalaureate Sermons and Occasional Addresses of Matthew Henry Buckham, D.D., LL.D.*, comp. John W. Buckham and J. E. Goodrich (Boston: Pilgrim Press, 1912), p. 19.
55. Matthew H. Buckham, "The Dynamic of Catechetical Instruction," in *The Very Elect*, p. 113.
56. John W. Buckham, "Ideals and Aims," p. 19.
57. Matthew H. Buckham, "Christianity and Social Reform," in *The Very Elect*, p. 233.
58. Ibid., p. 229.
59. Ibid., p. 234.
60. Dewey, "From Absolutism to Experimentalism," p. 20.
61. G. G. Atkins, "An Estimate of Professor Torrey's Christian Life,"

in *In Memoriam Henry A. P. Torrey, LL.D.* (Burlington: University of Vermont, 1906), p. 25.

62. Darwin P. Kingsley, "Remarks of Hon. Darwin P. Kingsley, 1881," in *In Memoriam Henry A. P. Torrey,* p. 17.
63. Dewey, "From Absolutism to Experimentalism," p. 14.
64. H. A. P. Torrey, review of *Facts and Comments,* by Herbert Spencer, *Philosophical Review* 12 (1903): 199.
65. John W. Buckham, "A Group of American Idealists," *Personalist* 1 (1920): 24.
66. Dewey, "From Absolutism to Experimentalism," p. 15.
67. Dewey found Marsh's *Memoir and Remains* of particular value at this time. In a talk at the University of Vermont, in celebration of Dewey's ninetieth birthday, Herbert W. Schneider declared, "Many years ago, when I was beginning to work on the history of American philosophy, Dewey handed me a volume, with the remark, 'This was very important to me in my early days and is still worth reading' " (Herbert W. Schneider, "John Dewey: A Talk Delivered by Professor Herbert W. Schneider in the Ira Allen Chapel, The University of Vermont, on October 26, 1949, at the Celebration of John Dewey's Ninetieth Birthday Anniversary," typewritten manuscript, University of Vermont, p. 5).
68. Dewey to Torrey, 17 November 1883, Dykhuizen Papers. I am indebted to Professor Henry C. Torrey of Rutgers University, grandson of H. A. P. Torrey, for permission to use this letter as well as the one sent by President Gilman to President Buckham, cited below.
69. "Address of President Buckham," in *In Memoriam Henry A. P. Torrey,* p. 22.
70. John W. Buckham, "Professor Torrey as Thinker and Teacher," in *In Memoriam Henry A. P. Torrey,* p. 31.
71. Ibid.
72. *Catalogue of the University of Vermont and State Agricultural College,* p. 18.
73. Dewey, "From Absolutism to Experimentalism," p. 15.
74. Ibid., pp. 19–20.
75. Ibid., p. 13.
76. Jane M. Dewey, ed., "Biography of John Dewey," in *The Philosophy of John Dewey,* The Library of Living Philosophers, ed. Paul A. Schilpp, vol. 1 (Evanston: Northwestern University, 1939), p. 11.
77. Dewey, "From Absolutism to Experimentalism," p. 19.

CHAPTER 2. INSTRUCTOR IN HIGH SCHOOL, 1879–1882

1. Wayland F. Dunaway, *A History of Pennsylvania,* 2d ed. (Englewood Cliffs, N.J.: Prentice-Hall, 1948), p. 624.
2. Charles A. Babcock, *Venango County, Pennsylvania: Her Pioneers and People,* vol. 1 (Chicago: J. H. Beers, 1919), p. 138.
3. Ibid., p. 309.

4. Ibid., p. 135; George W. Brown, *Old Times in Oildom* (Oil City, Pa.: Derrick Publishing Co., 1911), p. 12.
5. Babcock, *Venango County,* 1:302.
6. U.S. Census Office, *Compendium of the Tenth Census of the United States, 1880, Part I,* p. 279.
7. Babcock, *Venango County,* 1:163.
8. Ibid., p. 145.
9. Max Eastman, "John Dewey," *Atlantic Monthly* 168 (1941): 673.
10. Babcock, *Venango County,* 1:199; *Derrick* (Oil City-Franklin-Clarion, Pa.), 28 January 1965. Since Dewey's day the building has had its two upper stories removed and the ground floor converted into quarters for the central fire station of Oil City.
11. Robert B. Williams of Montclair State College in his "John Dewey and Oil City," *Peabody Journal of Education,* January 1969, pp. 223–26, reports on the scarcity of material on Dewey's years in Oil City and on current efforts to supply this "missing link" in Dewey's career.
12. *Derrick,* 28 January 1965.
13. Jane M. Dewey, ed., "Biography of John Dewey," in *The Philosophy of John Dewey,* The Library of Living Philosophers, ed. Paul A. Schilpp, vol. 1 (Evanston: Northwestern University, 1939), p. 13.
14. I am indebted to George H. Morris of Florida Southern College for the material in the two preceding paragraphs. Morris, in the spring of 1955, went to Oil City where he met three former students of Dewey's who gave him their memories and impressions. Professor Morris generously allowed me to use his unpublished manuscript.
15. Babcock, *Venango County,* 1:307.
16. Eastman, "John Dewey," p. 673.
17. Dewey to Harris, 17 May 1881, Hoose Library, University of Southern California, Los Angeles, Calif.
18. Dewey to Harris, 21 October 1881, Hoose Library.
19. Dewey to Harris, 22 October 1881, Hoose Library.
20. Dewey to Harris, 1 July 1882, Hoose Library.
21. Dewey, "The Metaphysical Assumptions of Materialism," *Journal of Speculative Philosophy* 16 (1882): 203–13 [*The Early Works of John Dewey, 1882–1898,* ed. Jo Ann Boydston, vol. 1 (Carbondale: Southern Illinois University Press, 1969), pp. 3–8].
22. Dewey, "The Pantheism of Spinoza," *Journal of Speculative Philosophy* 16 (1882): 249–57 [*Early Works of Dewey,* 1:9–18].
23. Dewey, "From Absolutism to Experimentalism," in *Contemporary American Philosophy,* ed. George P. Adams and William P. Montague, vol. 2 (New York: Macmillan Co., 1930), p. 16.
24. See Hamilton Child, comp., *Gazetteer and Business Directory of Chittenden County, Vermont, for 1882–83* (Syracuse, N.Y.: Hamilton Child, 1882), p. 166.
25. Ibid.
26. Flora S. Williams to Charles Root, 9 December 1954, George

Dykhuizen Papers and Correspondence, Special Collections, Guy W. Bailey Library, University of Vermont, Burlington, Vt.

27. Interview of 17 July 1938. Miss Byington's report was fully confirmed by Mr. Charles Root, also a former pupil of Dewey's.
28. Dewey, "From Absolutism to Experimentalism," p. 15.
29. Ibid., pp. 14–15.
30. Torrey to Morris, 11 February 1882, Special Collections, The Milton S. Eisenhower Library, The Johns Hopkins University, Baltimore, Md.
31. Dewey to Gilman, 11 August 1882, Daniel C. Gilman Papers, The Milton S. Eisenhower Library, The Johns Hopkins University, Baltimore, Md.

CHAPTER 3. THE JOHNS HOPKINS UNIVERSITY, 1882–1884

1. W. Carson Ryan, *Studies in Early Graduate Education* (New York: Carnegie Foundation for the Advancement of Teaching, 1939), p. 32.
2. Dewey had at least three different addresses while in Baltimore: 66 Saratoga Street, 91 Saratoga Street, and 266 North Howard Street.
3. Josiah Royce, "Present Ideals of American University Life," *Scribner's Magazine* 10 (1891): 383.
4. "Johns Hopkins University," *Michigan Argonaut* 3 (1885): 292.
5. These were: "Knowledge and the Relativity of Feeling," *Journal of Speculative Philosophy* 17 (1883): 56–70; "Kant and Philosophic Method," ibid. 18 (1884): 162–74; "The New Psychology," *Andover Review* 2 (1884): 278–89 [*The Early Works of John Dewey, 1882–1898,* ed. Jo Ann Boydston, vol. 1 (Carbondale: Southern Illinois University Press, 1969), pp. 19–33, 34–47, 48–60].
6. For a list of the courses offered in the department during the academic years 1882–83 and 1883–84 and for a list of the names of students (including Dewey) enrolled in them, see *The Johns Hopkins Circulars* for these years.
7. Dewey to W. T. Harris, 17 January 1884, Hoose Library, University of Southern California, Los Angeles, Calif.
8. See p. 18 of this volume.
9. Dewey to Harris, 17 January 1884, Hoose Library.
10. Dewey to Torrey, 5 October 1882, George Dykhuizen Papers and Correspondence, Special Collections, Guy W. Bailey Library, University of Vermont, Burlington, Vt.
11. Dewey to Harris, 17 January 1884, Hoose Library. For an excellent account of Peirce's years at the Johns Hopkins, see Max H. Fisch and Jackson I. Cope, "Peirce at The Johns Hopkins University," in *Studies in the Philosophy of Charles Sanders Peirce,* ed. Philip P. Wiener and Frederic H. Young (Cambridge: Harvard University Press, 1952), pp. 277–311.

12. Dewey to Torrey, 4 February 1883, Dykhuizen Papers.
13. The chief of these are: *British Thought and Thinkers* (Chicago: S. C. Griggs & Co., 1880), *Kant's Critique of Pure Reason: A Critical Exposition* (Chicago: S. C. Griggs & Co., 1882), and *Philosophy and Christianity* (New York: Robert Carter & Bros., 1883).
14. Dewey, "From Absolutism to Experimentalism," in *Contemporary American Philosophy*, ed. George P. Adams and William P. Montague, vol. 2 (New York: Macmillan Co., 1930), p. 19.
15. Dewey to Torrey, 5 October 1882, Dykhuizen Papers.
16. Dewey to Harris, 17 January 1884, Hoose Library.
17. See Dewey, ["George Sylvester Morris: An Estimate"], typescript, George S. Morris Papers, Michigan Historical Collections, University of Michigan, Ann Arbor, Mich.; published in *The Life and Work of George Sylvester Morris*, by Robert M. Wenley (New York: Macmillan Co., 1917), p. 313.
18. See George S. Morris, "Philosophy and Its Specific Problems," *Princeton Review* n.s. 9 (1882): 208–32.
19. Dewey to Torrey, 5 October 1882, Dykhuizen Papers.
20. Dewey, "From Absolutism to Experimentalism," p. 19.
21. Ibid.
22. Ibid., p. 18.
23. The Metaphysical Club was one of several departmental clubs at the Johns Hopkins at this time. It had both faculty and student members. Peirce, Morris, and Hall had turns as president. Monthly meetings were held at which papers on philosophical and allied subjects were given. The club was founded in 1879 and discontinued in 1884. For the titles of papers given and for the names of the speakers during the two years that Dewey was a member, see *The Johns Hopkins Circulars* for 1882–83 and 1883–84.
24. Dewey, "Knowledge and the Relativity of Feeling," *Journal of Speculative Philosophy* 17 (1883): 56–70 [*Early Works of Dewey*, 1:19–33].
25. Ibid., p. 70 [ibid., p. 33].
26. Dewey, "Kant and Philosophic Method," pp. 162–74 [*Early Works of Dewey*, 1:34–47].
27. Ibid., p. 169 [ibid., p. 42].
28. Ibid., p. 171 [ibid., p. 44].
29. Ibid.
30. Dewey to Torrey, 17 November 1883, Dykhuizen Papers.
31. Dewey to Harris, 17 January 1884, Hoose Library.
32. Ibid.
33. Dewey to T. R. Ball, 28 May 1888, Special Collections, The Milton S. Eisenhower Library, The Johns Hopkins University, Baltimore, Md.
34. Dewey to Torrey, 4 February 1883, Dykhuizen Papers.
35. Dewey, "The New Psychology," *Andover Review* 2 (1884): 278–89 [*Early Works of Dewey*, 1:48–60].
36. Ibid., p. 285 [ibid., p. 56].

37. Ibid., p. 288 [ibid., p. 60].
38. Ibid., pp. 278, 288 [ibid., pp. 48, 59–60].
39. Dewey, "From Absolutism to Experimentalism," p. 21.
40. Quoted by Jane M. Dewey, ed., "Biography of John Dewey," in *The Philosophy of John Dewey*, The Library of Living Philosophers, ed. Paul A. Schilpp, vol. 1 (Evanston: Northwestern University, 1939), pp. 17–18.
41. See *The Johns Hopkins Circular*, 1882–83.
42. Dewey to Torrey, 4 February 1883, Dykhuizen Papers.
43. Ibid.
44. Gilman to Buckham, 30 March [1883], Dykhuizen Papers.
45. Buckham to Gilman, 3 April 1883, Daniel C. Gilman Papers, The Milton S. Eisenhower Library.
46. Torrey to Gilman, 5 April 1883, Gilman Papers.
47. See Clayton C. Hall, "Early Memories of the University," *The Johns Hopkins Alumni Magazine* 1 (1913): 305.
48. "Johns Hopkins University," *Michigan Argonaut* 3 (1885): 292.
49. "Dewey Recalls Hopkins Days at Age 91," *The Johns Hopkins News-Letter*, 31 October 1950.
50. Morris to Gilman, 21 May 1884, Gilman Papers.
51. Dewey to Angell, 19 July 1884, James Burrill Angell Papers, Michigan Historical Collections, University of Michigan, Ann Arbor, Mich.

CHAPTER 4. EARLY UNIVERSITY POSITIONS, 1884–1889

1. Wilfred B. Shaw, *A Short History of the University of Michigan*, 2d ed. (Ann Arbor: George Wahr, 1937), p. 55.
2. Daniel F. Lyons, "Literary Department," *Castalian* 9 (1894): 101.
3. Jane M. Dewey, ed., "Biography of John Dewey," in *The Philosophy of John Dewey*, The Library of Living Philosophers, ed. Paul A. Schilpp, vol. 1 (Evanston: Northwestern University, 1939), p. 19.
4. Morris to Angell, 6 January 1885, James Burrill Angell Papers, Michigan Historical Collections, University of Michigan, Ann Arbor, Mich.
5. De Witt H. Parker and Charles B. Vibbert, "The Department of Philosophy," in *The University of Michigan: An Encyclopaedic Survey*, ed. Wilfred B. Shaw, vol. 2 (Ann Arbor: University of Michigan Press, 1951), p. 673.
6. "Cause for Congratulation," *Michigan Argonaut*, December 1885, p. 65.
7. Dewey to H. A. P. Torrey, 28 March 1888, George Dykhuizen Papers and Correspondence, Special Collections, Guy W. Bailey Library, University of Vermont, Burlington, Vt.
8. As a nonsectarian state institution, the University of Michigan rotated the appointments in the Department of Philosophy among

the clergy of the dominant denominations: Baptist, Methodist, Congregational, and Episcopal.

9. *Michigan Argonaut*, October 1883, pp. 23–24.
10. *Michigan Argonaut*, November 1883, p. 83.
11. *Michigan Argonaut*, October 1883, p. 24.
12. For the course offerings of Morris and Dewey, see the *Calendar of the University of Michigan*, 1885–89.
13. Dewey to Torrey, 16 February 1886, Dykhuizen Papers.
14. *Chronicle* 17 (1886): 155. Though Dewey's name was not attached to this notice, it is assumed from the style that he wrote it.
15. Dewey to Torrey, 28 February 1886, Dykhuizen Papers.
16. Henry S. Frieze, "George Sylvester Morris," *Michigan Argonaut*, December 1886, p. 69.
17. George S. Morris, *Philosophy and Christianity* (New York: Robert Carter & Bros., 1883).
18. Robert M. Wenley, *The Life and Work of George Sylvester Morris* (New York: Macmillan Co., 1917), p. 272.
19. Dewey, "Ethics and Physical Science," *Andover Review* 7 (1887): 577 [*The Early Works of John Dewey, 1882–1898*, ed. Jo Ann Boydston, vol. 1 (Carbondale: Southern Illinois University Press, 1969), p. 209].
20. Dewey, "The Philosophy of Thomas Hill Green," *Andover Review* 11 (1889): 345 [*The Early Works of John Dewey, 1882–1898*, ed. Jo Ann Boydston, vol. 3 (Carbondale: Southern Illinois University Press, 1969), p. 23].
21. Dewey, "Soul and Body," *Bibliotheca Sacra* 43 (1886): 239–63 [*Early Works of Dewey*, 1:93–115].
22. Ibid., p. 263 [ibid., p. 114].
23. Ibid., p. 259 [ibid., p. 111].
24. Ibid., p. 263 [ibid., pp. 114–15]. Dewey's position in this article as to the precise relation of body and soul is a confused one. At one point he said, "The sensation has its *occasion* from the nervous process; it has its *cause* from within [the mind or soul itself]" (pp. 253–54 [p. 106]). In another place, following Aristotle, he declared that "soul and body are related indeed as function and organ, activity and instrument" (p. 260 [p. 112]). In still another place, he asserted that the body is the phenomenal expression of the soul, and quoted with approval the words of James Marsh that the body is " 'the necessary mode of our existence in the world of sense. . . . *It is our proper self as existent in space,* in the order and under the laws of nature' " (p. 261 [p. 112]). (The quotation is from James Marsh, "Remarks on Psychology," in *The Remains of the Rev. James Marsh, D.D., with a Memoir of His Life*, ed. Joseph Torrey [Boston: Crocker & Brewster, 1843], pp. 256–57.) Dewey's article should be compared with that of George S. Morris entitled, "The Immortality of the Soul," published ten years earlier in *Bibliotheca Sacra* 33 (1876): 695–715.

25. Dewey, "Ethics and Physical Science," *Andover Review* 7 (1887): 573–91 [*Early Works of Dewey*, 1:205–26].
26. Ibid., p. 580 [ibid., pp. 212–13].
27. Ibid., p. 576 [ibid., p. 209].
28. Dewey, "The New Psychology," *Andover Review* 2 (1884): 278–89 [*Early Works of Dewey*, 1:48–60].
29. Dewey, "The Psychological Standpoint," *Mind* 11 (1886): 1–19 [*Early Works of Dewey*, 1:122–43].
30. Dewey, "Psychology and Philosophic Method," *Mind* 11 (1886): 153–73 [*Early Works of Dewey*, 1:144–67].
31. Cf., for example, Edward Caird, "Metaphysic," *Encyclopædia Britannica*, 9th ed., 14:79–102.
32. Dewey, "Psychology and Philosophic Method," p. 153 [*Early Works of Dewey*, 1:144].
33. Shadworth H. Hodgson, "Illusory Psychology," *Mind* 11 (1886): 480 [*Early Works of Dewey*, 1:xliii]. For Dewey's reply to Hodgson, see his " 'Illusory Psychology,' " *Mind* 12 (1887): 83–88 [*Early Works of Dewey*, 1:168–75]. William James, who was in correspondence with Hodgson at this time, writes him that he had read his paper on "poor Dewey" and in general agreed with what Hodgson had written. (James to Hodgson, 15 March 1887, quoted in *The Thought and Character of William James*, by Ralph B. Perry, vol. 1 [Boston: Little, Brown & Co., 1935], p. 641.)
34. "Minutes and Constitution of the Philosophical Society of the University of Michigan, A.D. 1884," Michigan Historical Collections, University of Michigan, Ann Arbor, Mich.
35. Typical topics discussed were: "University Education," "Goethe and the Conduct of Life," "Philosophy and Literature," "Herbert Spencer as a Biologist," "Lessing's 'Laocoön'," "Reason and Instinct," "History and Genius," and "The Greek Mysteries."
36. "Minutes and Constitution," p. 24.
37. "An Able Paper by Dr. Dewey on Mental Evolution," *Michigan Argonaut*, October 1884, p. 23. For a similarly favorable account, see *Chronicle* 16 (1884): 44. Dewey gave two other papers before the society during these first years at Michigan: "Hegel and Recent Thought," and "Sir Henry Maine's Conception of Democracy," "Minutes and Constitution," pp. 47, 53.
38. "Here Are the Figures," *Michigan Argonaut* 4 (1886): 127.
39. *Monthly Bulletin*, Students' Christian Association, University of Michigan, October 1884, p. 20.
40. "The Obligation to Knowledge of God" and "The Place of Religious Emotion" appeared, possibly in summary, in *Monthly Bulletin*, November 1884, pp. 23–25 [*Early Works of Dewey*, 1:61–63] and *Monthly Bulletin*, November 1886, pp. 23–25 [*Early Works of Dewey*, 1:90–92]. "Faith and Doubt" was mentioned in *Monthly Bulletin*, January 1886, p. 56, but never summarized.
41. Dewey joined on 2 November 1884. Ann Arbor, Michigan, Congregational Church Membership Roll, 1847–1906, Michigan Historical

Collections, p. 16. He joined by a letter of transferral from The First Congregational Church in Burlington, Vermont, which he had joined at the age of eleven. The letter confirming the transferral, written by the clerk of the Ann Arbor church to the clerk of the Burlington church, is in the files of the latter institution.

42. Dewey, *Psychology* (New York: Harper & Bros., 1887), p. 343 [*The Early Works of John Dewey, 1882–1898*, ed. Jo Ann Boydston, vol. 2 (Carbondale: Southern Illinois University Press, 1967), p. 295].
43. *Monthly Bulletin*, November 1887, p. 24.
44. Dewey presided at two of these. (Ann Arbor, Mich., Congregational Church Clerk's Record, 1847–1916, Michigan Historical Collections, pp. 292, 300.)
45. *Journal of the Michigan Schoolmasters' Club: Sixty-Second Meeting, Held in Ann Arbor, April 28, 29, 30, 1921* (Ann Arbor: The Club, 1927), p. 113.
46. Except for the first meeting, there are no records of the talks given during the early years of the club's existence. At the first meeting, Dewey was one of five speakers to address the group; he spoke on "Psychology in High-Schools from the Standpoint of the College," Michigan School-Masters' Club, *Papers, 1886* (Lansing, Mich.: H. R. Pattengill, 1886) [*Early Works of Dewey*, 1:81–88]. Dewey earlier had written two articles on an educational matter, namely, the effects of college study on the health of women. This topic was of great interest at the time because of agitation for woman suffrage and equal rights to a college education. The first article was entitled "Education and the Health of Women," *Science* 6 (1885): 341–42 [*Early Works of Dewey*, 1:64–68]; the second was named "Health and Sex in Higher Education," *Popular Science Monthly*, March 1886, 606–14 [*Early Works of Dewey*, 1:69–80].
47. Dewey, *The Ethics of Democracy*, University of Michigan Philosophical Papers, second series, no. 1 (Ann Arbor: Andrews & Co., 1888) [*Early Works of Dewey*, 1:227–49].
48. Ibid., p. 22 [ibid., p. 244].
49. Ibid., p. 25 [ibid., p. 246].
50. Ibid., p. 26 [ibid., pp. 246–47].
51. Report of Dewey's talk, "The Rise of the Great Industries," to the Political Science Association, in *Michigan Argonaut* 4 (1886): 224.
52. Jane Dewey, "Biography of John Dewey," p. 38.
53. S. Lawrence Bigelow, I. Leo Sharfman, and Robert M. Wenley, "Henry Carter Adams," *Journal of Political Economy* 30 (1922): 205.
54. Henry C. Adams, "The Social Ministry of Wealth," *International Journal of Ethics*, January 1894, p. 185.
55. Henry C. Adams, "An Interpretation of the Social Movements of Our Time," *International Journal of Ethics*, October 1891, p. 45.
56. Jane Dewey, "Biography of John Dewey," pp. 20–21.

57. Willinda Savage, "The Evolution of John Dewey's Philosophy of Experimentalism as Developed at the University of Michigan" (Ph.D. diss., University of Michigan, 1950).
58. Jane Dewey, "Biography of John Dewey," p. 21.
59. "Minutes and Constitution," pp. 11, 14.
60. "Course Reports, 1882–86," University of Michigan, Michigan Historical Collections.
61. *Proceedings of the Board of Regents of the University of Michigan from January 1881 to January, 1886* (Ann Arbor: Courier Book and Job Printing, 1886), p. 482.
62. *Proceedings of the Board of Regents of the University of Michigan from January 1886 to January 1891* (Ann Arbor, 1891), p. 34; also, *Michigan Argonaut* 4 (1886): 283.
63. *Calendar of the University of Michigan,* 1886–87 and 1887–88.
64. Jane Dewey, "Biography of John Dewey," p. 21.
65. Quoted in Fred N. Scott, "John Dewey," *Castalian* 6 (1891): 26.
66. Ibid.
67. Parker and Vibbert, "Department of Philosophy," p. 673.
68. G. Stanley Hall, review of *Psychology, American Journal of Psychology,* November 1887, p. 157.
69. James to Robertson, 1886, in *Thought and Character of James,* by Perry, 2:516.
70. Hall, review of *Psychology,* p. 156.
71. The quotations are taken from "A Psychical Study," *Oracle* 21 (1888): 18–20.
72. Dewey, *Leibniz's New Essays concerning the Human Understanding* (Chicago: S. C. Griggs & Co., 1888) [*Early Works of Dewey,* 1:250–435].
73. Ibid., p. 241 [ibid., p. 414].
74. Memorandum of late 1893 or early 1894, Tufts to Harper, Presidents' Papers, 1889–1925, Special Collections, The Joseph Regenstein Library, University of Chicago, Chicago, Ill. For Ladd's statement, see *New Englander and Yale Review* 50 (1899): 66–68.
75. James R. Angell, "The Clock Rambles," *Oracle* 21 (1888): 44.
76. *Oracle* 21 (1888): 92.
77. "Psychology," *Michigan Argonaut,* November 1888, p. 40.
78. Minutes of 28 January 1888, "University of Minnesota Board of Regents, Minutes, 1885–1905," Archives, University of Minnesota Libraries, Minneapolis, Minn., p. 304.
79. Dewey to Torrey, 28 March 1888, Dykhuizen Papers.
80. *Proceedings of Regents, 1886–91,* p. 208.
81. This statement appears in a newspaper clipping taken from either a Minneapolis or St. Paul paper and is without any notation as to source or date (University of Minnesota Library, Minneapolis, Minn.). The reference to the McCosh school of thought stemmed from the fact that the previous instructor, Thomas Peebles, was a graduate of Princeton and while an undergraduate had taken courses from McCosh and had been won over to the Scottish Re-

alism espoused by McCosh. This philosophy he had taught his classes at the University of Minnesota during the four years he was there.

82. *Ariel,* 1 March 1888, p. 61.
83. *The University of Minnesota: Catalogue for the Year 1888–89 and Announcements for the Year 1889–90* (Minneapolis: The University, 1889), pp. 38–39, 41.
84. Ibid., p. 39.
85. Ibid., p. 36.
86. Ibid.
87. Ibid., p. 47.
88. *The University of Minnesota: Catalogue for the Year 1887–88 and Announcement for the Year 1888–89* (Minneapolis: By the University, 1888), pp. 54–55; see also *The University of Minnesota: Catalogue for the Year 1886–87, and Announcements for the Year 1888* (Minneapolis: The University, 1887), p. 47.
89. *Ariel,* 27 April 1889, p. 156.
90. James Gray, *The University of Minnesota: 1851–1951* (Minneapolis: University of Minnesota Press, 1951), p. 348.
91. Dewey to Torrey, 3 January 1889, Dykhuizen Papers.
92. Dewey, "The Philosophy of Thomas Hill Green," *Andover Review* 11 (1889): 337–55 [*Early Works of Dewey,* 3:14–35].
93. Ibid., p. 339 [ibid., p. 16].
94. Dewey to Torrey, 3 January 1889, Dykhuizen Papers.
95. James A. McLellan, *Applied Psychology: An Introduction to the Principles and Practice of Education* (Toronto: Copp, Clark & Co., 1889).
96. Jo Ann Boydston, "A Note on *Applied Psychology,*" in *Early Works of Dewey,* 3:xvi.
97. *Chronicle* 20 (1889): 241.
98. *Ariel,* 27 April 1889, p. 156.
99. *Proceedings of Regents, 1886–91,* p. 298.
100. Dewey to Angell, 19 April 1889, Angell Papers.
101. Ibid.
102. *Ariel,* 21 May 1889, p. 175.
103. *Chronicle* 20 (1889): 266.
104. Minutes of 1 June 1889, "University of Minnesota Board of Regents, Minutes 1888–1905," University of Minnesota Archives, p. 398.

CHAPTER 5. THE UNIVERSITY OF MICHIGAN, 1889–1894

1. Later, when time permitted, Dewey often collaborated with Scott in a seminar in aesthetics. (*Calendar of the University of Michigan,* 1890–91, 1891–92.)
2. Ibid.
3. William James, *The Principles of Psychology,* 2 vols. (New York: Henry Holt & Co., 1890).

4. In a letter to William James at this time, Dewey referred to his course in Advanced Psychology, and said: "I don't know that I told you that I have had a class of four graduates going through your psychology this year, and how much we have all enjoyed it. I'm sure you would be greatly gratified if you could see what a stimulus to mental freedom, as well as what a purveyor of methods and materials, your book has been to us" (Dewey to James, 10 May 1891, in *The Thought and Character of William James,* by Ralph B. Perry, vol. 2 [Boston: Little, Brown & Co., 1935], p. 517).
5. Minutes of the meetings of 18 December 1889, 19 November 1891, and 12 December 1893, in "Minutes and Constitution of the Philosophical Society of the University of Michigan," Michigan Historical Collections, University of Michigan, Ann Arbor, Mich. The talks themselves are not extant.
6. *Monthly Bulletin,* Students' Christian Association, University of Michigan, June 1894, p. 147. But Dewey declined to be one of its Board of Directors in 1893 when the Association adopted as a requirement for student membership on the board that the student subscribe to the tenets of evangelical Christianity. (*Monthly Bulletin,* April 1893, p. 171.)
7. Dewey, "Christianity and Democracy," in *Religious Thought at the University of Michigan* (Ann Arbor: Register Publishing Co., Inland Press, 1893), pp. 60–69 [*The Early Works of John Dewey, 1882–1898,* ed. Jo Ann Boydston, vol. 4 (Carbondale: Southern Illinois University Press, 1971), pp. 3–10].
8. F. A. Manny, "The Bible Institute," *Monthly Bulletin,* November 1892, p. 45.
9. Dewey, "Reconstruction," *Monthly Bulletin,* June 1894, pp. 149–56 [*Early Works of Dewey,* 4:96–105].
10. These were: "The Scholastic and the Speculator," *Inlander,* December 1891, pp. 145–48, ibid., January 1892, pp. 186–88 [*The Early Works of John Dewey, 1882–1898,* ed. Jo Ann Boydston, vol. 3 (Carbondale: Southern Illinois University Press, 1969), pp. 148–54]; "Anthropology and Law," *Inlander,* April 1893, pp. 305–8 [*Early Works of Dewey,* 4:37–41]; and "Why Study Philosophy?" *Inlander,* December 1893, pp. 106–9 [*Early Works of Dewey,* 4:62–65]. Under the caption "The Angle of Reflection," Dewey also wrote six informal pieces for the *Inlander.* (See *Early Works of Dewey,* 3:195–210, lxiii.)
11. *Calendar of the University of Michigan,* 1889–94. The house in the meantime has been converted into a commercial establishment.
12. Archibald had been in Ann Arbor just a short time when he died in 1891, at the age of eighty. The records of the First Congregational Church in Ann Arbor refer to the death of "our brother Mr. Archibald S. Dewey, whom even in his short sojourn among us we have learned greatly to esteem and love" (see Ann Arbor, Mich., Congregational Church Clerk's Record, 1847–1916, insert between pages 340–41, Michigan Historical Collections).

13. De Witt H. Parker and Charles B. Vibbert, "The Department of Philosophy," in *The University of Michigan: An Encyclopaedic Survey,* ed. Wilfred B. Shaw, vol. 2 (Ann Arbor: University of Michigan Press, 1951), p. 674.
14. Jane M. Dewey, ed., "Biography of John Dewey," in *The Philosophy of John Dewey,* The Library of Living Philosophers, ed. Paul A. Schilpp, vol. 1 (Evanston: Northwestern University, 1939), p. 25.
15. See the *Chronicle* 21 (1890): 253.
16. "John Dewey, Ph.D.," *Chronicle* 21 (1890); 327–28.
17. Dewey, "Comments on Cheating," *Monthly Bulletin,* December 1893, p. 38 [*Early Works of Dewey,* 4:369–70].
18. Dewey, "From Absolutism to Experimentalism," in *Contemporary American Philosophy,* ed. George P. Adams and William P. Montague, vol. 2 (New York: Macmillan Co., 1930), p. 24.
19. In 1903, in a letter to James explaining the emergence of the pragmatic point of view at the University of Chicago, Dewey traced its beginnings back to the time when he, Mead, and Lloyd were at the University of Michigan. "As for the standpoint, we have all been at work at it for about twelve years. Lloyd and Mead were both at it in Ann Arbor ten years ago" (Dewey to James, March 1903, in *Thought and Character of James,* by Perry, 2:520).
20. For descriptions of Mead's courses, see *Calendar of the University of Michigan,* 1891–94.
21. Jane Dewey, "Biography of John Dewey," p. 26.
22. Alfred H. Lloyd, *Dynamic Idealism* (Chicago: A. C. McClurg, 1898), p. 122.
23. Ibid., p. 128.
24. Dewey, *Outlines of a Critical Theory of Ethics* (Ann Arbor: Register Publishing Co., Inland Press, 1891) [*Early Works of Dewey,* 3:237–388].
25. Ibid., p. vii [ibid., p. 239].
26. Ibid., p. viii [ibid.].
27. Dewey to James, 10 May 1891, in *Thought and Character of James,* by Perry, 2:517.
28. Dewey, *The Study of Ethics: A Syllabus* (Ann Arbor: Register Publishing Co., Inland Press, 1894) [*Early Works of Dewey,* 4:219–362].
29. Ibid., p. [iii] [ibid., p. 221].
30. Ibid., p. 29 [ibid., p. 251].
31. Dewey, "The Logic of Verification," *Open Court* 4 (1890): 2227 [*Early Works of Dewey,* 3:88].
32. Dewey's logical theory at this time is expounded mainly in the articles: "Is Logic a Dualistic Science?" *Open Court* 3 (1890): 2040–43; "The Logic of Verification," ibid. 4 (1890): 2225–28; and "The Present Position of Logical Theory," *Monist,* October 1891, pp. 1–17 [*Early Works of Dewey,* 3:75–82, 83–89, and 125–41].
33. Dewey, *Psychology* (New York: Harper & Bros., 1887), pp. 418, 422 [*The Early Works of John Dewey, 1882–1898,* ed. Jo Ann Boyd-

ston, vol. 2 (Carbondale: Southern Illinois University Press, 1967), pp. 358, 361].

34. Dewey, *Study of Ethics*, p. 24 [*Early Works of Dewey*, 4:246]; also "Self-Realization as the Moral Ideal," *Philosophical Review* 2 (1893): 653 [*Early Works of Dewey*, 4:43].
35. Dewey, *Outlines*, pp. 101–2 [*Early Works of Dewey*, 3:304].
36. Dewey, "Green's Theory of the Moral Motive," *Philosophical Review* 1 (1892): 597, 600 [*Early Works of Dewey*, 3:159, 161–62]; "Self-Realization as the Moral Ideal," ibid. 2 (1893): 653, 659 [*Early Works of Dewey*, 4:43, 49].
37. Dewey, *Study of Ethics*, p. 41 [*Early Works of Dewey*, 4:262].
38. Dewey, "Self-Realization as Moral Ideal," p. 664 [*Early Works of Dewey*, 4:53].
39. Dewey, *Psychology*, p. 343 [*Early Works of Dewey*, 2:294–95].
40. Dewey, *Outlines*, p. 170 [*Early Works of Dewey*, 3:347].
41. Dewey, "Christianity and Democracy," pp. 60–69 [*Early Works of Dewey*, 4:3–10].
42. Ibid., p. 65 [ibid., p. 7].
43. Dewey, *Study of Ethics*, p. 43 [*Early Works of Dewey*, 4:264].
44. Fred N. Scott, "John Dewey," *Castalian* 6 (1891): 27.
45. Dewey, "From Absolutism to Experimentalism," p. 20.
46. Dewey, "Present Position of Logical Theory," p. 1; *Outlines*, pp. 126–27; "Renan's Loss of Faith in Science," *Open Court* 7 (1893): 3515 [*Early Works of Dewey*, 3:125, 319–20; 4:17–18].
47. Dewey, *Outlines*, p. 127 [*Early Works of Dewey*, 3:320].
48. For example, Dewey wrote,

> When we remember that every forward step of science has involved a readjustment of institutional life, that even such an apparently distant and indifferent region as the solar system could not be annexed to scientific inquiry without arousing the opposing force of the mightiest political organizations of the day; when we recall such things it is not surprising that the advance of scientific method to the matters closest to man—his social relationships—should have gone on more slowly than was expected ("Renan's Loss of Faith in Science," p. 3515 [*Early Works of Dewey*, 4:17–18]).

49. Ibid. [ibid., p. 18].
50. Dewey, "Science and Society," in *Philosophy and Civilization* (New York: Minton, Balch & Co., 1931), p. 330.
51. For Dewey's account of Ford's influence on him, see Dewey to James, 3 June 1891, in *Thought and Character of James*, by Perry, 2:518–19.
52. Franklin Ford, *Draft of Action* ([Ann Arbor]: Printed by the News Association, [1892]), p. 8.
53. Ibid., p. 58.
54. Dewey, *Outlines*, pp. 123–27 [*Early Works of Dewey*, 3:317–20].
55. *University* [of Michigan] *Record*, April 1892, p. 22.
56. *Detroit Tribune*, 13 April 1892.

57. *Detroit Tribune*, 10 April 1892.
58. Letter to Willinda Savage, quoted in Willinda Savage, "John Dewey and 'Thought News' at the University of Michigan," *Michigan Alumnus Quarterly Review*, May 1950, p. 209. This article gives a detailed and interesting account of Dewey's proposed venture into journalism.
59. Dewey conducted a Bible class for students attending the church during 1889–90, and selected as the topic of study, "Ancient Life and Thought in Its Relation to Christianity" (*Michigan Argonaut*, March 1890, p. 127).
60. Dewey, "Christianity and Democracy," p. 62 [*Early Works of Dewey*, 4:5].
61. Ibid., p. 67 [ibid., p. 9].
62. Ibid., p. 66 [ibid., p. 8].
63. Ibid., p. 67 [ibid., p. 9].
64. Ibid., p. 68 [ibid.].
65. Dewey, "Reconstruction," p. 153 [*Early Works of Dewey*, 4:101].
66. Dewey, "The Relation of Philosophy to Theology," *Monthly Bulletin*, January 1893, pp. 67–68 [*Early Works of Dewey*, 4:367].
67. An organization in which Dewey became deeply interested during his last years in Ann Arbor was Hull House in Chicago, founded in 1889 by Jane Addams. He was considered "a valued friend" of the organization (see memorandum of late 1893 or early 1894, James H. Tufts to Harper, Presidents' Papers, 1889–1925, Special Collections, The Joseph Regenstein Library, University of Chicago, Chicago, Ill.), and, when he moved to Chicago, became a member of its Board of Trustees. Dewey and Jane Addams remained devoted and lifelong friends.
68. Ann Arbor, Mich., Congregational Church: Record of Communicants and Marriages, 1873–1905, Michigan Historical Collections, pp. 52–53.
69. Memorandum, Tufts to Harper, Presidents' Papers, 1889–1925.
70. Dewey to Harper, 15 February 1894, Presidents' Papers, 1889–1925.
71. Ibid.
72. Dewey to Harper, 19 March 1894, Presidents' Papers, 1889–1925.
73. "New Head Professors," *University of Chicago Weekly*, 5 April 1894, p. 5.
74. *University of Chicago Weekly*, 5 April 1894, p. 7.
75. *Monthly Bulletin*, May 1894, p. 130.
76. *Proceedings of Regents*, 1891–96, p. 274.

CHAPTER 6. THE UNIVERSITY OF CHICAGO, 1894–1904: I

1. Thomas W. Goodspeed, *A History of the University of Chicago: The First Quarter-Century* (Chicago: University of Chicago Press, 1916), p. 201.

2. D. G. Lyon, "The University of Chicago," *Baptist Courier* (Greenville, S.C.), 23 July 1896.
3. Memorandum, James H. Tufts to T. W. Goodspeed, 23 March 1915, Special Collections, The Joseph Regenstein Library, University of Chicago, Chicago, Ill.
4. Palmer to Harper, 4 June 1892, Presidents' Papers, 1889–1925, Special Collections, The Joseph Regenstein Library.
5. Charles A. Strong had left Chicago for Columbia University because his wife's health required a change of residence.
6. "The Department of Pedagogy," in *The University of Chicago Annual Register, July, 1895–July, 1896, with Announcements for 1896–7* (Chicago: University of Chicago Press, 1896), p. 52.
7. Dewey, "Pedagogy as a University Discipline," *University* [of Chicago] *Record* 1 (1896): 354 [*The Early Works of John Dewey, 1882–1898*, ed. Jo Ann Boydston, vol. 5 (Carbondale: Southern Illinois University Press, 1972), p. 282].
8. Ibid., pp. 362–63 [ibid., p. 288].
9. Dewey, *Pedagogical Collections*, University of Chicago Archives. This was a little brochure put out in May 1895.
10. Dewey to Harper, 19 March 1894, Presidents' Papers, 1889–1925.
11. *University of Michigan Daily*, 23 May 1894.
12. Jane M. Dewey, ed., "Biography of John Dewey," in *The Philosophy of John Dewey*, The Library of Living Philosophers, ed. Paul A. Schilpp, vol. 1 (Evanston: Northwestern University, 1939), p. 24.
13. *University of Chicago Weekly*, 17 October 1895, p. 567. This hotel is no longer standing, having made way for the International House of the University of Chicago. The present Del Prado Hotel on Hyde Park Boulevard is not the one where Dewey lived.
14. These were: 213 East 61st Street, 5813 Monroe Avenue (now Kenwood Avenue), 5238 Woodlawn Avenue, 6036 Jefferson Avenue (now Harper Avenue), and 6016 Jackson Park Boulevard (now Stoney Island Avenue). (See *University of Chicago Annual Register*, 1895–1904.) Most of the neighborhoods in which these dwellings were located have since badly deteriorated and have been included in slum clearance projects.
15. Goodspeed, *History of University of Chicago*, pp. 497–98.
16. "John D. Rockefeller," *University of Chicago Weekly* 5 (1896): 77. According to one report, this song is "dearest to the hearts of all Chicago students, the one that is sung at every student gathering, at every athletic event, and in all the halls of the campus" (ibid., p. 113).
17. *The President's Report, July 1902–July 1904* (Chicago: University of Chicago Press, 1905), p. 54.
18. *The President's Report, July 1892–July 1902* (Chicago: University of Chicago Press, 1903).
19. "The Department of Philosophy, in *University of Chicago Annual Register, July, 1894–July, 1895, with Announcements for 1895–6* (Chicago: University of Chicago Press, 1895), p. 42.

20. *University* [of Chicago] *Record* 8 (1904): 343.
21. For a complete list of the courses that Dewey gave in the Department of Philosophy at Chicago, see the *University of Chicago Annual Register*, 1895–1904.
22. *University of Chicago Weekly*, 24 December 1896, p. 128.
23. Edward S. Ames, *Beyond Theology: The Autobiography of Edward Scribner Ames*, ed. Van Meter Ames (Chicago: University of Chicago Press, 1959), p. 44.
24. Dewey to James, 19 December 1903, in *The Thought and Character of William James*, by Ralph B. Perry, vol. 2 (Boston: Little, Brown & Co., 1935), p. 525.
25. [Dewey with the cooperation of members and fellows of the Department of Philosophy], "Preface," in *Studies in Logical Theory*, University of Chicago Decennial Publications, 2d series, vol. 11 (Chicago: University of Chicago Press, 1903), p. xi.
26. Dewey, *The Study of Ethics: A Syllabus* (Ann Arbor: Register Publishing Co., Inland Press, 1894), p. 43 [*The Early Works of John Dewey, 1882–1898*, ed. Jo Ann Boydston, vol. 4 (Carbondale: Southern Illinois University Press, 1971), p. 264].
27. See pp. 99, 103 of this volume.
28. For a list of Dewey's writings during these years, see Milton H. Thomas, *John Dewey: A Centennial Bibliography* (Chicago: University of Chicago Press, 1962), pp. 9–26.
29. Quoted by Jane Dewey, "Biography of John Dewey," p. 18.
30. Dewey, "Some Stages of Logical Thought," *Philosophical Review* 9 (1900): 465–89.
31. Ibid., p. 487.
32. Ibid., p. 489.
33. "Preface," in *Studies in Logical Theory*, p. x.
34. Ibid., p. xi.
35. Dewey, "Thought and Its Subject-Matter," in *Studies in Logical Theory*, p. 14.
36. Ibid., p. 45.
37. Ibid., p. 13.
38. Ibid., p. 8.
39. Ibid., p. 75.
40. "Preface," in *Studies in Logical Theory*, p. x.
41. Dewey, "Thought and Its Subject-Matter," p. 51.
42. Ibid., p. 52.
43. James to Dewey, 17 October 1903, in *Thought and Character of James*, by Perry, 2:524.
44. William James, "The Chicago School," *Psychological Bulletin* 1 (1904): 1.
45. Ibid., p. 5.
46. Dewey to James, 19 December 1903, in *Thought and Character of James*, by Perry, 2:526.
47. James to Schiller, 3 April 1903, in *Thought and Character of James*, by Perry, 2:375.

48. James to Schiller, 15 November 1903, in *Thought and Character of James*, by Perry, 2:501.
49. Ferdinand C. S. Schiller, review of *Studies in Logical Theory, Mind* n.s. 13 (1904): 100.
50. Ferdinand C. S. Schiller, "In Defence of Humanism," *Mind* n.s. 13 (1904): 529–30.
51. Charles S. Peirce, review of *Studies in Logical Theory, Nation* 76 (1904): 220.
52. Arthur K. Rogers, "Philosophy and Life," *Dial* 36 (1904): 338. See also Rogers, "The Standpoint of Instrumental Logic," *Journal of Philosophy* 1 (1904): 208; Wilmon H. Sheldon, review of *Studies in Logical Theory,* ibid., pp. 100–105.
53. Andrew Seth Pringle-Pattison, review of *Studies in Logical Theory, Philosophical Review* 13 (1904): 674.
54. Francis H. Bradley, "On Truth and Practice," *Mind* n.s. 13 (1904): 309n.
55. Jane Dewey, "Biography of John Dewey," p. 29.
56. For a complete list of Dewey's courses in education at the University of Chicago, see the *University of Chicago Annual Register,* 1895–1904.
57. Though the official name of the school was the "University Elementary School," it became popularly known as the "Dewey School," and the "Laboratory School." Ella Flagg Young is credited with having suggested the last name.
58. "The Model School," *University of Chicago Weekly,* 16 January 1896, p. 707.
59. The continuing growth of the school necessitated changes in location. After its residence at 389 Fifty-seventh Street, the school moved to 5718 Kimbark Avenue, which building is still standing; then to South Park Club House at Fifty-seventh and Rosalie Court (now part of Harper Avenue); and finally, to 5412 Ellis Avenue. For an excellent history of the school, see Katherine C. Mayhew and Anna C. Edwards, *The Dewey School* (New York: D. Appleton-Century Co., 1936).
60. *University* [of Chicago] *Record* 2 (1897): 1.
61. *Maroon,* 15 January 1896, p. 4; *University* [of Chicago] *Record* 1 (1896): 27.
62. *University* [of Chicago] *Record* 1 (1896): 113–15.
63. *University of Chicago Weekly,* 5 November 1896, p. 58.
64. *University of Chicago Weekly,* 22 April 1897, p. 285.
65. *University* [of Chicago] *Record* 4 (1900): 271.
66. *University* [of Chicago] *Record* 2 (1897): 173–74. These resolutions were signed by C. P. Cary, Charity Dye, and Wickliffe Rose.
67. Minutes of 5 March 1901, "Board of Trustees, Minutes," vol. 3 (1900), p. 157.
68. Ibid.
69. Minutes of 11 June 1901, "Board of Trustees, Minutes," vol. 3 (1900), p. 285. For some of the correspondence relating to the con-

tinuation of the Dewey School, see: Dewey to Harper, 13 April 1901; Charles De Garmo to Harper, 22 April 1901; William Kent, Charles F. Harding, E. E. Chandler, and John F. Holland to the President and Trustees of the University of Chicago, 23 April 1901; Anita McCormick Blaine to Harper, 30 April 1901; Harper to Kent, Harding, Chandler, and Holland, 1 May 1901; Presidents' Papers, 1889–1925.

70. Minutes of 20 May 1902, "Board of Trustees, Minutes," vol. 4 (1902), p. 101.
71. Dewey, "Significance of the School of Education," *Elementary School Teacher,* March 1904, p. 448.
72. Dewey to Anita McCormick Blaine, 21 May 1902, McCormick Collection, The State Historical Society of Wisconsin, Madison, Wis.
73. *President's Report, July 1892–July 1902,* pp. lxxxiii–lxxxv.
74. Dewey, "Significance of the School of Education," p. 447.
75. Compare, for example, the list of titles of publications in philosophy and psychology with that of titles of publications in education, in Publications of the Members of the University, *University of Chicago Decennial Publications,* 1st series, vol. 2 (Chicago: University of Chicago Press, 1904), pp. 3–11, 12–13.
76. Ella F. Young, *Isolation in the School,* University of Chicago Contributions to Education, no. 1 (Chicago: University of Chicago Press, 1901); *Ethics in the School,* ibid., no. 4 (1902); *Some Types of Modern Educational Theory,* ibid., no. 6 (1902).
77. Dewey, "The Primary-Education Fetich," *Forum* 25 (1898): 327–28 [*Early Works of Dewey,* 5:269].
78. William H. Kilpatrick, "Dewey's Influence on Education," in *Philosophy of John Dewey,* p. 465.
79. Dewey, "How Much Freedom in New Schools?" *New Republic,* 9 July 1930, p. 204; see also Dewey, "In Remembrance: Francis Wayland Parker," *Journal of Education* 55 (1902): 199; and "In Memoriam: Colonel Francis Wayland Parker," *Elementary School Teacher,* June 1902, pp. 704–8.
80. Dewey, "Froebel's Educational Principles," *Elementary School Record* 5 (1900): 143.
81. James H. Canfield, "William Torrey Harris—Teacher, Philosopher, Friend," *American Monthly Review of Reviews* 34 (1906): 166.
82. Dewey, "The Theory of the Chicago Experiment," in *The Dewey School,* by Mayhew and Edwards, pp. 463–77.
83. Ellen E. De Graff, "Chicago Happenings of Interest to Evansvillians—Something about Psychology." This is a newspaper account appearing in a Chicago or Evansville paper sometime in late 1894. The clipping is in Colonel Parker's Scrapbook, University of Chicago Archives.
84. Dewey, *The School and Society* (Chicago: University of Chicago Press, 1899); *The Child and the Curriculum* (Chicago: University of Chicago Press, 1902); "The Results of Child-Study Applied to Education," *Transactions of the Illinois Society for Child-Study,*

January 1895, pp. 18–19 [*Early Works of Dewey*, 5: 204–6]; *Interest in Relation to Training of the Will*, Second Supplement to the Herbart Yearbook for 1895 (Bloomington, Ill.: Pantagraph Printing and Stationery Co., 1896), pp. 209–55 [*Early Works of Dewey*, 5:111–50]; "The Reflex Arc Concept in Psychology," *Psychological Review* 3 (1896): 357–70 [*Early Works of Dewey*, 5:96–110]; "Ethical Principles underlying Education," in *Third Yearbook of the National Herbart Society* (Chicago: The Society, 1897), pp. 7–33 [*Early Works of Dewey*, 5:54–83]; "Principles of Mental Development as Illustrated in Early Infancy," *Transactions of the Illinois Society for Child-Study*, October 1899, pp. 65–83; "Psychology and Social Practice," *Psychological Review* 7 (1900): 105–24; "The Place of Manual Training in the Elementary Course of Study," *Manual Training Magazine*, July 1901, pp. 193–99.

85. Dewey, "Results of Child-Study," p. 18 [*Early Works of Dewey*, 5:204].
86. *The School and Society*, pp. 49–50.
87. Dewey, *Interest in Relation to Will*, p. 29 [*Early Works of Dewey*, 5:141].
88. Dewey, "Manual Training," p. 194.
89. Dewey, *School and Society*, p. 49.
90. Dewey, "The Psychology of the Elementary Curriculum," *Elementary School Record* 9 (1900): 223; see also "Interpretation of the Culture Epoch Theory," *Public-School Journal*, January 1896, pp. 233–36 [*Early Works of Dewey*, 5:247–53].
91. Dewey, *School and Society*, p. 28.
92. Dewey, "Ethical Principles," p. 14 [*Early Works of Dewey*, 5:62].
93. Dewey, "Psychology and Social Practice," p. 108.
94. Ibid., pp. 108–9.
95. Dewey, "My Pedagogic Creed," *School Journal* 54 (1897): 79 [*Early Works of Dewey*, 5:91].
96. Dewey, *School and Society*, pp. 88–90.
97. Dewey, *Child and Curriculum*, p. 17; see also "The Psychological Aspect of the School Curriculum," *Educational Review* 13 (1897): 356–69 [*Early Works of Dewey*, 5:164–76].
98. Dewey, *Child and Curriculum*, p. 9.
99. Dewey, "Ethical Principles," pp. 7–12 [*Early Works of Dewey*, 5:54–61].
100. Dewey, *School and Society*, p. 27.
101. Dewey, "Introduction," in *The Dewey School*, by Mayhew and Edwards, p. xvi.
102. Dewey, *The School and Society* (Chicago: University of Chicago Press, 1900), p. 27.
103. Dewey, *School and Society* (1899), p. 32.
104. Ibid., pp. 16–20.
105. Ibid., pp. 27–28.
106. Harriet A. Farrand, "Dr. Dewey's University Elementary School," *Journal of Education* 48 (1898): 172.

107. Brief reviews appeared in *Education* in 1899; *Educational Record* in 1900; and by Dewey's colleague, Addison W. Moore, in *Review of Education* in 1901.
108. *University* [of Chicago] *Record* 5 (1900): 160.

CHAPTER 7. THE UNIVERSITY OF CHICAGO, 1894–1904: II

1. *University* [of Chicago] *Record* 1 (1896): 278.
2. Ibid., p. 311.
3. *University* [of Chicago] *Record* 6 (1901): 171; *Educational Lectures,* Summer School, Brigham Young Academy. Reports made by Alice Young and edited by N. L. Nelson. Privately printed, 1901. 241 pp.
4. *University* [of Chicago] *Record* 9 (1904): 92.
5. *University* [of Chicago] *Record* 1 (1896): 35.
6. *University* [of Chicago] *Record* 6 (1902): 358. This talk appeared in *Psychological Review* 9 (1902): 217–30; the earlier one, "Psychology and Social Practice," was printed in ibid. 7 (1900): 105–24.
7. *University* [of Chicago] *Record* 2 (1897): 158, 162. Published in the *Monist,* April 1898, pp. 321–41 [*The Early Works of John Dewey, 1882–1898,* ed. Jo Ann Boydston, vol. 5 (Carbondale: Southern Illinois University Press, 1972), pp. 34–53].
8. "The University Senate, October 1892–June 1896," p. 42.
9. Ibid., p. 89.
10. Ibid., p. 107.
11. "The University Senate, September 1896–January 1902," p. 57.
12. *University of Chicago Annual Register,* 1894–95 and 1895–96.
13. *University of Chicago Annual Register, July, 1894–July, 1895, with Announcements for 1895–6* (Chicago: University of Chicago Press, 1895), p. 377.
14. "Mr. Rockefeller's Investment," *Boston Herald,* 24 August 1895.
15. *Voice,* 18 August 1895.
16. T. W. Goodspeed, secretary of the Board of Trustees, University of Chicago, in a statement to *Chicago Tribune,* 17 February 1895.
17. Dewey, "Academic Freedom," *Educational Review* 13 (1902): 1–14.
18. Ibid., p. 10.
19. Ibid., p. 8.
20. Gates to Harper, 9 November 1904. Related letters are: Gates to Harper, 18 July 1899; Gates to Harper, 17 December 1903; Harper to Rockefeller, 31 December 1903; Archbold to Rockefeller, 25 May 1899 (Rockefeller passed this letter on to Gates, who in turn sent it to President Harper with the notation: "As I am accustomed to send you criticisms of the University that come to this office, I send you this"). All these letters are in William Rainey Harper Personal Papers, Special Collections, The Joseph Regenstein Library, University of Chicago, Chicago, Ill.
21. J. M. Rice, "The Public Schools of Chicago and St. Paul," *Forum* 15 (1893): 200–215.

22. Dewey, letter to *Chicago Evening Post,* 19 December 1895 [*Early Works of Dewey,* 5:423].
23. Dewey, "From Absolutism to Experimentalism," in *Contemporary American Philosophy,* ed. George P. Adams and William P. Montague, vol. 2 (New York: Macmillan Co., 1930), p. 20.
24. Bessie L. Pierce, *A History of Chicago,* vol. 3 (New York: Alfred A. Knopf, 1947), p. 252.
25. Albion W. Small, *The New Humanity* (Chicago: University of Chicago Press, n.d. [reprinted from the *University Extension World,* July 1894]), pp. 16–17.
26. Albion W. Small, letter to the editor, *Boston Herald,* 11 August 1894.
27. See especially his *The Ethics of Democracy,* University of Michigan, Philosophical Papers, 2d series, no. 1 (Ann Arbor: Andrews & Co., 1888) [*The Early Works of John Dewey, 1882–1898,* ed. Jo Ann Boydston, vol. 1 (Carbondale: Southern Illinois University Press, 1969), pp. 227–49].
28. Dewey, "My Pedagogic Creed," *School Journal* 54 (1897): 80 [*Early Works of Dewey,* 5:94].
29. Jane Addams, "John Dewey and Social Welfare," in *John Dewey: The Man and His Philosophy* (Cambridge: Harvard University Press, 1930), p. 147.
30. Ibid., p. 140.
31. Ibid., p. 141.
32. Wayne Andrews, *Battle for Chicago* (New York: Harcourt, Brace & Co., 1946), p. 153.
33. Henry D. Lloyd, "Story of a Great Monopoly," *Atlantic Monthly* 47 (1881): 317–34.
34. Dewey, "Foreword," in *The Philosophy of Henry George,* by George R. Geiger (New York: Macmillan Co., 1933), pp. x, xiii.
35. "The American Peril," *Chicago Commons,* June 1897, p. 9.
36. Dewey, "The Realism of Jane Addams," in *Democratic Versus Coercive International Organization: Peace and Bread in Time of War,* by Jane Addams (New York: King's Crown Press, 1945), p. xix.
37. Jane M. Dewey, ed., "Biography of John Dewey," in *The Philosophy of John Dewey,* The Library of Living Philosophers, ed. Paul A. Schilpp, vol. 1 (Evanston: Northwestern University, 1939), p. 30.
38. Dewey, "Author's Note," in *The School and Society* (Chicago: University of Chicago Press, 1900), pp. 15–16.
39. Quoted in *The Thought and Character of William James,* by Ralph B. Perry, vol. 1 (Boston: Little, Brown & Co., 1935), p. 376.
40. Max Eastman, "John Dewey," *Atlantic Monthly* 168 (1941): 676.
41. Jane Dewey, "Biography of John Dewey," p. 25.
42. Dewey, "Author's Note," p. 15.
43. Jane Addams, *The Excellent Becomes the Permanent* (New York: Macmillan Co., 1932), pp. 11–12, 61, 68.
44. Jane Dewey, "Biography of John Dewey," p. 30.

45. Dewey to Anita McCormick Blaine, 27 February 1900, McCormick Collection, The State Historical Society of Wisconsin, Madison, Wis.
46. Interview with Frederick Dewey, 19 April 1962.
47. Minutes of 23 April 1901, "Board of Trustees, Minutes," vol. 3 (1900), p. 226. President Harper wanted to give Dewey a total salary of $6,000. Dewey refused this and asked for $7,000. When Harper again hinted that the salary would be $6,000, Dewey wrote: "I presume my statement of a week ago that the proposed salary of $6,000 is not satisfactory, is understood. But as my previous remarks to the same effect were not taken as conclusive, I would state again that I cannot do the proposed work for less than $7,000" (Dewey to Harper, 13 April 1901, Presidents' Papers, 1889–1925, Special Collections, The Joseph Regenstein Library, University of Chicago, Chicago, Ill.).
48. Minutes of 24 June 1902, "Board of Trustees, Minutes," vol. 4 (1902), p. 121.
49. Minutes of 19 August 1902, "Board of Trustees, Minutes," 4:142.
50. Minutes of 19 May 1903, "Board of Trustees, Minutes," vol. 5 (1903), p. 261.
51. *Chicago Record Herald*, 18 May 1901.
52. For an excellent and detailed account of the events leading to Dewey's resignation from the University of Chicago, see Robert L. McCaul, "Dewey and the University of Chicago," *School and Society* 89 (1961): 152–57, 179–83, 202–6. The writer is very much indebted to Professor McCaul for his friendly and valuable assistance on this phase of Dewey's experience at the University of Chicago.
53. Dewey to Harper, 16 September 1901, Presidents' Papers, 1889–1925. Answering this letter, Harper assured Dewey that rubber stamps were being prepared that would add the name of Colonel Parker as Director and the words "on the Blaine foundation" to the application forms of the Parker School (Dewey to Jackman, 26 September 1901 [in which he refers to President Harper's assurance], Presidents' Papers, 1889–1925).
54. Dewey to Jackman, 26 September 1901, Presidents' Papers, 1889–1925.
55. Ibid.
56. Dewey to Jackman, 21 February 1903, Presidents' Papers, 1889–1925.
57. Jackman to Dewey, 21 February 1903, Presidents' Papers, 1889–1925.
58. Report by Blaine on her talk with Dewey, 17 April 1903, McCormick Collection.
59. Ibid.
60. Report by Blaine on her conversation with Emily R. Baber, 3 May 1903, McCormick Collection.

61. Report by Blaine on her talk with Dewey, 17 April 1903, McCormick Collection.
62. Report by Blaine on her conversation with Zonia Rice and Emily R. Baber, Spring 1903, McCormick Collection.
63. Ibid.
64. Blaine to Harper, 30 April 1903, McCormick Collection.
65. Miss Rice's explanation for her failure to speak against the nomination was that she could not very well oppose the nomination of Alice Dewey in the presence of her husband.
66. Dewey to Blaine, 30 April 1903, McCormick Collection.
67. Ibid.
68. Dewey, "Democracy in Education," *Elementary School Teacher* 4 (1903): 193–204.
69. Jackman to Harper, 4 May 1903, Presidents' Papers, 1889–1925.
70. Ibid.
71. "Minutes of Meeting of the Trustees of the Chicago Institute," 5 May 1903, McCormick Collection.
72. Blaine to Harper, 5 May 1903, McCormick Collection.
73. Harper to Dewey, 29 February 1904, Secretary of the Board of Trustees Correspondence, Special Collections, The Joseph Regenstein Library, University of Chicago, Chicago, Ill.
74. Harper to Dewey, 18 April 1904, Secretary of the Board of Trustees Correspondence.
75. Harper to Dewey, 30 April 1904, Secretary of the Board of Trustees Correspondence.
76. Ibid.
77. Harper to Alice Dewey, 30 April 1904, Secretary of the Board of Trustees Correspondence.
78. Ibid.
79. Dewey to Harper, 10 May 1904, Presidents' Papers, 1889–1925.
80. Dewey to Harper, 11 April 1904, Presidents' Papers, 1889–1925.
81. Dewey to Harper, 6 April 1904, Presidents' Papers, 1889–1925.
82. Dewey to Harris, 25 April 1904, Hoose Library, University of Southern California, Los Angeles, Calif. I am indebted to Edith Harris, daughter of W. T. Harris, for permission to use the letters exchanged between Mr. and Mrs. Dewey and Harris.
83. Dewey to Harris, 28 April 1904, Hoose Library.
84. Minutes of 2 May 1904, "Board of Trustees, Minutes," vol. 4 (1904), p. 449.
85. *University* [of Chicago] *Record* 9 (1904): 35–36.
86. "The President's Quarterly Statement on the Condition of the University," *University* [of Chicago] *Record* 9 (1904): 214.
87. Angell to Harper, 5 May 1904, University of Chicago Archives, as yet not located by the curator.
88. Harris to Dewey, 30 April 1904, Hoose Library.
89. Alice Dewey to Harris, 2 May 1904, Hoose Library.
90. Jane Dewey, "Biography of John Dewey," p. 35.

CHAPTER 8. COLUMBIA UNIVERSITY, 1905–1914

1. Cattell to Dewey, 14 April 1904; Cattell to Dewey, 18 April 1904; Cattell to Butler, 19 April 1904; Special Collections, Butler Library, Columbia University, New York City.
2. Butler to Cattell, 19 April 1904, Butler Library.
3. Cattell to Butler, 24 April 1904, Butler Library.
4. Minutes of 2 May 1904, "Columbia College, Minutes of the Trustees, 1903–1904," 24:169.
5. This wire is referred to in Butler to Cattell, 25 April 1904, Butler Library.
6. Minutes of 2 May 1904, "Columbia College, Minutes of the Trustees, 1903–1904," 24:168, 169.
7. This was the date fixed because Dewey's contract with the University of Chicago did not expire until 31 December 1904 and because Dewey wanted to be with his family, who were spending the year in Europe, during the month of January.
8. The other two were the Faculty of Political Science and the Faculty of Pure Science.
9. Minutes of 6 June 1904, "Columbia College, Minutes of the Trustees, 1903–1904," 24:216; "Resolutions, 6 June 1904," *Resolutions Adopted by the Trustees of Columbia College, 1903–1909,* vol. 24 (New York: Printed for the Trustees, 1910), p. 3.
10. Dewey to David E. Smith, 7 May 1904, Butler Library.
11. Brander Matthews, *A History of Columbia University, 1754–1904* (New York: Columbia University Press, 1904), pp. 183–84.
12. Frederick P. Keppel, *Columbia* (New York: Oxford University Press, 1914), p. xi.
13. Columbia University, *Annual Reports of the President and Treasurer to the Trustees, with the Accompanying Documents for the Year Ending June 30, 1905* (New York: Printed for the University, 1905), p. 7.
14. Columbia University, *Annual Report of the President and Treasurer to the Trustees, with Accompanying Documents for the Year Ending June 30, 1930* (New York: n.p., n.d.), p. 58
15. Columbia University, *Reports, 1905.*
16. Columbia University, *Report, 1930,* p. 58.
17. One source of the very sizeable income of Columbia has been its extensive real estate holdings in the city. Among these is the land on which Rockefeller Center stands. In 1929, this yielded a return of $700,000; in 1945, the return had increased to $3,743,295. (Horace Coon, *Columbia: Colossus on the Hudson,* American College and University Series, vol. 1 [New York: E. P. Dutton & Co., 1947], pp. 29, 30.)
18. The name "Department of Philosophy and Psychology," was changed to "Department of Philosophy" in 1920 when Psychology was assigned a department of its own. Because of ill-health, Fullerton retired from the university in 1917.

19. John H. Randall, Jr., "The Department of Philosophy," in *A History of the Faculty of Philosophy, Columbia University,* ed. Jacques Barzun (New York: Columbia University Press, 1957), p. 144. Professor Randall's excellent account should be read by those interested in the history of the department.
20. Editor's note in Herbert W. Schneider, "Religion as a University Concern," *Columbia University Quarterly,* June 1931, p. 93n.
21. Minutes of 4 October 1909, "Columbia College, Minutes of the Trustees, 1909–1910," 30:51.
22. Dewey to Woodbridge, 14 September 1908, Butler Library.
23. Dewey, "Experience, Knowledge and Value: A Rejoinder," in *The Philosophy of John Dewey,* The Library of Living Philosophers, ed. Paul A. Schilpp, vol. 1 (Evanston: Northwestern University, 1939), p. 522.
24. Frederick J. E. Woodbridge, "Confessions," in *Contemporary American Philosophy,* ed. George P. Adams and William P. Montague, vol. 2 (New York: Macmillan Co., 1930), p. 417.
25. Ibid., p. 419.
26. Dewey and Arthur F. Bentley, *John Dewey and Arthur F. Bentley: A Philosophical Correspondence, 1932–1951,* ed. Sidney Ratner and Jules Altman (New Brunswick, N.J.: Rutgers University Press, 1964), p. 66.
27. Woodbridge, "Confessions," p. 435.
28. Jane M. Dewey, ed., "Biography of John Dewey," in *The Philosophy of John Dewey,* p. 36.
29. Felix Adler, *An Ethical Philosophy of Life* (New York: D. Appleton & Co., 1918), pp. 116, 117.
30. Felix Adler, "Personality: How to Develop It in the Family, the School and Society," in *Essays in Honor of John Dewey on the Occasion of His Seventieth Birthday, October 20, 1929* (New York: Henry Holt & Co., 1929), pp. 3–22.
31. This address was published under the title *Democracy and Education in the World of Today* (New York: Society for Ethical Culture, 1938).
32. William P. Montague, "The Program and First Principles of Six Realists," *Journal of Philosophy* 7 (1910): 393–401. The other contributors were Edwin B. Holt of Harvard, Walter T. Marvin of Rutgers, Ralph B. Perry of Harvard, Edward G. Spaulding of Princeton, and Walter B. Pitkin of Columbia.
33. William P. Montague et al., *The New Realism: Coöperative Studies in Philosophy* (New York: Macmillan Co., 1912).
34. William P. Montague, *The Ways of Things* (New York: Prentice-Hall, 1940), p. 242.
35. Jane Dewey, "Biography of John Dewey," p. 37.
36. Randall, "Department of Philosophy," p. 127.
37. Ibid.
38. For a complete listing of these courses, see *Columbia University Catalogue,* 1905–15.

39. Wilmon H. Sheldon, "The Vice of Modern Philosophy," *Journal of Philosophy* 12 (1915): 5.
40. For a list of Dewey's writings from 1905 through 1914, see Milton H. Thomas, *John Dewey: A Centennial Bibliography* (Chicago: University of Chicago Press, 1962), pp. 26–42.
41. Dewey, "Rejoinder," p. 522.
42. Dewey, "The Postulate of Immediate Empiricism," *Journal of Philosophy* 2 (1905): 393–99.
43. Ibid., pp. 393, 394.
44. Dewey, "Some Implications of Anti-Intellectualism," *Journal of Philosophy* 7 (1910): 479–80. Another phase of the fallacy is the claim that every conscious experience is a knowing experience, which Dewey deals with in his theory of knowledge. The charge often made that Dewey is anti-intellectual in that he would abandon intelligence in solving problems, substituting some nonrational factor, does violence to a basic part of his philosophy. "It is anti-intellectualistic," said Dewey, "only with reference to certain theories about intellect, theories which seem to me to isolate knowledge from its connections, empirical and metaphysical" (quoted in William P. Montague, *The Ways of Knowing, or the Methods of Philosophy* [New York: Macmillan Co., 1925], p. 135n.).
45. Dewey, "Anti-Intellectualism," p. 480.
46. Dewey, "The Practical Character of Reality," in *Philosophy and Civilization* (New York: Minton, Balch & Co., 1931), p. 37; first published as "Does Reality Possess Practical Character?" in *Essays, Philosophical and Psychological* (New York: Longmans, Green & Co., 1908), pp. 53–80. These essays were written in honor of William James.
47. Evander B. McGilvary, "The Chicago 'Idea' and Idealism," *Journal of Philosophy* 5 (1908): 593.
48. Dewey, "A Short Catechism concerning Truth," in *The Influence of Darwin on Philosophy and Other Essays in Contemporary Thought* (New York: Henry Holt & Co., 1910), p. 157.
49. Ibid.
50. Dewey, "Reality as Experience," *Journal of Philosophy* 3 (1906): 253–57.
51. Ibid., p. 253.
52. Ibid., p. 254.
53. Ibid., pp. 254–55.
54. Ibid., p. 256.
55. Dewey, "Pure Experience and Reality: A Disclaimer," *Philosophical Review* 16 (1907): 419–22.
56. Dewey, "Reality as Experience."
57. Evander B. McGilvary, "Pure Experience and Reality: A Reassertion," *Philosophical Review* 16 (1907): 424.
58. Dewey, "Postulate of Immediate Empiricism," in *Influence of Darwin*, p. 240.

59. Ibid.
60. Dewey, *Experience and Nature,* Lectures upon the Paul Carus Foundation, 1st series (Chicago: Open Court Publishing Co., 1925).
61. Dewey, "Beliefs and Realities," *Philosophical Review* 15 (1906): 115.
62. Dewey, "Thought and Its Subject-Matter: The General Problem of Logical Theory," in *Studies in Logical Theory,* University of Chicago, The Decennial Publications, 2d series, vol. 11 (Chicago: University of Chicago Press, 1903), pp. 6–7.
63. Dewey, "The Control of Ideas by Facts," *Journal of Philosophy* 4 (1907): 198.
64. Dewey, "Brief Studies in Realism, II, Epistemological Realism: The Alleged Ubiquity of the Knowledge Relation," *Journal of Philosophy* 8 (1911): 553.
65. Dewey, "Control of Ideas by Facts," p. 197.
66. Ibid.; "Valid Knowledge and 'Subjectivity of Experience'," *Journal of Philosophy* 7 (1910): 173.
67. Dewey, "Pragmatism," in *A Cyclopedia of Education,* ed. Paul Monroe, vol. 5 (New York: Macmillan Co., 1913), p. 23.
68. James B. Pratt, "Truth and Ideas," *Journal of Philosophy* 5 (1908): 129–30.
69. Ibid., p. 130.
70. Dewey, "Judgment," in *A Cyclopedia of Education,* ed. Paul Monroe, vol. 3 (New York: Macmillan Co., 1912), pp. 571–72.
71. Dewey, "What Does Pragmatism Mean by Practical?" *Journal of Philosophy* 5 (1908): 88, 89; "Fact," in *A Cyclopedia of Education,* ed. Paul Monroe, vol. 2 (New York: Macmillan Co., 1911), pp. 567–68.
72. Dewey, "The Realism of Pragmatism," *Journal of Philosophy* 2 (1905): 325.
73. Dewey, "Anti-Intellectualism," p. 480.
74. Dewey, "Control of Ideas by Facts," p. 202.
75. Dewey, "The Experimental Theory of Knowledge," *Mind* n.s. 15 (1906): 305.
76. Dewey, "Short Catechism," p. 158.
77. Ibid., p. 162.
78. Dewey, "What Does Pragmatism Mean by Practical?" p. 85.
79. Dewey, "Short Catechism," pp. 159–60.
80. Ibid., p. 160.
81. Ibid., p. 159.
82. Dewey, "Reality and the Criterion for the Truth of Ideas," *Mind* n.s. 16 (1907): 337.
83. Dewey, "Beliefs and Realities," p. 124.
84. Dewey, "Experience and Objective Idealism," *Philosophical Review* 15 (1906): 473.
85. Dewey, "Reality and Ideas," p. 339.
86. Dewey, "Experimental Theory of Knowledge," p. 295.

87. Charles W. Bakewell, "The Issue between Idealism and Immediate Empiricism," *Journal of Philosophy* 2 (1905): 688, 690; see also Bakewell, "An Open Letter to Professor Dewey concerning Immediate Empiricism," ibid., pp. 520–22; Dewey, "Immediate Empiricism," ibid., pp. 597–99; Dewey, "The Knowledge Experience Again," ibid., pp. 707–11; and Dewey, "Brief Studies in Realism, II, Epistemological Realism," pp. 546–54.
88. Dewey, "Brief Studies in Realism, I, Naïve Realism vs. Presentative Realism," *Journal of Philosophy* 8 (1911): 395.
89. Dewey, "The Logical Character of Ideas," *Journal of Philosophy* 5 (1908): 376.
90. Ibid.
91. Dewey, "Valid Knowledge and the 'Subjectivity of Experience'," *Journal of Philosophy* 7 (1910): 173.
92. Dewey and James H. Tufts, *Ethics* (New York: Longmans, Green & Co., 1908).
93. Dewey, *The Influence of Darwin on Philosophy and Other Essays in Contemporary Thought* (New York: Henry Holt & Co., 1910).
94. Dewey, *How We Think* (Boston: D. C. Heath & Co., 1910).
95. The essay not previously published was "A Short Catechism concerning Truth," delivered before the Philosophical Club of Smith College in the spring of 1909.
96. Dewey and Tufts, *Ethics,* p. iii.
97. Norman Wilde, review of *Ethics, Journal of Philosophy* 5 (1908): 636.
98. Ibid.
99. Walter T. Marvin, review of *Ethics, Educational Review* 37 (1909): 416.
100. William Caldwell, review of *Ethics, Philosophical Review* 18 (1909): 226.
101. Dewey and Evelyn Dewey, *Schools of To-morrow* (New York: E. P. Dutton & Co., 1915), pp. 109–16.
102. "An Experimental School," *Columbia University Quarterly,* March 1917, p. 191.
103. Dewey's contacts with advanced students in education grew much closer when a special Department of Educational Research was set up in 1915 within the Faculty of Philosophy to administer Ph.D. programs in education; he was one of seven professors appointed to the department. For an excellent account of the history of Teachers College, see Lawrence A. Cremin, David A. Shannon, and Mary E. Townsend, *A History of Teachers College, Columbia University* (New York: Columbia University Press, 1954).
104. Paul Monroe, ed., *A Cyclopedia of Education,* 5 vols. (New York: Macmillan Co., 1911–13).
105. Dewey, "The Bearings of Pragmatism upon Education, First Paper," *Progressive Journal of Education,* December 1908, pp. 1–3; "The Bearings of Pragmatism upon Education, Second Paper," ibid., January 1909, pp. 5–8; "The Bearings of Pragmatism upon

Education, Concluding Paper," ibid., February 1909, pp. 6–7; "Teaching That Does Not Educate," ibid., June 1909, pp. 1–3; "Is Co-education Injurious to Girls?" *Ladies Home Journal,* June 1911, pp. 22, 60–61; "Reasoning in Early Childhood," *Teachers College Record,* January 1914, pp. 9–15; "Report on the Fairhope [Alabama] Experiment in Organic Education," *Survey,* 16 May 1914, p. 199.

106. Dewey, *Moral Principles in Education,* Riverside Educational Monographs, ed. Henry Suzzallo (Boston: Houghton Mifflin Co., 1909).
107. Dewey, "Ethical Principles underlying Education," in *Third Yearbook of the National Herbart Society* (Chicago: National Herbart Society, 1897), pp. 7–33 [*The Early Works of John Dewey, 1882–1898,* ed. Jo Ann Boydston, vol. 5 (Carbondale: Southern Illinois University Press, 1972), pp. 54–83].
108. Dewey, *Interest and Effort in Education,* Riverside Educational Monographs, ed. Henry Suzzallo (Boston: Houghton Mifflin Co., 1913).
109. Dewey, *Interest in Relation to Training of the Will,* Second Supplement to the Herbart Yearbook for 1895 (Bloomington, Ill.: Pantagraph Printing and Stationery Co., 1896) [*Early Works of Dewey,* 5:111–50].
110. Dewey, "Evolution.—The Philosophical Concepts," in *Cyclopedia of Education,* 2:529.
111. Dewey, *How We Think,* pp. 57, 58.
112. Ibid., p. iii.
113. Henry A. Bruce, "Psychology of Education," *New York Times Saturday Review of Books,* 5 November 1910, p. 617.
114. Frank A. Fitzpatrick, review of *How We Think, Educational Review* 60 (1910): 97.
115. Boyd H. Bode, review of *How We Think, School Review* 18 (1910): 642, 645.
116. William H. Kilpatrick, "Dewey's Influence on Education," in *Philosophy of John Dewey,* p. 469.
117. In this shift no one played a more effective role than Kilpatrick. Through his "project method," he popularized Dewey's problem approach to learning, and saw it become an accepted part of American elementary classroom procedure. "So great was the Kilpatrick influence during the Nineteen Twenties and Thirties," declared one writer, "that he has been accused by the critics of progressive education of having indoctrinated a whole generation of teachers and administrators in Dewey's ideas, and of having formed, with his colleagues at Columbia University's Teachers College, a tightly knit movement of progressive educators who controlled the American educational system" (Harold Taylor, "Debate over 'The Progressive Idea'," *New York Times Magazine,* 26 November 1961, p. 30).
118. *Journal of Philosophy* 2 (1905): 41. Dewey became the organiza-

tion's fifth president. The preceding four were: J. E. Creighton of Cornell, A. T. Ormond of Princeton, Josiah Royce of Harvard, and George T. Ladd of Yale.

119. "'Control' of Vocational Education," *Survey*, March 1913, p. 893.
120. Paul U. Kellogg, "Vocational Education Measures in Illinois," *Survey*, March 1913, p. 832.
121. Dewey, "An Undemocratic Proposal," *American Teacher*, January 1913, p. 2.
122. Ibid., p. 3.
123. Dewey, "Some Dangers in the Present Movement for Industrial Education," *Child Labor Bulletin*, February 1913, pp. iv, 69–74; *Some Dangers in the Present Movement for Industrial Education*, Pamphlet no. 190 of the National Labor Committee (New York: National Labor Committee, 1913); "Industrial Education and Democracy [Pt. 2]," *Survey*, March 1913, pp. 870–71, 893.
124. Dewey, "A Policy of Industrial Education," *New Republic*, 19 December 1914, pp. 11–12; "Industrial Education—A Wrong Kind," ibid., 20 February 1915, pp. 71–73; "Education vs. Trade-Training —Dr. Dewey's Reply," ibid., 15 May 1915, pp. 42–43.
125. This address was published in *Bulletin 18* (Peoria, Ill.: National Society for the Promotion of Industrial Education, 1913), pp. 27–34.
126. Dewey, "The Need of an Industrial Education in an Industrial Democracy," *Manual Training and Vocational Education*, February 1916, pp. 409–14; also in *Proceedings of the Second Pan-American Scientific Congress*, vol. 4 (Washington, D.C.: Government Printing Office, 1917), pp. 222–25.
127. Dewey, "Religion and Our Schools," *Hibbert Journal*, July 1908, p. 799.
128. Ibid., p. 800. In 1940, the question of released time for instruction in religion in the New York City schools again came up. The City's Board of Education called an open meeting for hearings at its headquarters at 110 Livingston Street in Brooklyn on 13 November. About five hundred parents, teachers, civic and religious leaders attended. The board heard twenty successive speakers representing various organizations. Of these twenty, seventeen opposed the plan, three supported it. Dewey, representing the Committee for Cultural Freedom of which he was honorary chairman, was one of those who spoke in opposition to the plan. As reported by the press, Dewey argued that

> we are a people of many races, many faiths, creeds and religions. I do not think that the men who made the Constitution forbade the establishment of a State church because they were opposed to religion. They knew that the introduction of religious differences into American life would undermine the democratic foundations of this country. What holds for adults holds even more for children, sensitive and conscious of differences. I certainly hope that the Board of Education will think very, very seriously before it introduces this division and antagonism in our public schools.

Despite the opposition, the board by a six to one vote adopted a resolution granting released time for religious instruction. ([Statement on Released Time Bill], *New York Times*, 14 November 1940, pp. 1, 18.)

129. The Commission on Educational Reconstruction, *Organizing the Teaching Profession: The Story of the American Federation of Teachers* (Glencoe, Ill.: Free Press, 1955), p. 31.
130. "A Call to Organize," *American Teacher*, February 1913, pp. 27, 28.
131. Dewey, "Professional Spirit among Teachers," *American Teacher*, October 1913, pp. 114–16.
132. Ibid., p. 114.
133. Ibid., p. 115.
134. Ibid., p. 114.
135. Paul U. Kellogg, *Lillian D. Wald, Settler and Trail-Blazer* (New York: n.p., 1927).
136. Lillian D. Wald, *Windows on Henry Street* (Boston: Little, Brown & Co., 1934), pp. 44–60.
137. Ibid., p. 255.
138. Dewey, "Introduction," in *Directory of the Trades and Occupations Taught at the Day and Evening Schools in Greater New York*, by Henry Street Settlement, Committee on Vocational Scholarships, rev. ed. (New York, 1916), p. v.
139. "Psychology Lectures by Prof. Dewey," *Columbia Spectator*, 21 February 1905, p. 2.
140. "The University," *Columbia University Quarterly*, June 1906, p. 307.
141. "Prof. Dewey to Lecture on Education," *Columbia Spectator*, 14 March 1906, p. 2.
142. "The University," *Columbia University Quarterly*, June 1907, pp. 381–82.
143. Dewey, "Darwin's Influence upon Philosophy," *Popular Science Monthly*, July 1909, pp. 90–98; reprinted as "The Influence of Darwin on Philosophy," in *Influence of Darwin*, pp. 1–19.
144. Dewey, *Ethics* (New York: Columbia University Press, 1908); reprinted as "Intelligence and Morals," in *Influence of Darwin*, pp. 46–76.
145. *Columbia University Quarterly*, June 1910, p. 351.
146. "Morals and Their Growth," *New York Times*, 18 December 1911, p. 6.
147. "The University," *Columbia University Quarterly*, March 1913, p. 186.
148. "The University," *Columbia University Quarterly*, June 1913, p. 302.
149. Ibid.
150. "Prof. Dewey's Lectures," *New York Times*, 11 January 1914, p. 9.
151. "The University," *Columbia University Quarterly*, June 1907, pp. 381–82.
152. "Dewey Gives First Lecture of Series," *Daily Illini*, 10 December 1907.
153. "The University," *Columbia University Quarterly*, June 1908, p. 388.

154. See *Influence of Darwin*, p. 154n.
155. *Columbia University Quarterly*, June 1910, p. 351.
156. Ibid.
157. Ibid.
158. "The Problem of Truth," *Old Penn, Weekly Review of the University of Pennsylvania*, 11 February 1911, pp. 522–28, ibid., 18 February 1911, pp. 556–63, ibid., 4 March 1911, pp. 620–25.
159. "The University," *Columbia University Quarterly*, December 1911, p. 103.
160. John L. March, "The Ichabod Spencer Lectures, 1914," *Union Alumni Monthly*, September–October, 1914, p. 309.
161. During the academic year 1905–6, the Deweys lived at 431 Riverside Drive; during 1906–7, they lived at 505 West 122nd Street; during 1907–9, they resided at 1700 Broadway; during 1909–10, they were at 130th Street and St. Nicholas Avenue; during 1910–11, they lived at 49 St. Nicholas Terrace; during 1911–12, their home was at 112th Street and Broadway; and during 1912–13, at East 41st Street. After 1913, with some of the older children gone, the family was smaller and more settled. From 1913–27, the Deweys lived at 2880 Broadway. In 1927 Mrs. Dewey died, and one or the other of Dewey's daughters lived with him. From 1927–38 Dewey lived with his daughter Evelyn at 125 East 62nd Street; when Evelyn married, his daughter Jane came to live with her father at 1 West 89th Street from 1939–45. In 1945 the two moved to 1158 Fifth Avenue. Jane lived with her father here until December 1946 when her father married Mrs. Roberta Grant. John lived with Roberta Dewey at 1158 Fifth Avenue till his death in June 1952. (For Dewey's residences while he was affiliated with Columbia, see *Columbia University Catalogue* for the years 1905 to 1940.)
162. Dewey, *How We Think*, pp. iii–iv.
163. "University Tea," *Columbia Spectator*, 20 February 1906, p. 1.
164. Dewey, statement in "Symposium on Woman's Suffrage," *International* 3 (1911): 93, 94.
165. "Professor for Suffrage," *New York Times*, 9 August 1912, p. 3.
166. Ibid.
167. "The University," *Columbia University Quarterly*, March 1913, p. 186.
168. "Riot of Enthusiasm Greets Maxim Gorky," *New York Times*, 11 April 1906, p. 6; "Gorky and Mark Twain Plead for Revolution," ibid., 12 April 1906, p. 4; "Gorky and Actress Asked to Quit Hotels," ibid., 15 April 1906, pp. 1, 3; "Gorky Is Now Hiding," ibid., 16 April 1906, pp. 1–2; "Gorky Will Go to Boston," ibid., 16 April 1906, p. 2.
169. Max Eastman, "John Dewey," *Atlantic Monthly* 168 (1941): 684.
170. The farm has since been divided into suburban lots. The original farm house has been modernized but in a way to preserve its earlier charm. The family of Mr. Gene Goodman now occupy the place.

171. The writer is indebted to Mr. Sabino Dewey of Huntington, Long Island, for information concerning Dewey's experience on the farm. Sabino Dewey was in his early teens at the time, and remembers vividly much of the life on the farm. (Interview with Sabino Dewey, 11 June 1964.)
172. Max Eastman is authority for the story that

> [Dewey] was pleased when one day a hurry call came from a wealthy neighbor for a dozen eggs, and, the children being in school, he himself took the eggs over in a basket. Going by force of habit to the front door, he was told brusquely that deliveries were made at the rear. He trotted obediently around to the back door, feeling both amused and happy. Some time later he was giving a talk to the women's club of the neighborhood, and when he got up to speak, his wealthy customer exclaimed in a loud whisper, "Why, that looks exactly like our egg-man!" (Eastman, "John Dewey," p. 681).

173. For some statements of these differences, see William James, *The Meaning of Truth* (New York: Longmans, Green & Co., 1909), pp. xvi–xix, 56, 169; Dewey, "What Does Pragmatism Mean by Practical?" pp. 85–99; Dewey to James, 24 February 1909, in *The Thought and Character of William James,* by Ralph B. Perry, vol. 2 (Boston: Little, Brown & Co., 1935), pp. 529–31; Perry, *Thought and Character of James,* 2:514–15.
174. Perry, *Thought and Character of James,* 2:533.
175. Dewey, "William James," *Independent* 69 (1910): 533.
176. Dewey, "William James," *Journal of Philosophy* 7 (1910): 506, 507, 508.
177. Dewey, "William James," *Independent,* p. 533.
178. Dewey, "William James," *Journal of Philosophy,* p. 508.

CHAPTER 9. COLUMBIA UNIVERSITY, 1914–1919

1. For a good statement of this argument, see John H. Muirhead, *German Philosophy in Relation to the War* (London: J. Murray, 1915).
2. These lectures were published in book form under the same title (*German Philosophy and Politics* [New York: Henry Holt & Co., 1915]). See also Dewey, "On Understanding the Mind of Germany," *Atlantic Monthly* 117 (1916): 251–62.
3. Dewey, *German Philosophy and Politics,* p. 121.
4. Ibid., p. 28.
5. Dewey, "Progress," in *Characters and Events,* ed. Joseph Ratner, vol. 2 (New York: Henry Holt & Co., 1929), pp. 820–21; first published in *International Journal of Ethics,* April 1916, pp. 311–22.
6. Ibid., p. 821.
7. Ibid., p. 827.
8. Ibid., p. 824.
9. Ibid., p. 820.

10. Quoted by Dewey in "Universal Service as Education," in *Characters and Events*, 2:466; first published in *New Republic*, 22 and 29 April 1916, pp. 309, 334–35.
11. Ibid., p. 467.
12. Ibid.
13. Ibid., p. 468.
14. Ibid., p. 467.
15. Theodore Roosevelt, "America Needs Hughes," *New Republic*, 7 October 1916, p. ii.
16. Dewey, "The Emergence of a New World," in *Characters and Events*, 2:445; first published as "In a Time of National Hesitation," *Seven Arts*, May 1917, pp. 3–7.
17. Ibid., p. 443.
18. Dewey, "The Future of Pacifism," in *Characters and Events*, 2:582; first published in *New Republic*, 28 July 1917, pp. 358–60.
19. Woodrow Wilson, "Flag-Day Address of President Wilson," *Congressional Record*, 65th Congress, 1st session, vol. 55, Appendix, p. 334.
20. Dewey, "Democracy and Loyalty in the Schools," *New York Evening Post*, 19 December 1917.
21. Dewey, *Enlistment for the Farm*, Columbia War Papers, series 1, no. 1 (New York: Division of Intelligence and Publicity of Columbia University, 1917).
22. Ibid., p. 5.
23. Ibid., pp. 5–6.
24. Dewey, "Democracy and Loyalty."
25. Dewey, "Conscription of Thought," in *Characters and Events*, 2:570; first published in *New Republic*, 1 September 1917, pp. 128–30.
26. Dewey, "In Explanation of Our Lapse," in *Characters and Events*, 2:574; first published in *New Republic*, 3 November 1917, pp. 17–18.
27. Ibid.
28. An earlier incident of this kind had occurred at Columbia. When Count Ilya Tolstoi, son of Count Leo Tolstoi, was invited to address the Russian night meeting of the International Club of the university on the evening of 10 February 1917, some three hundred persons assembled to hear him. When the meeting opened, it was announced that the Count would not be allowed to give his talk because his radical political and social views were distasteful to Professor J. O. Prince, head of the Department of Slavonic Language and Literature at the university. This suppression of freedom of speech upset both students and faculty alike; Dewey was among those condemning the act. In a statement to the press he declared, "I think it was unfortunate that one individual member of the Faculty had the opportunity by means of purely technical rules to put the university in the wrong light before the public. As a matter of fact, freedom of speech and liberty of opinion have always existed at Columbia. That makes the occurrence the more

regrettable" ("Tolstoy Incident Divides Columbia," *New York Times*, 14 February 1917, p. 5).

29. Dewey to Seligman, 25 September 1917, Special Collections, Butler Library, Columbia University, New York City.
30. Randolph Bourne, "Those Columbia Trustees," in *The History of a Literary Radical & Other Papers* (New York: S. A. Russell, 1956), p. 185. This article appeared originally as a letter to the editor of *New Republic*, 20 October 1917, pp. 328–29.
31. Dewey, "Future of Pacifism," p. 583.
32. Ibid., p. 582. The different positions of Dewey and Jane Addams on the war were "a source of pain on both sides" but did not impair the long and close friendship of the two. (See Jane M. Dewey, ed., "Biography of John Dewey," in *The Philosophy of John Dewey*, The Library of Living Philosophers, ed. Paul A. Schilpp, vol. 1 [Evanston: Northwestern University, 1939], p. 30.)
33. Dewey, "Future of Pacifism," p. 583.
34. Dewey, "Force, Violence and Law," in *Characters and Events*, 2:636; first published in *New Republic*, 22 January 1916, pp. 295–97.
35. Ibid.
36. Dewey, "Force and Coercion," in *Characters and Events*, 2:784; first published in *International Journal of Ethics*, April 1916, pp. 359–67.
37. Dewey, "Force, Violence and Law," p. 638.
38. Ibid.
39. Ibid., p. 637.
40. Ibid., p. 638.
41. Ibid., p. 639.
42. Ibid.
43. Ibid.
44. Dewey, "Conscience and Compulsion," in *Characters and Events*, 2:577–78; first published in *New Republic*, 14 July 1917, pp. 297–98.
45. Ibid., p. 578.
46. Ibid.
47. Ibid., p. 580.
48. For more information about Bourne, see Max Lerner, "Randolph Bourne and Two Generations," *Twice a Year* (double number, 1940–41): 54–78; Alfred Kazin, *On Native Grounds: An Interpretation of Modern American Prose Literature* (New York: Reynal & Hitchcock, 1942), pp. 183–85; Van Wyck Brooks, "Introduction," in *History of a Literary Radical*, by Bourne, pp. 1–20; Sidney Kaplan, "Social Engineers as Saviors: Effects of World War I on Some American Liberals," *Journal of the History of Ideas* 17 (1956): 347–69; A. F. Beringause, "The Double Martyrdom of Randolph Bourne," *Journal of the History of Ideas* 18 (1957): 594–603.
49. Bourne, "Twilight of Idols," in *History of a Literary Radical*, p. 242; first published in *Seven Arts*, October 1917, pp. 688–702. This essay which details Bourne's break with Dewey has been referred to as "one of the most poignant pieces of writing in our political

literature, for the break with Dewey was a painful one for Bourne" (Lerner, "Randolph Bourne and Two Generations," p. 68).

50. Dewey, "Force and Ideals," in *Characters and Events*, 2:630; first published as "The Discrediting of Idealism," *New Republic*, 8 October 1919, pp. 285–87.
51. Ibid., p. 631.
52. See Lightner Witmer, *The Nearing Case* (New York: B. W. Huebsch, 1915); "A Puritan Revolutionist," *World Tomorrow* 13 (1930): 305–8. The author's name is not given.
53. "The Philadelphia Martyr," *New York Times*, 10 October 1915, p. 16.
54. Dewey, "Professorial Freedom," *New York Times*, 22 October 1915, p. 10.
55. Charles A. Beard, the distinguished historian at Columbia, gave dramatic expression of his dissatisfaction with conditions there when he resigned on 8 October 1917, one week after the dismissal of Cattell and Dana. In his letter to President Butler explaining his action, Beard wrote that he could no longer endure the autocratic and high-handed manner in which a small clique of trustees over the years had been running the university. He described the trustees as men "who have no standing in the world of education, who are reactionary and visionless in politics, narrow and mediaeval in religion" and who completely lack a sense of "the true function of a university in the advancement of learning" ("Professor Beard's Letter of Resignation from Columbia University," *School and Society* 6 [1917]: 446). He declared that in their treatment of faculty members they have acted arbitrarily and in almost complete disregard of faculty wishes, making "the status of the professor lower than that of the manual laborer, who, through his union, has at least some voice in the terms and conditions of his employment" (ibid., p. 446). Beard gave another and more detached statement of his reasons for leaving Columbia in "A Statement by Charles A. Beard," *New Republic*, 29 December 1917, pp. 249–51.

    Dewey commented to the press: "I regard the action of Professor Beard as the natural consequence of the degrading action of the trustees last week. I personally regret the loss to the university of such a scholarly man and a teacher of such rare power" ([Statement], *New York Times*, 9 October 1917, p. 3).
56. Dewey, "The Case of the Professor and the Public Interest," *Dial* 62 (1917): 435–37.
57. Ibid., p. 435.
58. Ibid.
59. Ibid., p. 437.
60. Dewey, "Democracy and Loyalty," p. 10. Dewey also discussed the De Witt Clinton High School case in the article "Public Education on Trial," *New Republic*, 29 December 1917, pp. 245–47.

61. Dewey, "Professional Organization of Teachers," *American Teacher*, September 1916, pp. 99–101.
62. Ibid., p. 101.
63. Arthur O. Lovejoy, "Origin of the American Association of University Professors," *Science* n.s. 41 (1915): 153–54.
64. Dewey, "The American Association of University Professors: Introductory Address," *Science* n.s. 41 (1915): 150.
65. Dewey, "Annual Address of the President," *Bulletin of the American Association of University Professors*, December 1915, p. 12.
66. For an interesting and detailed account of the early period of the New School, see Alvin Johnson, *Pioneer's Progress: An Autobiography* (New York: Viking Press, 1952), pp. 271–87.
67. For an account of the origin and history of the American Civil Liberties Union, see Donald O. Johnson, *The Challenge to American Freedom: World War I and the Rise of the American Civil Liberties Union* (Lexington: University of Kentucky Press, 1963).
68. I am indebted to Roger N. Baldwin, long-time Executive Director of the union, for this account of Dewey's relation to the organization. (See Roger N. Baldwin to Dykhuizen, 22 September 1970, George Dykhuizen Papers and Correspondence, Special Collections, Guy W. Bailey Library, University of Vermont, Burlington, Vt.)
69. For a listing of Dewey's writings during the years 1914–18, see Milton H. Thomas, *John Dewey: A Centennial Bibliography* (Chicago: University of Chicago Press, 1962), pp. 41–47.
70. Dewey, "The Subject-Matter of Metaphysical Inquiry," *Journal of Philosophy* 12 (1915): 337–45.
71. Dewey, "Introduction," in *Essays in Experimental Logic* (Chicago: University of Chicago Press, 1916), pp. 1–74.
72. Dewey, "The Postulate of Immediate Empiricism," *Journal of Philosophy* 2 (1905): 393–99.
73. Ibid., p. 399.
74. Dewey, "Some Implications of Anti-Intellectualism," *Journal of Philosophy* 7 (1910): 479.
75. Dewey, "Metaphysical Inquiry," p. 340.
76. Ibid., p. 340n.
77. Ibid., p. 340.
78. Ibid., p. 341.
79. Ibid., p. 340.
80. Ibid., p. 345.
81. Ibid., p. 343.
82. Ibid., p. 344.
83. Ibid., pp. 343–44.
84. Ibid., p. 345.
85. Ibid., p. 344.
86. Ibid., p. 345.
87. Ibid., p. 344.
88. Dewey, "A Short Catechism concerning Truth," in *The Influence*

of *Darwin on Philosophy and Other Essays in Contemporary Thought* (New York: Henry Holt & Co., 1910), p. 157.

89. Dewey, "Objects, Data, and Existences: A Reply to Professor McGilvary," *Journal of Philosophy* 6 (1909): 19n.
90. Dewey, "Introduction," in *Essays in Experimental Logic*, p. 6.
91. Ibid.
92. Ibid., p. 7.
93. Ibid., pp. 7–8.
94. Dewey, *The School and Society*, 2d ed. (Chicago: University of Chicago Press, 1915).
95. Dewey and Evelyn Dewey, *Schools of To-morrow* (New York: E. P. Dutton & Co., 1915). An interesting account of how this book came to be written is that by Burges Johnson, then manager of the educational department of E. P. Dutton and Company of New York who published the book:

> I had recommended to Mr. John Macrae, the president of the concern, that we bring at once some books of distinction to prove the house was now educationally minded, and I proposed that we ask Professor John Dewey for a book about the new "progressive" schools.
>
> Armed with authority to contract for such a book I went to see Dr. Dewey. I had the title already planned in advance, if I could persuade him to accept it—"Schools of Tomorrow"—and I had read enough of his talks about several of these schools to suggest the direction such a book might take. I knew that if I went with a concrete plan, good or bad, I would be more likely to get something than if I had no plan at all.
>
> He liked the title and purpose of such a book but said he had decided not to publish any more for a time, and talked to me about the danger of writing too much. It was easy, he said, for a teacher to find himself bound down by a book he had written a year ago, fearing the charge of inconsistency if he grew a little wiser as time passed.
>
> But I had a sudden notion as I listened to him that there might be a way of getting that book. I had brought along a couple of tentative chapter titles and I asked him to help me phrase enough additional titles to cover the subject properly. After ten or twelve were written out and lying there before us, I asked him whether he really had not completed some of those chapters already in addresses, or articles for learned journals. He looked them over thoughtfully and then looked up with a little smile. "Yes," he said, "I think that book is about half written already."
>
> In due time the manuscript of *Schools of Tomorrow* was on my desk at Dutton's and I started to read it. The first chapter seemed to me written in a style that never would attract the general reader but only the educational technician. I wanted a book that would sell as widely as possible through all channels and establish our young educational department in the good graces of the firm. But the second chapter greatly cheered me. It was simply expressed, and parents interested in schools but knowing little about them could understand it. So I went back to Columbia with the manuscript and all my supply of tact ready to hand. I explained to Dr. Dewey in halting phrases that the opening chapter was rather forbidding; but then I burst into fulsome praise of chapter two, and asked him whether he would be willing to have the book begin with that chapter, and move the opening pages over to the middle of the book. He listened to me quietly and

then said in his gentle voice, "What you say interests me greatly. I wrote the first chapter, and my daughter Evelyn wrote the second." (Burges Johnson, *As Much as I Dare: A Personal Recollection* [New York: Ives Washburn, 1944], pp. 186–87).

I am indebted to Dr. Homer Dodge for calling this anecdote to my attention.

96. Dewey, *Democracy and Education: An Introduction to the Philosophy of Education*, Text-Book Series in Education, ed. Paul Monroe (New York: Macmillan Co., 1916).
97. See Dewey's account of this school in his "Report on the Fairhope [Alabama] Experiment in Organic Education," *Survey*, 16 May 1914, p. 199.
98. Ernest C. Moore, "A Prophet among Schoolmasters," *Survey*, 8 January 1916, p. 438.
99. Dewey, "From Absolutism to Experimentalism," in *Contemporary American Philosophy*, ed. George P. Adams and William P. Montague, vol. 2 (New York: Macmillan Co., 1930), p. 23.
100. Walter Lippmann, "The Hope of Democracy," *New Republic*, 1 July 1916, p. 231.
101. Dewey, *Democracy and Education*, p. 11.
102. Ibid., p. 59.
103. Ibid., pp. 89–90.
104. Ibid., p. 388.
105. Ibid., p. 305.
106. Ibid., p. 378.
107. Ibid., p. 383.
108. Ibid., p. 387.
109. Dewey, "Absolutism to Experimentalism," p. 21.
110. Dewey, *Democracy and Education*, p. 383.
111. T. P. Beyer, "What Is Education?" *Dial* 61 (1916): 101.
112. During the years 1915 to 1935, Dewey wrote 160 articles and 5 letters in *New Republic*.
113. Dewey to Levinson, 27 February 1918, Salmon O. Levinson Papers, Special Collections, The Joseph Regenstein Library, University of Chicago, Chicago, Ill. Dewey did, however, have an editorial relationship with another liberal magazine at this time. On 6 June 1918, when the publishers of *Dial* announced that their publication offices were being moved from Chicago to New York, they also announced some additions to the board of editors. Dewey was among those added, and thereafter, for a number of years, his name appeared with those of the editors. (See *Dial* 64 [1918]: 521.)
114. Bliven to Dykhuizen, 9 June 1964, Dykhuizen Papers.
115. Published in *Manual Training and Vocational Education*, February 1916, pp. 409–14; reprinted in *Proceedings of the Second Pan-American Scientific Congress*, vol. 4, sec. 4, pt. 1 (Washington, D.C.: Government Printing Office, 1917), pp. 222–25.

116. Published in *National Education Association Addresses and Proceedings* (Ann Arbor: The Association, 1916), pp. 183–89.
117. Published in *Psychological Review* 24 (1917): 266–77.
118. Published in *School and Society* 5 (1917): 331–35.
119. Dewey, "Federal Aid to Elementary Education," *Child Labor Bulletin*, May 1917, pp. 61–66.
120. Dewey, "Vocational Education in the Light of the World War," Vocational Education Association of the Middle West, *Bulletin No. 4* (Chicago, 1918).
121. See Dewey, "America in the World," *Nation* 106 (1918): 287.
122. Frederick M. Alexander, *Man's Supreme Inheritance: Conscious Guidance and Control in Relation to Human Evolution in Civilization* (New York: E. P. Dutton & Co., 1918).
123. Dewey, "Introductory Word," in *Man's Supreme Inheritance*, by Alexander, p. xv.
124. Quoted by Jane Dewey, "Biography of John Dewey," pp. 44–45. For other comments on Dewey's experience with Alexander, see Max Eastman, "John Dewey," *Atlantic Monthly* 168 (1941): 683, and Corliss Lamont, ed., *Dialogue on John Dewey* (New York: Horizon Press, 1959), pp. 24–29. See also Randolph Bourne's review of Alexander's book under the title "Making over the Body," *New Republic*, 4 May 1918, pp. 28–29, and Dewey's "Reply to a Reviewer," ibid., 11 May 1918, p. 55.
125. Dewey, "Fiat Justitia, Ruat Cœlum," in *Characters and Events*, 2:593, 595; first published in *New Republic*, 29 September 1917, pp. 237–38.
126. Woodrow Wilson, "Address by the President of the United States," *Congressional Record*, 65th Congress, 2d Session, 56:680–81.
127. Dewey, "The Fourteen Points and the League of Nations," *Dial* 65 (1918): 463.
128. The four articles were: "The Approach to a League of Nations," *Dial* 65 (1918): 341–42; "The League of Nations and the New Diplomacy," ibid., pp. 401–3; "The Fourteen Points and the League of Nations," ibid., pp. 463–64; and "A League of Nations and Economic Freedom," ibid., pp. 537–39. All but the third of these were reprinted in *Characters and Events*, vol. 2.
129. Dewey, "The Approach to a League of Nations," in *Characters and Events*, 2:604.
130. Ibid.
131. Dewey, "A League of Nations and Economic Freedom," in *Characters and Events*, 2:610.
132. Dewey, "The League of Nations and the New Diplomacy," in *Characters and Events*, 2:606.
133. Dewey, "League of Nations and Economic Freedom," p. 614.
134. Dewey, "Shall We Join the League?" in *Characters and Events*, 2:626, 625; first published in *New Republic*, 7 March 1923, pp. 36–37.

135. Dewey, "Our National Dilemma," in *Characters and Events*, 2:615; first published in *New Republic*, 24 May 1920, pp. 117–18.

CHAPTER 10. THE FAR EAST, 1919–1921

1. Dewey to Levinson, 9 December 1918, Salmon O. Levinson Papers, Special Collections, The Joseph Regenstein Library, University of Chicago, Chicago, Ill.
2. Dewey to Levinson, 21 December 1918, Levinson Papers. For a detailed and informative account of Dewey's visit to Japan, see the excellent article by Lewis S. Feuer, "John Dewey's Sojourn in Japan," *Record* (Teachers College), September 1969, pp. 123–45.
3. For accounts of Dewey's arrival and reception at the dock see: *Jiji Shimpo* (Tokyo), Evening Edition, 9 February 1919, and ibid., Morning Edition, 10 February 1919; *Nichinichi Shimbun* (Tokyo), 10 February 1919; *Asahi Shimbun* (Tokyo), 10 February 1919; *Yomiuri Shimbun* (Tokyo), 10 February 1919; *Asahi Shimbun* (Osaka), 11 February 1919. I am indebted to the late Professor Nagano Yoshio of Tokyo University and to Professor Miura Norio of Tohoku Gakuin University in Sendai, for photostatic copies of passages relating to Dewey in the above-named newspapers. I am especially grateful to Professor Miura for translating into English these and other Japanese passages used in this chapter.
4. Dewey and Alice Chipman Dewey, *Letters from China and Japan*, ed. Evelyn Dewey (New York: E. P. Dutton & Co., 1920), pp. 20–21.
5. For this list, see Nagano Yoshio, *Philosophy of John Dewey* (Tokyo: Chuwa Book Store, 1946), pp. 1–18; *Bulletin of the Alumni Association* (Tokyo), March 1919, pp. 21–22; Dewey, "Dewey's Lectures in Japan," *Journal of Philosophy* 16 (1919): 357–64.
6. *Jiji Shimpo* (Tokyo), Morning Edition, 26 February 1919; *Asahi Shimbun* (Tokyo), 27 February 1919; *Journal of Philosophy* (Tokyo) 34 (1919): 304.
7. Dewey and Alice Dewey, *Letters*, p. 52.
8. Nagano to Miura, 2 December 1965 (while Professor Miura was in Burlington), George Dykhuizen Papers and Correspondence, Special Collections, Guy W. Bailey Library, University of Vermont, Burlington, Vt. Professor Nagano, then a graduate student at Imperial University in Tokyo, heard Dewey through to the end.
9. Dewey, *Reconstruction in Philosophy* (New York: Henry Holt & Co., 1920), p. iii.
10. Ibid.
11. Victor N. Kobayashi, *John Dewey in Japanese Educational Thought* (Ann Arbor: University of Michigan Press, 1964), p. 40.
12. That Dewey's talks did not always favorably impress his listeners is manifest in some of the comments made of them. On 26 February 1919, Dewey addressed a group at Keio University in Tokyo on "Business and Democracy." Professor Shumi Kobayashi of the university commented that the lecture contained no new or fresh

material but merely stated in a very ordinary way what most of his listeners already knew. (See his "Impressions of Professor Dewey's Lecture," *World of Experimental Education* [Tokyo] 40 [1919]: 11–14.) On 8 and 15 March, Dewey spoke at Waseda University, also in Tokyo, on "Philosophic Basis of Democracy." On this occasion also, according to one editorial report, many of his listeners declared that they found nothing new or particularly stimulating in Dewey's remarks. (See *World of Experimental Education* [Tokyo] 40 [1919]: 9–10.) On still another occasion, on 19 March, Dewey addressed a gathering of Japanese Christians in a Tokyo church on "The Moral Meaning of Democracy." Referring to this talk in his diary, the famous Japanese Christian, Uchimura Kanzo, wrote: "If I had given the same lecture in Japanese, the audience would have complained" (quoted by Victor Kobayashi, *Dewey in Japanese Educational Thought*, p. 39).

13. See Victor Kobayashi, *Dewey in Japanese Educational Thought*, pp. 29–40, for a fuller account of these and other followers of Dewey.
14. Ibid., p. 137.
15. Ibid., pp. 40, 41.
16. Dewey, "On the Two Sides of the Eastern Sea," in *Characters and Events*, ed. Joseph Ratner, vol. 1 (New York: Henry Holt & Co., 1929), p. 170; first published in *New Republic*, 16 July 1919, pp. 346–48.
17. Dewey, "Liberalism in Japan," in *Characters and Events*, 1:149; first published as "I. The Intellectual Preparation," *Dial* 67 (1919): 283–85; "II. The Economic Factor," ibid., pp. 333–37; "III. The Chief Foe," ibid., pp. 369–71.
18. Dewey, "Liberalism in Japan," p. 150.
19. Dewey, "Japan Revisited: Two Years Later," in *Characters and Events*, 1:181; first published as "Public Opinion in Japan," *New Republic*, 16 November 1921, sup. to no. 363, pp. 15–18.
20. Dewey, "Liberalism in Japan," p. 160.
21. Dewey, "Japan Revisited," p. 182.
22. Dewey, "Liberalism in Japan," p. 166.
23. Dewey and Alice Dewey, *Letters*, p. 38.
24. Dewey, "Liberalism in Japan," p. 166.
25. Dewey, "Japan and America," *Dial* 64 (1919): 501.
26. Dewey, "Liberalism in Japan," p. 160.
27. Ibid., p. 158.
28. Dewey, "Japan and America," p. 503.
29. Ibid., p. 502.
30. Dewey, "Liberalism in Japan," p. 169.
31. Ibid., p. 167.
32. Dewey and Alice Dewey, *Letters*, p. 148.
33. Ibid., p. 149.
34. See *Asahi Shimbun* (Tokyo), 23 March 1919; and *Jiji Shimpo* (Tokyo), Morning Edition, 23 March 1919.

35. *Jiji Shimpo* (Tokyo), Morning Edition, 23 March 1919; *Asahi Shimbun* (Tokyo), 24 March 1919.
36. Dewey and Alice Dewey, *Letters*, p. 59.
37. Ibid., p. 50.
38. *Bulletin of Alumni Association* (Tokyo), 20 May 1919, p. 42; Dewey and Alice Dewey, *Letters*, pp. 141, 143.
39. *Bulletin of Alumni Association* (Tokyo), 20 June 1919, p. 44.
40. Max Eastman, "John Dewey," *Atlantic Monthly* 168 (1941): 683.
41. Hu Shih, "John Dewey in China," in *Philosophy and Culture: East and West*, ed. Charles A. Moore (Honolulu: University of Hawaii Press, 1962), p. 762.
42. Dewey, "Chinese Social Habits," in *Characters and Events*, 1:215; first published as "What Holds China Back?" *Asia* 20 (1920): 373–77.
43. Dewey and Alice Dewey, *Letters*, p. 176.
44. Ibid., p. 184.
45. Dewey, "Chinese Social Habits," p. 220.
46. Dewey and Alice Dewey, *Letters*, p. 166.
47. Hu Shih, "John Dewey in China," pp. 764, 765.
48. Hu Shih, ed., *Dewey's Five Major Series of Lectures in Peking* (Peking: *Morning Post*, 1920).
49. Robert Clopton and Tsuin-chen Ou, eds., *John Dewey: Lectures in China, 1919–1920* (Honolulu: University of Hawaii Press, 1973).
50. O. Brière, *Fifty Years of Chinese Philosophy, 1898–1950*, translated from the French by Laurence G. Thompson (London: George Allen & Unwin, 1956), p. 26.
51. Dewey to John J. Coss, 13 January 1920, Special Collections, Butler Library, Columbia University, New York City.
52. Hu Shih, "John Dewey in China," p. 765.
53. Dewey to Coss, 22 April 1920, Butler Library.
54. Ibid.
55. Coss to Dewey, 10 June 1920, Butler Library.
56. Dewey to Coss, 22 April 1920, Butler Library.
57. "To Moscow," *Time Magazine*, 4 June 1928, p. 16.
58. Bertrand Russell, *The Problem of China* (New York: Century Co., 1922), pp. 236–37.
59. "Bertrand Russell Reported Dead," *New York Times*, 21 April 1921, p. 13.
60. Ralph Schoenman, "Preface," in *Bertrand Russell, Philosopher of the Century: Essays in His Honor*, ed. Ralph Schoenman (Boston: Little, Brown & Co., 1967), pp. 8–9.
61. Interview with Lucy (Dewey) Brandauer, 28 June 1967.
62. Dewey to Coss, 22 April 1920, Butler Library.
63. Hu Shih reports that Dewey visited eleven of the twenty-two provinces of China ("Dewey in China," p. 764). But during some remarks in Fuchow Dewey declared that Fukien Province was the twelfth he had been in. To these twelve must be added Kwangtung Province to which he went after his lecture in Fukien.

64. Lucy (Dewey) Brandauer to Dykhuizen, 6 March 1967, Dykhuizen Papers.
65. This account of the Deweys' lectures in Fukien Province is taken from the pamphlet, written in Chinese, entitled *Record of Dewey's Talks in Fukien Province* (undated, but probably published in the summer or fall of 1921) and put out by the Ministry of Education of Fukien Province. I am indebted to my colleague, Professor David C. Lai, for translating this pamphlet into English.
66. Lucy (Dewey) Brandauer to Dykhuizen, 6 March 1967, Dykhuizen Papers.
67. Dewey, "Young China and Old," in *Characters and Events*, 1:256; first published as "Old China and New," *Asia* 21 (1921): 445–50, 454, 456.
68. Dewey was paid for the articles he wrote from Japan and China, and in a letter to Coss he refers to them as "pot boilers" (Dewey to Coss, 7 November 1920, Butler Library).
69. Dewey, "The Student Revolt in China," *New Republic*, 6 August 1919, pp. 16–18.
70. Ibid., p. 18.
71. Dewey and Alice Dewey, *Letters*, p. 247.
72. Dewey, "The Growth of Chinese National Sentiment," in *Characters and Events*, 1:222–36; first published as "Chinese National Sentiment," *Asia* 19 (1919): 1237–42.
73. Dewey, "Justice and Law in China," in *Characters and Events*, 1:244–54; first published as "The New Leaven in Chinese Politics," *Asia* 20 (1920): 267–72.
74. Dewey, "A Political Upheaval in China," *New Republic*, 6 October 1920, pp. 142–44.
75. Dewey, "Industrial China," *New Republic*, 8 December 1920, pp. 39–41.
76. Dewey, "Conditions for China's Nationhood," in *Characters and Events*, 1:237–43; first published as "Is China a Nation?" *New Republic*, 12 January 1921, pp. 187–90.
77. Dewey, "Transforming the Mind of China," in *Characters and Events*, 1:285–95; first published in *Asia* 19 (1919): 1103–8.
78. Dewey, "Chinese Social Habits," in *Characters and Events*, 1:211–21; first published as "What Holds China Back?" *Asia* 20 (1920): 373–77.
79. Dewey, "New Culture in China," in *Characters and Events*, 1:270–84; first published in *Asia* 21 (1921): 581–86, 642.
80. Ibid., p. 277.
81. Dewey, "On the Two Sides of the Eastern Sea," *New Republic*, 16 July 1919, pp. 346–48.
82. Dewey, "Shantung, as Seen from Within," *New Republic*, 3 March 1920, pp. 12–17.
83. Dewey, "The Far Eastern Deadlock," *New Republic*, 16 March 1921, pp. 71–74.

84. Dewey, "China's Nightmare," in *Characters and Events,* 1:193–98; first published in *New Republic,* 30 June 1920, pp. 145–47.
85. Dewey, "America and China," in *Characters and Events,* 1:296–303; first published as "The American Opportunity in China," *New Republic,* 3 December 1919, pp. 14–17.
86. Dewey, "The Consortium in China," *New Republic,* 13 April 1921, pp. 178–80.
87. Dewey, "Shantung Again," *New Republic,* 28 September 1921, pp. 123–26.
88. Dewey, "China's Nightmare," p. 196.
89. Dewey and Alice Dewey, *Letters,* pp. 263–64.
90. Dewey, "The International Duel in China," *New Republic,* 27 August 1919, pp. 110–12.
91. Ibid., p. 110.
92. Ibid., p. 112.
93. Dewey, "New Culture in China," p. 279.
94. See especially Thomas Berry, "Dewey's Influence in China," in *John Dewey: His Thought and Influence,* ed. John Blewett (New York: Fordham University Press, 1960), pp. 199–230.
95. See Homer H. Dubs, "Recent Chinese Philosophy," *Journal of Philosophy* 35 (1938): 350; and Wing-tsit Chan, "Hu Shih and Chinese Philosophy," *Philosophy East and West,* April 1956, p. 4.
96. Quoted by Hu Shih in "John Dewey in China," p. 766. The quotation is from *People's Education* (Peking), October 1959.
97. Ibid., p. 767. The quotation is from *Wenhui Pao* (Shanghai), 28 February 1955.
98. Dewey to Coss, 13 January 1920, Butler Library.
99. Dewey to Coss, 7 November 1920, Butler Library.
100. Dewey to Coss, 13 January 1920, Butler Library.
101. Jane M. Dewey, ed., "Biography of John Dewey," in *The Philosophy of John Dewey,* The Library of Living Philosophers, ed. Paul A. Schilpp, vol. 1 (Evanston: Northwestern University, 1939), p. 42.

CHAPTER 11. COLUMBIA UNIVERSITY, 1921–1925

1. Dewey to John J. Coss, 22 April 1920, Special Collections, Butler Library, Columbia University, New York City. In this same letter, referring to his *Reconstruction in Philosophy,* Dewey wrote: "I tried to sum up my past in that, and get rid of it for a fresh start."
2. Dewey, *Human Nature and Conduct* (New York: Henry Holt & Co., 1922).
3. Dewey and James H. Tufts, *Ethics* (New York: Henry Holt & Co., 1908).
4. Dewey, *Human Nature and Conduct,* p. 16.
5. Ibid., p. iii.
6. Horace M. Kallen, "The Twilight of the Moralists," *New Republic,* 24 May 1922, p. 381.
7. Hartley B. Alexander, "The Paul Carus Foundation," in *Experi-*

ence and Nature, by Dewey, Lectures upon the Paul Carus Foundation, 1st series (Chicago: Open Court Publishing Co., 1925), p. xi.

8. *Journal of Philosophy* 19 (1922): 720–21.
9. Dewey, *Experience and Nature,* Lectures upon the Paul Carus Foundation, 1st series (Chicago: Open Court Publishing Co., 1925).
10. Ibid., p. 41.
11. Walter B. Veazie, a former student of Dewey's, wrote: "Sometime during the academic year 1915–16 several graduate students at Columbia were attempting to draw up a classification of recent philosophers and philosophical systems. Where to place Dewey was a delicate question. Someone suggested, 'Why not ask him?' Dewey's reply: 'That is easy. With the revival of Greek Philosophy'" ("John Dewey and the Revival of Greek Philosophy," in *University of Colorado Studies,* Series in Philosophy, no. 2 [Boulder: University of Colorado Press, 1961], p. 3). John H. Randall, Jr., remarked: "Dewey was not, like Woodbridge, inside the classic tradition looking out. He stood outside it, looking in. . . . He was fascinated by it" ("John Dewey, 1859–1952," *Journal of Philosophy* 50 [1953]: 7).
12. Dewey, *Experience and Nature,* p. 2.
13. Ibid., p. 51. In an earlier essay, "The Subject-Matter of Metaphysical Inquiry," *Journal of Philosophy* 12 (1915): 337–45, Dewey wrote that metaphysics has to do with "certain irreducible traits found in any and every subject of scientific inquiry" (p. 338). Though different, this statement is not inconsistent with what Dewey said later.
14. Dewey, *Experience and Nature,* p. 44.
15. Ibid., p. 71.
16. Ibid., p. 261.
17. Ibid., p. 35.
18. Ibid., p. 272.
19. Ibid., p. 104.
20. Dewey, *Experience and Nature,* 3d ed. (La Salle, Ill.: Open Court Publishing Co., 1958), p. 88.
21. Dewey, *Experience and Nature,* p. 96.
22. Ibid., p. 413.
23. Ibid., p. 265.
24. Ibid., p. 267.
25. Ibid., p. 265.
26. Ibid., p. 114.
27. Ibid., p. 361.
28. Dewey, *Experience and Nature,* 2d ed. (New York: W. W. Norton, 1929), p. v.
29. Dewey, *Experience and Nature,* p. 136.
30. Ibid., p. 26.
31. Dewey, *Experience and Nature,* 2d ed., p. vi.
32. Dewey, *Experience and Nature,* p. 303.
33. Ibid., p. 389.

34. Dewey, *Experience and Nature*, 2d ed., p. viii.
35. Dewey, *Experience and Nature*, pp. 358, 359, 361.
36. Ibid., p. 358.
37. Ibid., pp. 392–93. Dewey's theory of art is most fully developed in his *Art as Experience* (New York: Minton, Balch & Co., 1934).
38. Dewey, *Experience and Nature*, 2d ed., p. ix.
39. Dewey, *Experience and Nature*, p. 398.
40. Ibid., p. 405.
41. Ibid., p. 408.
42. Ibid., p. 413.
43. Ibid.
44. Joseph K. Hart, "*Experience and Nature*," *Survey*, 15 November 1925, p. 239.
45. Mark De Wolfe Howe, ed., *Holmes-Pollock Letters*, vol. 2 (Cambridge: Harvard University Press, 1941), p. 287.
46. Randall, "John Dewey, 1859–1952," p. 9.
47. Dewey, *Experience and Nature*, 2d ed., p. 3a.
48. Herbert W. Carr, review of *Experience and Nature*, *Philosophical Review* 35 (1926): 64.
49. George P. Adams, review of *Experience and Nature*, *International Journal of Ethics*, January 1926, p. 201.
50. Ibid., p. 204.
51. George Santayana, "Dewey's Naturalistic Metaphysics," *Journal of Philosophy* 22 (1925): 678.
52. Ibid., p. 680.
53. Ibid., p. 678.
54. Dewey, "Half-Hearted Naturalism," *Journal of Philosophy* 24 (1927): 58.
55. Ibid.
56. Dewey, *Experience and Nature*, 2d ed., pp. 3a–3b.
57. Ibid., p. 3a.
58. Ibid., p. iii.
59. Ibid., p. 4a.
60. Dewey, "Shall We Join the League?" in *Characters and Events*, ed. Joseph Ratner, vol. 2 (New York: Henry Holt & Co., 1929), pp. 620–28; first published in *New Republic*, 7 March 1923, pp. 36–37, and ibid., 28 March 1923, pp. 139–40.
61. Ibid., p. 624.
62. Ibid., p. 625.
63. Dewey, "Our National Dilemma," in *Characters and Events*, 2:615–19; first published in *New Republic*, 24 March 1920, pp. 117–18.
64. Ibid., p. 616.
65. Ibid., p. 619.
66. For an excellent and detailed account of Levinson and the part he played in the outlawry of war movement, see John E. Stoner, *S. O. Levinson and the Pact of Paris* (Chicago: University of Chicago Press, 1943).

67. Interview of 12 April 1960 with Ronald B. Levinson, son of Salmon O. Levinson, of the University of Maine.
68. Salmon O. Levinson, "The Legal Status of War," *New Republic*, 9 March 1918, pp. 171–73.
69. Dewey, "Morals and the Conduct of States," *New Republic*, 23 March 1918, pp. 232–34.
70. American Committee for the Outlawry of War to Mrs. Charles R. Miller, 15 November 1924, Special Collections, The Joseph Regenstein Library, University of Chicago, Chicago, Ill.
71. Dewey, "Ethics and International Relations," *Foreign Affairs*, March 1923, pp. 85–95; "Political Combination or Legal Cooperation," *New Republic*, 21 March 1923, pp. 89–91; "If War Were Outlawed," ibid., 25 April 1923, pp. 234–35; "What Outlawry of War Is Not," ibid., 3 October 1923, pp. 149–52. This last article was written in reply to one by Walter Lippmann entitled "The Outlawry of War," *Atlantic Monthly* 132 (1923): 245–53, in which Lippmann spoke slightingly of the movement. John Haynes Holmes, prominent Unitarian minister in New York City, declared in a letter to Levinson: "I read John Dewey's article in answer to Walter Lippmann last night and I have been in a state almost of hysterics ever since. Lippmann's article was so clever that it disturbed me more perhaps than I ever intimated to you. The way Dewey's mind, however, has found the weaknesses in Lippmann's armor is positively uncanny. All in all, Dewey's article is one of the most brilliant pieces of controversial writing that I have ever seen and one more evidence that Dewey's mind is well nigh unmatched in our world today. Think of what it means to have such an intellect on your side!" (Quoted in Levinson to Dewey, 4 October 1923, Salmon O. Levinson Papers, The Joseph Regenstein Library.) "Shall the United States Join the World Court?" *Christian Century* 40 (1923): 1329–34; "War and a Code of Law," *New Republic*, 24 October 1923, pp. 224–26.
72. Dewey, *Outlawry of War: What It Is and Is Not* (Chicago: American Committee for the Outlawry of War, 1923).
73. Levinson to Dewey, 23 November 1923, Levinson Papers.
74. Levinson to Dewey, 28 March 1923, Levinson Papers.
75. Dewey, "Outlawry of War," in *Encyclopedia of the Social Sciences*, vol. 11 (New York: Macmillan Co., 1933), p. 510.
76. "Backed for Nobel Prize: S. O. Levinson of Chicago Is Sponsored by Professor Dewey," *New York Times*, 28 May 1930, p. 24.
77. Stoner, *S. O. Levinson*, p. 343. For a quite different account of the importance of the role played by Levinson in preparing the way for the Kellogg-Briand Pact, see James T. Shotwell, *The Autobiography of James T. Shotwell* (Indianapolis: Bobbs-Merrill Co., 1961), pp. 213–19.
78. Dewey to Levinson, 21 December 1918, Levinson Papers.
79. Dewey, "Dewey Aids La Follette," *New York Times*, 23 October 1924, p. 2.

80. William Shack, *Art and Argyrol: The Life and Career of Dr. Albert C. Barnes* (New York: Thomas Yoseloff, 1960), p. 101.
81. For example, see Sidney Hook, "Some Memories of John Dewey," *Commentary* 14 (1952): 249–50.
82. "Albert Coombs Barnes," in *Current Biography: Who's News and Why, 1945,* ed. Anna Rothe (New York: H. W. Wilson Co., 1945), p. 39.
83. For Dewey's dedicatory address, see "Dedication Address," *Journal of the Barnes Foundation,* May 1925, pp. 3–6.
84. Albert C. Barnes, *The Art in Painting* (Merion, Pa.: Barnes Foundation Press, 1925), p. [v].
85. "Albert Coombs Barnes," p. 38.
86. Dewey, *Art as Experience* (New York: Minton, Balch & Co., 1934).
87. Ibid., p. viii.
88. Shack, *Art and Argyrol,* p. 191.
89. Ibid., p. 315.
90. *L.I.D. Monthly,* February 1931, p. 2. For a history of the league, see Harry W. Laidler, ed., *League for Industrial Democracy: Forty Years of Education, the Task Ahead, A Symposium* (New York: League for Industrial Democracy, 1945).
91. I am indebted to the late Harry W. Laidler, longtime executive director of the league, for this account of Dewey's connections with the organization.
92. Typewritten manuscript, 34 pp., undated, Special Collections, Butler Library, Columbia University, New York City. [Dewey, *Report and Recommendation upon Turkish Education* (n.p.: Research and Measurement Bureau of the Ministry of Education, 1960). Published in Turkish, 1939.]
93. Dewey, "Secularizing a Theocracy: Young Turkey and the Caliphate," *New Republic,* 17 September 1924, pp. 69–71; "Angora, the New," ibid., 15 October 1924, pp. 169–70; "The Turkish Tragedy," ibid., 12 November 1924, pp. 268–69; "Foreign Schools in Turkey," ibid., 3 December 1924, pp. 40–42; "The Problem of Turkey," ibid., 7 January 1925, pp. 162–63.

CHAPTER 12. COLUMBIA UNIVERSITY, 1926–1930

1. Dewey, *The Public and Its Problems* (New York: Henry Holt & Co., 1927).
2. Walter Lippmann, *The Phantom Public* (New York: Harcourt, Brace & Co., 1925).
3. Dewey, "Practical Democracy," *New Republic,* 2 December 1925, pp. 52–54.
4. Ibid., p. 54.
5. Dewey, *Public and Its Problems,* pp. 15–16.
6. Ibid., p. 33.
7. Ibid., p. 126.

8. Ibid., p. 117.
9. T. V. Smith, *Philosophical Review* 38 (1929): 180. Among other reviews were: William E. Hocking, *Journal of Philosophy* 26 (1929): 329–35; O. de Selincourt, *Mind* n.s. 37 (1928): 368–70; Robert M. Lovett, *New Republic*, 24 August 1927, pp. 22–23; and Harold J. Laski, *Saturday Review*, 15 October 1927, pp. 198–99.
10. Dewey, "Why I Am for Smith," *New Republic*, 7 November 1928, p. 320.
11. Ibid., p. 321.
12. Dewey, *Public and Its Problems*, p. 202.
13. Benjamin C. Marsh, *Lobbyist for the People: A Record of Fifty Years* (Washington, D.C.: Public Affairs Press, 1953), pp. 87–88.
14. "Attacks Wage Disparity," *New York Times*, 26 December 1929, p. 28.
15. "Child Relief Steps Urged on Congress," *New York Times*, 30 December 1929, p. 19.
16. Dewey, "Asks Federal Fund to Aid Unemployed," *New York Times*, 12 May 1930, p. 35.
17. Dewey, "Asks Hoover to Act on Unemployment," *New York Times*, 21 July 1930, p. 17.
18. Dewey, "Puts Need of Idle at Two Billions," *New York Times*, 26 October 1930, p. 21.
19. "John Dewey Assails the Major Parties," *New York Times*, 14 October 1929, p. 2.
20. "Liberals Here Plan an Opposition Party; Prof. Dewey Heads National Organizing Group," *New York Times*, 9 September 1929, p. 1.
21. Dewey, "What Do Liberals Want?" *Outlook and Independent* 153 (1929): 261.
22. Dewey, "Why I Am a Member of the Teachers Union," *American Teacher*, January 1928, p. 4.
23. Ibid., p. 6.
24. Dewey, "The Manufacturers' Association and the Public Schools," *Journal of the National Education Association* 17 (1928): 61–62.
25. "Finds Mothers Fail as Home Teachers," *New York Times*, 9 March 1928, p. 52. For Dewey's address, see "Progressive Education and the Science of Education," *Progressive Education*, July–September 1928, pp. 197–204.
26. Dewey, "Labor Politics and Labor Education," *New Republic*, 2 January 1929, p. 213.
27. These articles were: "Church and State in Mexico," *New Republic*, 25 August 1926, pp. 9–10; "Mexico's Educational Renaissance," ibid., 22 September 1926, pp. 116–18; "From a Mexican Notebook," ibid., 20 October 1926, pp. 239–41; and "Imperialism Is Easy," ibid., 23 March 1927, pp. 133–34.
28. Jane M. Dewey, ed., "Biography of John Dewey," in *The Philosophy of John Dewey*, The Library of Living Philosophers, ed. Paul A.

Schilpp, vol. 1 (Evanston: Northwestern University, 1939), p. 42.

29. Dewey to David E. Smith, 12 August 1927, Special Collections, Butler Library, Columbia University, New York City.
30. See telegram, Dewey to Mr. and Mrs. S. O. Levinson, 14 July 1927; telegram, Levinson to Dewey, 14 July 1927; Dewey to Levinson, 22 July 1927; Salmon O. Levinson Papers, Special Collections, The Joseph Regenstein Library, University of Chicago, Chicago, Ill. See also Dewey to David E. Smith, 12 August 1927, and Dewey to John J. Coss, 22 July 1927, Butler Library.
31. Dewey, "In Response," in *John Dewey, the Man and His Philosophy: Addresses Delivered in New York in Celebration of His Seventieth Birthday* (Cambridge: Harvard University Press, 1930), p. 177. Dewey's children resented Max Eastman's account of their mother's last years in which he said that toward the end of her life Mrs. Dewey became, "although still full of witty charm, impossible except for saints to live with." They have denounced the account as grossly unfair and have been at a loss to explain it, especially when they recall that Eastman when a student at Columbia had so often enjoyed their mother's hospitality. (Interview of 25 August 1967 with Jane Dewey and Lucy [Dewey] Brandauer. See "John Dewey," *Atlantic Monthly* 168 [1941]: 671–85.)
32. Dewey to Levinson, 22 July 1927, Levinson Papers; Dewey to David E. Smith, 12 August 1927, Butler Library.
33. Dewey, "Psychology and Justice," in *Characters and Events*, ed. Joseph Ratner, vol. 2 (New York: Henry Holt & Co., 1929), pp. 526–36; first published in *New Republic*, 23 November 1927, pp. 9–12.
34. Ibid., p. 536.
35. Among others on the committee were Jane Addams, Albert C. Barnes, Walter Lippmann, George H. Mead, Helen Parkhurst, Roscoe Pound, and James H. Tufts. Though Epstein's usual fee for a bust was $5,000, he agreed to do the Dewey bust for half that amount. (See Ratner to Levinson, 12 May 1928, Levinson Papers.)
36. "Columbia Unveils John Dewey Bust," *New York Times*, 10 November 1928, p. 17. The bust, for many years on display in the library room of Teachers College, is now at the Center for Dewey Studies in Carbondale, Illinois, on loan from the John Dewey Foundation.
37. In May 1924, an item in the press said that Dewey had been invited to Russia by the widow of Lenin to assist in establishing a Russian school system along the lines of the American system. (See "Educator Dewey Sought by Russia for Schools' Aid," *New York World*, 5 May 1924, and "Says Russia Uses America as Model: Invitation from Mme. Lenin to Dewey," *New York Times*, 6 May 1924, p. 3.) When S. O. Levinson congratulated Dewey on the honor, Dewey replied, "I don't know anything more about the Russian

business than what I read in the papers" (Levinson to Dewey, 9 May 1924, Levinson Papers; Dewey to Levinson, 10 May 1924, Levinson Papers.) Nothing further was heard of the matter; Dewey's 1928 visit to the Soviet Union was without any invitation to help develop the Soviet school system.

38. "American Educators in Russia," *School and Society* 27 (1928): 779. This account gives also a complete list of the names of the delegates.
39. For many of the details of Dewey's trip, I am indebted to Elizabeth [Mrs. Frederick] Dewey who kindly allowed me to use the diary she kept of her travels.
40. Diary of Elizabeth Dewey, 3 July 1928.
41. Dewey, *Impressions of Soviet Russia and the Revolutionary World: Mexico—China—Turkey* (New York: New Republic, 1929), p. 30.
42. Ibid., p. 31.
43. Ibid., p. 33.
44. Walter Duranty, "Russians Entertain for John Dewey," *New York Times*, 22 July 1928, p. 6.
45. Dewey, "Impressions of Soviet Russia," *New Republic*, 17 November 1928, pp. 343–44; ibid., 21 November 1928, pp. 11–14; ibid., 28 November 1928, pp. 38–42; ibid., 5 December 1928, pp. 64–67; ibid., 12 December 1928, pp. 91–94; and ibid., 19 December 1928, pp. 134–37.
46. Dewey, *Impressions*, p. 61.
47. Ibid., p. 105.
48. Ibid., p. 94.
49. Ibid., p. 82.
50. Ibid., p. 4.
51. Ibid., p. 24.
52. Ibid., p. 8.
53. Ibid., p. 7.
54. Ibid., p. 114.
55. Ibid., p. 130.
56. "Labor Expunges Tribute to Dewey," *New York Times*, 29 November 1928, p. 12. See also Dewey, "Mr. Woll as a Communist Catcher," *New Republic*, 13 March 1929, p. 99.
57. R. E. Darnell to the Dean, College of Arts and Sciences, University of Vermont, 18 November 1961, George Dykhuizen Papers and Correspondence, Special Collections, Guy W. Bailey Library, University of Vermont, Burlington, Vt.
58. Ewing to Dewey, 12 March 1928. Photostatic copies of the letters, cablegrams, and telegrams involved in the correspondence between the University of Edinburgh and Dewey were kindly sent to the writer by Miss C. M. Masterton, Administrative Assistant at the university.
59. Dewey, *The Quest for Certainty* (New York: Minton, Balch & Co., 1929).

60. Ibid., p. 13.
61. Ibid., p. 14.
62. Ibid., p. 17.
63. Ibid.
64. Ibid., p. 26.
65. Ibid., p. 8.
66. Ibid., p. 111. The quotation is from Percy W. Bridgman, *The Logic of Modern Physics* (New York: Macmillan Co., 1927), p. 5.
67. Ibid., p. 111n. The quotation is from A. S. Eddington, *The Nature of the Physical World* (New York: Macmillan Co., 1928), p. 255.
68. Ibid., p. 137.
69. Ibid., p. 259.
70. Ibid., p. 114.
71. Ibid., p. 287. [In early printings of this book the phrase appeared as "Copernican evolution"; it was subsequently corrected.]
72. Ibid., p. 304.
73. Max C. Otto, review of *The Quest for Certainty, Philosophical Review* 40 (1931): 81.
74. John W. Buckham, "Progressive Pragmatism," *Methodist Review* 113 (1930): 729.
75. Ferdinand C. S. Schiller, review of *The Quest for Certainty, Mind* n.s. 39 (1930): 374.
76. T. V. Smith, "Dewey's *The Quest for Certainty*: A Symposium," *Religious Education* 25 (1930): 73.
77. Otto, review of *The Quest for Certainty*, p. 79.
78. Julius S. Bixler, "Professor Dewey Discusses Religion," *Harvard Theological Review* 23 (1930): 219.
79. Herman H. Horne, *John Dewey's Philosophy, Especially the "Quest for Certainty"* (Boston: Boston University School of Religious Education and Social Service, n.d., probably written in 1930 or 1931), pp. 23–24.
80. *Essays in Honor of John Dewey on the Occasion of His Seventieth Birthday, October 20, 1929* (New York: Henry Holt & Co., 1929).
81. James R. Angell, "The Toastmaster's Words," in *John Dewey, the Man and His Philosophy: Addresses Delivered in New York in Celebration of His Seventieth Birthday* (Cambridge: Harvard University Press, 1930), pp. 136–37.
82. Ibid., pp. 137–38.
83. Dewey, "In Response," in *John Dewey, the Man and His Philosophy*, p. 180.
84. Ibid., p. 181.
85. *John Dewey, the Man and His Philosophy: Addresses Delivered in New York in Celebration of His Seventieth Birthday* (Cambridge: Harvard University Press, 1930).
86. *New York Times*, 21 October 1929, p. 26.
87. *New York Herald Tribune*, 19 October 1929.
88. *New York World*, 20 October 1929.

89. Irwin Edman, "Our Foremost Philosopher at Seventy," *New York Times Magazine*, 13 October 1929, pp. 17, 74, 75.
90. Herbert W. Schneider, "He Modernized Our Schools," *New York Herald Tribune*, 13 October 1929.
91. Scott Buchanan, "John Dewey," *Nation* 129 (1929): 458–59.
92. Robert M. Lovett, "John Dewey at Seventy," *New Republic*, 23 October 1929, pp. 262–64.
93. Dewey, *Individualism, Old and New* (New York: Minton, Balch & Co., 1930). Most of the material in the book was first presented as a series of articles in the *New Republic* from 24 April 1929 to 2 April 1930.
94. Ibid., p. 82.
95. Ibid., p. 168.
96. Ibid., p. 93.
97. Ibid., p. 32.
98. Ibid., p. 83.
99. Ibid., p. 99.
100. Ibid., p. 167.
101. Ibid.
102. John Chamberlain, "John Dewey Looks toward a New Individualism," *New York Times Book Review*, 21 December 1930, p. 2.
103. Butler to Dewey, 24 December 1929, Dewey Papers, Morris Library, Southern Illinois University, Carbondale, Ill.
104. Butler to Dewey, 3 March 1930, Dewey Papers. Dewey's salary as of 1 July 1928 was $12,000, the highest given at that time to a full professor at Columbia. (See Butler to Dewey, 5 April 1928, Dewey Papers.)
105. Horace Coon, *Columbia, Colossus on the Hudson*, American College and University Series, vol. 1 (New York: E. P. Dutton & Co., 1947), p. 34.
106. Howard L. McBain, "Report of the Dean for the Academic Year Ending June 30, 1930," in Columbia University, *Annual Report of the President and Treasurer to the Trustees, with Accompanying Documents for the Year Ending June 30, 1930* (New York: n.p., n.d.), p. 225.
107. See John H. Randall, Jr., "The Department of Philosophy," in *A History of the Faculty of Philosophy, Columbia University*, ed. Jacques Barzun (New York: Columbia University Press, 1957), pp. 126, 127.
108. Lawrence A. Cremin, David A. Shannon, and Mary E. Townsend, *A History of Teachers College, Columbia University* (New York: Columbia University Press, 1954), p. 46.
109. In the account which follows, I have relied mainly on the following works, all written by former students of Dewey: Irwin Edman, *Philosopher's Holiday* (New York: Viking Press, 1938), pp. 138–43; Sidney Hook, *John Dewey: An Intellectual Portrait* (New York: John Day Co., 1939), pp. 3–27; Harold A. Larrabee, "John Dewey

as Teacher," in *John Dewey: Master Educator,* ed. William W. Brickman and Stanley Lehrer (New York: Society for the Advancement of Education, 1959), pp. 50–57; and Randall, "The Department of Philosophy," pp. 102–45.

110. Hook, *John Dewey: An Intellectual Portrait,* p. 18.
111. Edman, *Philosopher's Holiday,* p. 141.
112. Ibid., pp. 142–43.
113. Randall, "Department of Philosophy," p. 129.

CHAPTER 13. EMERITUS, COLUMBIA UNIVERSITY, 1930–1935

1. *News Bulletin of the League for Independent Political Action,* November 1930, p. 3.
2. Dewey to Norris, 23 December 1930. Quoted in *News Bulletin of the League,* January 1931, p. 1.
3. *News Bulletin of the League,* January 1931, pp. 1–2.
4. Norris to Dewey, 26 December 1930. Quoted in *News Bulletin of the League,* January 1931, p. 2.
5. *News Bulletin of the League,* January 1931, p. 2.
6. "Senate Insurgents Afraid, Says Dewey," *New York Times,* 31 December 1930, p. 3. See also the editorial "Smoking Them Out," *New York Times,* 1 January 1931, p. 28.
7. "The Press on a Third Party," *New York Times,* 14 January 1931, p. 24.
8. "The Professor and the Senator," *New York Times,* 27 December 1930, p. 12.
9. Dewey, "The Need for a New Party," *New Republic,* 18 March 1931, pp. 115–17; ibid., 25 March 1931, pp. 150–52; ibid., 1 April 1931, pp. 177–79; ibid., 8 April 1931, pp. 202–5.
10. Dewey voted for the Socialist candidate, Norman Thomas, in the presidential elections of 1932 and 1936.
11. For a detailed statement of the League's 1932 platform, see "Platform and Program of the League for Independent Action," *News Bulletin of the League,* September–October 1932, p. 4.
12. Dewey, "The Imperative Need for a New Radical Party," *Common Sense* 2 (1933): 7; reprinted as "Imperative Need: A New Radical Party," in *Challenge to the New Deal,* ed. Alfred M. Bingham and Selden Rodman (New York: Falcon Press, 1934), pp. 269–73.
13. Dewey, "No Half Way House for America," *People's Lobby Bulletin,* November 1934, p. 1.
14. Ibid. Political liberals and radicals such as Dewey were not alone in demanding fundamental changes in the methods of conducting the nation's economy. The churches were almost unanimous in declaring that laissez-faire methods must give way to national economic planning, that competition and exploitation must yield to cooperation and sharing. (See extracts of the statements of the spokesmen for: the Federal Council of the Churches of Christ, the Methodist Episcopal Church, the Congregational-Christian Church,

the Protestant Episcopal Church, the Roman Catholic Church, the Unitarian Association, the Jewish Commission on Social Justice, in "The Church Does Not Mince Words," *Social Frontier*, December 1934, p. 27.)

15. Dewey, "Full Warehouses and Empty Stomachs," *People's Lobby Bulletin*, May 1931, pp. 1–3; "Challenge to Progressive Senators to Ask for Relief," ibid., June 1931, p. 5; "You Must Act to Get Congress to Act," ibid., May 1932, p. 1; "Voters Must Demand Congress Tax Wealth Instead of Want," ibid., June 1932, p. 1; "Get Mayor and Governor to Demand Relief," ibid., November 1932, p. 1; "Relief Is Vital," ibid., February 1933, pp. 1–2; "The Drive against Hunger," *New Republic*, 29 March 1933, p. 190; "President's Policies Help Property Owners Chiefly," *People's Lobby Bulletin*, June 1934, pp. 1–2.
16. Levinson to Dewey, 16 June 1931, Salmon O. Levinson Papers, Special Collections, The Joseph Regenstein Library, University of Chicago, Chicago, Ill.
17. Dewey to Levinson, 18 June 1931, Levinson Papers.
18. Levinson to Dewey, 11 April 1932, Levinson Papers.
19. Dewey to Levinson, 1 November 1932, Levinson Papers.
20. Levinson to Dewey, 2 March 1933, Levinson Papers.
21. Dewey to Levinson, 8 March 1933, Levinson Papers.
22. See Edwin C. Broome, "The Present Crisis and Public Education," *School and Society* 35 (1932): 302.
23. Dewey, "Education and Our Present Social Problems," *School and Society* 37 (1933): 474.
24. Ibid., p. 478.
25. Ibid., p. 475.
26. Dewey, "Teachers as Citizens." For an account of this talk, see Anna L. P. Collins in *American Teacher*, October 1931, p. 7. Dewey, "The Economic Situation: A Challenge to Education," *Journal of Home Economics* 24 (1932): 495–501; "The Crisis in Education," *American Teacher*, April 1933, pp. 5–9; "Shall We Abolish School 'Frills'? No," *Rotarian*, May 1933, pp. 18–19, 49; "The Teacher and the Public," *Vital Speeches*, 28 January 1935, pp. 278–79; "Can Education Share in Social Reconstruction?" *Social Frontier*, October 1934, pp. 11–12.
27. For example, in 1932 fifty-two writers, artists, and intellectuals signed a manifesto supporting the Communist party and endorsing William Z. Foster for president. For the names of some of the more outstanding signers, see Daniel Bell, "The Background and Development of Marxian Socialism in the United States," in *Socialism and American Life*, ed. Donald D. Egbert and Stow Persons, vol. 1 (Princeton, N.J.: Princeton University Press, 1952), p. 354.
28. Nelson M. Blake, *A History of American Life and Thought*, 2d ed. (New York: McGraw-Hill Book Co., 1972), p. 547.
29. See Dewey, "On the Grievance Committee's Report," *Union*

Teacher, May 1933, p. 3; see also Henry R. Linville, "Can the Union Solve the Left-Wing Problem?" ibid., pp. 4–5.

30. William W. Wattenberg, *On the Education Front: The Reactions of Teachers Associations in New York and Chicago* (New York: Columbia University Press, 1936), p. 147.
31. Jane M. Dewey, ed., "Biography of John Dewey," in *The Philosophy of John Dewey*, The Library of Living Philosophers, ed. Paul A. Schilpp, vol. 1 (Evanston: Northwestern University, 1939), p. 39.
32. Dewey and James H. Tufts, *Ethics*, rev. ed. (New York: Henry Holt & Co., 1932).
33. Dewey, *How We Think*, rev. and expanded ed. (Boston: D. C. Heath & Co., 1933).
34. Dewey, *Art as Experience* (New York: Minton, Balch & Co., 1934).
35. Ibid., p. 35.
36. Ibid., p. 46.
37. Ibid., pp. 132–33.
38. Ibid., p. 65.
39. Ibid., p. 325.
40. Ibid., p. 54.
41. Ibid., p. 326.
42. Ibid., p. 270.
43. Ibid., p. 271.
44. Ibid., p. 270.
45. Dewey, *Experience and Nature*, Lectures upon the Paul Carus Foundation, 1st series (Chicago: Open Court Publishing Co., 1925), ch. 9, especially pp. 392–93.
46. Dewey, *Art as Experience*, p. 274.
47. Ernest S. Bates, "John Dewey's Æsthetics," *American Mercury* 33 (1934): 253. See also Samuel L. Faison, Jr., "Three Critics of Modern Art," *Yale Review*, September 1934, pp. 188–89.
48. David W. Prall, review of *Art as Experience*, *Philosophical Review* 44 (1935): 390.
49. Dewey, *A Common Faith* (New Haven: Yale University Press, 1934).
50. Ibid., p. 9.
51. Ibid., p. 13.
52. Ibid., p. 27.
53. Ibid., p. 9.
54. Ibid., p. 57.
55. Ibid., p. 52.
56. Ibid., p. 51. Sidney Hook has some interesting comments about his discussion with Dewey as to the appropriateness of Dewey's use of the term "God":

> I worked closely with him on the manuscript of his *A Common Faith*. It is a thoroughly naturalistic approach to religion. The only thing I disagreed with was his use of the term "God" for faith in the validity of moral ideals. Dewey's God is not the God of Abraham, Isaac, and Jacob; nor of Plato, Aristotle, and Aquinas, nor of Spinoza, Kant, or

Hegel; nor of James or Schiller. Why then use it, I asked. He argued that the term had no unequivocal meaning in the history of thought; that there was no danger of its being misunderstood (in which he was shortly proved wrong); and that there was no reason why its emotive associations of the sacred, profound, and ultimate should be surrendered to the supernaturalist, especially since for him not religion but the religious experience is central. All this seemed to me to be legitimate if not sufficient grounds. But then he added something which men like Russell or Cohen would never have dreamed of saying: "Besides there are so many people who would feel bewildered if not hurt were they denied the intellectual right to use the term 'God.' They are not in the churches, they believe what I believe, they would feel a loss if they could not speak of God. Why then shouldn't I use the term?" (Sidney Hook, "Some Memories of John Dewey," *Commentary* 14 [1952]: 253).

As Hook foresaw, Dewey's use of the term "God" did lead to misunderstanding. Some of his readers, especially in theological circles, believed that by extending the meaning of the term "God" to include nonhuman or superhuman forces operating in and through nature, Dewey had adopted a position similar to that of historic theism. This misapprehension of his views prompted Dewey to reaffirm his naturalism and humanism, denying having made important concessions to traditional theism. (See, for example, Henry N. Wieman, "John Dewey's Common Faith," *Christian Century* 51 [1934]: 1450–52; reply to Wieman by Edwin E. Aubrey, "Is John Dewey a Theist?" ibid., p. 1550; reply to Aubrey and Wieman by Dewey, ibid., pp. 1551–52; reply to Dewey by Wieman, ibid., pp. 1552–53.)

57. Dewey, *A Common Faith*, p. 53.
58. Ibid., p. 55.
59. Ibid., p. 83.
60. Ibid., p. 87.
61. For some reviews of Dewey's *A Common Faith*, see Robert Scoon, *Journal of Philosophy* 31 (1934): 584–85; Ferdinand C. S. Schiller, *Mind* n.s. 44 (1935): 397–99; Reinhold Niebuhr, "A Footnote on Religion," *Nation* 139 (1934): 358–59; Max C. Otto, *Philosophical Review* 44 (1935): 496–97; Henry Hazlitt, "But Is It Religion?" *Yale Review*, September 1934, pp. 166–68.
62. John H. Randall, Jr., "Art and Religion as Education," *Social Frontier*, January 1936, p. 110.
63. See the brochure, *South African Education Conference of the New Education Fellowship to Be Held at Cape Town 2nd to 13th July, 1934; Johannesburg 16th to 27th July, 1934* ("printed in South Africa," n.d., n.p.). I am indebted to Miss Florence Anderson of the Carnegie Corporation of New York for a Xeroxed copy of the brochure.
64. E. G. Malherbe, "Editor's Introduction," in *Educational Adaptations in a Changing Society: Report of the South African Education Conference Held in Capetown and Johannesburg in July, 1934, under the Auspices of the New Education Fellowship*, ed.

E. G. Malherbe, J. J. G. Carson, and J. D. Rheinallt Jones (Capetown and Johannesburg: Juta & Co., 1937), pp. iii, iv.

65. Malherbe, ed., *Educational Adaptations*, p. 539. The corporation defrayed the traveling expenses of four other specially invited overseas speakers who came long distances. For a list of the specially invited overseas speakers, see the above-mentioned brochure.
66. Dewey, "The Need for a Philosophy of Education," "What is Learning?" "Growth in Activity," in *Educational Adaptations*, pp. 22–28, 91–93, 120–22.
67. Jane Dewey to Dykhuizen, 5 March 1967, George Dykhuizen Papers and Correspondence, Special Collections, Guy W. Bailey Library, University of Vermont, Burlington, Vt.
68. Dewey, *Liberalism and Social Action* (New York: G. P. Putnam's Sons, 1935).
69. Ibid., p. 21.
70. Ibid., p. 54.
71. Ibid., p. 62.
72. Ibid., p. 55.
73. Dewey, *Philosophy and Civilization* (New York: Minton, Balch & Co., 1931), p. 330.
74. Dewey, *Liberalism and Social Action*, p. 58.
75. Ibid., p. 86. Dewey's one exception to his doctrine of nonviolence was "when society through an authorized majority has entered upon the path of social experimentation leading to great social change, and a minority refuses by force to permit the method of intelligent action to go into effect. Then force may be intelligently employed to subdue and disarm the recalcitrant minority" (ibid., p. 87).
76. Horace M. Kallen, "Salvation by Intelligence," *Saturday Review*, 14 December 1935, p. 7.
77. Sidney Hook, *John Dewey: An Intellectual Portrait* (New York: John Day Co., 1939), p. 158.
78. Reinhold Niebuhr, "The Pathos of Liberalism," *Nation* 141 (1935): 303.
79. Dewey, "When America Goes to War," *Modern Monthly*, June 1935, p. 200.
80. For a detailed account of the establishment of the University-in-Exile, see Alvin Johnson, *Pioneer's Progress: An Autobiography* (New York: Viking Press, 1952), pp. 332–48.
81. "Exiles' University Opens Here Oct. 1; Faculty German," *New York Times*, 19 August 1933, pp. 1, 5.
82. Dewey to Bentley, 20 March 1940, in *John Dewey and Arthur F. Bentley: A Philosophical Correspondence, 1932–1951*, ed. Sidney Ratner, Jules Altman, and James E. Wheeler (New Brunswick, N.J.: Rutgers University Press, 1964), p. 74.
83. Dewey to Bentley, 19 February 1942, in *Dewey-Bentley Correspondence*, p. 89.

84. See *New York and the Seabury Investigation: A Digest and Interpretation of the Reports by Samuel Seabury concerning the Government of New York City* (New York: City Affairs Committee of New York, 1933).
85. Dewey, "George Mead as I Knew Him," *University* [of Chicago] *Record* 17 (1931): 174.
86. King Albert was represented by the Belgian ambassador.
87. Interview of 28 June 1967 with Jane Dewey and Lucy (Dewey) Brandauer.
88. "[University of Paris] Honors Professor Dewey," *New York Times,* 9 November 1930, p. 12.
89. "$7,887,111 in Gifts Made to Harvard," *New York Times,* 24 June 1932, p. 14. At its meeting on 10 December 1931, the trustees of the University of Chicago "in accordance with the approval of the University Senate expressed at its meeting on November 21" voted to confer the Doctor of Laws degree on Dewey. (See, Minutes of 10 December 1931, "Board of Trustees Minutes, January–December, 1931.") There is no record of Dewey's accepting the degree and no account of why he did not. Dewey's refusal to accept the degree could very well have stemmed from President Hutchins's attempt earlier in the year to appoint Mortimer Adler to a post in the Department of Philosophy over the vigorous protest of its members. Hutchins's act led to the resignation of Mead, E. A. Burtt, Arthur E. Murphy, and others from the department. Dewey undoubtedly felt that the university's offering him a degree at this time was an attempt by Hutchins to smooth troubled waters, and Dewey did not care to be used in this way.
90. William D. Boutwell, "The Atlantic City Meeting of the National Education Association, June 25 to July 1, 1932," *School and Society* 36 (1932): 42. For an account of the alleged political maneuvering preceding the election in which Dewey was made "the butt for a coarse jest," see H. E. Buchholz, "Dewey Mocked by the NEA," *Educational Administration and Supervision* 18 (1932): 413–21.
91. Dewey to Ruth Levinson, 24 July [1931], Levinson Papers.
92. Levinson to Dewey, 26 July 1931, Levinson Papers.
93. "John Dewey, 13, Dies," *New York Times,* 30 December 1934, p. 17.
94. Levinson to Dewey, 31 December 1934, Levinson Papers.

CHAPTER 14. EMERITUS, COLUMBIA UNIVERSITY, 1935–1939

1. The *Social Frontier* began publication in October 1934 and continued to publish under that name till 1939. A section called "John Dewey's Page" was set aside for Dewey's use; articles by him appeared in each issue of the magazine from January 1935 to November 1937.
2. Dewey, "The Teacher and His World," *Social Frontier,* January 1935, p. 7.

3. Dewey, "Youth in a Confused World," *Social Frontier*, May 1935, pp. 9–10; "The Need for Orientation," *Forum* 93 (1935): 333–35.
4. Dewey, "The Crucial Role of Intelligence," *Social Frontier*, February 1935, pp. 9–10.
5. See *Social Frontier*, February 1935, pp. 3–8. The major portion of this issue is devoted to a discussion of the conservative press and the struggle to maintain freedom in the schools.
6. Dewey, "The Social Significance of Academic Freedom," *Social Frontier*, March 1936, p. 166. In the same issue appears a group of articles dealing with the significance, scope, and limitations of academic freedom.
7. Ibid., p. 165.
8. See, for example, Paul F. Douglass, "Keep the Public Schools Public," *Social Frontier*, November 1937, pp. 42–46.
9. Dewey, "Religion and Our Schools," in *Characters and Events*, ed. Joseph Ratner, vol. 2 (New York: Henry Holt & Co., 1929), p. 514; first published in *Hibbert Journal*, July 1908, pp. 796–809.
10. "School Time Voted for Church Study," *New York Times*, 14 November 1940, p. 1. Despite the large number of people speaking in opposition to the resolution, the Board of Education passed it by a 6 to 1 vote.
11. Dewey, "How Much Freedom in New Schools?" *New Republic*, 9 July 1930, p. 204. This essay was Dewey's contribution to a symposium "The New Education Ten Years After," sponsored by the *New Republic*. The ten years referred to are 1919–29, 1919 being the year the Progressive Education Association was founded. Progressive education began, of course, long before the association was formed.
12. Ibid., p. 205.
13. Ibid., p. 206.
14. Dewey, *Experience and Education* (New York: Macmillan Co., 1938). This volume is the published version of Dewey's Kappa Delta Pi Lecture delivered in Atlantic City at the 1 March 1938 meeting of the fraternity.
15. Ibid., p. 114.
16. Ibid., p. 19.
17. Ibid., pp. 16–17.
18. Ibid., p. 115.
19. Robert M. Hutchins, *The Higher Learning in America* (New Haven: Yale University Press, 1936).
20. William H. Kilpatrick. Quoted by Eunice F. Barnard, "A Teachers' Teacher Tells What Education Is," *New York Times Magazine*, 21 March 1937, p. 5.
21. Dewey, "President Hutchins' Proposals to Remake Higher Education," *Social Frontier*, January 1937, pp. 103–4. See also "Rationality in Education," ibid., December 1936, pp. 71–73, and " 'The Higher Learning in America,' " ibid., March 1937, pp. 167–69. See

also Hutchins's reply, "Grammar, Rhetoric, and Mr. Dewey," ibid., February 1937, pp. 137–39.

22. Dewey, "Hutchins' Proposals," p. 104.
23. Among its first members were George Axtelle, Boyd H. Bode, John L. Childs, George S. Counts, Sidney Hook, H. Gordon Hullfish, Alvin Johnson, William H. Kilpatrick, Jesse H. Newlon, Harold Rugg, and V. T. Thayer.
24. The Society's latest membership directory lists three hundred and sixty-four members from forty-one states and five foreign countries.
25. Similar committees had already been formed in France, England, and Czechoslovakia.
26. For the names of those signing the statement, see Eugene Lyons, *The Red Decade: The Stalinist Penetration of America* (New Rochelle, N.Y.: Arlington House, 1941), pp. 254–55.
27. Quoted in ibid., pp. 327, 329.
28. "Whitewash Expedition Leaves U.S. to Visit Trotzky in Mexico," *Daily Worker*, 3 April 1937, pp. 1–2.
29. "Trotsky Investigates Himself," *New Masses*, 20 April 1937, p. 28.
30. James T. Farrell, "Dewey in Mexico," in *John Dewey: Philosopher of Science and Freedom*, ed. Sidney Hook (New York: Dial Press, 1950), pp. 364–65.
31. *The Case of Leon Trotsky: Report of Hearings on the Charges Made against Him in the Moscow Trials by the Preliminary Commission of Inquiry*, John Dewey, Chairman; Carleton Beals (resigned); Otto Ruehle; Benjamin Stolberg; Suzanne La Follette, Secretary (New York: Harper & Bros., 1937), p. 585.

    The Preliminary Commission was not without internal dissension. Toward the end of the sessions one of its members, Carleton Beals, resigned from the commission on the ground that he was not allowed to question Trotsky along certain lines and because he felt that the commission was not conducting a really serious inquiry. In a statement to the press, Beals declared:

    > I am merely passing a fair judgment on the commission and its intolerable methods. . . . To label their efforts an investigation is to sully a fair word. The hushed adoration of the other members of the commission for Mr. Trotzky has defeated all spirit of honest investigation. . . . When our lawyer, Mr. Finerty, got through with his long-winded and meaningless cross-examination of Trotzky, the Russian leader actually had wings sprouting from his shoulders. The methods thus far followed by the commission have been a schoolboy joke and I do not wish further to be a party to something so utterly ridiculous. Thus far, no investigations have been conducted, but merely a pink tea party with every one but myself uttering sweet platitudes" (quoted in "Beals Brands 'Trial' of Trotzky Ridiculous," *Daily Worker*, 20 April 1937, p. 4).

    For Dewey's version of Beals's resignation, see *The Case of Leon Trotsky*, pp. xvii–xviii.

32. New York: Harper & Bros., 1937.
33. *Not Guilty: Report of the Commission of Inquiry into the Charges Made against Leon Trotsky in the Moscow Trials* (New York: Harper & Bros., 1938). Suzanne La Follette did the actual writing of the report.
34. "John Dewey, Great American Liberal, Denounces Russian Dictatorship," *Washington Post*, 19 December 1937.
35. Ibid.
36. Dewey, *Logic: The Theory of Inquiry* (New York: Henry Holt & Co., 1938).
37. Ibid., p. 117.
38. Ibid., p. iv.
39. Ibid., p. 16.
40. Ibid., p. 124.
41. Ibid., p. 309.
42. Ibid., p. 120.
43. Ibid., p. 310.
44. Ibid., p. 287.
45. Ibid., p. 4.
46. Ibid., p. 11.
47. Ibid., p. 104.
48. Ibid.
49. Ibid., p. 143.
50. Ibid., p. v.
51. Ibid., p. 514.
52. Ibid., p. 534.
53. William Gruen, "The Naturalization of Logic," *Nation* 147 (1938): 427.
54. For a list of reviews, articles, and symposia prompted by the *Logic,* see Milton H. Thomas, *John Dewey: A Centennial Bibliography* (Chicago: University of Chicago Press, 1962), pp. 124–25.
55. Dewey, "Logical Conditions of a Scientific Treatment of Morality," in *Investigations Representing the Departments, Part II: Philosophy, Education,* University of Chicago, The Decennial Publications, 1st series, vol. 3 (Chicago: University of Chicago Press, 1903), pp. 113–39; "The Problem of Values," *Journal of Philosophy* 10 (1913): 268–69; "The Objects of Valuation," ibid. 15 (1918): 253–58; and "Valuation and Experimental Knowledge," *Philosophical Review* 31 (1922): 325–51.
56. Dewey, *Experience and Nature,* Lectures upon the Paul Carus Foundation, 1st series (Chicago: Open Court Publishing Co., 1925), pp. 394–437.
57. Dewey, *The Quest for Certainty* (New York: Minton, Balch & Co.), pp. 254–86.
58. Dewey, *Theory of Valuation,* International Encyclopedia of Unified Science, vol. 2, no. 4 (Chicago: University of Chicago Press, 1939).

59. Ibid., p. 27.
60. Ibid., p. 51.
61. Ibid., pp. 51–52.
62. Ibid., p. 4.
63. Dewey, "Some Questions about Value," *Journal of Philosophy* 41 (1944): 449.
64. Ibid., pp. 449–55.
65. Ibid., p. 455.
66. Ray Lepley, ed., *Value: A Cooperative Inquiry* (New York: Columbia University Press, 1949).
67. Dewey, "The Field of 'Value,'" in *Value: A Cooperative Inquiry,* pp. 64–77.
68. Ibid., p. 64.
69. Lepley, *Value: A Cooperative Inquiry,* p. v.
70. Charles A. Baylis, review of *Value: A Cooperative Inquiry, Journal of Philosophy* 48 (1951): 705.
71. Bertrand Russell et al., "If War Comes, Shall We Participate or Be Neutral?" *Common Sense* 8 (1939).
72. Dewey, "No Matter What Happens—Stay Out," *Common Sense* 8 (1939): 11.
73. Ibid.
74. Dewey, *Freedom and Culture* (New York: G. P. Putnam's Sons, 1939).
75. Ibid., pp. 18–19.
76. Ibid., p. 76.
77. Ibid., p. 77.
78. Ibid., p. 80.
79. Ibid., p. 87.
80. Ibid., p. 101.
81. Ibid., p. 173.
82. Ibid., pp. 125–26.
83. Ibid., p. 167.
84. Ibid., pp. 175–76.
85. Ibid., p. 126.
86. James D. Adams, review of *Freedom and Culture, New York Times Book Review,* 6 July 1941, p. 2.
87. Edwin T. Buehrer, "Democracy, the Long, Hard Way," *Christian Century* 57 (1940): 178.
88. William Gruen, "The Battleground of Democracy," *Nation* 149 (1939): 622.
89. "Manifesto," *Nation* 148 (1939): 626.
90. More than one hundred and forty men and women prominent in the world of scholarship and art signed the Manifesto before it was made public. For the complete list of signers, see Lyons, *Red Decade,* pp. 343, 345.
91. "Liberty and Common Sense," *New Republic,* 31 May 1939, p. 89. In a letter replying to this editorial, Dewey declared that the Mani-

festo nowhere condemns socialist commonwealths as such but only the Russian communist variety. (Dewey, "The Committee for Cultural Freedom," *New Republic*, 14 June 1939, pp. 161–62.)

92. "To All Active Supporters of Democracy and Peace," *Nation* 149 (1939): 228.
93. Ibid., p. 228. This letter won the support of and was signed by some four hundred well-known figures in the academic, literary, and artistic world. For the complete list of signers, see Lyons, *Red Decade*, pp. 348–51.
94. See *The Bertrand Russell Case*, ed. Dewey and Horace M. Kallen (New York: Viking Press, 1941), pp. 7–10, 57–74.
95. For some of these lists, see Lyons, *Red Decade*, pp. 374–76.
96. Dewey, "Democracy and Educational Administration," *School and Society* 45 (1937): 457–62.
97. Dewey, "Anniversary Address," *Journal of the Michigan Schoolmasters' Club 1936*, 25 July 1936, pp. 5–13; abridged in *Education Digest*, November 1936, pp. 1–3.
98. Dewey, "Authority and Resistance to Social Change," *School and Society* 44 (1936): 457–66.
99. Dewey, "Education, the Foundation for Social Organization," in *Educating for Democracy: A Symposium* (Yellow Springs, Ohio: Antioch Press, 1937), pp. 37–54.
100. "Teach Realities, Dr. Dewey Urges," *New York Times*, 14 November 1936, p. 21.
101. Dewey, "The Challenge of Democracy to Education," *Progressive Education*, February 1937, pp. 79–85.
102. Dewey, "Education and Social Change," *Social Frontier*, May 1937, pp. 235–38.
103. Dewey, "Education: 1800–1939," *Vermont Alumnus*, May 1939, pp. 169–70, 188–89; *Vermont Cynic*, 1 May 1939, p. 7.
104. "College Youth Better Mannered," *Vermont Alumnus*, June 1939, p. 196.
105. Ibid. As was his custom when visiting in Burlington, Dewey stayed at the home of Mrs. Edward V. Hoyt at 195 South Prospect Street, located across the street from the house where the Dewey family lived while John was attending the university. Mrs. Hoyt, as Violet Underwood, was a childhood friend of Dewey. When in Vermont, Dewey also regularly visited his cousin and college classmate, John Parker Rich, who lived some six miles north of St. Albans on his estate, Richwood.
106. For a list of some of the members of the club, see Jane M. Dewey, ed., "Biography of John Dewey," in *The Philosophy of John Dewey*, The Library of Living Philosophers, ed. Paul A. Schilpp, vol. 1 (Evanston: Northwestern University, 1939), pp. 37–38.
107. Dewey, *Characters and Events*, ed. Joseph Ratner, 2 vols. (New York: Henry Holt & Co., 1929).
108. Dewey, *Intelligence in the Modern World: John Dewey's Philoso-*

phy, ed., with an introduction by Joseph Ratner (New York: Modern Library, 1939).

109. Dewey, *Education Today*, ed., with a foreword by Joseph Ratner (New York: G. P. Putnam's Sons, 1940).
110. Welling, one year older than Dewey, was a New York lawyer who since the early 1900s had done pioneer work in encouraging student self-government in high schools and colleges throughout the United States. Student self-government, he believed, was good training for responsible adult citizenship. He founded and for a number of years was chairman of the National Self-Government Committee, Inc. As a member of the Committee's Associate Council, Dewey became acquainted with Welling. Welling's book *Self Government and Politics in School* (Bound collection of articles and reprints, New York, 1936) contains a short introduction by Dewey.
111. See Dewey to Welling, 19 February 1934; Dewey to Welling, 20 March 1935; Dewey to Welling, March 1937; Dewey to Welling, 26 October 1939. See also Welling to Dewey, 23 October 1939, and Welling to Dewey, 30 October 1939. Richard W. G. Welling Papers, Manuscript Division, The New York Public Library, Astor, Lenox and Tilden Foundations.
112. Richard Welling, *As the Twig Is Bent* (New York: G. P. Putnam's Sons, 1942), p. 248.
113. Dewey to Welling, 5 March 1949, Welling Papers.
114. These were: The American Civil Liberties Union, American Philosophical Association, Conference on Methods in Philosophy and the Sciences, Department of Philosophy of Columbia University, John Dewey Labor Fellowship, New School for Social Research, New York Teachers Guild, Progressive Education Association, and the Society for Ethical Culture in New York City. (See "Dr. Dewey Is Hailed on 80th Birthday," *New York Times*, 21 October 1939, p. 19.)
115. Among these were William H. Kilpatrick of Teachers College at Columbia; Eduard C. Lindeman, professor of social philosophy at the New York School of Social Work and president of the Institute for Propaganda Analysis; John L. Childs of Teachers College; John L. Elliott of the Society for Ethical Culture in New York City; Ned Dearborn, dean of the New York University education division; Horace M. Kallen of the New School for Social Research; Boyd H. Bode, professor of education at Ohio State University; Charles W. Morris, professor of philosophy at the University of Chicago; Albert C. Barnes of the Barnes Foundation; Arthur E. Murphy of the University of Illinois; Willard W. Beatly, director of education, Office of Indian Affairs, Washington, D.C.; Charles Beard, formerly of Columbia; and T. V. Smith, professor of philosophy at the University of Chicago and serving as Congressman-at-Large from Illinois. (See "Dr. Dewey Is Hailed on 80th Birthday," p. 19.)

116. Dewey to Nathanson, 27 June 1939, private collection of Jerome Nathanson. See also Dewey to Levinson, 21 October 1939, Salmon O. Levinson Papers, Special Collections, The Joseph Regenstein Library, University of Chicago, Chicago, Ill.
117. Dewey, "Creative Democracy–The Task Before Us," in *The Philosopher of the Common Man: Essays in Honor of John Dewey to Celebrate His Eightieth Birthday,* ed. Sidney Ratner (New York: G. P. Putnam's Sons, 1940), p. 220.
118. Ibid., p. 228.
119. *Philosophical Review* 48 (1939): 190, and ibid. 49 (1940): 169.
120. *The Philosopher of the Common Man: Essays in Honor of John Dewey to Celebrate His Eightieth Birthday* (New York: G. P. Putnam's Sons, 1940).
121. Paul A. Schilpp, ed., *The Philosophy of John Dewey,* The Library of Living Philosophers, vol. 1 (Evanston: Northwestern University, 1939).
122. Sidney Hook, *John Dewey: An Intellectual Portrait* (New York: John Day Co., 1939).
123. "Philosopher of Americanism," *New York Times,* 20 October 1939, p. 22.
124. Samuel J. Woolf, "A Philosopher's Philosophy," *New York Times,* 15 October 1939, p. 5.
125. Ibid., p. 17.
126. "Butler, Dr. Dewey Honored by China," *New York Times,* 21 December 1939, p. 20.

CHAPTER 15. RETIREMENT YEARS, 1939–1952

1. One of the publications of the Conference on the Scientific Spirit and Democratic Faith was significantly entitled *The Authoritarian Attempt to Capture Education: Papers from the Second Conference on the Scientific Spirit and Democratic Faith,* Preface by Jerome Nathanson (New York: King's Crown Press, 1945).
2. The Reverend Geoffrey O'Connell in a talk at one of the sessions of the National Catholic Alumni Federation in New York City on 26 October 1939, and as reported in "John Dewey's Aims Held Un-American," *New York Times,* 27 October 1939, p. 14. For other Catholic denunciations of Dewey's philosophy, see the *Tablet,* 2 December 1939, p. 1; ibid., 16 December 1939, p. 14; and ibid., 16 November 1940, p. 4.
3. Wilfred Parsons, in a talk before the Columbus Forum in New York City, as reported in *Tablet,* 9 December 1939, p. 20.
4. Thomas F. Woodlock, *The Real Threat to American Liberties,* (San Francisco: National Council of Catholic Women Convention, 1939), p. 8. See also "The Spiritual Basis of Democracy," in *Science, Philosophy and Religion: Second Symposium* (New York: Conference on Science, Philosophy and Religion in Their Relation to the Democratic Way of Life, 1942), pp. 251–57. This essay was

drawn up by seven members of the faculty of Princeton University and the president of Princeton Theological Seminary.

5. Mortimer Adler, "God and the Professors," in *Pragmatism and American Culture*, ed., with an introduction by Gail Kennedy (Boston: D. C. Heath & Co., 1950), p. 72. For a reply to Adler's charges, see Sidney Hook, "The New Medievalism," in ibid., pp. 76–80.
6. See, for example, Dan W. Gilbert, "Sovietizing Our Children," *National Republic*, August 1936, pp. 16–17, 32.
7. Dewey, "Investigating Education," *New York Times*, 6 May 1940, p. 16.
8. Ibid. See also the letter of Merwin K. Hart, president of the New York State Economic Council, in reply to Dewey's letter, "Dr. Dewey's Stand Disputed," *New York Times*, 9 May 1940, p. 22, and Dewey's rejoinder, "Censorship Not Wanted," ibid., 14 May 1940, p. 22.
9. "Bishop Manning Makes Protest against Russell's Appointment," *New York Times*, 1 March 1940, p. 23.
10. "Campaign against Appointment of Russell Widens," *Tablet*, 16 March 1940, pp. 1, 24.
11. "An Appointment," *Tablet*, 2 March 1940, p. 11.
12. "Statement of the Committee on Cultural Freedom," in *The Bertrand Russell Case*, ed. Dewey and Horace M. Kallen, (New York: Viking Press, 1941), p. 227.
13. Dorothy Thompson, quoted by Horace M. Kallen "Behind the Bertrand Russell Case," in *Bertrand Russell Case*, p. 28.
14. See "Decision of Justice John E. McGeehan," in *Bertrand Russell Case*, pp. 214–18.
15. Quoted by Kallen, "Behind the Bertrand Russell Case," pp. 20, 21.
16. "Decision of McGeehan," p. 222.
17. Ibid., p. 225.
18. "Russell Defended by Four Educators," *New York Times*, 12 March 1940, p. 27.
19. Dewey to Welling, 4 April 1940; see also Dewey to Welling, 8 April 1940, noting the similarity of the attacks on Russell and himself and declaring that, if he were to be a candidate for a position in a New York City college, he would be subjected to the same kind of assaults as those directed at Russell. (Richard W. Welling Papers, Manuscript Division, The New York Public Library, Astor, Lenox and Tilden Foundations.)
20. Dewey, "The Case for Bertrand Russell," *Nation* 150 (1940): 732.
21. In his introduction to the book, Dewey credits Albert C. Barnes with suggesting the idea of such a work and a group representing the Committee for Cultural Freedom with getting writers for the project.
22. Dewey, "Social Realities *versus* Police Court Fictions," in *Bertrand Russell Case*, pp. 55–74.
23. Ibid., p. 72.

24. "Dr. Butler's Address to the Columbia Faculties," *New York Times*, 4 October 1940, p. 14.
25. "Dr. Butler's Edict Scored in Senate," *New York Times*, 5 October 1940, pp. 1, 7.
26. Dewey, [Statement on Academic Freedom], *New York Times*, 5 October 1940, p. 7.
27. Joseph E. Davies, *Mission to Moscow* (New York: Simon & Schuster, 1941).
28. Ibid., p. 43.
29. Ibid., p. 455.
30. Ibid., pp. 509–10.
31. Ibid., p. 303.
32. Dewey, "Russia's Position: Mr. Davies's Book Regarded as Incorrect Picture," *New York Times*, 11 January 1942, p. 7.
33. Ibid.
34. Ibid.
35. Dewey and Suzanne La Follette, ["Several Faults Are Found in 'Mission to Moscow' Film"], *New York Times*, 9 May 1943, p. 8E.
36. Ibid. Dewey's criticism of the film did not go unchallenged. Arthur U. Pope, organizer and director of the Committee for National Morals, accused Dewey of being unreasonable in what could be expected of a film. For the ensuing exchange of letters, see response by Pope, *New York Times*, 16 May 1943, p. 12E; reply by Dewey and La Follette, ibid., 24 May 1943, p. 14; reply by Pope, ibid., 12 June 1943, p. 12; and reply by Dewey and La Follette, ibid., 19 June 1943, p. 12.
37. C. P. West, "Pragmatism: The Logic of Capitalism," *New Essays*, Winter 1943, pp. 61–70. Quoted in part in Jim Cork, "John Dewey and Karl Marx," in *John Dewey: Philosopher of Science and Freedom*, ed. Sidney Hook (New York: Dial Press, 1950), p. 334.
38. M. Dynnik, "Contemporary Bourgeois Philosophy in the U.S.," trans. and abridged by Mirra Ginsburg, *Modern Review* 1 (1947): 657. First published in *Bolshevik* for March 1947.
39. Joseph Nahem, "What Is 'Progressive Education'?" *Worker*, 30 September 1951, p. 8, quoted by Mark Starr, "John Dewey Attacked by the Communists," *Progressive Education*, November 1951, p. 58.
40. Starr, "Dewey Attacked," p. 58.
41. Ibid.
42. Dynnik, "Bourgeois Philosophy," p. 657.
43. See the article on John Dewey in the 1952 edition of the *Large Soviet Encyclopaedia* as reproduced in Martin Levit, "Soviet Version of John Dewey and Pragmatism," *History of Education Journal* 4 (1953): 138–39.
44. Dynnik, "Bourgeois Philosophy," p. 657. For an extended critical analysis of Dewey's philosophy by a Communist writer, see Harry K. Wells, *Pragmatism: Philosophy of Imperialism* (New York: International Publishers, 1954).

45. For a list of Dewey's writings during the 1940s, see Milton H. Thomas, *John Dewey: A Centennial Bibliography* (Chicago: University of Chicago Press, 1962), pp. 131–49.
46. Dewey, *Problems of Men* (New York: Philosophical Library, 1946). The volume contains also one earlier article by Dewey, "Logical Conditions of a Scientific Treatment of Morality," written in 1903.
47. Arthur F. Bentley, *Linguistic Analysis of Mathematics* (Bloomington, Ind.: Principia Press, 1932); *Behavior, Knowledge, Fact* (Bloomington, Ind.: Principia Press, 1935).
48. Dewey and Arthur F. Bentley, *Knowing and the Known* (Boston: Beacon Press, 1949). The collaboration involved in writing this volume resulted in a massive correspondence between Dewey and Bentley. A selection of items—letters, drafts of essays, and postcards, combined with the earlier and later correspondence between the two men—was published in book form under the title *John Dewey and Arthur F. Bentley: A Philosophical Correspondence, 1932–1951,* ed. Sidney Ratner, Jules Altman, and James E. Wheeler (New Brunswick, N.J.: Rutgers University Press, 1964). The book provides fascinating insights into the workings of two gifted philosophical minds as well as into the nonprofessional, human sides of the writers. An extended, informative introductory essay by Sidney Ratner greatly enhances the value of the work.
49. Dewey and Bentley, *Knowing and the Known,* p. 37.
50. Among these were: Rudolf Carnap, *Introduction to Semantics* (Cambridge: Harvard University Press, 1942); Morris R. Cohen and Ernest Nagel, *An Introduction to Logic and Scientific Method* (New York: Harcourt, Brace & Co., 1934); Curt J. Ducasse, "Is a Fact a True Proposition?—A Reply," *Journal of Philosophy* 39 (1942): 132–36; Clarence I. Lewis, "The Modes of Meaning," *Philosophy and Phenomenological Research,* December 1943, pp. 236–49; Charles W. Morris, *Foundations of the Theory of Signs* (Chicago: University of Chicago Press, 1938); and Alfred Tarski, "The Semantic Conception of Truth and the Foundations of Semantics," *Philosophy and Phenomenological Research,* March 1944, pp. 341–75.
51. Dewey and Bentley, *Knowing and the Known,* p. 162.
52. Ibid., p. 276.
53. Ibid., p. 311.
54. Ibid., p. 296.
55. Ibid., pp. 296, 297.
56. Ibid., p. 304.
57. Ibid., p. 298.
58. Ibid., p. 300.
59. Ibid., p. 74.
60. Ibid., pp. 51, 297.
61. See, for example, the comments of Charles W. Morris, review of

Knowing and the Known, Annals of the American Academy of Political and Social Science 268 (1950): 224.

62. Sidney Ratner, review of *Knowing and the Known, Social Research* 17 (1950): 249. Other reviews are: Paul Ziff, *Journal of Symbolic Logic* 15 (1950): 156; James Collins, *Modern Schoolman*, May 1950, pp. 322–26; Max Black, *Philosophical Review* 59 (1950): 269–70; Solomon Weinstock, "Kennetic Inquiry," *Scientific Monthly* 72 (1951): 135–36.
63. For this correspondence, see *The Morning Notes of Adelbert Ames, Jr., Including a Correspondence with John Dewey*, ed., with a preface by Hadley Cantril (New Brunswick, N.J.: Rutgers University Press, 1960), pp. 171–231.
64. Dewey to Ames, 17 November 1950, in *Morning Notes of Ames*, pp. 230–31.
65. "Dr. John Dewey Weds," *New York Times*, 12 December 1946, p. 31.
66. "Dr. Dewey Loses Estate," *New York Times*, 19 June 1947, p. 2. Dewey's children were criticized in some quarters for taking the money. Some of their acquaintances believed that Dewey should be allowed to continue to receive income from the estate for his few remaining years. The children's position was that Dewey had no special need of the money and that there was therefore no good reason to break the terms of the will. Dewey was receiving a pension from Columbia University and another from the Albert C. Barnes Foundation, as well as substantial amounts in royalties from his writings. Besides, Roberta herself had considerable wealth derived from the American Glass Company of Greensburg, Pennsylvania, of which her late brother had been president.
67. Irwin Edman, "America's Philosopher Attains an Alert 90," *New York Times Magazine*, 16 October 1949, pp. 17, 74, 75.
68. Lester Grant, "John Dewey at 90, Finds Tension of World May Result in Good," *New York Herald Tribune*, 15 October 1949.
69. "Perpetual Arriver," *Time*, 31 October 1949, pp. 35–36; "*Life* Congratulates John Dewey," *Life*, 31 October 1949, p. 43.
70. "John Dewey," *New Republic*, 17 October 1949, pp. 10–39.
71. *Saturday Review*, 22 October 1949, pp. 11–15, 36–38, 44.
72. "Salute to John Dewey," *New Leader*, 22 October 1949.
73. See Jerome Nathanson to Dewey, 9 September 1949, and Dewey to Nathanson, 18 September 1949, private collection of Jerome Nathanson.
74. For an account of these meetings, see "700 Honor Prof. Dewey," *New York Times*, 22 October 1949, p. 19; "U.S. Seen Nearing Crisis in Learning," and "Dewey Denounced in Moscow," ibid., 23 October 1949, p. 62.
75. For a detailed account of the dinner including some of the greetings and addresses, see Harry W. Laidler, ed., *John Dewey at Ninety* (New York: League for Industrial Democracy, 1950).
76. William P. Montague, "Citation from the Committee," in *John Dewey at Ninety*, p. 31.

77. Dewey, "John Dewey Responds," in *John Dewey at Ninety,* p. 32.
78. Ibid., p. 33.
79. Ibid., p. 34.
80. Ibid., p. 35.
81. "The John Dewey 90th Anniversary Fund," in *John Dewey at Ninety,* p. 38. Actually, less than $4,000 was ever raised for the fund.
82. The volume appeared the following spring under the title *John Dewey: Philosopher of Science and Freedom,* ed. Sidney Hook (New York: Dial Press, 1950).
83. The writer of the article was L. H. Bailey of Cornell University, author of *The Holy Earth* (New York: Charles Scribner's Sons, 1915).
84. See "Dewey's Entire Life an Inquiry, Says Dr. Schneider," *Burlington Free Press,* 27 October 1949; *Burlington Daily News,* 27 October 1949; *Vermont Cynic,* 2 November 1949; *Alumni News,* December 1949.
85. "Burlington, Vt., Fetes John Dewey; at 90, He Visits Childhood Scenes," *New York Times,* 27 October 1949, pp. 29, 40.
86. Dewey to Lyman, 27 October 1949, Special Collections, Guy W. Bailey Library, University of Vermont, Burlington, Vt.
87. Dewey, [Contribution to a Symposium], in *Democracy in a World of Tensions: A Symposium Prepared by UNESCO,* ed. Richard McKeon and Stein Rokkan (Chicago: University of Chicago Press, 1951).
88. Dewey, "Modern Philosophy," in *The Cleavage in Our Culture: Studies in Scientific Humanism in Honor of Max Otto,* ed. Frederick Burkhardt (Boston: Beacon Press, 1952). For a list of Dewey's writings in 1950–52, see Thomas, *Dewey Bibliography,* pp. 149–51.
89. Dewey and Bentley, *Dewey-Bentley Correspondence,* p. 643.
90. "Sectarian Education," *New York Times,* 1 October 1947, p. 28.
91. Dewey, "Communists as Teachers," *New York Times,* 21 June 1949, p. 24.
92. Dewey, "Mr. Acheson's Critics: Their Attacks Feared Damaging to Our World Prestige," *New York Times,* 19 November 1950, p. 14.
93. "Liberals Forecast '53 Victory in City," *New York Times,* 4 May 1952, p. 55.
94. "Yale Honors Educator Dismissed by California over Loyalty Oath," *New York Times,* 12 June 1951, pp. 1, 25.
95. Butler to Dewey, 22 October 1943; Dewey to Butler, 6 November 1943, Special Collections, Butler Library, Columbia University, New York City; Jane Dewey to Dykhuizen, 1 August 1970, George Dykhuizen Papers and Correspondence, Special Collections, Guy W. Bailey Library, University of Vermont, Burlington, Vt.
96. Dewey to Ames, 9 October 1949, in *Morning Notes of Ames,* p. 220.
97. Dewey to Bentley, 9 April 1951, in *Dewey-Bentley Correspondence,* p. 646.

98. I am indebted to the late Roberta Dewey for this account of her husband's last days.
99. "John Dewey Memorial Service, June 4, 1952" (mimeographed).
100. Minutes of 17 April 1953, "Faculty of Philosophy Minutes, 1941– ," vol. 3.
101. Donald Harrington to Dykhuizen, 7 July 1952, Dykhuizen Papers.
102. See "UVM May Have Dewey Memorial," *Burlington Free Press,* 5 June 1952, and "500 Attend Rites for John Dewey," *New York Times,* 5 June 1952, p. 31.
103. Telegram, Roberta Dewey to Dykhuizen, 10 October 1952, Dykhuizen Papers.
104. "Checklist of Writings about John Dewey, 1886–1972," in preparation at the Center for Dewey Studies, Southern Illinois University, Carbondale.
105. Jo Ann Boydston with Robert L. Andresen, comps. and eds., *A Checklist of Translations, 1900–1967* (Carbondale: Southern Illinois University Press, 1969).
106. Henry S. Commager, *The American Mind: An Interpretation of American Thought and Character since the 1880's* (New Haven: Yale University Press, 1950), p. 100.
107. Morris R. Cohen, *American Thought: A Critical Sketch,* ed., with a foreword by Felix S. Cohen (New York: Collier Books, 1962), p. 364.

Index